MARKS IN THE SAND …

William's Story

William Sutherland

Marks in the Sand … William's Story

Published 2019 by William Sutherland
www.self-sufficiency.net

Typeset by John Owen Smith

Cover: Photo by Will Sutherland – Design by John Owen Smith

ISBN 978-1-9161714-0-4

Printed by KDP

LOVE

MAGIC &

POLITICS

William Sutherland in 2019

Let's Make a Start!

For some, this short summary may be enough to satisfy curiosity. After all, what greater purpose do "memoirs" have except to inflame our interest in love and romance?

For others, there is a larger story to tell – and it's set out in the pages that follow. The people described in this book are real people. Some of them may disagree with the way I see things. This they are perfectly entitled to do. My purpose is simply to set out my own feelings and memories of how my life unfolded – and I make no apology for that.

My story is some kind of chronicle showing how a reasonably energetic and thoughtful human has battled with the routine challenges of daily life and the wider challenges posed by our present civilisation's global cultural system. For my children, grandchildren and future generations, it may provide useful clues to why things were, and are, the way they are.

Love!

They were sexy; I was sexy – and we loved it!

Sarah was the first, the most fun and bore our four children
Nada was the wildest
Denise was the saddest
Liesi was probably the wisest
Ros was (and is) the kindest
Priscilla was the most sensible
Sue was the most lovable – mother of Hal
Paget was the most complex
Ariel was the most intellectual
Angela was the best cook with the worst temper – mother of Roisin and Liam
Estie was the most mysterious

With these 11 ladies I shared some of the great puzzles and joys of life's cosmic roller coaster. They were/are all wonderful people. I do not regret one moment of the time I spent with them.

Magic

From all the unfathomable magic of these physical and emotional couplings came not only greater wisdom but seven wonderful children. They have brought me great joy and satisfaction over the 43 years of my life during which their upbringing has been one of my main tasks. I am proud of all of them – all smart, strong and independent citizens of planet Earth. I hope they enjoyed their childhoods as much as I enjoyed the challenge of looking after them.

Most of the key events in my life have also happened "by magic". By that I mean they have not been planned but usually came about by "seizing the moment". Planting trees, building golf courses, managing windsurfing and politicians, constructing houses, writing Alternative Treaties, winning golf matches, teaching self-sufficiency and playing music – these are all part of the mix.

Politics

From a very early age I have been fascinated by how the world works and, in particular, why so many apparently successful human civilisations have crashed. I have studied physics, mathematics, economics and agriculture. I have worked in government, in business and in alternative politics. I have met many people and visited many places. I know the answer to most of my questions now but I have not found anybody who has any idea of a solution.

I can see now that all human societies become trapped by the power and stubborn inertia of their own cultural institutions. Systems of rules and behaviours which were invented for one purpose eventually outlive their usefulness as circumstances change; in effect, they become the bars of a cultural cage. Systems that once seemed life-enabling now become life-threatening. In the past, disaster has often come from soil erosion and tree felling as governments based in cities lose touch with the realities of the natural world. We live in a similar dynamic today.

Of all the human institutions, the one which is almost invariably the most life-threatening is "money". Originally invented to fight wars and found nation states, money ends up giving us wrong signals which ultimately encourage destruction and exhaustion of the resources we need and the life support systems we depend upon.

The theme of "My Quest" runs through all of this narrative. And this quest continues.

Contents

William Sutherland – His Story

Introduction

This is a story about my life and some of the family history that came before it. It's been a busy and exciting life with some unexpected twists and turns. Could I have done things differently? I really don't know – all I know is that I gave it my best shot. It would be nice to think that some of the things I have done have made life better for the wider world. It would be nice to think my children did not find being part of the Sutherland clan too frustrating or annoying. I did my best to give them self-confidence, a good education (in the true sense of that word) and an independent and inquisitive mind. That has not always been comfortable but I look back on 40 years of child-rearing with great pleasure and satisfaction. We had a lot of fun and good times. Of course, my life has been woven into Sarah's life ever since we met on Seahouses pier – was it in '62 or '63? We, too, have had a lot of fun and good times despite occasional discomforts.

For those who don't know much about me, I've had a strange and perhaps unusual life! It started in Northumberland, moved to London, then to Millbrook in Bedfordshire, next to Ireland, briefly to France and finally back to Northumberland again. I've always had a restless spirit of enquiry – first about how the physical Universe works and then, for the last 50 years, about how human society works (or doesn't work!). I started as a farmer; became a golf course developer; worked in Whitehall and Westminster; pioneered the development of windsurfing both in the UK and internationally; co-ordinated, edited and published the Alternative Treaties from the Rio Earth Summit; lived a life of self-sufficiency in Ireland, where I pioneered running self-sufficiency courses with John Seymour and later revised and significantly expanded his original book to produce "The New Complete Book of Self Sufficiency". Currently I still teach self-sufficiency and grow most of my own fruit and vegetables. In between I have shared my life with some wonderful women: Sarah Gilbert, Priscilla Russell, Sue Woodward, Paget Butler, Angela Ashe and Ros Cattliff. I loved them all as best I could and each of them taught me something different – what a “roller coaster”! Each of my seven children has given me the wonderful excitement and satisfaction of guiding an energetic and intelligent young human into the challenges and realities of life.

I’m not writing any of this to try and justify or excuse the occasional discomforts, irritations and disagreements which always punctuate human experience. I am not writing this to try and set out and/or explain why we made all the decisions we made about educating and bringing up our children. This is essentially a narrative which follows the focus and activities of my own life as I now see them. Fate and chance have certainly played their part – for the most part, fate has been kind although some do say that you can make your own luck! Everyone will have their own views and opinions – but here, at least, is my version of the facts. And many of these facts arose many years before most of the readers of this piece have memories.

Early days at Dunstan Steads – William on the left

“Marks in the Sand”

This carbon life form in a weird chain of chance
Soon finds its place in the world’s cosmic dance
From tottering first steps to a spreading of wings
Making children and dreaming magnificent things
Struggling to make sense of the meaning of life
Struggling to thrive with four kids and a wife
Getting up every day with a zip and a dash
Often taking actions which some think are rash
Never daunted by thinking “outside the box”
Never stymied by life’s unforeseen knocks
Building magical golf courses, one right from scratch
Building five fine houses with skills few can match
Managing windsurfing races all over the world
Creating the rules as this fine sport unfurled
Enjoying the challenge of working in Whitehall
Before Westminster madness where winner takes all
Donning tie and fine suits at smart Arthur Young
Telling Managers and Councils how things should be done
Then off to Rio for the Earth’s first true Summit
Editing and publishing the Treaties that came from it
Planting a great forest, many thousands of trees
Growing food, making beer and all things like these
Teaching and campaigning for healthy “right living”
Raised three more kids with music and singing
I’ve loved many fine women and have no regrets
Played games, brought up children, took care of my pets
Played my ‘cello in orchestras as well as in pubs
Watched great movies and theatre that everyone loves
My time on the Earth, I don’t think it’s been wasted
Life’s frustrations and pleasures have all been tasted
So here is my story where fate played such a hand
A lifetime’s achievements or just “marks in the sand”?

Chapter 1: 1945–1966

Beginnings

My earliest memories are of running over the scented turf of Dunstanburgh Golf Course on the way to our chalet-styled beach hut where there would be gritty sandwiches for tea and luke-warm orange juice to drink. In those days just after the Second World War (and before ferocious selective weedkillers) the dunes were ablaze with wild flowers and butterflies. The grass felt soft and cool under bare feet but the sea was always freezing cold. I had to struggle to cope with wearing glasses from an early age because I had inherited my father's "lazy" left eye. Wearing a black patch over the right eye made me look a fool at the village school and there were frequent visits to Mr Ingram, the eye consultant in Newcastle, in attempts to train both eyes to work together. It seems to have been reasonably successful!

My parents were hard-working (and conscientious) farmers and land owners with many additional "leadership" roles in the local village community. Rationing was still in force after the war and our lives were frugal; luxury was generally frowned on as being akin to waste! Our old farm house was big and cold – especially during one winter when one of our house cows put its back-end through the kitchen window! Most of our vegetables were grown in our own walled vegetable garden by the full-time gardener, Willie Train (who also led the bell ringers in Embleton Church). We had two house cows and they provided all the milk and butter both for ourselves and the farm workers (Annabel was our dairy maid). There were pigs and chickens for eggs and meat. The pig killing every November provided great drama (and squealing) – lots of fresh meat and we boys got the blown up bladders to kick about in the garden (the origins of football, I'm sure).

Soon it was time for me to go to the Embleton village school to begin my long run on the treadmill of life. We played marbles very keenly in the muddy playground and enjoyed the excitements of conkers in the autumn. We learned our times-tables by rote under the kind and patient guidance of Mrs Winter. I think we must also have learned to read although I don't think I was very good at it – certainly I had to have remedial spelling classes for many years when I went on to prep school. In fact when it came to it, I think "O" level English Language is the only exam I've ever failed!

Grandparents

The contrast between my 2 sets of grandparents could hardly have been greater. My father's father, Sir Arthur Munro Sutherland, was a huge and serious public figure who had been a leading light in the political and business life of Newcastle. My mother's parents, Bert and Elsie, played games, bought us ice-creams, and their house in Chalfont St Giles always seemed to be bathed in sunshine and joy.

Sir Arthur Sutherland Bt., KBE, Dl, DCL, KG (St John), JP had been Lord Mayor of Newcastle, multiple philanthropist, Lord Lieutenant of the County, multi-millionaire and an almost legendary figure in the history of the City of Newcastle. As a committed Methodist he donated to numerous charities as well as providing funds for major hospitals and for his old school, the Royal Grammar School, where he was Chairman of the Governors for many years. In the speech which he made in 1936 when presented with the Honorary Freedom of the City, he urged the boys of the RGS to follow his motto of INDUSTRY, THRIFT AND AMBITION!

Sir Arthur had borrowed money from his father to buy his first ship and set up his first shipping company when he was just 25 years old. He had left school as early as he could (at the age of 16) to begin work in the business of his dreams, shipping, and worked his way up to become Chief Clerk in one of the local shipping companies by the time he was 21. He certainly followed the tenets of the Sutherland family motto – *Sans Peur* – "Without Fear". Just as he took a big risk in buying his first ship – a small second-hand tramp steamer just over 3,500 tons – he continued to make quick decisions and accept big risks throughout his life. He was particularly famous for his decision to invest £1 million – a huge sum in those days – in commissioning the building of 17 modern diesel ships during the big depression of the 1930s. The employment and jobs this created around Tyneside quickly helped bring the depression in the north east to an end.

Originally the Sutherland family (Sir Arthur's Grandfather) had come down from Orkney to Thurso, in the north of Scotland, seeking work as a cobbler. This had been a success and eventually Sir Arthur's family came down to Newcastle but the links to Scotland always remained strong. It was a great surprise to me to find the family motto, "Sans Peur", written large across the hallway of Dunrobin Castle, which is home to the Dukes of Sutherland. I had seen this motto on many items of my grandfather but had no idea that this was its true source!

As children we were never told much about our Newcastle grandfather. I believe his impact on the life of my father had been so immense that my parents felt we should not have to grow up in its shadow. Certainly we could see for ourselves (on visits to Thurso House for example) the grand style in which he lived but I have only found out the details of his life, business and philanthropy by doing my own research. Sir Arthur wrote his own biography – "Tynesider" – and there is now a booklet about his life written by Nigel McMurray.

Sir Arthur's household was run on strict lines – 3 immaculate motor cars looked after by Wallace – the chief servant, butler and manager of the household. Registration numbers of his Rolls Royce cars were AMS 1, 2 and 3. He had big beautiful houses in Newcastle and Hethpool in the Cheviots. We children entered his presence well-scrubbed and well behaved. He gave us the occasional humbug but mostly we were farmed off to be fed tinned peaches by Mrs Wallace. Often our visits to Thurso

House in Newcastle coincided with the dreaded journey to boarding school at Mowden Hall – how we got to hate those tinned peaches! The very idea that Sir Arthur might once have had a loving wife simply did not occur to us.

The Dunstanburgh Estate – After my grandfather bought this large and beautiful estate along the Northumbrian coast (in 1919, I think), I was told (by my father) that Sir Arthur had a vision of creating an Embleton Riviera-style resort. He saw the potential for high-class residential development by completing an imposing crescent of 23 (I think it was) fine villas curving from Embleton towards Dunstan Steads. In the event this never happened and the 4 villas which had been built in 1911 remain as a token of this wider vision. It was Sir Arthur who commissioned James Braid to redesign and extend the golf course which had been founded in 1900. (Golf was one of Sir Arthur's very few hobbies!) It was Sir Arthur who encouraged the building of the duneland "bungalows" both as an integral part of the golf course and as part of his efforts to bring city people out to play golf and enjoy the beaches. The golf course was all part of his Methodist ethos of providing healthy recreational facilities for the local working people. And he saw that with the right kind of tourist development, jobs could be created and money brought into the area.

As a wealthy "self made" shipowner in Newcastle and leading Methodist, Sir Arthur had been granted his baronetcy after his success in using his ships (and his special relationship with Sweden) to bring desperately needed foodstuffs into Britain during the First World War. His Danish wife was very well connected with the Swedish Royal family and somehow they managed to get permission to sail about 70 ships (trapped in the Baltic) through Sweden's coastal territorial waters so as to avoid the dangerous German U-boat blockade.

Immediately after the war Sir Arthur was elected Mayor of Newcastle. He became a major philanthropist – donating £ millions to build the University Medical School, the Dental

School and provide new facilities for his old school, the Royal Grammar School. He built several churches and finally (after his death) bequeathed Thurso House to the City of Newcastle. (There's more information in Wikipedia /Arthur Sutherland.)

After Sir Arthur died in 1953 my father told me that he, my father, had been offered the choice between inheriting the College Valley estate or the Dunstanburgh estate. My father chose the latter and our family managed that whole estate for many years before it was gradually sold off by my brother Owen. We also kept the golf course going as an important local asset despite it making continual losses. In fact I took on the management of the course myself while I was still an undergraduate at Cambridge because I did not want my parents to give it up and convert the fairways back to farmland.

Visits to Thurso House – As children we often visited Sir Arthur at Thurso House in Newcastle. He very much liked lobster so we would collect these live and wrapped in damp newspapers from Seahouses. We could hear the lobsters rustling about in the back of the car on the way to town! Of course he was an old man then but the house was run on almost military lines by Wallace. Sir Arthur insisted that all the clocks, and there were quite a few in the house, must keep perfect time and all strike on the hour together! This they did, which was very entertaining for us children.

We had to be "seen and not heard" at fancy formal meals in his dining room. I remember the elaborate silver galleon that was an ornament in the centre of the table. Our main enjoyment on those visits involved sliding around on the varnished parquet flooring under the huge snooker table. Sir Arthur would invite us into his (very formal) study occasionally to give us jars of sticky humbugs!

Sir Arthur left Thurso House (almost as a monument to himself) in his will as a gift to the City of Newcastle. It is used now as a wedding venue as well as providing luxury accommodation for the Lord Mayor and important visitors to the City (including the Queen!). One thing which still puzzles me is the use and unchanged state of Thurso House. There seems to be nothing specific in Sir Arthur's Will regarding future use of the house and garden and what happens when, and if, the City decides to cash them in! It is wonderful that the City has left so much of the house exactly as it was on the day Sir Arthur died. His bedroom still has the old fittings and even the exercise bike he used. This makes the place rather like it's been frozen in time! It seems remarkable that the City, often governed by Labour, has not cashed in the house and garden since I cannot believe it makes much of a profit and the land alone must be worth millions! As a family I think we are very glad to see the City using the Mansion House as Sir Arthur intended.

The Wallaces – We knew the Wallaces very well because we always went for tea in their little cottage beside Thurso house on our way to prep school (also long after Sir Arthur had died). Wallace was very proper and a stickler for having things done correctly. He always kept Sir Arthur's 3 cars perfectly polished in their spotlessly clean garage with its perfect shiny tiled floor. (Sir Alan Sugar of TV fame has his number AMS 1 now!) Every summer Wallace would take his holidays fishing for salmon in the north of Scotland. He would show us photos of his catches each year – some enormous salmon over 50lb weight which you would rarely see today. Mrs Wallace was a lovely bosomy slow spoken Scots lady with a soft Scottish accent. She provided lavish teas and spoiled us thoroughly although, as I said, I did get heartily sick of her tinned peaches because I always associated them with going back to the prep school which I hated.

Hethpool – was another beautiful place up in the Cheviots which we often visited. The gardens were immaculate, the lake serene and the water turbines a source of wonder as we watched the lights fluctuating up and down as the governors "hunted" (as my father told us). (The quantity of water going through the turbines was controlled by valves operated by the governors which were spinning weights – if the speed was too high they would fly out closing the valves, too slow and they would drop to open them. When they "hunted" they were simply oscillating in an unstable way.) We learned to row from the storybook boathouse and had to mind out for the swans which always nested at the north end of the lake. Hethpool house had a fine selection of fishing rods (and watering cans!) which we used to fish both in the lake and off the bridge over the Lynn (the deep gorge where we invariably caught eels rather than trout). Today I'm sad to see the pretty summer house run down and the old paths overgrown with nettles – but we still take walks down beside the lake so we can bathe in the big pool below the waterfall in the Lynn. Each year I usually go along with my scythe and clear a way through the "secret" overgrown path in the woods beside the lake. Where the College burn flows over rushing waterfalls in the Lynn there is a magic deep pool for "wild" swimming. It's also a wonderful secluded place for picnics.

Bert and Elsie Owen – My mother's parents always seemed easy going, fun loving and sporty – again with a strong Methodist instinct for community service. Their small house up the bumpy incline of Stylecroft Road in Chalfont St Giles always seemed sunny as they whistled and sang their way through each day. Lots of games were provided for us kids – we loved pushing the lawnmowers to cut the grass. Gramp would be serious though when he was watching the test matches on the small black and white TV. We all loved it when they drove north to see us because they always brought each of us a small interesting toy. There was plenty of singing and laughter as we played games together.

Our visits south were exciting expeditions in those days. They generally began with a 5 o'clock early morning start in the dark – I can remember the moths, white in our headlights, as we crossed the railway at Little Mill. We'd drive for what seemed like hours down the single-lane A1, often having to stop to scrape the squashed insects off the windscreen. (Some cars were fitted with what looked like small plastic snowploughs on the front of their bonnets in attempts to divert the insects – it seems hard to imagine now!) We'd often stop overnight either in York with Peggy and Walter Smith or in Doncaster with Stella and Ernie Walker – friends of my Mum. It took 2 days to reach London where the sun always seemed hotter and the ice cream more delicious.

Grampa Bert was a busy bee who knew everyone, arranged and compered the local dances and was a leading light in the local theatre and bowls club. His real sport had been hockey which he played until in his 40s and then became a referee. It would seem that the games and sporty side of my life came from Bert. Apart from the games he made for us, Bert fascinated us because he was a professional teacher of Pitt's shorthand so we often saw those mysterious strokes and curves of his shorthand. He had worked in some kind of insurance, done office work during the First World War and was a very senior official in the local Masonic Lodge (we saw his ribbons and insignia in their special velvet box – but this work was never talked about.) Our Granny, Elsie, was simply a bundle of smiles and love – you could not imagine a single cross word. She suffered from high blood pressure (a family weakness) and died from liver damage caused by the primitive blood pressure medicines. It happened whilst I was still at the Leys – I can remember the day.

Our trips south also brought us boys into contact with our cousins – John and Diana. My Mum's sister Doreen was a vivacious young teacher who had married a handsome naval officer (Leslie), who had served on minesweepers in the Far East during the Second World War. After the War they both taught at what was then called a Secondary Modern School (for those who failed the 11 plus exam). Soon they became joint Heads of their school and were totally committed to its success – often achieving amazing results with kids who had been in nothing but trouble before. They were great believers in the value of teaching supposedly non-academic kids practical skills. Success in practical things soon changed the mindsets of these "difficult" cases and very often they went on to achieve excellent exam results in the academic studies that had made them so miserable before. For us 3 boys it was a new experience to meet a real girl – Diana – and to find that Doreen was so much less inhibited about discussing progressive subjects than my very serious-minded parents. Later Diana and her girlfriends at the Friends School, Saffron Walden, would provide my first education about how the female of our species behaved so differently from the males. A lesson I learned much more thoroughly when I finally had my own daughters!

Parents

My father, Sir Ivan Sutherland Bart, was a short muscular man of rather few words. As the third child of Sir Arthur Sutherland he had never expected to inherit the Baronetcy. "Work" was his recreation and he was always focussed and cheerful when he had a spade or a saw in his hand. He hated pomp and privilege. He was extremely uncomfortable in suits and ties and smart hotels. He enjoyed listening to the radio – especially when people were talking about science or philosophy. His life was devoted to improving the farm and estate and making sure his workers had a fair deal. I learned a lot from watching him work – especially the good sense of doing a job properly so it would last a long time and would not break or fail even in exceptional circumstances.

As children we knew that 2 events had made a great impact on our father's life. The first when he was barely 20 was the petrol explosion which had severely burned much of his body, including his face which remained very scarred. (He had mistakenly put petrol into a primus stove from a mislabelled bottle.) The second was the messy and very unhappy divorce from his first wife Marjorie Brewer where her unfaithfulness (we understood) had separated him from his children, John and

Michael, as well as leaving him bitterly sad to lose what must have been the love of his life. The scar tissue from the burns on his face made it difficult for him to smile; it also made him very sensitive to public view.

I soon realised that my father really wanted nothing to do with the high-profile public world which his "larger than life" father had occupied. This often made me cross because I thought his ideas often very sensible – ideas which the public should hear about.

My mother, Peggy, brought with her all the characteristics of a well-trained nanny. Exceptionally resourceful, patient and conscientious – she always made sure we were well looked after. Perhaps her training created a degree of formality in her treatment of her own children – things had to be done properly with nothing remotely slap dash or easy going. After being sent away to school it was never easy to share personal feelings with either parent. Our emotional lives at boarding school were very much our own affairs where we had to "cut our own furrows" as best we could. But on the credit side, my Mum did like to teach us to play games and we enjoyed many winter evenings together in front of the sitting room fire playing cards or board games with her.

My parents were both serious people (with Methodist backgrounds) who did their best to fulfil what they saw as their responsibilities as major local landowners. They treated their workers well, building purpose-built homes for them to the north of Dunstan Steads (now holiday cottages) and giving the Council money to build the small cottages in Quakers Row, Embleton, for retired farm workers. My father found his responsibilities as a major landlord irksome – the regular meetings with his agent (Mr Campbell from Wooler) were tiresome affairs where problems were the normal order of the day. Both my parents hated all the legal mumbo jumbo and government laws which seemed designed to make their lives difficult. My father never farmed for a "profit"; he farmed to build up his estate, its buildings, soil, roads, fences, drains and woodlands – as well as providing much needed employment for local people. Every morning my father would be up to start work at first light and at 9 o'clock he would meet with the farm Steward (John Dodds and later Ron Cox) in the office at the east end of the house (which was out of bounds to us) to decide the business of the day. Every morning at 9 o'clock the gardener, Willie Train, would call at the kitchen end of the house to see what vegetables my mother required from the walled kitchen garden. His wife, Elsie, would start her 2 hours of regular daily cleaning in the house – and so life went on. Willie Train's old cottage in the garden was part of the old blacksmith's forge (every large farm had one) – a magical place which still had all the working parts of the furnace with its massive bellows. As teenagers my brothers and I would get the forge going, melting brass and watching the sparks fly from white hot steel.

My mother was the clever, conscientious and resourceful nanny who had (through working as a nanny for my father's best friend, Norman Burrell) become the wife of Ivan, the heir to the large and beautiful Dunstanburgh estate. Almost always cheerful and busy, she provided an ideal well-run home. Whilst my father often seemed to carry the cares of the world on his shoulders, our mother was often humming or singing and a great companion in playing games. Every evening she would sit in her big chair beside the sitting-room fire either knitting or darning. There was never any fuss over house-work or meals – everything seemed calmly well organised. Every Sunday (when we were not away at school) there would be a delicious roast beef joint (on the bone) with, perhaps, a steamed lemon pudding to follow. Once we were all safely away at boarding school our mother took on more and more important roles in the local community. She learned to calm her nerves at public speaking and she succeeded in getting things done where many have failed because of her cheerful tact and calm patience. Although quiet and softly spoken, she was a resolute campaigner for the things she believed to be right. She invariably kept her cool when others were panicking and she was always prepared to wait for as long as necessary to get what she wanted.

We often saw my father's brother Gordon and his elder sister Kath. Gordon was always charming and exuded infectious enthusiasm about his great love – the motor car. He lived in beautiful houses with his charming and elegant wife and sons – often letting us drive some of his fancy sports cars when we were older. Gordon had been a leading figure in motor racing in the Brooklands era before the Second World War – driving 4 litre racing Bentleys. Gordon was the driving force behind the design and success of Aston Martin (which he owned) in racing (Le Mans). Unfortunately the beautiful cars he designed and built were well ahead of their times – too expensive to find a ready market. Eventually he had to sell the business to David Brown (hence the DB1, etc.). Kath was a forceful and strong-minded lady who did not suffer fools… We had to be on best behaviour when we made our regular visits to have tea with her (and her yappy terriers) in Wooler. I was fortunate to be one of her favourites (she generally did not like children and had none of her own) – she always gave me lovely China tea, ginger biscuits and Terry's bitter chocolate – yummy. Kath was very wealthy but her wealth was swallowed up by clever and unscrupulous lawyers after she died. It now languishes in some dusty old Trust (run by these lawyers) supposedly for use to help village life in Northumberland.

My father's eldest brother Munro and Munro's son Peter were both killed in wartime service. But we often heard from my father how Sir Arthur had deceived Munro over the purchase and later sale of the Newcastle Chronicle newspaper. Munro had had a very hard time during the First World War after being taken prisoner early in the war when his aircraft was shot down. When he finally returned to England after the war he was at something of a loose end. This was one reason why Sir Arthur bought the paper to save it in hard times, promising he would look after the workforce and putting Munro in charge. Later when the paper ran into hard times he sold it regardless of his promise – Munro never spoke to him again. Because my father disliked publicity and did not wish to be a "public figure" he was not happy when the baronetcy fell to him. My father was fortunate that my Mum took up the responsibilities expected of local gentry – running the important groups in the village and becoming a councillor, harbour commissioner, president of the Women's Institute, prison visitor, magistrate and school governor etc..

Farming

My feelings about farming were strongly affected first by the fact that we (as a family) had to take on uncomfortable farm work during holiday periods (often in winter) and second by the sometimes inconvenient and unexpected dramas which we had to deal with when animals were sick or had escaped. Chucking cold turnips off the back of a trailer early on a frosty winter morning was not much fun especially when we knew the rest of the world was on holiday. And the needs of sick or injured animals would often require getting up and out in the black darkness of night. My parents always told us that they did not expect us to go into farming as it required constant hard work for very little financial reward.

After leaving school (at Uppingham which he hated) my father began work as an engineer in the shipyards – a skill which he always enjoyed. But after his accident the direction of his life changed. My father had been trained in traditional methods of farming after being apprenticed to a very strict (and somewhat forbidding) local farmer. Mr Robertson dressed in smart tweeds, drove a Rolls Royce and was almost treated like royalty by the local people. Asked what he thought about going to church he replied that although he did not much care for it, he would be extremely worried if his workers stopped going. Clearly he felt that the threat of "hell", so often uttered by the clergy, was an important incentive for ensuring good behaviour amongst the "working" classes!

We still used horses on the farm after the war. Cereals were harvested with the old fashioned “binder” (before the invention of the combine harvester). The sheaves were stacked, first in the field to dry out naturally and then in carefully built stacks in the stack yard close to the farm buildings (the ‘onsteads’ as we called them). This allowed the thrashing to take place at a more convenient time during the winter when everyone was less busy with harvesting. We had a large mixed farm so the beef animals were brought into the covered “courtings” during winter where they could be fattened up for sale. The cowman, Jack Swanston, worked full time in the ‘onsteads’, feeding the cattle and making sure their bedding was fresh. All the winter supplies of hay, turnips and grain were stored in the ‘onsteads’. As kids we loved to eat the freshly chopped turnip slices – and we loved the smell of Jack Swanston’s pipe with the black shag tobacco he sliced up so carefully before closing down the perforated steel cap which prevented sparks lighting the hay!

The farm had small Massey Ferguson tractors which started with petrol then turned over to diesel. And our great thrill was to drive the ex-US army jeep which my father used to get around the farm – so we all learned to drive even before we became teenagers. Before I went to primary school the farm took delivery of its first really powerful tracklaying tractor – a massive Fowler Field Marshall 6-litre single-cylinder diesel machine that had to have its engine heated by burning rags before being started with a 12-bore blank cartridge that got the huge flywheel spinning. Getting this machine going in the morning was quite a performance! What a contrast with the quiet dignity of our 2 gentle shire horses that we used to feed on our way back from school with handfuls of grass as they turned for another furrow. We often walked the 1 mile between home and the village school – at the age of 6 or 7 – and nobody thought twice about it. We’d often meet the roadman. Each local road had a permanent roadman who looked after the drains, kept the hedges cut neatly with a skilful use of his hedging knife and scythed the verges during summer. The roadman knew where all the birds’ nests were and would show us these golden secrets.

At the village school we all spoke in broad Northumbrian as we learned our tables and the rudiments of reading. The first form teacher was a lovely lady called Mrs Winter but the headmaster was the terrifying Mr Smith for us 5-year olds. We all knew Mr Smith because he had a little mongrel terrier dog that could find golf balls – and golf balls were soon to become one of my great pre-occupations because all my efforts at golf were dependent on having enough golf balls. There was plenty of rough and tumble in the playground – playing various forms of tig as well as marbles. The local boys would brag about how they'd had gas to have all their teeth removed – this saved them any further expense and discomfort from toothache as they would have false teeth for ever after! Each year there were dramas over who had passed the 11 plus (with a ticket to a smart grammar school) and who had failed. But this was not to affect me because I was destined to follow the private school system.

My Brothers – Owen and Ben

We three Sutherland boys were well marshalled, polished and conscientiously educated by our dedicated parents. How many times did fellow hotel guests tell my parents what wonderfully "well behaved" boys they had? We grew up together, played together and all went to the same schools. As the eldest of the three, I had the challenge of "trail blazing" within the sometimes rigorous boarding school system. Whether this was a good or bad thing for my younger siblings I find it hard to tell, but it may well have been tricky for them to make their way somewhat in the "shadow" of my earlier passage. I certainly do not think my very visible successes and often high-profile positions of authority, can have made life easy for them; probably more difficult for Owen, who was closer to me in age and aptitudes.

In many ways Owen was virtually a smaller version of me – better looking, of course, and he was the only one of the three who did not need to wear glasses. I don't think we ever argued or came to cross-purposes during the entire period of our schooling. Owen did fine both in sports and study but Ben was a left-handed maverick who followed his own course in a life which was dominated by a fascination (and great skill) with practical electrical devices. Our parents continually worried about Ben because he found reading and writing extremely challenging. Ben, on the other hand, never doubted for one moment that his life would be a huge success because of his skills with electronics, which he saw then as a great force for the future.

There are really only two things I remember about teaming up with Owen at school and then at University. (We did not have much contact outside sport because we were in different years.) The first took place in the final of the inter-house rugby competition at the Leys. We did not appear to have a particularly strong side as North B House were clear favourites to win with many of the first XV in their team. Somehow we found ourselves in the final against North B. The match took place on the first team playing field in front of the whole school. (These climactic events are of enormous significance in the public school culture!) As Head of House and regular first team player, I was captain of our side as we doggedly held off North B who already had a small lead over us. In the final moments of this desperate game Owen had the presence of mind to kick the ball forward into an open space behind the opponent's line of backs. Playing in the centre, I was the fastest runner on the pitch and found myself first to reach and gather the ball. It was a simple matter from there to score the try which won us the match. What drama and rejoicing there was as we paraded back to the House around the school quad as victors "against the odds". The second occasion was when Owen and I rowed together in the St Catharine's College 4th boat and achieved the memorable (and uncommon) feat of "getting our oars" by making 4 bumps in the May races. The oar I received that day hung for years in the north sitting room at the Old Farm House in Newton! (The "bumps" are a strange old Cambridge rowing tradition where the river is too narrow to race one against one – so the boats are lined up one and a half boat lengths apart. They then start together, each boat trying to catch and 'bump" the boat in front. Once a "bump" is achieved both boats drop out – they then change position on the next race day. There are 4 race days – you have to achieve four bumps to "get your oar"!)

Ben's school days were dominated by his obsession with electronics. Brilliant at practical tasks Ben did not find academic work easy because his brain did not work well with letters (some kind of dyslexia). He plodded along with academic study and had no real interest in sport. Ben was fortunate in being able to work away and experiment with all the radio equipment which was kept by the school Combined Cadet Force. Later Ben would win a scholarship with Marconi to study electronics at Essex University and he went on from there to work for Marconi.

Let's jump forward now to our post-University lives. Owen graduated with a degree in Natural Sciences from Cambridge. He was a great lover of fast sports cars and rather shocked us all by buying a bright yellow Lotus. The Lotus was a perfect backdrop for his smart girlfriend Maggi, who he had met at Cambridge. They made a fine show as they zipped about together! We (the rest of the family) all realised that change was in the air after the dramatic refusal of Maggi to allow any children to be taken into the reception after her wedding to Owen. Rupert and Ceri had been very smart and well-behaved page and bridesmaid at the wedding. It was an unpleasant surprise when the hotel staff told us we were not welcome with our children at the reception. This ban applied to all children. The hotel staff themselves were upset about it and quickly offered to provide us all (the cousins were all there) with food and refreshments for our own party in the hotel garden. Later when we called by to see Owen and Maggi in their new home, it was made very clear to us that the children were not welcome. Owen seemed to have got himself into a "hard place" between a forceful wife and a mother who also had her own ideas about his future. As stated elsewhere in my story, my mother had her own plans for Owen which would ensure he stayed near home and remained within her orbit. To this day I do not know how much Owen pushed himself forward to take the central role in managing the family estate or how far this was determined by my mother's own plans. One way or another it was clear to me that the role he was taking as manager of the family trust could only lead to serious conflicts of interest but all my pleading was in vain and the die was cast! It would only be a matter of time before my easy-going relationship with Owen was turned into conflict and we would not speak to each other for more than 30 years.

Owen continued to manage the family estate and business over the years that followed. Many things were done which I profoundly disagreed with but, mercifully, I was able to escape and make my own way in the world. I have no doubt Owen was very successful in making money from the development of beautiful old farm buildings into modern expensive farm conversions. Most of these are now used as holiday cottages at the top end of the market. Finally he was able to sell-off virtually all of the land and buildings. The greatest surprise of all came "out of the blue" when Owen eventually divorced Maggi and suddenly transformed himself into a fun-loving eligible man with fast cars and yachts. He became a keen and excellent dancer and dated various capable women, seemingly found from internet dating sites for professionals. His dalliances soon ended when he met and married Jan, an ex-teacher, brilliant at languages and art. They then moved off to live in Spain, where Owen took leading roles acting with local dramatic societies. Together they took part in many dance competitions – with great success.

Ben was the brother who became very keen on sailing at an early stage in his life. He went on many sea-going expeditions with the Ocean Youth club and later became a regular mate helping to run the expeditions himself. So it was perhaps not surprising that sailing and electronics became dominant themes in his later life and successful career. Ben committed himself wholeheartedly to these pastimes. As far as I remember, Ben never took sides in the family arguments over managing the estate – he simply let things go along as he ploughed his own independent furrow through life (as he always had). Just as Owen surprised us all (much later) by starting a new life after divorcing Maggi so Ben staged a similar transformation after he had bought his yacht "Flying Angel". It came about like this.

For several years after leaving University Ben worked for Marconi but clearly he had other plans of his own for how his life should turn out. After one of the very first solo trans-Atlantic sailing races Ben was able to buy one of the competing yachts, the beautiful 42-foot ketch "Flying Angel" as virtually a bare hull and rigging. She had just taken part in the race and had no internal comforts or fittings whatever (for lightness) but she was a fine, deep-keeled, well-founded ocean-going yacht. Ben had moved down to live near Poole (which had harbour facilities suitable for Flying Angel) and began working on his yacht to install all the missing internal furniture and fittings. This was work he was extremely skilled at – a very practical man with his hands (like his father before him).

It took months and even years for him to finish his work. Once the work was finished, he simply sold up his house and set sail – never to return. His yacht was his home, his office and his business for many years afterwards. He chartered her in warm tropical islands and wherever he went he was welcome because of his legendary skill in fixing all and any faulty electronic equipment (and there is plenty of this expensive stuff in any modern marina!). We hardly ever heard from him except for the occasional message from some far-off harbour.

The next significant development in Ben's life came as a result of his regular winter stop-overs in the harbour at Annapolis, near Washington on the East Coast of the US. One day he turned up at my mother's house with new friends Bonna and her husband. Ben did occasional work for Bonna ferrying boats and yachts for her for customers in her yacht brokerage business. Next thing we know Ben and Bonna are married and living and working together in Annapolis. Bonna is smart, energetic and attractive – a perfect business partner for Ben. Ben is, in fact, a good businessman too but he has no real interest in making money for its own sake – his passion is centred on exploring what technology can do both in electronics and really any big complicated machine. Together they make a fantastic team. Ben virtually adopts Bonna's two elder boys; they build a fabulous home on the waterfront and soon have their own daughter Lesley.

Ben at home with young Lesley

Life goes on … but one day Ben turns up again (it must have been around 1980) telling us he may have made a big mistake because he has just bought the first concession offered in the US for the use of mobile phones in the Washington DC area. He will be installing the first phones in people's cars very shortly. Nobody knows at this stage what the future will hold… Of course we know now – as so often before (and like his grandfather Sir Arthur) Ben was able to see the future before anyone else and the rest is, as they say, history. Ben and Bonna's business exploded and they had a wonderful loving marriage together. Later Ben would pioneer the building of phone units that could be operated outside cars – the first generally available "mobile" phones; they sold like hot cakes.

Bonna *Clayton and Lesley*

Before his premature death (from acute leukaemia) Ben was exploring the ways in which computers, mobile phones and electronics could be matched together to transform the way we live in our homes. No doubt he would have made a success of that too. His lovely yacht "Flying Angel" had been sold but the name lives on with his beautiful powerboat. With twin turbo-charged diesel engines producing 900 horsepower, this fine piece of furniture thunders over the water at enormous speed, sounding like a spitfire reborn from World War II! Despite their sad loss, Lesley and Bonna seem to go from strength to strength. Lesley and her husband Clayton now have their own young family, so it would seem that the small piece of the Sutherland dynasty which inhabits the US is doing well.

Cousins

We saw more of our cousins on my mother's side because we regularly stayed down in Stylecroft Road (Chalfont St Giles) where they lived next door to my grandparents. Doreen's children, John and Diana, were also similar ages to ourselves whilst cousins Ian and David (Uncle Gordon's children) were rather older. Somehow John and Diana always seemed rather sophisticated and "cool" compared to we "country bumpkins" from the north. Their parents were witty and enterprising, often singing and even playing modern jazz on radio or gramophone (which seemed quite daring to us). John would listen to radio Luxembourg and follow their rendering of the famous Eagle comic story of Dan Dare and the Mekon. All this seemed rather exotic to us. Diana, of course, was the only female (of our age) that we ever encountered and that also brought a new dimension to the Sutherland boys. Later her friends at the Friends School in Saffron Walden would give me my first chance as a teenager to get to know girls rather better!

We saw comparatively little of Ian and David. Ian had sophisticated charm in abundance and appeared super-worldly-wise. We were slightly in awe of him because he had been head-boy at our public school (The Leys). I remember him as a suave salesman for the newly introduced Rank Xerox copying machines. Like his father, he loved fast cars and it was a real thrill to slide down into his Porsche (I think it was) to be taken out to dinner at the University Arms hotel in Cambridge. David seemed rather remote; we never got to hear much about him because he spent considerable time in Ireland at Trinity College in Dublin. He died very young and rather mysteriously so he never featured much in our lives.

Mowden Hall 1953 – A Prep School from "Hell"

Just before I was sent away to board at the Mowden Hall prep school I had to have a major eye operation to cure a squint in my left eye – a faulty family gene which, fortunately, does not seem to have appeared in any of my children. It was quite a traumatic and uncomfortable experience for a 7-year-old but all turned out well. Then the great watershed came in my life as I was wrenched away from a comfortable home life, put into uniform and taken 50 miles away to boarding school. I'm sure my mother found the wrench pretty tough too but all the local "well off" families sent their children off to be trained in this way. I knew my father had had a pretty miserable and unsuccessful time during his school time at Uppingham. He had never enjoyed the pompous attitude adopted by senior boys within the "fagging" system. He had excelled at gymnastics and swimming but (possibly because of his bad eyesight) had been hopeless at other sports. As we drove the final unhappy miles towards Stocksfield he did his best to encourage me, telling me he promised to give me £100 to buy a motorbike if I ever became head boy. (This was, I think, such a remote possibility in his view that he thought no more about it.)

Without any doubt, the first year I spent as a boarder at Mowden was the worst year of my life. I hated every minute of it but I was determined never to show it. Certainly I was not going to weep like many of the more feeble specimens! It was certainly a case of keeping a "stiff upper lip" – any boy that showed weakness was going to be bullied. My strong Northumbrian accent was not acceptable and I was hopeless at reading and writing compared to the other kids. I was a very shy, self-conscious boy with ugly and uncomfortable glasses; every night I lay in bed cursing my bad fortune to be in such a hostile place. My academic performance was so bad I was not allowed to go up to the second form and had to spend my next year repeating the lessons of the first form. The school cross country runs were horrific – running in rain and mud with a painful stitch and coming back to freezing changing rooms. Then there was the tedious crocodile walk (in formal Sunday suits) a couple of miles to the local church for service every Sunday – what a dirge that was. Sundays were the worst days because the kitchen was closed so there was no hot evening meal, just a banana and some half sour milk. After supper the headmaster's wife, Mrs Marchbank, would play the same hymn for us to sing – "The day thou gavest Lord is ended…" It always seemed a sad end to the day – I will never forget it.

At meals we had to eat everything that was put on our plates – stinking cauliflower and foul-smelling butter beans (I'm sure the cooks tapped their cigarette ash into the stews). The boiled eggs at breakfast frequently had half-developed chick embryos in them. The school uniforms, jackets and ties, were restrictive and uncomfortable. And the culture certainly had many elements found in the "Lord of the Flies". You certainly did not want to make enemies. If you could make friendships and alliances with the popular boys – usually those good at sport – your position was safe. The weak and oddballs were bullied (more emotionally than physically) but you are very much "on your own" when dumped in a closed society like a boarding school. Masters and prefects cannot protect you all the time.

Some time towards the end of my second year at Mowden my approach to life began to change. I can still remember very clearly the sunny morning I woke up in the yellow dorm when I made a definite decision – I WAS NOT GOING TO BE MISERABLE ANY MORE. Being miserable suddenly seemed pointless so why not simply make the best of every day and enjoy whatever perks life had to offer. In a sense the school had changed the foundations of my being and I resolved to tackle the world on my own terms from that moment on. I accepted the challenges of school life – its petty competitions and jealousies. I decided I would climb the ladder of social prestige not simply by joining its conventions but by becoming a "winner" within those conventions. I would "play the game" but never let my own integrity and inner independence be swallowed up by the game. This is probably an attitude which has stayed with me throughout my life!

My change in approach was one thing but having the mental and physical resources to achieve my objective was quite another. My reading and writing were hopeless. My physique was pretty spindly and my glasses got in the way of rough sports. But salvation was at hand from another quarter. It came from mathematics. After surviving the disgrace of a second year in the first form I was moved straight to form 3. Here my fortunes began to change. The school maths teacher was a formidable man, an ex-commando with a famous war record at D-Day. Major Coulson was fierce but fair – and a good teacher. Every Saturday morning he had the entire school assemble in the big dining room to answer 80 – yes 80 – quick-fire questions of mental arithmetic. Your answers were scribbled in an exercise book which was then passed to your neighbour for marking immediately the 80 questions were finished. Finally all the scores were entered on a big sheet that was posted on the school noticeboard – names listed in order of best scores. There was no hiding place – scores for each week were added up to produce a running league table showing the position of every boy in the school.

No doubt Major Coulson felt this type of ruthless competition mirrored the kind of army training he had endured. The teachers of today would no doubt be horrified by the brutal nature of the competition – there was no succour for the weak. In fact I think most of the boys enjoyed the challenge and it certainly provided great training for passing exams! Luckily for me I soon became one of his star players – this mental arithmetic was something I could do. The faster and more challenging the questions became the more I was focussed and enjoying the challenge. As a relatively new boy it was a good feeling to be top of Coulson's list. Suddenly I found myself with new friends and the world seemed a much better place.

Quite apart from the pressure-cooker dynamics of the close

social relations which boarding school required, Mowden had two other memorably unpleasant features. One was boxing – which was compulsory for all boys – brutal and often bloody. I refused to take part – and used my tendency to have copious nosebleeds as my excuse. The other was swimming – in a smelly and sweaty greenish pool under a large greenhouse roof. Again I refused point blank to take part – and excused myself on the grounds of a perforated eardrum I had suffered from an earlier mastoid infection. I'm pretty sure the authorities found my refusals annoying as there was very strong pressure for everyone to fall in with their plans. So I did not learn to swim at Mowden and I did not learn to box!

After four years at school my fortunes were improved dramatically as I discovered my body had changed and quite suddenly I could run and jump with amazing power. I could run faster than any boy in the school – win races and score tries at rugby. This is the strange thing about finding you have a good mix of genes which come from parents and grandparents. Masters and school friends began to take notice – I had my own "platform" for power within the norms of school culture. It became easy to conform to the conventions required by school life but I always remained a secret rebel and had no compunction about breaking rules if it suited me. I regularly raided the headmaster's wine cellar together with a couple of pals. We simply unscrewed the door fittings in the wine cellar then filled the bottles we drank with water and replaced them. I often wonder what must have happened long after I had left when the losses were discovered. I had always disliked the headmaster, Mr Marchbank, and I'm sure he disliked me too. He was a small rather unattractive little man who did nothing to inspire respect. Certainly he caned me a couple of times with some relish – 4 lashes on the hand were extremely painful. It must have been irritating for him when he finally made me head boy!

I realise now that most of the masters in the school must have gone through all sorts of stress and adventures in the war which had just finished. Our poor Latin master, Mr Cook, always seemed sorry for himself and was often drunk after a lunch at the local pub. The booze did not put him in the best of tempers – we all had to learn Latin, of course, in order to pass the Common Entrance exam for entry to Public School. Mr Lowe, the woodwork teacher, had been in the Royal Engineers and was a calm and powerful Scotsman. Mr Sullivan was neat and polite – a nifty rugby coach and a very nice man. Mr Dakin, who took over as headmaster if my memory serves, was a great pal because he let us borrow his smart new golf clubs. We had a very business-like "matron" who looked after our bathing and our ailments – Miss Nightingale. (One of her pretty young assistants was Judy Turnbull, who later would do so much to help my aged mother in Embleton!)

Kipper McKinley and David Nicol were my two best pals at Mowden – though I never kept up with them later. Kipper McK was a lively fellow and a good sportsman. I remember staying with him in Redcar and going to my first football match to watch Middlesbrough play. David Nicol was, like me, mad on golf and it seemed his whole family simply lived for the game. His big sister was county champion and his big brother, John Nicol, would play golf with me later in old boys' public school events.

The Leys – 1958-63

Miraculously I did pass the Common Entrance exam for Public School and my parents decided to send me to the country's leading Methodist school – the Leys in Cambridge. (My cousin Ian had already been Head Boy there.) It was a long way to Cambridge in those days! Getting the school trunk packed was a major exercise and my Mum was a conscientious expert at getting it all right. Exact numbers of shirts, collars, socks, vests, sports shirts etc. were required. I had to learn how to put on the detached collars which could be changed every couple of days – to make the white shirts last a bit longer. Everything for school went in the trunk and then the trunk was taken to Christon Bank station (yes, there was a main line station) for delivery to the school "Passenger Luggage in Advance" or PLA as the railway called it. So all would be waiting to be unpacked when I finally arrived to take my place as a new boy, or "sprog", in North A House, which was right beside Coe Fen Street – a major trunk (and very noisy) road through the town.

Being a new "sprog" was quite a scary business. There was no "fagging" at the Leys – possibly because it was a staunchly Methodist establishment – but "sprogs" were treated like dirt. My father had been determined I should not go to any school with "fagging" because he had found it so unpleasant when he went to Uppingham school. I was told that all "sprogs" had to go through an initiation ceremony which involved singing a song in front of the whole common room. (There were about 75 boys in each of the 5 school "houses" – so each year-group contained about 15 boys.) So my first conflict with authority and tradition took place almost immediately as I refused point blank to play the game. I also, as at Mowden, refused to take part in the compulsory swimming sessions – the school was unusual in having an excellent full-sized swimming pool.

Classes in the school were streamed by ability. Thanks to the training I'd had at Mowden I was a scholarship boy and put straight into the A-section of the second form (which was called V2(a). I had also been inspired by finding a broken old 'cello in the attic at Mowden so I had enrolled for 'cello lessons. These took place once each week with Miss Allen – a sweet birdlike lady who I liked very much and she was a very enthusiastic teacher. Later she would have a romantic affair with Mr Moore, my (excellent) maths teacher – so both were sadly sent away from the school! I hope they were happy together.

Now we began a high-intensity school life with chapel every morning and every evening and games at least 3 times each week. Every Wednesday we had to turn out in our uncomfortable army uniforms to parade and train with the Combined Cadet Force (the CCF). This was absolutely compulsory and a grim reminder of the recent war. Apart from routine square-bashing we did do pretty dramatic initiative training and arduous survival exercises. We all had to learn to shoot and do marksman tests, first with small-bore (.22) rifles and then with the extremely powerful .303 Lee Enfield service rifles. I opted to join the Royal Artillery section and we sometimes went over to the military range at Thetford to fire real 25-pounder guns – they lobbed a big shell about 15 miles over neighbouring farms and villages. It was amazing to see how the sheep which grazed on the range began to run from the place where they knew a shell was going to land. We had to do officer training in the Corps and I suppose it was simply accepted that the good public school leaver would be a natural leader either in industry or the community. Perhaps I would have made a good army officer as I passed out second in the school's officer selection board! Eventually in my later years at the Leys I was excused CCF duties so that I could put in extra time studying to take the Oxford and Cambridge scholarship exams.

Virtually all the discipline and day-to-day housekeeping chores were in the hands of the prefects. There were 12 school prefects who had important school duties – ringing the chapel bell was one, enforcing school discipline was another and reading out school notices in front of the whole school in the big refectory was another. The duty rota gave each school prefect a one week turn of duty every term. I remember that one of the tricky jobs we had to master was ringing the chapel bell properly – the whole school would be laughing when a beginner had his first try!

However, most of school life took place within the House. Here the role of the prefects was key – there were about 4 house prefects and something like 8 sub-prefects. The prefects were chosen by the housemaster (who lived in a house adjacent to North A) and the deputy housemaster who lived in a small flat on the first floor of North A. It was a very rare occurrence for a master to come into the House so discipline and the ethos of House life were set almost entirely by the boy prefects. The punishment system was administered by the prefects who could award a boy a "Y" mark for any kind of bad behaviour, a "T" mark for having both hands in your pocket and a "C" mark for shoddy dress. These punishment marks were written up on a central noticeboard in the House common room so everyone could see who had what. Boys had to work off their punishments by getting up very early before breakfast and being in class room number 6 (a big class room beside the library) before 7.15 am to write out the school line 15 times. I can remember it well!

"Few things are more distressing to a well ordered mind than to see a boy who ought to know better disporting himself at improper moments."

Boys who collected more than a certain number of "Y" marks would be "gated", which meant they were not allowed to go into town as the other boys were on school holidays. And those who collected 3 "T" marks had both their pockets sewn up by Lulu (the caretaker's wife). Fred, the caretaker, and his wife Lulu looked after the fabric of the place, sweeping floors, mending broken furniture and getting all the laundry done. They had a small flat deep in the basement of North A.

For the first 2 years boys simply had a locker in the common room for their books and personal bits and pieces. We kept our sports gear hanging in the (smelly) changing rooms where noisy, steamy showers and baths washed off the copious amounts of mud we picked up from rugger or hockey. We also were allowed "tuck boxes" for which each boy had his own key or combination lock. "Tuck" was a highly prized luxury – sometimes most exotic if gifts came in from rich parents. I remember my study mate Bill Heaney was the son of a rich American newspaper owner and he got sent all sorts of stuff – including smoked mussels and chocolate covered locusts which were very crunchy.

The common room was a buzzy busy place with a few comfy seats, a table tennis table and an old radio where we all listened to "Round the Horn" every Sunday. We also had a quiet room with soft seats where you could go to read or play cards. The daily routine was brisk and full-on. Breakfast at 8.15 am, morning chapel at 9.00, lessons starting at 9.30 with two 45-minute periods before break at 11.00 and two after. In break all boys had to do PE outdoors – star jumps, press ups, stretching etc. – and those on special teams did circuits in the gym. This left 15 minutes for a quick slice of hot toast and a cup of tea. Lunch was at 1.00 pm and everyone had to be ready for games on the field at 2.30 pm. Games finished about 4.00 pm so there was just time for showering etc. and a hot drink before the 2 afternoon lessons from 4.40 pm. Supper (all meals were taken together with 350 boys in the dining hall) was at 6.30 pm followed by "Prep" from 7.30 pm until 8.15 pm. "Prep" was the time we had to do our homework – it was supervised by one of the House prefects. After "prep" the junior boys had to be upstairs in their dorms by 9.00 pm with lights out at 9.20 pm. Once again it was the job of the sub-prefects to make sure all this happened by the book within the confines of each House.

There were three large dormitories in North A House. The two large dorms had about 24 beds each – at least two being occupied by prefects. The smaller dorm had about 20 beds. Boarding school life was community life with a vengeance – there was no privacy until boys were sufficiently senior to have their own "study". Only boys in the third year or above were allocated to "studies" where they could keep their books, their gramophones etc. and other personal possessions. Third-year boys would share a study between 3 or 4 boys. Fourth-year boys and older shared 2 to a study and the Head of House had his own study.

The ethos and culture of each House was strongly affected by the approach of its Housemaster and the personalities of the prefects. Quite how boys with different talents were allocated between Houses I'm not sure – some simply followed in the footsteps of parents or relatives. Of the 5 Houses, School House had the most musicians and artists and its housemaster was the school organist and musician, Ken Naylor. North B House was the most sporty, having the least academic achievement but probably the most fun as their house-master was the senior sports coach, ex-Olympic hockey player, Barbarian rugby player and generally gifted sportsman Neil White. Later I would continue my friendship with Neil after he became Secretary at Worlington Golf Club.

It was a tricky matter learning to keep discipline as a 16-year-old boy with 30 or 40 younger boys to manage. One's credibility, respect and effectiveness depended on minute by minute decisions. It was vitally important not to issue a command or instruction that was unlikely to be obeyed – so timing and some instinctive empathy was crucial. Prefects who were able to be fair and reasonable would steadily build up respect – their job became easier and easier. Within the school culture of that time, success at sport was the touchstone for popularity. The whole school was required to turn out on the touchline to watch the first team play at rugby or hockey. Every Friday afternoon there was a crush of interested boys looking at the team lists for the weekend. (There were matches against other schools at least once each week – sometimes more often.)

Here again I was fortunate. After a couple of years at school my physique again changed dramatically – or so it seemed to me. Muscles appeared where there had been none before and I could run like the wind. I was a regular member of the "Minor Colts" teams for both rugby and hockey – which meant serious training and frequent school matches where results were taken very seriously. There were also great sporting rivalries between the different Houses in the school – one inter-House competition in each of the rugby and hockey teams. My athletic prowess continued to grow – so much so that the authorities had to limit the number of events anyone was permitted to enter in the County Championships (I won the 100 yards, the 220 yards, the 120 yds hurdles, the 440 yards, the long jump, the shot putt and the discus). In both my final school years I represented the county in the Schools National Championships – first year in the 440 yards and second year in the 120 yards high hurdles. It was a daunting experience running in front of a huge stadium of spectators and I was nowhere near big enough (there were some giant 17 and 18-year-olds !) to win anything. High hurdling is a brutally explosive event and I still suffer today from the battering my right hip took during all those leaps over the obstacles.

One feature of uniformed school life was the possibility of wearing different ties when (and if) one achieved sporting or community honours. Even the smallest differences in clothing and accessories were extremely significant. Almost everyone had an ambition to become entitled to wear one of the special school ties. Everybody knew precisely the significance of each different tie. Even the socks you wore to sports matches reflected whether or not you had been awarded your "colours" (only those putting in exceptional performances would get their colours). I can remember very well when I became one of the youngest boys ever to wear the black and yellow striped tie which was awarded as house colours after I played (right wing) at the age of 16 in the winning house hockey team. With a special tie you really became a "somebody" and it was certainly a good feeling! There were ties for the different grades of prefects and ties for sports, including shooting but, strangely, there were no ties for academic achievements or for music. There were also ties for different school societies – the Kelvin club for science, the Glee club for singing, etc..

My younger brothers, Owen and Ben, soon joined me in North A House. I'm not sure this was the best arrangement as it was inevitable that the successes or failures of the eldest created expectations for the others. Brother Owen was also good at sport but he had a much smaller physique than me. Ben had no interest either in sport or conventional school work since his total focus was on electronics and machines. Everybody worried about Ben and how he would get on in the world – everybody that is EXCEPT Ben. Ben had complete confidence in his own unique ability to create and fix complex electrical devices. He spent hours fiddling with the sophisticated military radios which were used by the CCF. As events showed, he was right as he later became one of the most successful pioneers of the cellphone or mobile phone. His fortune was assured after he became the first person in the world to purchase the first concession ever offered for mobile phones for the area of Washington DC where he lived.

After surviving the first couple of weeks, life for me at the Leys was good. I played rugby and hockey for the first teams and was one of the boys who started the school athletics team instead of playing the (slow) game of cricket. I won many of the sporting events both at school and County level, going on to compete for Cambridgeshire in the national athletics championships in both of my last two school years. I was marked out for special training to take the Oxford and Cambridge university scholarship exams – a very important matter as far as the school's reputation was concerned. The benefit to me was that I was given special leave to miss the chore of going to the CCF parade every Wednesday – this so I could spend the time studying. The annoyance was that I was persuaded to stay on to repeat my last year in an effort to improve my chances of University success. That worked (I did get awarded an Exhibition to St Catharine's College, Cambridge) but I was bored and really wanted to get on with my life as by that time I had met Sarah, who was to be my future wife.

Although I never got along well with the headmaster, Mr Barker (the Pot), I did enjoy the bombastic company of his wife Jean Barker. She was a "no nonsense" super-forceful Canadian woman (she had worked at Bletchley Park during the war) who invited a select group of (bullet proof) boys to play bridge with her on Sunday afternoons. I was one of her young card players. This experience was a bit scary but we certainly learned a lot about life and tactics in cards. Proper card etiquette was absolutely required. One particular tip which has served me well is her advice that it is quite permissible to "ask your partner the score"; this is a device to signal caution in bidding if you already have a part-score below the line! Of course Mrs Barker went on to become a successful Lord Mayor of Cambridge and then a junior government minister. Finally, as Baroness Trumpington, she became an outspoken and very popular member of the House of Lords – famously being filmed making a V sign at a fellow peer who had irritated her.

I have no doubt that all the "leadership" training provided by my school experience probably made me an insufferably self-confident and brash young man. Being an officer in the CCF was one thing, whilst being head of House and deputy head prefect for the school did force you to take responsibility. The boys could be merciless towards those they did not respect – and no amount of formal authority could compensate. I'm sure my progress and success must have been quite a shock for my parents – particularly for my father, who was a man who hated being in the public eye.

Girls

Like most public schools, the Leys was a single-sex boys' school. I had no sisters and my Mum was such an ordered and calm person that (as I slowly realised later) she provided no clue as to how real girls might behave. My only girl relative was my mother's sister's daughter, Diana, (my cousin). So it was thanks to Diana and her girlfriends at the Friends' School, Saffron Walden, that I started my long apprenticeship of trying to understand women. It is true that the Leys did its bit by offering senior boys the chance to go to organised dancing classes in the town – which we did. This gave us a chance to touch the opposite sex but no real opportunity to get to know them. One or two boys who were more experienced and sophisticated did manage to form relationships – but they had grown up in cities which provided much more worldly wisdom than the open countryside of Northumberland.

So in my later years at school I would take the train over to Saffron Walden to try my hand at the challenging business of finding a girlfriend. The girls at the co-ed Quaker school were much more advanced in these matters than I – experts at "snogging" as it was called. I had some brief "love affairs" which were mostly carried on in the exchange of handwritten letters. But the girls of Saffron Walden would soon be replaced by my falling in love with the exciting, wild and wilful Sarah. You will find out more about that later!

Home Life

The first thing you have to realise is that from the age of 8 onwards home life played a relatively minor role in my own and my brothers' development. For more than two thirds of each year we boys were at boarding school where full attention was required every waking minute to build and maintain your place in what was a sort of pressure-cooker society. Every moment of the boarding school day could bring an unexpected challenge where success or failure could seriously affect one's standing. So home life was a great escape from these pressures. Home life was orderly, meals came on time and we fell in easily with the routine of the farm although our parents discouraged us from becoming too involved with farm work. As we got older we helped out by driving tractors, feeding animals and stacking hay. We played in the farm buildings and chatted with the farm workers. At Christmas and Easter we were cleaned up and polished to be taken around all the workers' cottages to give them presents and receive biscuits or chocolates in return. We also had to help out with the farm chores while the regular workers took their holidays.

We simply took for granted the fact that we had 1,000 acres of farmland to play in, not to mention the huge open spaces of Embleton beach and the links. We became keen hunters using bow and arrows which we bought with our pocket money from Murray's sports shop in Alnwick. Pigeons were our chief prey until we graduated to using air rifles. By the time we were teenagers we were already experienced drivers and well used to hunting hares, pheasant and partridge with .22 rifles and 12-bore shotgun. At that time the whole place was running with hares;

we could shoot 50 each week and make some pocket money by taking them up to the meat factory in Berwick where they were made into game pate. My father was extremely strict about safety and not making animals suffer by badly placed bullets which only wounded rather than killed. If we did wound an animal then it had to be followed until it could be killed cleanly by a shot in the head.

Sailing

As a young teenager my brother Owen was the first of the three of us to became keen on sailing. Our parents wanted to encourage him and booked him on a sailing course one long holiday weekend when we were taken from school to the Norfolk Broads. Ben and I had to "twiddle our thumbs" while Owen received his special sailing lesson. In later years we would all be sent off to various sailing schools, one at Bosham, another at Falmouth, during the summer holidays. Sailing on the Norfolk Broads would become a regular and much-loved feature of our family holidays together. Eventually we were bought an 11-foot-long Gull dinghy which we could take on holidays on a trailer. After a couple of years this was replaced by an Enterprise (built by Mr Garrett in Alnmouth) which we sailed for many years. Now that I have had the experience (and hassle) of towing a boat on a trailer myself I realise how patient and hard-working my father must have been to put up with our sailing hobby. The paradox here is that it was Ben and myself who ended up devoting a lot of our lives to sailing whilst it was only ever a small part of Owen's life! Such are the vagaries of life.

As a family we made regular trips to sail on the Norfolk Broads. As we drove south towards Potter Heigham, Owen and I would be scanning the trees to see if there was any wind. The family would hire a 6 or even 8-berth motor cruiser (our base camp) and we boys (usually just Owen and myself) would sail one of the lovely old traditional "half-deckers" – catching up with the family for delicious meals every evening. Our old family friend, Mrs Donkin (Mrs D to us) would almost always come along with us to lend a hand. Her cheery smile provided us boys with some relief from my father's often seriously careful and measured approach to life.

'Cello

The story of my love of the 'cello begins in the hot sunny attic of Mowden Hall school – a place we sometimes escaped to for a bit a peace during my final year. Lying in the attic was the remains of what turned out to be a beautiful old 'cello. Only a couple of strings were left – but they made a wonderful resonant sound when I plucked them. The shape and structure of the old instrument fascinated me since I had never seen such a thing close up before. It was a logical next step to choose 'cello lessons as a music option when moving on to the Leys. Prior to that I had been taken to piano lessons with a sweet but rather feeble lady in Seahouses (Mrs Lambert) – so I could at least read music.

Sadly, my parents were never enthusiasts about my musical interests (or talent). I only discovered later that there had been keen and very capable musicians on both sides of the family! But my parents simply held the view that you were either gifted with musical talent or you weren't. As I stumbled along with my early efforts they very soon decided I did not have the gift so I never received much encouragement. I remember the vicar calling one day when I was trying to play a new piano piece – his comment was "persevere my son and you will succeed" – it was not exactly encouraging. The only person in the family who did support my musical endeavours was my Aunt Doreen. As one of my early Christmas presents she gave me a small musical manuscript book which contained the complete score of the Hebrides Overture by Mendelssohn. This fascinated me but, at the time, just seemed rather amazing. I little thought then that I would one day (several times) be actually playing this piece as part of an orchestra.

Before I went to the Leys my parents had the good fortune to find an old 'cello for sale in the local Gazette. A recently widowed lady was selling her husband's old instrument – the 'cello for £10 and the old wooden case for £5. It was a beautiful thing – if rather fragile. I found out later that it must have been more than 200 years old. It had no maker's label (unfortunately) – just a label inside from the firm that repaired it in Germany in 1815. This was the 'cello which was sent down to the Leys for me to learn on (by Passenger Luggage in Advance on the railways).

Miss Allen was a quiet but inspirational teacher – because she could play so beautifully. She was a small but pretty birdlike creature and certainly gave the impression that she believed I could play! We made speedy progress through the various fingerboard positions until I was good enough to join the school orchestra. The House I was in at school had no musical tradition – the real musicians all came from School House, where the housemaster was the wonderful school music master Mr Naylor. As far as the school establishment was concerned my sporting prowess was my greatest and most important talent – so my musical efforts were largely ignored.

Fortunately my musical talent (such as it was) was "discovered" by Cecil Crouch, the school's gay art master. One of my good pals in North A House was a great artist. He had suggested to me that I might earn some pocket money by acting as a life model in the art school. My athletic prowess and genes had, fortunately for me, provided a good physique – just what the arty fellows wanted. So I regularly did my hour or so as a model (stripped down to my underpants!). Mr Crouch had his own tradition of inviting 3 or 4 of his chosen boys to join him at his home in Girton for a splap-up Sunday lunch. He was an excellent cook, a charming civilised man and a good pianist. He would invite me to bring my 'cello and after lunch we would repair to his sunbathed sitting room to have a go at playing sonatas by Brahms or Beethoven. Riding out on my bike with a 'cello swinging beside me was always rather a chancy affair! But the music was great although I did not share Mr Crouch's vision that I might become a wonderful ballet dancer! Later I played more advanced orchestral music in the Cambridge holiday orchestra.

One sad aspect to my school musical career was the early disappearance of my lovely 'cello teacher. After about 3 years of tuition she was suddenly sacked by the school. We soon found out why. The school authorities had discovered that Miss Allen was having an illicit love affair with (of all people) my favourite maths teacher, Mr Moore. I suppose, being a strict Methodist establishment, the school felt they had no alternative but to get rid of these two lovers (Mr Moore was still married) as they set such a bad example. So in a moment I lost 2 of my best teachers. We never did find out what happened to them, but I certainly hope they were happy. They were both excellent people as far as I was concerned.

After leaving school my poor old 'cello was confined to a cupboard. University life was too busy – not to mention my rapidly growing family and business commitments. I only got the 'cello out again much later after I met Sue, who not only encouraged me to take up music again but also brought so many new things into my life (including our son Hal). It must have been around 1987 that we took the 'cello out of its case. Sadly it had a nasty crack, what they call a "sound post crack" in the back. This came from being kept in houses that were centrally heated and therefore too dry – the pressure on the sound post created stresses which in turn caused the 'cello to crack. Sue persuaded me to take it to a luthier in Cambridge and we left it to be repaired – which it was, most beautifully. I messed about with my newly reborn instrument but it was not until I went to live in Ireland that I decided to play seriously again.

There were a number of different factors which encouraged me to play again. I regularly read articles in the New Scientist magazine. One of these described a large-scale research project which seemed to show that there was no such thing as natural musical talent. The researchers had questioned more than 1,000 student musicians about their training and experience. They did not find a single one of the top musician students who had done less than 10,000 hours of practice. They concluded that it is purely practice that creates musical talent. 10,000 hours is about 3 hours each day for 10 years! Clearly you have to enjoy doing this and enjoy your relationship with both teachers and parents if this is to be possible. But I decided then and there that I would put this theory to the test – if I just did 10 minutes each day over the next year we would see what happened. The second important influence was the completely different attitude to music and singing in Ireland compared to England. In Ireland almost everyone is expected to be able to sing or play something – as I discovered after every Irish dinner party!

Sarah and Seahouses Pier

It was a wild, wet and windy Bank Holiday Monday in August 1962 when I went along to help my parents run the Embleton Women's Institute's stall at the annual Lifeboat fete in Seahouses. Little did I know it then but that day was to change my life! By afternoon there were very few punters prepared to brave the weather to perambulate around the various stands. I was bored and climbed up onto the top of the harbour wall (it's prohibited now) to watch the waves as the cold grey drizzle continued. There I chanced to meet another brave soul – did she join me or did I join her? One way or another we fell into conversation – and a spark had been kindled that would release great mutual energies over the next 50 years, including four wonderful children.

Sarah was up from Newcastle staying at the old farmhouse in Christon Bank with her fierce granny (Gaga) and grampa Nash (an ex-tax inspector). Strong and somewhat rebellious, she too was a mathematician, a lover of golf, swimming and all things outdoors. We were two teenagers full of pent-up energy and it was not long before we were dreaming about the family we would have and the great adventures of life that awaited us. The forces of destiny could not be denied and our lives became woven together from that moment onwards. I have never for one minute regretted it – despite its sometimes difficult and uncomfortable consequences. We have, like many others before us, battled through hard times as well as good. We have launched four capable "new" people into the world and we have always stood by each other when events required it. One way and another, I think we can look back on it all as a "job well done"! I certainly realise now that without the energy and confident commitment of Sarah behind me I would not have achieved so much or taken on such "risky" commitments. I was always a much more cautious parent than she was and she certainly put the children through some challenging experiences but always with the exact judgement of what they could actually cope with.

Golf

Golf was another important part of home life. I must have been about 8 or 9 years old when I started to swing a club. Probably the most important thing my father ever taught me was how to grip a golf club! He did not play golf himself although his father had been keen (and had been a big influence in developing Dunstanburgh Golf Course, which he owned). But I can very well remember being in the garden room at Dunstan Steads and my father telling me that the most important thing to get right at the beginning was your grip. He showed me how and his advice has stayed with me for all of my life.

The golf course was only a few hundred yards from our front door and it was owned and managed by my parents. So it was easy to go down and bash a few balls about whenever time allowed. But neither of my parents played so my golfing education was entrusted to the Donkin family. Mrs Donkin was a great friend of my parents. Her whole family was golf mad. Her husband, Dixon Donkin, was general manager of the Co-op store which was then a big and important shop in Embleton selling everything from butter to buttons, boots to beeswax. The honours board in the golf house still shows many Donkins as Captains and winners, both ladies and men. When my parents had to go away for any reason we were dropped off to stay with Mrs D. We enjoyed her cheerful company, playing dominoes and card games and learning that there was a less serious side to life. (My parents generally took life and their responsibilities seriously so laughter was not a very common feature of our home life.)

The first thing I had to learn about golf from Mrs D was the vital importance of golfing etiquette. We also learned about the strange, and perhaps unfair, ethos of golf where players had to accept the "rub of the green" (so even a great shot could finish in a divot mark and you could do nothing about it). These lessons gave the golfing experience something of a spiritual or semi-religious dimension. But my crude swishing at the ball was soon to be revamped and retrained by taking lessons from the wise old Glaswegian, Eddie Fernie, at the (very smart) course at Foxton. Fernie was chief coach for the Northumberland county teams and a wizard at giving his pupils both skills and the confidence to use them. His opening gambit with new pupils was to ask them to show him their swing. He would then contemplate what he had seen for a few moments before telling them they had the best natural swing he had ever seen. Of course he would go on to suggest various small changes – each one moving the swing to something more reliable and repeatable.

When I was 17 years old I was able to apply and get a provisional driving licence. This enabled the holder to drive on public roads provided there was another person in the car who held a current driving licence. Here again Mrs D proved a great help because, although she had never driven a car, she had paid to get a driving licence before any test was required. So she would jump in the car so I could drive down to Alnmouth for my weekly lesson during the summer holidays.

Mr Fernie was going to have another very important influence on my life although I did not know it at the time. It came about because he was the official coach to both the boys' and ladies' Northumberland county golf teams. Sarah was one of the girls who went along to Fernie for this county coaching and whilst doing so met a young man from Whitley Bay, Jim Rumbellow, who would later become Captain of the Cambridge University Stymies golf team. She had not hesitated to tell him that she had a boyfriend who could hit the ball much better than he could! As a result Jim later got in touch with me when we were at Cambridge together and invited me to play golf for his team. This I was glad to do and soon became a regular member of the Stymies golf team. Jim has been a great friend ever since and I've made many other life-long friendships as a result. Jim himself (although not the strongest player in the world) became Captain of one of Britain's premier golf clubs (Royal St George's in Kent) and actually held this position when the British Open was played there in 2011.

Golf in the long summer evenings was a regular part of the time I spent at home between school and University. Sometimes I'd play 4 rounds in the day; sometimes I'd be working on the course mowing or scything. Scything was a vital ingredient of my golf in those days because it produced large quantities of golf balls! I had learned to scythe by watching the beautiful smooth movements of Jock Arnott – the gamekeeper who also worked as a greenkeeper. Obtaining a regular supply of balls was a necessary requirement as buying a new ball was a major outlay – not just the money but going into Alnwick. In those days, the best golf balls – small English size, the US larger ball came later – were Dunlop 65s, each individually wrapped in crinkly black paper. The Dunlops cost 4s 9d and it was a nervous business to hit the first shot with one after carefully unwrapping the paper. Just below the Dunlop was the Warwick at 4s 6d, then you had the unwrapped Bogeys at 3s and even cheaper the GBDs at 2s 6d.

At the end of the long summer days it was always a pleasant prospect to be plodding up the hill home to Dunstan Steads as twilight fell, knowing there was hot supper waiting. I had regular golfing partners from the village – about my age – Glyn Barrs (an exact contemporary at the village school who became a local butcher) and Alan Breeze (a young lab technician from Newcastle University who lived in the village). During summer holidays I would drive the three of us up to Scotland with golf clubs and tent in the family's nippy Fiat 1600 estate car. We were mad young enthusiasts in those days, lacking experience I must admit. On our first trip we had camped overnight in a wood near Gullane. Glyn had brought a big bag of his sausages and we were looking forward to a big meaty breakfast. The question was – how could we brew up tea and cook the sausages? In desperation we started up the car and tried to boil a kettle on top of the exhaust manifold. Quite a crazy idea and hopelessly ineffective! We never did get those sausages eaten! We played the Gullane courses then went on up to St Andrews, where we could camp without interference on the east sands (beside the Old Course). It was easy to play on all the municipal courses in those days – and we did. A lot has changed since those days in the 1960s and the Scots have turned their famous golf courses into money-spinning businesses squeezing as much as they can from gullible Americans. Not a pleasant prospect because these people tend to take 5 hours to play a round and have no idea of sensible golfing etiquette!

My other (important) golfing pals were Sarah and the girls from the bungalows – Ros Cattliff and Jenny Lee Smith. We were all mad keen, often playing in bare feet. We felt somewhat sorry for Jenny Lee Smith because she had a dragon for a mother and this mother was determined to make her daughter famous. Of course she duly did and Jenny Lee Smith became a significant pioneer of women's professional golf, winning some major championships. We did not realise at that time that Jenny was one of a pair of adopted twins. In fact I only discovered this 40 years later when Jenny wrote a book (My Secret Sister) about how she had managed to finally discover and meet her missing twin!

More about my Father – and his suicide

As a teenager I began to try and understand what made my father tick! I knew from the rather stiff visits we paid to his father, the famous wealthy philanthropist Sir Arthur Sutherland, that he had not had a happy home life. His mother had died relatively young. Business, both private and public, had clearly been at the centre of his father's life. This was obvious from what we overheard during visits to my father's elder sister Kath, who lived in Wooler. No doubt the experience of having to witness all the pomp and high-profile fame of his father had made my father want to retreat from this world of privilege and money. One result was that my father utterly despised the ways of the local landed gentry who strutted around in their tweeds giving orders like local royalty. My father played this out by being proud of being a working farmer who got up at 6 every morning and put on his working clothes. He loved his work improving the farm infrastructure – drains, fences, roads and buildings. He had a well-equipped workshop with big power saws, planes and drills and he would often be found there listening to his radio and making the next piece of gear for the farm. He was always a strong believer in the motto that if something is worth doing then it's worth doing well. All the things he made were made to last.

My father wanted to be seen as a good working man. He often dressed in an old gabardine raincoat tied up with string. The farm workers all tell the story of how a travelling salesman had told them that he'd taken directions on the road from an old tramp wearing a mac tied up with string. The salesman could not believe it when the workers told him that his directions had come directly from Sir Ivan Sutherland himself!

I think it was a mystery to my father when my mother decided to get into local government – even though there was no politics in local government then! Her frequent public activities often took her away from family life but she had amazing patience and strength in getting things done through all the conflicting local opinions and inertia. My father's only ventures onto the public stage were either to argue with the vicar and the Church over the doctrine of "original sin" or to exchange letters in the paper with our outspoken (and tweed-clad) neighbour Sir Jock Craster. My father had been at Uppingham with Jock Craster and had always disliked what he regarded as his bombastic and self-appointed expertise on country matters. He regarded Craster as a pompous fool – more pity for those who took Craster's words at face value. We were always encouraged to shoot the pheasants which Sir Jock reared if they strayed onto our farm and became "fair game".

My father's strong feelings about what he regarded as the wickedness of the Church's doctrine on original sin always surprised me. He wrote to the newspapers about this and had quite outspoken (very uncharacteristic) arguments with the various vicars who came to the Parish. My father thought it very wrong that the church had made so many ordinary people feel bad about what he regarded as quite natural desires and instincts. The established Church seemed to have simply invented this doctrine for its own purposes – so that "sinners" would come to them to be "saved". I found my father's arguments very persuasive although I have come to see that the Church's invention of "Hell" was a great way to keep ordinary people "in line"! Try as I might, I cannot find anyone who can tell just when "Hell" was invented nor how the "powers that be" convinced ordinary people of its potential horrors.

From time to time we children did see parts of my father's wilder side. When we drove up beyond Holy Island around Lowick, where he once lived, he used to point out the telegraph pole which had nearly killed him on his motorbike. Evidently the bike had got out of control at high speed, gone off the road, doing an aerial cartwheel in the process which threw him off and resulted in the exhaust pipe being impaled through the telegraph pole. We knew of course that he had blown himself up in his younger days. Occasionally we would hear snippets of stories from either of his two great friends, Norman Burrell or Basil Mahon. They had been companions in the Home Guard during the war and told the story of how my father had been obsessed by explosives. On one occasion he and his friends had just finished learning how to set explosives off under water so they set out to give this a try in the local quarry pond. No sooner had they thrown their parcel of explosives into the water when a party of nuns appeared – they were in for a nasty shock! On another occasion – or so it is said – my father tried to blow up the cliff face near the rumbling kern at Dunstanburgh Castle.

At home I can remember how my father used to enjoy getting the small steam engines going that you could buy to go with the Meccano sets. We'd have steam and smoke in our comfy sitting room as we tried to operate a crane or some other mechanical creation. Another favourite hobby was his jet powered cars which whizzed around on the end of a short piece of string on the lino floor in his office. These were powered by a small solid cylinder of slow burning brown explosive (solid rocket fuel!). You popped this into the metal jacket of the "jet", connected a fuse and applied a lighted match. Once again there was plenty of smoke and fumes. Sometimes my father would create a much larger version of this rocket experiment by tying a wire to a rocket firework on Guy Fawkes night. The other end of the wire was then tied to a strong upright post. When the rocket was ignited it fairly thrashed around in a circle before the wire snapped and the whole lot zipped off into the night. He told us he used to do this trick with the out-of-date ship's distress rockets which he got from his father's business. The most exciting incident had been when he lashed several of these rockets around the edge of the big wheel which turned the mangle for squeezing water out of newly washed clothes.

We did a lot of shooting with my father. He was very keen that we should become good shots so we practised with him either in the 'onsteads' (against the hay bales with a .22 rifle) or down the hall in our house (when our mother was out at one of her meetings!). We did become good shots and later became proficient at shooting flying game with his 12-bore shotgun.

My father's other great interest was movie photography. Immediately after the war he bought a state-of-the-art "wind-up" 8mm movie camera. He used this to take a good number of family photos which have now been transferred onto a digital format. He had an expensive film projector for showing movies in the house – a very rare treat in the days before TV. We would watch movies of Felix the Cat or Mr Magoo – silent movies, of course. At this time all the film was made of nitro-cellulose. Occasionally my father would show us how violently this would burn. All such film was discontinued after 1951 but the Health and Safety Executive have meanwhile issued a very dramatic leaflet warning of how dangerous it can be. The cellulose nitrate was a major ingredient in wartime explosives. It ignites extremely easily (a temperature as low as 38 degrees C can set it off) and, once lit, it requires no oxygen so it is almost impossible to put out. Putting it in water just makes the fumes even more toxic.

Later in his life when he had more or less retired from active farming, my father bought a very modern set of equipment for showing movies. He took his big projector, screen and sound system around the local villages where he would show the films he had bought to groups such as the Women's Institutes. It was when he was taking some ladies with him in his Landrover that he damaged his leg when he slipped trying to get the overweight Mrs Swanston (the widow of Jack Swanston, our cowman) up into the vehicle. The pain from the injured nerves was so intense it virtually crippled my father. When he was sent to hospital for examination the doctors told him that there was nothing they could do without an operation and, worse still, they found the blood circulation in his legs was very poor. Gangrene and amputation was a real possibility. My father was 79 at the time and made the fateful decision to shoot himself. He kept his decision secret – something which he apologised for in his final letter to my mother. She describes the day of the event very vividly in her own life story and her shock at seeing the brown envelope on the kitchen table on that wet November morning with the words "I have killed myself" written on the outside. My father was 15 years older than my mother and had already made arrangements so the Smithy in Embleton would be available for my mother to live in after he died.

I am sure my father realised that if he had become a dependent invalid this would not only have been a "hell on Earth" for him, but it would have trapped my mother in a way he could never have accepted. As it was, his death freed my mother to be able to travel, seeing the world and visiting the many relatives she would not otherwise have been able to meet. My mother always said her life was in three distinct parts – first her youth and training to be a child nurse, second life as a farmer's wife and finally life as a "free agent" travelling to see relatives and having time to enjoy the expanding family and grandchildren.

I did not go to my father's funeral service in Embleton because the entire sad drama took place when I was already fully committed in Jamaica with a specially chosen group of senior sports people invited by the Jamaican government. I knew in any case that my father would not have wished his action to cause major disruption in other people's lives. As my mother says in her own story "*Ivan always said that life must go on – if you said you would do something you must still do it.*" I was able to make a contribution to the service by letter – as follows:

I asked for the opportunity to contribute to this service today in my own way – first because I am grateful to have been my father's son and second because I want to add my own thoughts and feelings to those which are already in your minds today.

A thanksgiving ceremony may seem unusual to many but its purpose is perceptive, simple and honest. Those adjectives are chosen with care because they parallel exactly the qualities I most admired in my father. The same qualities which led to his last decisive act; qualities which are becoming increasingly rare in our slick technological society where ideas and products are spoon-fed through the media, and human life is dispensed through plastic wrappers and gaudy tin cans. It was a great sadness to my father that he lived in a world which had little time for his ideas; a world where statesmen and politicians are more prone to count their TV ratings than the effect their decisions have on the realities of the ordinary man's life.

But the conventional battle to influence minds was not my father's style and, alas, in his lifetime he found few friends to share his straightforward philosophy. I can hear him now talking about death – the arguments are hard and, as is often the case, the truth hurts. Man is alone among species in his ability to prolong the infirmities of age, but whether we have the philosophical strength to use this power wisely is a more open question. Strangely this is one of the key issues covered by the Reith Lectures this year on the radio – a programme often followed by my father.

On Thursday when I was told of my father's decision and its consequences, the effect was blinding. But my great sadness was joined very soon by a feeling of great pride that I was the son of a man who had died because of his beliefs. That's not very common any more. There's an old saying that actions speak louder than words. My father knew he was right and had the ultimate courage to act accordingly. His strength in this will never be forgotten; in a strange way too his act passes part of that strength on to us – as a challenge and as an example.

One could say more but what more is there really to say. My father was no lover of pomp and ceremony. Our tribute will lie in what we make out of the rest of our lives and how far we can make the simple principles he believed in become reality.

The Family's Failed "love affair" with the National Trust!

The estate which my father inherited from Sir Arthur included the entire coastal strip stretching from the north side of Craster to the Long Nanny at Beadnell. (Sir Arthur had already given

Dunstanburgh Castle to the Nation – Ministry of Works.) This was just part of the larger properties which included the 5 farms of North farm (sold to Manners), High and Low Newton farms (run by the Gregorys), Dunstan Square and Dunstan Steads (run by my father). The estate included many houses in Embleton, including the Dunstanburgh Hotel (which was sold to the Robsons), and Low Newton. My father had been offered the choice of taking this coastal property or Sir Arthur's College Valley estate (Hethpool) when Sir Arthur died. Wisely he chose Embleton.

Most of the day-to-day management of the estate outside the farming was handled by my father's agent, Mr Campbell, whose office was in Wooler. He was a crusty old-school sort of fellow who collected rents and dealt with correspondence and queries – of which there were many. Mr Campbell would pay regular visits to Dunstan Steads to discuss these matters – for which we had to be on our best behaviour and my father had to put on his shirt and tie!

The golf links, adjacent duneland and beaches were always a concern to my parents. They were totally opposed to any kind of commercial development but well aware that this land was an extremely valuable asset for the village community. The problem was that the golf course made no profits and took up valuable time to run whilst the long stretch of duneland and beach was virtually impossible to "police". Horse riders, bikers, walkers, campers and fishermen all used the beaches as they wished – often very much to the detriment of other users and the natural life which flourished there. There was no way my family had the resources to try and control this large and vulnerable expanse of coastline.

One of my father's more distant relatives, Mr Ben Proud, was associated in some way with the National Trust. At that time the Trust was organised into regions – each region being managed by a regional committee of the "great and the good" (usually land-owners who had already given property to the Trust). Ben Proud knew some of these folk and began to have discussions with my father about the potential advantages of handing over (gifting) the links, duneland and beaches to the National Trust. My father was assured that the National Trust had its own powerful set of byelaws and would be able to use these to "police" the dunes much more effectively than any private individual. Furthermore by giving this land to the Trust it would be removed from any assessment of death duties, which at that time were at a very high, almost confiscatory, level.

As with all such affairs, the lawyers for the two parties got together to see how the various deeds of gift could be drafted. Strongly-worded restrictive covenants were incorporated into the deeds. My father wished to ensure that there would be no development, no vehicles, no animals permitted on the dunes – nothing that would detract from the natural state of the land and nothing that might cause annoyance to any successors in title.

At this time the state of affairs on the duneland was rather different from what it has become now. The bungalow owners played a much more active role as "stakeholders" in the golf course and duneland. Not only did they have a vested interest in "looking after" the duneland, they also played an important part in keeping the golf course going as a viable business. All the rents from the 40 bungalows were paid towards the upkeep of the golf course and all the bungalows were required to pay at least one annual green fee to the golf course. At the northern end of Embleton Bay, the group of bungalow owners whose shacks were near to Low Newton all used the access road to Risemoor Cottage to get close to their bungalows. They parked their cars on the dunes. There was no control of this access and during busy summer days there would always be a large number of day trippers who also tried to find space to park in the dunes along this route. This produced a chaotic and dangerous state of traffic congestion as well as serious erosion of the dunes.

The other group who wanted access to the dunes were the traditional fishermen at Low Newton who had always launched their cobles from the beach. At that time there was no ramp down to the beach in the Low Newton village – only steps.

During winter and storms the four cobles were drawn up and parked on the duneland immediately to the south of what were then operational farm buildings.

In the Low Newton village square itself there was often severe traffic congestion because there were no double yellow lines along the access road and no public car park at the top of the hill. The area which is now used as a village green (and as additional drinking space for the pub) was then taken up by untidy allotments which were allocated to the residents. The allotments (so important for growing food in earlier times) were hardly used and were covered in weeds and ramshackle old sheds. We had to have careful negotiations with our tenants to get agreement to remove the allotments and create an open grass space for recreation.

So there was effectively single-file access into Low Newton village when the entire roadside was taken up by parked cars. At weekends the traffic situation became extremely congested, dangerous and chaotic. The farm buildings (which Owen and Ben later converted into cottages) were still in use at the time so there was also a need for tractors and farm traffic to pass down the narrow access road immediately beside our family home (the Farmhouse) where I lived with Sarah and the children.

After the land was gifted by my father to the National Trust in 1961, there was an expectation that they would take control of these problems by enforcing their byelaws and honouring the covenants in the deed of gift. But it soon became clear that the promises made by Ben Proud and other representatives of the Trust were not going to be kept. The National Trust now had what it wanted and claimed that it could not do anything because it had no money! The Trust suddenly decided to try and get the bungalows cleared off the dunes – an attempt which was strongly resisted by my parents. Next the Trust began a public campaign to have a tarmac access road constructed so that the public could drive along the coast from Craster to the castle! My father still owned this land and categorically refused to be bullied into meeting this demand. As a family we had already been under pressure for many years to provide public car parking space so that more people could access the dunes and beach. Again my father had refused although he could have made large profits by doing so as there was virtually no planning control at this time.

The problems of controlling public access to sensitive areas of natural beauty had increased rapidly after the Second World War in line with the number of people who could afford cars. Despite huge public pressure and the potential to make big profits, my father steadfastly refused to provide any parking space whether at Newton, Embleton golf course (just the golf car park), Dunstan Steads road end or Craster. He wanted to protect the duneland and castle from being ruined by an influx of too many people. As he said often in exchanges of letters to the press, if people want to go there they can walk!

My father's frustrations with the broken promises and inaction of the Trust finally reached a point where he wrote to the Times warning other landowners about the fact that you could not trust the Trust. This did produce more weasel words of apologies from the Trust but no substantive action – just more of the same old excuses. No doubt other potential donors made sure they used good lawyers to protect themselves against abuses by the Trust.

I was a sad witness to all these struggles as I passed through Cambridge University. I realised that my father had been naïve and his lawyers had been incompetent – despite their smart manners and even smarter suits. Little did I realise then that I would soon be at the front line fighting my own battles against the Trust. I certainly realised that having an understanding of law might be useful in managing one's affairs in the real world. More of all this later!

My American Gap Year

After staying on at the Leys for a final winter term to take the Cambridge scholarship exams, I was finally able to move on to the next phase of my life. After being awarded an "Exhibition" to enter St Catharine's College, I had 9 months to kill before going up to Cambridge. It was decided I should make a 3-month trip to the USA to visit my Mum's relatives and generally explore the "New World". My Mum's American aunt, Auntie Win, was her mother's sister, who had moved to live in the US after a whirlwind romance with Pev, the American who became her husband. Win and Pev ran a bouncy happy household which had all the positive characteristics of my Mum's family and none of the inhibitions of life at Dunstan Steads – they even hugged and kissed each other! Pev had been a successful executive in the baby clothing firm Carters – so later Sarah and I were able to use "Babygrows" for our kids before they were available in the UK!

The warm family environment in Westfield (near Boston) was really a life-changing experience for me. Win and Pev had two grown up daughters, Joan and Marge, and we saw a lot of them (also bright and bouncy people) with their young daughters – each had 3 daughters. Marge and her husband Ted lived just a couple of doors down along Llewellyn Drive and I often went out 10-pin-bowling with Ted, who was mad keen on sport. It was winter time so Win and Pev often took me up to the local ski resort where I taught myself to ski. The rope tows were rather vicious contraptions – you needed specially reinforced leather mittens to use them – and even they got worn through pretty quickly. The scenery was beautiful, the weather cold but clear and dry. I always took a bag of tuna sandwiches (as did many others) and we simply hid them off piste somewhere so we could retrieve them when hunger struck.

Each morning in Llewellyn Drive started with a delicious breakfast, with fresh fruit juice and wonderful toasted cheese sandwiches. The house was centrally heated to a ridiculously high temperature so we would all be in light clothes and shirt sleeves while we watched the thermometer outside the window climb up from 20 below zero as the sun rose. Auntie Win was a brilliant cook and her speciality was meat balls and spaghetti.

We often went together to the local butchers so she could buy the ingredients – I think I must have put on plenty of weight there! I kept in touch with Sarah by frequent letter writing and my parents sent me the airmail version of the Times newspaper.

One story I will always remember was told me by Auntie Win. She told me how easy and important it was to say "thank you" for good things – but many people often forgot how much pleasure this could give. On one occasion Pev had bought her a very expensive evening dress made and designed by one of the country's top dress designers. She had thought it lovely so she wrote to the designer just to say "thank you". To her surprise, a few days later she received a reply from New York from the designer himself, saying how much he appreciated her writing and would she like to come up to New York where he would be glad to take her out to dinner. It is a lesson I have always tried to remember – saying "thank you`" really does not cost much!

Win and Pev took me on a long road trip in true American style – staying at roadside motels and driving much further south to Williamstown and through Pennsylvania and Virginia. It was amazing how the weather warmed up as we went further south and the spring approached. We became experts on spotting the famous Howard Johnson restaurants with their bright orange roofs along the freeways.

I went down to stay with Joan and her husband Bill (near Boston) just before I was due to fly back to England. One of their neighbours had a daughter, Lorinda Wilder, who was obviously very keen to get to know me in rather a forceful American way. She later came over to stay with us in England but I was never captivated by the charms she offered! At Joan's I was introduced to my first pizza – such things were completely unknown in England at the time. Then finally, as my time to leave approached there was a massive snowfall – literally 4 or 5 feet. All the roads were blocked, the local school roof collapsed because of the weight and Bill and I had a major task to clear the massive snowdrifts so we could get out of the house. This job was made much worse by the local snowploughs which ploughed all the snow off the road into our driveway. My flight was postponed so I had a few extra days in the snow.

All in all, my US trip opened up a whole new way of being for me. Life could evidently be much more fun than the serious and dutiful life my parents seemed to live – we shared plenty of jokes and laughter as well as sharp intelligence and effective living. I had a great time romping about with the 6 young granddaughters – particularly little Mary Beth Hellstein. She was only 4 or 5 years old then but remains a good friend even today.

MY QUEST

I first became conscious of "my quest" when I was about 7 years old. This happened as I read a beautiful picture book about the "Wonders of the World". I can remember the time quite clearly. I was lying in bed, cosy under my soft green and gold eiderdown, looking at all these extra-ordinary photos of beautiful things in nature that I had never seen before. So – how did it all work? What were the mechanisms that could produce such amazing things? And this was how my "quest" began. True, it would metamorphose into new directions but the imperative to discover remained the same.

"My quest" is a theme which runs throughout my story. I suppose that searching for answers is one strange consequence of having consciousness. In fact I sometimes think that much of what we do is driven by a need to find "displacement activities" which keep our brains occupied precisely so we don't have to think about the great questions of existence. But time and time again in my own life my decisions on what to do next have been governed by the needs of "my quest".

My time at school provided my first insights into the workings of the physical world around me. Mathematics seemed to be an essential tool for grappling with these unknowns – it was evidently very powerful as it had been applied by Sir Isaac Newton to "explain" many of the mysteries that had previously been thought of as the work of "Gods" of one kind or another. Then we had the beauty of the periodic table: its manifestation of the simple concept of the atom and its sub-atomic components as imagined by Rutherford. Finally, we had the bizarre mystery of relativity which showed that time and space could stretch and bend, and then the uncomfortable findings of quantum theory showing the duality between photons and electromagnetic waves.

All these theoretical and experimental insights which humans had deduced from science clearly had a profound effect on our relationship with the natural world. They had been applied to the development of machinery which used the stored energy of sunlight (in fossil fuels) to "amplify" the power of humans over nature. We had moved from a world dominated by superstition and "gods" to a new world where humans believed they could (given time and application) manage everything using science and technology.

But late in my teenage years in my preparation to take A-level physics, I began to see that these "certainties" had been seriously undermined by the "discovery" of relativity and quantum theory. Einstein's realisation that the implications of James Clerk Maxwell's famous equations (that light always travels at the same speed in any frame of reference) were actually correct had led him to develop his theory of relativity. Then the explanation (by Max Planck) of "black body radiation" and the insights of Heisenberg (his uncertainty principle) had been taken up by Schroeder to formulate his equations for quantum mechanics. It was becoming clear that the Universe was very far from being the passive and predictable machine that humans had previously imagined.

As a teenager there were 2 projects in particular which I found both fascinating and scary. The first concerned the development of power through nuclear fission (the first nuclear power stations were being built at this time). Although the potential to produce massive quantities of power from tiny quantities of radioactive material was truly fantastic (as the atom bomb had shown), it was clear to me that the dangers created by disposal of radioactive waste would persist for thousands of years. Dealing with this waste properly would be very problematic and expensive. This made the prospect of nuclear fission power profoundly life threatening – it seemed madness. The second almost magical project was the possibility of containing light elements (like Hydrogen) in a magnetic "bottle" so that the process of nuclear fusion (which happens in stars) could take place safely (without serious problems of radioactive waste) to produce almost unlimited power on Earth. The British had become pioneers exploring this possibility during the 1950s in a machine called ZETA.

So this was my state of mind when I went up to Cambridge to study mathematics and theoretical physics with the cleverest minds of the day! I remained excited and hopeful that the teaching of these great minds would yield new insights for me.

Cambridge University

At Cambridge I found myself billeted with the college mathematicians under one of St Catharine's College's most revered old dons – Canon Whadams. I think there were 10 mathematicians in our year – Richard Lewis was the scholar and extremely bright, Les Hales and myself were the two exhibitioners (not quite so bright!). I was allocated to digs outside the college with the imposing Mrs Day in Station Road. Richie was in the same digs and we had a lot of good times together. Unfortunately Mrs Day found our revelries too much for her and I was forced to move out to smaller digs across Coe Fen in Hardwick St. In fact this was a great bonus for me because I was on my own there and had no temptations to party. Often I would do 3 hours work then go off to the golf course on the Goggs to practise for an hour – this way the exercise and fresh air kept my brain from getting muddled.

At Cambridge the college rules were still very strict. All undergraduates had to "keep term" in order to get their degrees –

that meant spending 59 nights (I think it was) in college every term. You needed a special dispensation to miss a night. All undergraduates were required by University rules to wear a gown in town after dusk. These rules were strictly enforced by the University Proctors and the Bulldogs who worked under them. College gates were locked at midnight so many of us became expert at climbing in after returning from late night parties. Women were strictly banned from the all-male college after midnight. Anyone found breaking these rules could be "sent down" and might have to redo a whole year of study.

My first challenge was to find a way to have a car at Cambridge since by that time I was well used to having my own car. My father's best friend, Norman Burrell, had advised me to buy a BMW – at that time a very new German make just becoming available in the UK. My parents had very kindly bought this for me as a present – the cost was about £1,600. The road holding and general performance of the early BMWs was far superior to most of the British makes. Independent suspension and a double overhead camshaft were pretty sophisticated specifications in those days. Bizarrely the first BMW I had (a red 1600cc) had 6-volt electrics but the gearbox was silky smooth and the performance excellent.

Owning cars at Cambridge was strictly forbidden for undergraduates unless they could justify its use because of their involvement in University team sports which required transport. I pondered this question with an old friend from the Leys – a crafty fellow called Frank Allen. He'd spent his gap year walking and fishing for trout in the mountains of Norway – and had many great tales of his experiences staying in remote farms where the ladies of the house had been extremely hospitable. Frank suggested we try and get onto the University Ice Hockey team – we were both good hockey players and could skate. The team was mostly made up of American postgraduates who were brilliant, almost professional, players. But they were short of team members so we were welcomed in. Each week we would travel down to Richmond ice rink by car or bus because they let us use the rink after public skating finished at midnight. We had quite a few adventures – particularly climbing back into college at 4am in the morning carrying all our ice hockey kit. I remember one night in particular when I had to climb in through one of the basement study windows which was always left open on the Kings Parade side of college. It was a bit of a battle getting in through the window with all my kit – especially as I was being watched (I think with some amusement) by a local policeman. So imagine my frustration when I found that the outer door of the study had been locked! I had to climb out again – with all my kit – and go around to the back wall which was about 12 feet high. What the policeman thought I cannot imagine.

So my membership of the University ice hockey team meant I could apply for a permit to have my car. This was successful so I always parked over the other side of the Backs in Queen's Road (which was a free parking area in those days). I did get included in the team which played Oxford but was never called to play because the US players were very much the top dogs.

But life does move in mysterious ways. Out of the blue I found a note in my college pigeon hole from someone called Jim Rumbellow. He had heard about me up at Alnmouth when he and Sarah were both being coached as potential golfing stars in the Northumberland Juniors by Eddie Fernie. Jim, a man of boundless charm and charisma, was now Captain of the CU Stymies – the second golf team of the University. Did I want to meet up and possibly join the Stymies? And so began one important strand of the great golfing odyssey which has run throughout my life. Almost every Saturday morning in the winter and easter terms we would be up at 6am, rushing down over the Backs (the name for the grouping of canals, rivers and meadows behind the major colleges) to see if the car would start after we cleared off the ice. Then I'd drive around several colleges to pick up other members of the team before heading off (no speed limits in those days) – often for a couple of hours driving to make a tee-off time of 9am at some remote golf club.

This was a combination of something like rally driving and golf – also there were no breathalysers in those days so evening carousing was the norm.

The Stymies of that year were a splendid lively bunch who squeezed every bit of enjoyment out of every moment of every weekend – golf sometimes being incidental to partying. Quite how we survived the driving and the drinking without disaster I don't know – but we did and we all made good friends for life in the process. The one morning I will always remember was the day we went out to play against Oxford at the Royal West Norfolk Golf Club (Brancaster). It was a long drive up north on a March winter morning. We reached the village of Brancaster and found the signpost directing us towards the golf course. For the moment there was nothing to be seen but tall white rushes then, suddenly like a ship rising from the waves, we saw the famous Brancaster clubhouse perched on the edge of the beach. There was still no sign of the golf course itself. Little did I know then that Brancaster would become a place for several regular annual golfing pilgrimages – and many of my friends would become members there.

I think virtually all of the Stymies went on to have great business careers during their lives – a testament perhaps to my theory that interpersonal skills are much more important in life than high academic achievement. Tony Abrahams went on to become Chairman of the English selectors for the Walker Cup, Peter Dawson became a very successful Chief Executive for the Royal and Ancient, Jim Rumbellow became Captain of Royal St George's, Tim Dickson founded the Golfing Quarterly (also becoming Captain of Royal Wimbledon), Richard Dyson became Chairman of the Institute of Chartered Accountants, Chris Radbone founded "Countdown", Danesh (always a man who seized the main chance) set up Bookers.com and sold it for many millions … and so it goes on.

Throughout my life I have kept in touch with old Stymie friends – we meet up for golf and to catch up on each other's news at least 2 or 3 times each year. These meetings do have an element of pilgrimage about them – it takes a broken leg or a broken arm for anyone to miss one!

College Life

College life was full-on – both work, as well as sport and social life, were all extremely busy. The University provided courses of lectures which were open to any student but the direction and day-to-day tuition of all subjects was in the hands of your college. Our Director of Studies, Canon Whadams, would suggest the lecture courses we should attend and allocate us to specialist college supervisors. The college supervisors were generally fellows of the college or post-graduate students with the necessary specialist knowledge. We would attend supervisions in small groups of 2 or 3 for several hour-long sessions every week. The essentially Cambridge philosophy of constantly questioning conventional thinking was always encouraged. Radical ideas were welcome and we were expected to be able to defend them robustly in open debate.

There were 2 University lecturers I remember in particular. Dr Smithies taught "Analysis" which was the pure mathematics pioneered by people like GH Hardy and his strange protegé Ramanujan ("The Man who knew Infinity" is the name of a film about his extra-ordinary genius). Smithies was the "driest stick" one can imagine. He had been giving the same lecture course for years and would write up his notes very neatly on the blackboard. Smithies always started to write (and talk) precisely 5 minutes after the hour when his lecture was due to start. And he stopped writing and talking exactly on the hour when his lecture finished. So precise was his habit that he would stop writing on the hour even if he was in the middle of some complex proof. Then, next time, he would simply start writing again from precisely the point he had got to at the previous lecture. I can remember (with bafflement) his introduction to statistics when he announced "probability is any number between 0 and 1" – almost everything after that was pure fantasy. The other lecturer I can well remember was called Dr Bretherton. His style and character was in complete contrast to that of Dr Smithies. His lectures were chaotic as he rushed about with great enthusiasm tossing his mop of bright ginger hair from side to side with a glint of madness in his eye. He taught theoretical physics, such things as the inner structure of stars and the mechanisms of the newly emerging field of radio telescopes. He also taught fluid dynamics and would often be seen watching the "hydraulic jumps" visible when drinking a beer down at the Mill pub on the Cam. It was said that Bretherton often crashed on his bike because his mind was wandering into some theoretical abyss. The other thing I remember about Bretherton was his exposition and explanation of the wonderfully powerful and elegant equations of James Clerk Maxwell. It is only recently that the Scots seem to have come to realise the true genius of Maxwell. He produced his equations purely by thinking about the consequences of Faraday's earlier experiments with electricity and magnetism. And these equations went on to form the basis for Einstein's later insights into special and general relativity.

MY QUEST 1

After two years studying maths and theoretical physics at Cambridge, I began to see that humans would never be able to "understand" the workings of the cosmos. The search for answers to fundamental questions of existence would always be like some infinitely complex Russian doll. Each doll opened (each problem understood) would simply reveal yet another slightly smaller (and possibly even more complex) doll – for ever and ever. It was already clear that more and more abstract and complex mathematics was necessary to describe the phenomenon we already knew.

So it became evident that my early hopes of finding answers to "how the Universe worked" were doomed to failure. But what I did learn from these exposures to the latest theoretical thinking was that the unfolding of the Universe seemed to be some kind of battle, or struggle, between one phenomenon we call "life" and another called "entropy". "Life" was always trying to make things ordered and beautiful whilst "entropy" was always determined to mess things up and destroy order and beauty. It seemed to me that we humans had, whether we liked it or not, some crucial role to play in this epic cosmic struggle. Our brains were almost certainly the most complex ordered structure which the unfolding of the Universe had yet produced (after 14 billion Earth years since the "Big Bang"). The question now was whether we could use the powers of this brain to enhance life – or were we to remain simply short-term pleasure seekers driven largely by greed?

My disillusionment with science was matched by an increasing realisation that my parents' own lives had often been dominated by the requirements of human institutions such as income tax, economics and law. I began to take more interest in the history of the human race – how had other societies organised themselves and, in particular, why had so many evidently sophisticated human civilisations simply allowed themselves to be destroyed by one folly or another? Why was it that humans in the mass (civilisations) made such bad decisions when most individual humans were much too intelligent to make such serious mistakes?

Law

The next step in my "quest" was to change from studying theoretical physics to studying law. In my third year at Cambridge I was able to begin a new phase of my "quest", looking at how human societies govern themselves through developing systems of law. I slowly began to turn my attention to trying to understand how the political and economic world of human civilization was constantly messing up. Already I had seen how my parents' lives had been mixed up and stressed by every contact they had with their lawyers. It seemed that some understanding of the legal process might be one starting point for my new mission to better understand society.

The lawyers were an urbane and articulate bunch. Words were their tools and precedent their lodestone. We had to read a lot of stuff – much of it waffly and seemingly imprecise – particularly the topic they called "constitutional law". I had to study 5 topics and pass an exam on each at the end of the year – land law, tort (the law of negligence), criminal law, constitutional law and "equity". University life continued to be busy – with early morning rowing training, weekend golf (all over the south of England) and some study.

Chapter 2: Marriage 1966

Our Wedding Day!

In November this year Sarah and I were married – a simple Registry office affair because Sarah was already pregnant with Rupert and neither of us were churchgoers. I took a good few friends up from Cambridge and we had a great party at Christon Bank farmhouse after the formalities. Sarah was studying maths at St Andrews so the powers that be made her move out of hall; she found herself sharing a room in the home of the University chaplain (Roger Stirrup). In the end it all worked out pretty well, the Stirrups were nice and very supportive. Rupert was born in April 1967 and my parents very kindly went up to babysit so Sarah could take her final exams.

For some of the time Sarah and I rented a small flat in St Andrews. Those were the days when ratepayers of the town were able to play a round of golf any time on the famous "Old Course" for just 2s 6d! We would often put a lovely stew in the slow oven and come back to enjoy it after a round of golf. Then we moved down to live in a house in Girton near Cambridge – 13 Fairway was the address, right beside the (terrible) Girton 9-hole golf course.

The Strange New Idea

One day in early summer 1968 my Mum decided she would pay us a visit at our home in Girton. It soon became clear that she had a very specific purpose. The estate needed a new tenant for one of the farms and she had decided that I should be asked if I would like to take this on. I was still studying at Cambridge and was flabbergasted to be asked to get into farming after all the occasions when my parents had told me time and time again that they did not want their children to be farmers. As a result I knew practically nothing about farm management and even less about the country society I might become part of – we had all been away at school since the beginning of time! The possibility that I might become a farmer was very much a "strange new idea"! Both Sarah and I were extremely surprised at this new proposal which just came "out of the blue".

My parents seemed desperate for me to "help them out" so I agreed to take on the challenge but with two important conditions – first, I would study "Farm Management" which was a one-year course currently on offer at the School of Agriculture in Cambridge; second, I would want to spend at least one year working as a normal farm worker so I would have a proper understanding of how things worked. And so it came to pass that I signed up for a fourth year at Cambridge with more golf, more rowing, more study and another baby – Ceri was born in 1968.

During this last year at Cambridge we lived a domestic life in Girton. We had friendly American neighbours, Burt and Edie, who I later stayed with in their home near Tacoma. A huge proportion of the farm management course was devoted to biometric analysis and the design of experiments. The University prided itself on having attracted several students from 'developing'' countries – special provisions were made to enable them to achieve their diplomas even though their general standard of education was extremely limited. One tribal chief from Nigeria surprised us all after the first farm visit. He had appeared rather nervous throughout the visit and we discovered why in the Q and A session at the end of the afternoon. He asked rather tentatively if those strange white animals were dangerous – he was referring to sheep – which he had never seen before! He ended up passing his Diploma but actually spent most of the year simply learning how to use the Brunsviga manual calculating machines (there were no pocket calculators or computers in those days!).

The Big Event

The "big event" of 1968 (apart from the birth of Ceri) was the University golf match against Oxford. There was stiff competition to get into the team – and I was on the margins of ability. The team captain was "God" as far as this decision was concerned. Our Captain, David Morkill, was a splendidly old fashioned ex-army officer with a strong Welsh pedigree. He was good at knitting and got on well with Sarah. But he was not very confident of my rather adventurous golfing style. I had played many very tough matches as No.1 for the Stymies – the University second team. But the "Blues" (the first team) took their game rather more seriously – players like Peter Dawson and Peter Moody went on to have glowing golfing careers. I was never a reliable medal golfer because I took too many risks – taking on difficult shots that wiser players would have avoided. I did hit the ball a long way and I did win a lot of my matches against good opponents. My chances came good one day when we played the army at Fleet. It was a bright winter day, I remember. About half way around the course we came to a longish par-3 hole, slightly uphill and slightly against the wind. The length was about 200 yards so I took my 2-iron. Morkill had just finished playing the hole and whilst walking on towards the next tee looked back to watch my shot. I hit a wonderful 2-iron finishing about 20 feet from the flag. After the round he told me that after seeing me hit that shot he knew then he wanted to have me in his Blues side.

Getting what is called a "full Blue" in 1968 was quite a big deal because it opened doors to many smart and important places (and the influential people who inhabited such places). So I was now entitled to wear the Blue's special tie and, even better, be elected to the elite Cambridge sports club – the Hawk's club with its distinctive deep red and gold striped tie. The dramas of the Varsity match itself still lay ahead. Morkill had decided the match would take place on the venerable old links at Porthcawl – in his native Wales. We duly traipsed west – and Sarah came along with baby Rupert.

Royal Porthcawl is a demanding links course with far more nasty bunkers than any modern architect would recommend! The Atlantic waves are not far away and as the match days finally arrived so did a wild set of Atlantic weather – constant gales and wind. I had a secret weapon in the shape of my thermal long johns which kept me warm despite the storm. Carrying my bag I could use my umbrella in one hand whilst keeping my other hand warm and dry in a trouser pocket. We played the match over 2 days – a 36-hole foursomes match on day 1, and a 36-hole singles match on day 2. Captain Morkill was a wily old bird and had chosen his team order carefully so that the players at the bottom of the order were solid players who would not quit under pressure. This was key in the match situation because it was often the last couple of matches that would decide a final result. It is a strange thing – the way different people respond to emotional pressure. I enjoyed the pressure of matchplay golf and always felt confident that I could win! Morkill put me down as number 10 – the last group. Everyone knows that what happens in this high-profile public spectacle can (if things go badly) leave scars that last a lifetime. There are hundreds of people watching as well as the Press and one's team mates.

So we duly donned our blue team-jerseys (there was no sponsorship in those days!) and got ready to play. There are 4 shots I remember very well. Number 1 was my drive off the first tee against a wild gale. Watched by the crowds, it was a good one – the driver snapped the tee and the ball sailed off down the fairway. So the 36-hole game was on. As my partner (Mervyn Lloyd) and I came to the 18th hole just before lunch, we were one hole down. The 18th hole is a good long hole downhill against the gale. Both our partners hit good drives, my partner's being a few yards longer than our opponents'. My Oxford opponent hit a superb fairway wood straight into the heart of the green about 200 yards away. A great cheer and applause came back on the wind from the crowd of spectators around the green. It was now my turn to strike. Again I took my trusty 2-iron which made a perfect contact and the ball sailed off precisely on target. Against the wind it would surely stop dead on the green, probably very close to the flag. But there was only a mysterious silence from the spectators – so where had the ball gone? We were puzzled as we walked down towards the green, seeing only one ball (our opponents') on the green. Then there was a sort of buzz in the crowd as they saw our mystified faces. Yes, yes – they said – it was the most amazing thing we have ever seen. Your shot was dropping straight down exactly on target for the flagstick, falling vertically in the wind. Next thing the ball bounced right on the top of the flag stick, went back up 20 feet into the air and finished 10 yards over the back of the green! This was indeed a cruel "rub of the green" but there was no relief. We lost the hole but went on to halve the match in the final 18 holes of the afternoon. What a drama that was – and I have never heard or seen any other shot be so unlucky – the odds are millions to one. Cambridge lost the first day's foursomes matches 31/2 to 11/2.

The third memorable shot came on the putting green. On the 13th hole I was joined in my singles match against the Oxford Secretary (Baxter) by a very enthusiastic bouncy strong rugby Blue who then offered to carry my clubs. These he grabbed and marched along beside me happily. I think I was one hole up at the time in the final round of the 36 holes as the whole match reached its climax. Next thing I knew this lusty fellow had tossed my clubs onto the ground as we reached the next tee for the short 14th hole. Unfortunately the impact snapped off the head of my home-made putter which had simply been glued into position with araldite. We both hit the green with our tee shots and I decided the best bet was for me to use my 2-iron as a putter. Baxter rolled his putt up close for a gimme par but my first attempt to putt with my long 2-iron sent the ball a good 8 feet past the hole. I could see my opponent was immediately cheered up by this, thinking he would soon be back to all square. Miraculously my next putt (still with the 2-iron) went straight into the hole for a half. Baxter's disappointment was magnified tenfold when he saw my drive on the long par-4 15th sail over the big cross bunkers. This was shot number 4 which clinched my victory as Baxter crumbled under the pressure. The famous golf correspondent of the Daily Telegraph, Leonard Crawley, described my victory as being the result of Baxter being dominated by "Sutherland's swashbuckling driving"! The Times reporter had the temerity to suggest that my putter was broken in a fit of rage – hmmm – most unlikely!

So the great event was over – successfully as Cambridge came out winners and I was the only player not to lose a match. But it was an epic struggle in wild weather which has left me with great memories and many great lifetime golfing friends. On a big match day on a golf course there is no place to hide – all those years of practice have to prove their worth as the golfer's mind struggles to battle those inner demons.

We arrive at Newton and have our first row with the family

With the sophisticated excitements of Cambridge behind us, Sarah and I arrived back north to take up residence in No. 5 Coastguard Cottages. Our only cooker and heater was the wonderful old coal-fired range. There was no heating in the bedrooms but it never seemed to bother the two young babes, Rupert and Ceri. It was time to start my apprenticeship on the farm and time to master the paperwork and finances needed to manage the Dunstanburgh Golf Course.

My parents had become reluctant owners of Dunstanburgh GC simply because it had always been a part of the estate which had been bought after the First World War by my grandfather, Sir Arthur Sutherland. My grandfather had been quite keen on golf. He had spent time and money developing the course as well as encouraging friends and enthusiasts from Newcastle to construct bungalows on the dunes adjacent to the course. Indeed these bungalow owners were a vital component of the golf business because each one had to pay an annual green fee to the course as well as paying their ground rent. This continued to be the case when the dunes and the golf course were re-opened to the public after the military occupation of the Second World War. My grandfather's grandiose plans to make Embleton, with its beautiful beach, a premier smart resort town had come to nothing as old age and other pre-occupations took their toll.

Now I had always had a great love for the golf links. Not simply to play golf but often working as a greenkeeper when I was a teenager during school holidays. In those days there were no poison sprays to kill worms and leatherjackets, no petrol driven lawnmowers to cut greens and certainly no irrigation of any kind. The fairways were cut by a magnificent converted WW2 lorry which was fitted with massively wide steel-spiked rear wheels which not only gave a good grip but also aerated fairways as they turned. The trusty Lloyds gangmowers were housed in the double-ended machine shed (with doors at both ends) at the bottom of the Dunstan Steads sea lane (obviously they could not be reversed so had to go in one door and out the other). The wonderful estate game keeper, Jock Arnott, would take one end of the course which he could walk to from his home in Newton, and I would take the south end. Every morning we picked up our long switch (2 bamboo poles lashed together to make a 12 foot length) and our rake and walked over the course, before players arrived, to switch the worm casts and crow pecks off the greens and make sure all bunkers were raked. Then we would take out the beautifully engineered hand mowers which we used to cut the greens. These were mounted on big travelling wheels so they could be pushed between greens. We cut each green, carefully choosing to make our strips so that the cuttings would be blown by the breeze onto the next strip to be cut. The hand mowers simply purred along as we pushed them over the turf! Any weeds were dug out by hand and very little fertiliser was ever needed because the cuttings were not boxed off and taken away. In fact, the greens were top-dressed twice each year using a home-made mixture of riddled sandy loam which we simply dug out of the hillside of Tom Ha's Hill to which dried blood and bone meal were added. This low-intensity regime meant the greens took no harm when they dried out brown and dormant during hot summers – they were hard and fast of course, but that was just the way links golf was. It all changed when TV brought the amazing deep-green heavily watered American greens into the public domain!

My parents had no real interest in golf other than feeling they should provide this facility as part of the villagers' need for recreation. They had brought the course back into use after the war but it had always been a drain on resources with expenditure on wages and upkeep far exceeding the small revenues from green fees and the bungalow ground rents. My father had passed the management over to my mother as he became fed up with all the constant fuss and criticism he received from the golfers. She, too, was getting fed up with the constant drain on time and resources and I discovered the family had started negotiations to pass the course over to a consortium of bungalow owners. It came as a shock to me when I discovered my parents had been making these plans without telling me even though they knew how much I was involved with golf and the course. I had always found Mr Sinton (Chairman of the Bungalow Owners Association) and Mr Neesham (Secretary of the Golf Club) rather pompous know-alls and the prospect of having them take over running our wonderful golf links horrified me.

So we came to what would be the first of several unpleasant confrontations between myself and my parents. When I tried to discuss the golf course proposals with the aim of persuading them not to give up the family's involvement I got nowhere. So finally, in frustration, I told them I was disgusted with their idea of giving up the course and their lack of interest in my strong feelings. I told them that I would gladly take on running the course and if they were not prepared to agree to this option then Sarah and I would simply upsticks and make our lives somewhere else. Somewhat reluctantly they agreed. My mother gave me a crash course on how to do the wages, the accounts and the complicated payment of income tax via PAYE. I soon got the hang of things (with help from head greenkeeper John Carss and his wife Nellie) and what was to be a long saga of my golfing management had begun.

Four Kids!

I suppose it may be unusual to be looking after four kids by the time you are 24 years old! Sarah and I never gave the matter a second thought. We were young, fit and full of "get-up and go"! We told our (more cautious?) friends how easy it was to have your children all in a bundle when you were young enough to cope with being up half the night. Better still, you had never had the chance to get used to a comfortable easy-going middle-class lifestyle. With just three and a half years between the four kids, they all seemed to muck in together like a litter of puppies – full of energy and keen to get to grips with life. Naturally Sarah bore the brunt of the physical challenge of actually producing the kids – strong brave girl that she is – but I was able to play a big part, too, in minding them because my work (either on the farm or at University) gave me good flexibility.

Rupert was born in St Andrew's in April 1967, Ceri was born in Cambridge in June 1968 (the same birthday as my mother),

Gael was born in Alnwick in May 1969 and Dylan was born, also in Alnwick, in November 1970.

We had what many people would call a "liberal" approach to raising the four children. In this we liked to follow the philosophies of the author Dr Spock, who famously said that you should try to treat your children like intelligent beings from outer space who knew nothing about how things were done on Earth. Spock's childcare book was published in 1946 and was strongly critical of the strictly timetabled routines which had previously dominated childcare. Our children were encouraged to express themselves and from the very start we all used our Christian names (William and Sarah) so we were simply other (grown-up) people rather than holding more formal roles as Mummy and Daddy. Visitors were sometimes shocked by all the kids' writing and painting on our house walls. We made every effort to remedy "bad" behaviour by careful explanation rather than mindless discipline. Above all we wanted our children to be calmly self-confident and able to make up their own minds, independent of custom or social convention.

In those days there were no seatbelt laws so we could just toss all the kids into the back of our Volvo estate (together with Goldie, the dog) and drive off without a care. They would usually settle down together but if there was trouble we always tried to avoid blaming a single child – all were held responsible for the trouble and all would be punished if necessary.

When the kids were very young it was normally my job to deal with hunger, nappies etc. at night. For quite a few years we would often have a strange "merry-go-round" during the night – first one child would slip into our bed for some comfort, then another .... Sometimes we'd find ourselves sleeping in one or other of the kids' beds whilst all four of the kids ended up taking over our bed.

There is no doubt that one of the greatest skills needed by any parent is the correct judgement of just exactly what challenges a child is ready and able to deal with. Here, Sarah had much more nerve than I, encouraging the kids to take on all sorts of excitements. For my part, I believed that it was largely a waste of time trying to stop kids taking risks by lecturing them. Kids do, in fact, have a strong sense of self-preservation (they've been at it for thousands of years, don't forget!) so my belief is that all non-fatal/non-permanent injuries are a real bonus. They are the best possible way for kids to learn to take care of themselves.

I must say that my parents were very easy-going about the way we brought up the four kids. Sarah's mother, on the other hand, was frequently scandalised by what she saw. Poor Sarah did often have to endure being on the wrong end of her mother's (very sharp) tongue! 20 years later, when the results of our efforts seemed to be extremely successful, Ruth Gilbert did apologise – indeed she was very proud of all her Sutherland grandchildren and what they had achieved.

We enjoyed the company of our kids and the challenge of introducing them to the many wonders of the world. Playing games was always an important part of our "training" – teaching children (at a very young age) to make their own decisions in the face of uncertainty and showing them, very directly, that some days you are lucky and some days you are not. It's good if you can avoid feeling it's your fault if things don't always turn out well – if you've done your best then that's all you can do. I also had a "bee in my bonnet" about "fairness". Life, as we all know, is not always "fair"! My own parents, on the other hand, had always taken a strong position that everything should be "fair" between their three children. So when I won £100 with a Premium Bond given me by Bert, my grandfather, they insisted the money be divided between all three of us (this did not seem "fair" to me of course!). If there was one piece of cake left then it would be carefully cut into three … and so on. If I, the eldest and strongest, achieved some public success then the other kids would often be compensated with some present or treat. (So it was a double shock to me when my parents broke their own cardinal rule and entrusted the management of the family Trust to Owen.) It certainly did not seem a good plan to me to teach children that life was always ``fair". My answer was to go to what might be seen as the opposite extreme – if there was one piece of cake left for 4 kids we would toss a coin or throw a dice to see who would be lucky that day. There might well be groans from the losers but these soon faded as they realised that next time it might be their turn to be lucky. Choosing the lucky "winner" by chance could become fun and was, I believed, a much better training for life. I use the same approach with my grandchildren today.

Our Children

Our family, ready to face the world, in 1969

I should make it clear here that this story is not about the detail of my regular family life or the talents and characters of my seven children. It's a story mainly about the other things I did in the wider world and the events which shaped the course of my life. My children have their own first-hand experience of life in a Sutherland household – mostly busy, mostly fun, often challenging, sometimes exhausting but always spiced with a dash of life's great mysteries. I have done my best to give them the love and stimulation they deserved – it has been a wonderful and rewarding experience. As Kahlil Gibran has said so perceptively – your children are like arrows shot from a bow. Mine are all flying free now – making their mark on the world. I watch on with wonder and satisfaction. It is good now to see the next generation of grandchildren and be able to share with them some of the magical things in life.

Introducing energetic and intelligent young people to the world is always a fascinating and rewarding task. They learn from you and you learn, too, from their constant stream of questions. Of course, it's wonderful to see how each new bundle of genes will develop into another human being. It's strange to see how little their personalities change from almost the very moment they are born – some calm and reflective, others bouncy and outgoing. Their multiple talents, of course, appear later, given the right opportunities and stimulation.

Nobody seems quite clear about the relative influence of nature over nurture! As parents we certainly like to think the environment (social, physical, educational, etc.) and stimulation we provide must have some effect on future behaviours. Probably the greatest gifts that a parent can give a child are an independent questioning mind and a good dose of self-confidence. Self-confidence is surely one characteristic that education (in the true sense of the word) and training can provide. And self-confidence is a characteristic of both physical, emotional and mental competence. In the Sutherland household I would like to think that we constantly provided graduated challenges in all these areas which gave the children the chances they needed to spread their wings – provided their parents measured up the challenges to a level which was always just within the reach of the child. Sarah was always much braver than I (and a better judge of what the kids could cope with) in giving the kids responsibilities and challenges.

My First Motorbike!

I acquired my first motorbike (I think it was in 1966) in rather a strange way. Not, as you might imagine, because my father had promised me £100 so I could buy a motorbike IF I became headboy at Mowden Hall. In the event, I did become headboy but the £100 my father had promised me did not materialise without a big fuss. For whatever reason my father found it extremely difficult to bring himself to actually hand over the money. There was a considerable argument between my parents – a VERY rare occurrence – as my mother (eventually) persuaded him that he simply had to keep his word. This did not make a good impression on me. Anyway, by the time 5 years had passed, the price of a new motorbike had gone up.

My first motorbike was "won" in a golfing wager against one of my great teenage golfing pals – Alan Breeze. Alan was a splendid entertaining fellow who always arrived at the golf house on a big noisy Norton 500. One day when we were playing one of our regular games we decided we'd play for £5 a corner. However, when I won the game, Alan turned to me and asked if I'd like to take his old Norton instead of the cash. He had decided it was no longer roadworthy as it blew smoke and flames out of the exhaust and evidently was on the point of total collapse. This seemed like an exciting option so I took it. The Norton was a meaty machine with tremendous power from its single cylinder 500 cc engine. It could be a bit of a pig to get started as you had to make sure you had retarded the ignition before hitting the kick-start – if you forgot, it could backfire and throw you over in a somersault as you kicked the starter (no electric start in those days). It was no longer fit or licenced for road use but we had many exciting trips along the beach or over the farm. Sometimes we'd have three of us on the big bike (myself, Sarah, and her sister Caroline). I learned a lot about handling a motorbike by riding fast over the fields. You needed a delicate touch to avoid skidding and falling off! Often golf balls would fly up if we went over them at speed on the fields adjacent to the golf course.

The thrill and instant response of a motor bike was pretty addictive but my first road bike was just a tiny Honda 50. Sarah and I rode this slow little machine all the way from Newton to Cambridge when we moved into the house in Girton. We each did about 5 hours as we bumbled along the minor roads because the engine was too small to use motorways. It was a long and gruelling trip. But the little bike was great for nipping into college. It had no fuel gauge – a fact which gave me a very long cold walk home one late night when I returned after a marathon cross county golfing extravaganza and the fuel ran out halfway down Huntingdon Road.

When I started work on the farm a year later I bought a lovely little Honda 160 twin. Very quiet and smooth. This little bike whizzed me from Newton to work at Dunstan Steads every day. I thought it better not to buy a more powerful machine but a couple of months later, when I got to know the men better, they told me how disappointed they had been to find their boss's son with such a feeble bike! My next bike was a rather flashy Honda 250 twin with a smart white fairing and lots of chrome. It was faster and noisier than the 160 but the chrome soon rusted and the large fairing made it rather wild in strong wind. When we went down to live in London I swapped the cumbersome 250 for a neat little Honda 90. This was my commuting bike for work every day. It's little fairing gave some protection from wet and my big gabardine riding mac provided full protection for my smart work suits. My gumboots could be changed easily in the Department's carpark before going in to work. The 90 was quick enough to beat the black-cab taxis off the lights but I found the aggressive behaviour of many car drivers rather irksome. I decided to move up a notch and in 1973 bought my first BMW boxer – a second-hand R75, very smooth and comfortable, a "thinking man's bike" as the adverts would have it – hardly any chrome, beautifully simple engineering and a maintenance-free shaft drive.

In 1974 BMW brought out the second series of their

upgraded R90S boxer and I noticed that the Park Lane showrooms had a lovely black and silver ex-demo bike for sale at £1,400. It was the first production BMW of the super-bike class with drilled double disks on the front and a top speed over 125 mph, 0-60mph in less than 4 seconds! Certainly I will never forget my first trial trip down Park Lane where the powerful bike surged forward like a magic carpet with hardly a whisper from the engine. I suppose it was "love at first sight" and I was to have 27 years of enjoyment partnered with that machine. It was still going well when I sold it (for £1,700) to buy another ex-demo BMW – the much faster K100RS which could reach over 140 mph and reach 60 mph in just over 3 seconds. You could really gobble up the miles with this machine and most years I would take it for a drive down the French motorways or through the Spanish mountains. It was at its best when cruising down the autoroute at 100 mph. It always amazed me to be overtaken by much faster bikes in the long Alpine tunnels where the howl of their engines was magnified by tunnel walls and the strips of lights flashed past like a psychedelic experience. I did get one speeding ticket, just one, when nipping down the M1 (as I frequently did from Millbrook to London). The police car chasing me claimed I was going more than 100 mph but this was simply because he could not match the super-fast acceleration of the bike from 60 – 95 in a couple of seconds as I whizzed past slow traffic. As I explained to the magistrates, I never ever drove above 100 because I knew it was classed as dangerous driving, leading to disqualification. The police were rather surprised to discover that they had not caught a wild rocker but a smartly suited well-spoken professional management consultant. I got off with 5 days disqualification, no fine and no endorsement on my licence!

In 2002 I finally passed the K100RS on to Ron Mills when Millbrook was sold. After more than 40 years of trouble-free motorbiking – often at somewhat reckless speeds – I decided to quit while I was ahead. The modern bikes are so fast and so smooth they give a completely unreal sense of safety but one slip or one silly motorist and you are the one who will be maimed or dead. I had just 3 “crashes” in those 40-plus years. Once on my Honda 90 when I was following a red London bus which pulled over and appeared to be stopping at a bus stop. I proceeded carefully past only to find he had actually stopped to let a large builder’s lorry come out of a building site – I had a slow-motion collision with the lorry – no real damage done. I got a nasty shock, an important lesson and emerged unscathed but wiser. The second bump happened when the K100RS anti-lock braking cut in on a wet day in the east end of London and I found myself unable to stop the bike gently bumping the car that had stopped suddenly in front of me. Again no damage was done. The third crash happened after midnight as I was returning from a golf match in Norfolk. It was a clear dry summer night, very dark, and I was very much enjoying burning up the smooth country roads with very little traffic. I came up quickly behind a slow moving car onto a straight piece of road as we came out of a bend so I opened the throttle and whizzed past him. Before I could react, my bike hit a large lump of wood which had been left in the middle of the road. This had been hidden behind the car I was overtaking and I hit it square on at about 80 mph. Luckily for me, the heavy bike remained stable and quickly came to a halt at the side of the road – the car passed by and I was left in the dark to examine the damage. The tyre was undamaged but the alloy front wheel rim had been completely bashed in so I could no longer even turn the wheel through the front forks. Clearly I could not continue and it was about 1 o’clock in the morning. 5 minutes later, as I pondered my options, a white builder’s van pulled up and a cheery fellow jumped out to see what had happened. When he saw the front wheel he went straight back to his van and brought out a large rubber hammer. A couple of minutes later he had hammered out the buckled wheel and I went on my way (cautiously) back to Millbrook. The only other real drama I had was when a pigeon hit me full in the chest at 90 mph as I overtook a big lorry in heavy rain on the M1. That was a shock and I got a big bruise and a lot of feathers but again the bike stayed on course and my journey continued.

Fast motorbikes have certainly provided some great fun and wonderful experiences throughout most of my life. You could tell a great deal about the bravery and character of your girlfriends when they were hanging on around your waist at 100 miles an hour – some loved it, others were terrified. You certainly have to trust the driver if you are sitting pillion on a powerful bike. I remember how the children used to go to sleep on long journeys when I tied them to my waist with a strong leather belt! Quite amazing! How lucky I was to win that robust Norton 500 ES2 all those years ago!

Hard Work at the Farm!

Once settled with the family at Newton my farming apprenticeship began. My father had promoted one of his workers, Ron Cox, to become farm manager – and an excellent manager he was. Ron was a fascinating man – very well read. He'd spent time in the army and worked as a hill shepherd, arriving at the farm as an ordinary farm hand. But his bright conversation and wide learning soon attracted great admiration from my father – and the two men became good friends. Ron would arrive in my father's office every morning at 9 o'clock sharp to discuss the day's happenings – and probably much more besides.

I can well imagine it must have been potentially threatening for Ron now to find he had a rather bumptious young Cambridge graduate, and the eldest son of the owner, moving into his patch. For my part, I was determined to be humble as I was certainly well aware that I did not really know much about how to run a farm with 1,000 acres and a dozen workers. I knew my father would never want to become a source of farming knowledge for me – he had always made it clear in the past that he did not want his children to go into farming. I always felt that he never really took my participation in the farm seriously – perhaps not surprising in view of all the negative comments he had always made to us children. No doubt my father felt my mother had rather foisted this situation onto him as part of her own plans to keep her sons about her – I simply don't know. Anyway, one way or another I duly turned up in my working clothes on my little Honda 160 motorbike – and made a start. I never went to a single 9 o'clock meeting with Ron and my father but reported for work with the rest of the labour force in the 'onsteads' at 7.15am every morning. I dare say the other workers were equally puzzled as to what exactly I was trying to do but they took it in good heart and I just mucked in to help with the daily chores – feeding animals, clearing out muck and making sure fresh hay and straw was provided. Like the other fellows, I brought sandwiches and a drink for the communal breakfast we all took, sitting on hay bales at around 8.30am when the early morning chores had been finished.

At 9am most of the men would head off to their tractors or the work which they had been doing on previous days. The farm steward might give new instructions or there might be some emergency to be dealt with. One way or another, the day soon picked up its own momentum. But I am getting a bit ahead of myself here. Ron Cox was a canny fellow so the first thing he wanted to do was to find out what sort of a chap this potentially cocky newcomer might be. Was I just a one-day-wonder or could I really stick it out as a solid worker? On my first day of work Ron presented me with a lump hammer, a cold chisel and a hacksaw and asked me to cut up a huge reinforced concrete beam which was lying in the stackyard. The objective was to make three 7-foot-long concrete posts which I would then take down onto the rocks beyond the Castle. The posts would be concreted in so as to extend the fences towards the low tide mark and prevent sheep escaping from one field to the next via the rocks. Nowadays we could have done that job with a diamond cutting disk on a big power saw – it would probably have taken 10 minutes. It took me 3 days of hammering, chipping and sawing to cut up the beam – it was a tough task. Then the pieces had to be carted off and put in place with concrete. So that was my first week of farm work! But I felt I had passed Ron's first test.

The next job was to be challenging in rather a different way. The farm still sowed turnips in mid-summer to provide winter fodder for cattle and sheep. The turnips were sown as row crops so the weeds could be controlled by hoeing but (at this time) the seeds were sown very close together so the small seedlings had to be "singled" – also by hoeing. Turnips could only grow to their full size if the distance between healthy seedlings was about a foot rather than one or two inches. I joined a team of 6 men and we started work to "single" the turnips by hand hoeing over a 13-acre field. That's a lot of turnips to single. Every dry day we would start work at 9am, working as a team, each man to one row, heads down and hoes at the ready. Once singled the ground between the rows could be cleared of weeds using a steerage hoe – but it took us 2 weeks to finish that field. Each day was the same as the last. As we talked and I got to know the men, I realised how different their lives had been to mine. Most of them had left school at the age of 14 and started work soon after – with no qualifications of any kind, just the expectation that they would continue as farm workers for the rest of their lives. They had hoed turnips every year for the last 20 years or more and easily settled into almost a meditative rhythm which allowed them to think and talk and be part of the natural world around them. They had no ambition to do anything else – the excitements in their lives came from families, friends, hobbies and sports. Their satisfaction came from honest work and happy families. When I asked if they ever felt like visiting foreign countries they looked at me as if I were crazy. Why on earth would we want to do that? was their answer. We have everything we need here. Some of the men had never been further away from home than Alnwick – and that was fine as far as they were concerned.

It was a great lesson to me to begin to understand a different way of living that did not depend on jumping through the hoops of exams or building a successful career at school. The powerful dynamic of a working team was wonderful to behold – how the different personalities melded together to help each other – some as jesters, some as leaders, some as fixers, each with different skills which were happily blended together to get a job done. There was George, whose character was very much a mixed blessing. George was a great drinker and party man who often had such a serious hangover he failed to turn up on a Monday morning (or even another day). This was a great irritation because it meant that others had to step in to do his work. But George was the great joker in the team – always able to make a foul job easier by his ready quips and jokes. Angus, on the other hand, was at the other extreme: a very conscientious and hard-working man who took his responsibilities seriously and would even go out in snowstorms to check the animals. Wiry and incredibly strong for his size, Angus was a gem among men – always behaving politely, never sick and never spending beyond his means. On one occasion I found Angus in tears after he had hurt himself (so could not work) and found that social services would not help him because he had saved too much money. He was in despair because everybody knew that George, who spent all his money on drink, was given help by social services because he had no savings. Such are the realities of our strange welfare state.

So I survived my first month – and it was a true education. Ron and I became good friends and I, too, found the breadth and depth of his knowledge and experience quite remarkable. Ron had married late and we were all delighted when (by some miracle) his 45-year-old wife finally produced a baby girl – Elspeth. My father had built a fine new house for them at Dunstan Square. Ron was making the farm run at a profit and everything in the garden looked "rosey".

Strange Things were Afoot!

At the same time as I began work as a farm labourer my brother Owen had finished his degree in Natural Sciences. He had returned to live at home in Dunstan Steads and began to look for jobs and decide what he would do next. I did not see much of him as I was extremely busy with my job, the running of the golf course and a young family. But it soon became clear that Owen had a very different idea about life as he drove around in his Lotus sports car in smart tweed suits and clean shoes! I was shocked to discover that he was able to drive into Alnwick in his sports car and collect money for being "on the dole". The very fact that he felt able to do this amazed me, as did the fact that government rules allowed it. From what I heard, Owen did go to various job interviews – whether he was actually offered a job by any of the big companies I never knew. What I did know was that he never took any outside job and my mother did what she could to make his life at home comfortable.

Because of the complications of income tax and potential inheritance tax (death duties), my parents had been advised by lawyers and accountants to set up various partnerships and trusts. We three brothers were the beneficiaries in the main Trust which now held ownership of a large part of the estate properties – the Trust being vested in Barclays Bank, Newcastle. The farms themselves were run as a business by a partnership which included all three sons and my mother. After I had been working as a farm labourer for 4 or 5 months I had already felt we were in rather a strange situation. I was getting up in pitch black at 6am in the mornings and going off to shovel cow shit for an hour before breakfast while my able-bodied brother lay in a comfortable bed enjoying all the comforts of life at Dunstan Steads – being waited on hand and foot by our Mum. I was also battling with the help of head greenkeeper John Carss to save the golf course from going bankrupt. Not to mention looking after a busy young family.

An Even Bigger row with the Family

The next thing I knew was that Owen was starting to take on some kind of role in managing the farms and properties – he even started to go along to the morning office meetings with Ron and my father. This seemed even more peculiar and puzzling since his role had never been discussed with me. Soon after this my mother informed me that they (my parents) had decided to make Owen the manager of the family Trust – since he had not yet got a job. This put me in a very difficult position where it was clear that Owen must have potentially serious conflicts of interest "managing" a Trust of which he was just one of the beneficiaries. It now seemed that whatever success I might make of my farming efforts I would eventually end up with Owen managing the major aspects of the business. This was not something I could accept. Things were now very different from my expectations after all the work and commitments I had made in trying to achieve what my mother had asked only a year before. I pleaded with my mother to change her mind, telling her in plain terms that this proposal would almost certainly lead to family argument and disaster. But all to no avail – my mother's mind was made up – she wanted to keep Owen at home and believed my energy and interests would inevitably take me on an independent course. My poor father simply stood by and watched feeling unable to intervene. I suspect he, too, found my energy and independence something of a threat!

Faced with an implacable "NO" from my parents, I packed up my farming ambitions and decided to give up any idea of being part of the family business. A completely new direction was needed. Sarah and I decided to move our base into Newcastle, where I could study for a PhD at the University and we could raise the children together with nurseries nearby. This was close enough to Embleton to enable me to keep up my close involvement with running Dunstanburgh Golf Course. I could follow my interest in researching how society worked and test my own belief that the theories of economics were only a very partial explanation of why people did what they did.

Newcastle University

We moved to Newcastle and bought a small new suburban house in Kenton Bar. By this time we were also living in the old Farm House at Newton after moving from the small cottage at 5 Coastguard Cottages – so we became a 2-home family dividing our time between Newton and Newcastle. We had had extensive work done at Newton to add on a sun lounge and extra bedroom plus bathroom before we moved in.

In Newcastle we soon established a new routine. I went in to work each day in the Department of Agricultural Economics under Professor John Ashton (ex Ministry of Agriculture civil servant) while, at the same time, I was able to plan how to reshape and extend the Dunstanburgh Golf Course. Rupert was able to go to the Montessori nursery school in Jesmond and we soon learned to get along with our new neighbours in Kenton Bar – making great friends with Margaret and John Tweddle (who now live in Los Angeles).

Studying at Newcastle was quite a shock after the hot-house intellectual atmosphere of Cambridge. Any suggestion that students might question any of the lecturer's assertions were strongly discouraged – we were being trained to "parrot" out the official line in all our answers. Most of the fancy economic theory was just a bit of relatively simple mathematical mumbo jumbo wrapped up in longwinded specialist language. I was quickly convinced that conventional economic theories provided very few real insights into why people, businesses and governments did what they did. My thesis topic tackled this issue head-on since its title was "The effect of institutional constraints on rural change". This idea had a very mixed following in the Department – but I pressed on nevertheless.

The time at Newcastle gave me a great opportunity to read widely and do my own research into social and societal change. I became increasingly fascinated by how democratic governments actually worked, given that most of the internal workings were kept secret by the rules imposed by the Official Secrets

Act. My interest was increased by the publicity which surrounded trail-blazing efforts by the then head of the Whitehall civil service, Sir William Armstrong, to modernise and bring in more people with scientific training. His efforts bore fruit in the form of the Fulton Report which had just been published (in 1968). New arrangements for entry into the civil service, based on the findings of this report, were set up in 1971. Candidates with scientific training were clearly going to be given more opportunities and the whole pay structure was being revised to make a career in the public service more attractive. I became determined to give it a shot!

Meanwhile I was getting on with taking the management and development of the golf course in hand. Unfortunately all my predictions about the potential conflicts within the family Trust began to come true. Much as I tried, I could not get my parents to see my point of view – if anything they tended to side with Owen. For whatever reason Owen's wife, Maggi, had clearly taken against us and no doubt Owen was charged with carrying out his part in the hostilities which continued down the years.

As far as the family estate was concerned, Owen steadfastly followed his own agenda with the full support of my parents and with minimal consultation with us. It was not long before we reached a serious impasse over the valuation of the farmland when I finally asked to leave the partnership a few years later. Owen would not budge from his offer of a tenanted valuation only for the farmland – this was a fraction of the amount of the vacant possession value. We ended up going to court as we had a perfect right to do, so the land would be put onto the market at auction to achieve a true value. Owen was forced to bid to buy back the family land – and we did in this way get a fair price. Not surprisingly this whole farce caused a very long break in our relationship and Owen and I did not speak for over 30 years. My views about Owen were further compounded when he sold the land opposite our home in Newton to the local council to be used as a turning circle without any consultation with us. Things got no better over the years that followed as Owen steadily cashed in the farming assets, first converting farm buildings and selling them off, then finally (after our father's death) selling the farms themselves. From my point of view, it seemed as if all our father's work was being cashed in for easy money.

My First Golf Course experience

In the early 1960s Dunstanburgh was, as now, a fine 18-hole golf course set in wonderful coastal scenery. The lay-out of the course had changed little, if at all, from the plans set out by James Braid in 1920 but golf equipment and golfing techniques had moved forward a great deal since then. The course had pottered along for years, mostly making small losses and simply giving my parents constant headaches as members demanded this or that improvement. Anyone could play on the course (as they can today) if they paid a subscription or green fee to the course management (which was me in those days). The golf Club, which ran competitions and set members' handicaps under the rules of the English Golf Union, was run quite separately by those members who wished to play competition golf by paying an additional small subscription to the golf club rather than the course management. This is not a common arrangement since most courses are managed by the Clubs themselves but it is the normal way for a "proprietary club" to be managed.

This arrangement often caused tensions because golf club members had no financial responsibilities nor did they have control of how the course was maintained and developed. They had free licence to grumble and campaign for changes because they did not have to carry the costs. My own position was severely constrained by the serious limitations imposed by the ridiculous lease which my parents had agreed when the land was given to the National Trust in 1961. The Trust's lawyers must have run rings around my parents because it transpired that the "term" of the lease (the number of years it would run) was limited to the lifetime of the last of my father's 3 sons. After this the golf course would revert entirely to belong to the Trust.

The indefinite and uncertain "term" of the lease made it impossible to raise any bank loan which could have enabled me to buy better equipment and significantly improve the club-house. But we did have carte blanche to work on and improve the golf course without having the need to consult (and get agreement from) the National Trust. I realised that the course as it had been laid out by James Braid was hopelessly short for the modern game. Both clubs and balls had improved so much that ordinary players could hit the ball well over 200 yards. The length of the holes on the James Braid course went roughly as follows:

Hole 1 – 320 yards down to the corner

Hole 2 – 245 yards up over Tom Ha's Hill – a completely blind second shot

Hole 3 – 340 yards straight down to the present 3rd green

Hole 4 – 170 as now

Hole 5 – 285 as now

Hole 6 – 385 as now

Hole 7 – 255 just over the hill in the bottom of the hollow

Hole 8 – 160 strange blind short hole to steep valley green

Hole 9 – 285 this was the 8th hole as now but with no back tee

Hole 10 – 250 yards to green on the mound beside present 9th bunker

Hole 11 – 195 short hole to present 9th green

Hole 12 – 420 as 10th now

Hole 13 – 205 short hole from pillbox to present 12th green

Hole 14 – 525 as now

Hole 15 – 120 as now

Hole 16 – 265 from present ladies tee – there was no back tee

Hole 17 – 395 as now

Hole 18 – 380 from what is now front winter tee

Total length – 5,220 yards

I decided that radical changes were required to make the course competitive for modern equipment. We prepared for the changes by close mowing of various parts of the rough so that we would have sufficient new turf (matching the existing sward) to make new greens and tees. This was easily done and we knew we could lift the turf from existing greens that were going to be taken out of use – so turfing the new greens would be straightforward. A couple of years later we hired a big drott with a good driver for a few days so that the 5 new greens (1st, 2nd, 7th, 11th and 13th) could be carved out of the sandy subsoil. New tees had to be made for the 2nd, 3rd, 8th, 11th, 13th, 16th and 18th. The head greenkeeper, John Carss, the greenstaff and myself worked away steadily and it only took a few weeks to complete the transformation which created the course which is in use today. All in all we created 10 new holes and lengthened some of the others. Dunstanburgh was re-born, its length extended by more than 1,000 yards!

Dramas with the National Trust at Newton

After we moved into the old Farm House at Low Newton (1968) the traffic situation on the road, around the house and on the sand dunes got steadily worse. The National Trust refused point blank to abide by the restrictive covenants in the deed of gift so dozens of cars were continually racing alongside our garden wall and parking on the dunes. The Northumberland County Council made all sorts of objections to my proposal that there should be no parking on the road and a new car park built away from the beach at the top of the hill (for which we could provide land).

Faced with this blank wall of refusals and a wall of negativity from my parents I decided to "take the bull by the horns" and shut the road onto the dunes myself. We owned the road and we owned Risemoor cottage and the farm buildings for which the road provided access. I told the Trust that if they were not going to take action to enforce the covenants and protect the duneland then I was going to precipitate a crisis by closing the road with a locked gate myself. Anyone wishing entry would have to get the key from me. At the same time I put a proposal to the bungalow owners who used the road to give them their own designated parking area to the west of the farm buildings – as they would no longer be able to park on the dunes or drive along the road to Risemoor. We also replaced the steps which gave access to the beach from the square by a ramp so that small-boat users could still launch from the beach.

With help from Ron Cox and the farm workers we duly put the gate into position. A huge fuss and bother ensued. At first the gate was ripped off by the fishermen and thrown into the sea. We had great coverage in the local press where I was able to explain why we had done this because of the failures of the National Trust. After the first gate was smashed we came back with a much stronger gate. When a local crowd of villagers and fishermen were again trying to rip it off I decided to film the whole thing (since I could not stop it). As soon as they saw my camera the crowd fled in terror. Soon afterwards the National Trust agreed to do what they should have done in the first place and put their own gate up across the access road to Risemoor. It was agreed that the traditional fishermen would continue to have the right to leave their boats (free of charge) on the duneland immediately adjacent to the southern farm building (as they always had done in storms and winter conditions). Special arrangements would be made on designated days with the National Trust when vehicles would be allowed to tow these boats in, or out, of the dunes.

Note that these original arrangements have now been totally modified by the Trust completely disregarding what was agreed. All our complaints have fallen on deaf ears as the Trust now try to make money by charging for boat parking (while, at the same time, refusing to clear up the site from broken-down old boats and trolleys).

Arguments with the National Trust did not stop there. As has been said, the Trust wilfully ignored the promises it had made to my father that it would enforce its byelaws to protect this vulnerable coastal strip. I now faced these problems of control directly myself as tenant and manager of the golf course and as resident of Low Newton. Racehorses were frequently being taken onto the beaches for training so their hooves ripped up the sand dunes. Campers left litter and old fires. Out-of-control dogs ran loose disturbing wild life and leaving their mess. In 1970 I met Major Orde (then Chairman of the NT Regional Committee) and he agreed that if I passed over the bungalow rents to the Trust they would use these to employ a designated warden for the Craster to Beadnell coastal strip. (Previously the Trust always came up with the excuse of having no money to do this work.) Later I persuaded my parents to offer up the Risemoor cottage specifically so it would be occupied by a resident warden. A 24-hour presence was clearly necessary if activities like the commercial harvesting of lug worms during night time low tides were to be stopped.

For several years these arrangements worked well but the management structure and commercial ethos of the National Trust became more and more profit oriented. Old local loyalties were swept away, the Trust's Regional Management arrangements were scrapped and "commercial" local managers appointed under direction from the Trust's head office in Swindon. Instead of looking after Embleton, the Trust took the bungalow moneys and used them to help wardening up at their profitable tourist outlets on the Farne Islands. Next they got rid of the resident warden and converted Risemoor into a very expensive holiday let. Then they began to try and operate (very badly) the boat park on the dunes as a commercial outlet by charging the users an annual fee which was completely contrary to our family's original agreement. This contrary behaviour from the Trust has been further compounded because they continually refuse to abide by the restrictive covenants my father had written into the Deed of Gift – namely to, so far as possible, maintain the dunes in their natural state and not allow any motor vehicles or animals to be on them. The Charity Commission, who have the responsibility to "police" the so-called charities, simply look on as the Trust's operation becomes more and more focussed on generating cash to pay big salaries and decent pensions for its staff. Step by step, the officers of the Trust have emasculated the influence of the membership by subtle changes in the complex constitution which governs their activities.

MY QUEST 2

My years studying agriculture, working on the farm and then spending 3 years immersed in economics at Newcastle moved "my quest" forward in new directions. On the one hand, I saw that man's relationship with the soil and food production was not one that should be governed solely by economics and the price mechanism. The long-term need to maintain and improve soils was never going to be served by such a dependency. To make a profit, farmers would simply "mine" the fertility of their land, leaving future generations the challenge of restoring it. On the other hand, I saw more and more clearly that the entire machinery of economics and what seemed like a blind belief in the wonderful power of the free market, were dangerous fictions. Humans were very good at inventing complex systems of rules and behaviours (we call them "institutions") to solve one problem but hopelessly ineffective at modifying such institutions when their long-term consequences became toxic. The clash between the influence of institutions (for example family traditions and/ or the whims of the local bank manager) and the power of economics was the focus of my 3-year thesis topic. It certainly seemed to me that the theories of economics did not provide explanations for a large number of important human decisions! Nor could economics produce good predictions of what humans would actually do!

The more I looked at human history, the more I became frustrated at not understanding why civilisations had become trapped in what were ultimately life destroying behaviours. Surely the leaders (and the populations) could have seen what was coming and taken action to avoid disaster? Just what were the internal mechanisms of government and why did they so often fail?

It was not easy (at this time in the late 1960s) to find out what happened within the "ivory towers" of Whitehall and/or the padded corridors of Parliament. Both my professor (John Ashton) and my supervisor (Brian Davies) had worked in the Ministry of Agriculture but they, too, were merely "professionals" and not "administrators". As such they were excluded from the inner workings of the government system. They were, as I later discovered, merely "professionals" who were employed to provide "professional" advice but they were excluded from the inner sanctums of power. These inner sanctums were the preserve of the elite "administrative" class – the so-called Whitehall Mandarins.

At that time, the workings of the civil service were strongly protected and kept secret by the strict rules of the Official Secrets Act (which all public servants had to sign). There were no books or academic studies of the inner workings of the Whitehall machine. It would be some years yet before the revelations of Clive Ponting broke the barriers of secrecy (he ended up defending his "leaking" of sensitive information before the Criminal Courts).

So how did decisions get taken in Government? This was why I decided the next step in my quest must be to join the civil service so I could discover at first hand how things worked.

Teeth! 1971

Most of those who have lived or worked with me over the last 45 years will know that my two broken front teeth have often been a source of uncomfortable misery. Here again the fates have a strange part to play.

During the time we lived in Kenton Bar (Newcastle) I would often play squash with our good friend Peter McMeekin. We often went out to dine with Peter and his lovely wife Pam and we knew their children well. During one particularly hard-fought squash-game Peter (a keen tennis player) took a big follow-through with his backhand and, as a result, snapped off both my beautiful front teeth with his racquet. By a miracle neither my face nor my eyes were hit – the two teeth were simply neatly smashed off. Peter was, of course, our dentist! And, up until that point, I had had a perfectly intact set of teeth.

Once recovered from the shock, we repaired to his surgery where he was able to stick on a couple of temporary crowns. Thus with the teeth at least partially repaired, we went home to enjoy a glass of gin and tonic. You can imagine that the comic side of this situation was pretty evident to all – especially Sarah when she heard the sad news. Clearly I was going to have to come to terms with the loss and all the fuss and bother needed to drill out the root canals and put on proper long-term crowns. My discomfort was multiplied on the morning after this accident when, as I was helping get the children ready for nursery school, I suddenly sneezed. The resulting blast of air blew out my two temporary crowns which promptly disappeared behind the radiator in our hallway. What a performance!

Despite all of Peter's careful efforts to keep my teeth and their crowns in good health I was constantly (every 3 or 4 years) plagued by painful infections which either required antibiotics or more root surgery. Finally, when I moved back to Northumberland in 2013, I could stand the fuss no longer and had my dentist pull out what remained of my poor old front teeth – what a relief it was to finally get rid of the nuisance. The modern dentures (which replace the teeth) are wonderfully well made and you soon get used to the strange material in your mouth.

Chapter 3: The Move to London 1972

By 1971 I had become determined to join the so-called "Mandarins" who ran the senior civil service in Whitehall. My ambition seemed particularly appropriate after the publication of the Fulton Report. The civil service wanted more people who could work with numbers – not just those who had studied history, classics or philosophy. And they were offering higher pay and fast promotion to those that made the grade. Both Sarah and my professor encouraged me to have a go.

At this time, the civil service entry examinations for the so-called "fast stream" were very challenging and very competitive. The first requirement was to have at least a second class honours degree. Over 5,000 candidates applied each year but only 70 places were on offer. It was not an easy exam to prepare for. I tried to widen my regular reading so as to get a better understanding of current affairs.

The first hurdle for applicants took the form of 2 days of exams, taken in regional centres (Newcastle in my case). These were strange exams – part IQ tests, part use and comprehension of English and part fictitious casework examples. We all, 60 or 70 of us, scribbled away frantically and metaphorically wiped the sweat from our brows. I later discovered that these tests had been devised by a mathematician (statistician) called Edgar Anstey. After taking the tests I found his book in the library describing how he had based his questions on many years of experience with army officer selection tests. He had done this simply on the basis of finding good correlations between each officer's test results and the actual success of his career. Those tests where high marks correlated well with actual success were developed whilst others which showed no such correlation were discarded.

With the first hurdle tests completed it was simply a matter of waiting for the post to arrive each day to see if there was an official brown envelope! Yes – it finally arrived, telling me I had passed the first stage and would now be required to attend 2 days of group tests and interviews in London. Luckily for me Sarah had a good friend from her time at St Andrews, Lorraine, who was working as a nurse in London with a flat right underneath the post office tower (then just opened). So it was off to London for the group tests under the constant scrutiny of 3 observers – one of whom, it turned out, was actually Edgar Anstey himself! It was a great challenge and very enjoyable to face up to the group exercises. We also had long and detailed interviews with each of the 3 observers. We had to choose 3 topics to discuss and defend. One of my topics was a bad choice – as I realised afterwards – discussing the links between "chance" and "free will". I dropped that one on my second attempt at the Civil Service Selection Board.

Once again we had to wait for that important brown envelope. Yes – it arrived and "yes" I had passed the tests but they had no place for me in that year – the letter suggested I apply again next year. 1972 duly arrived and I did apply again. This time it was a pass and I was invited for a final interview at the Final Selection Board (a group of crusty old generals and retired grandees of one kind or another). This one-hour interview I can remember very well because the door handle on the interview room door was faulty – this was in the centre of Admiralty Arch in London. I remember thinking that this must be a clever army type of initiative test – how would the baffled student react when he/she could not open the door? Anyway I did get the door open and I told the panel about the problem.

Bingo I was finally accepted with an A-fast-stream-grade and posted to the newly created and rather flashy large Department of the Environment under its flamboyant Secretary of State, Peter Walker. I bought myself 3 smart suits in Newcastle and Sarah and I began to research possible places to live in London.

Family Life from 1972

The first big challenge facing us in our move to London was to find a suitable house in a sensible location. We took a good look at the map and made a definite decision that we should try and avoid any long commutes – if possible, staying within 15 minutes of Westminster (travelling by motorbike). We also wanted to be somewhere in north London to make it easier to get up to my business at Dunstanburgh and our house in Newton. If we could be near a decent park that would be good too. The "hot spot" from all these points of view seemed to be near Regents Park or Primrose Hill. We decided to take the whole (young) family (aged 5, 4, 3 and 1) down to London on the train for an exploratory trip.

On the map it did not look too far to walk from Kings Cross up to Primrose Hill. We duly set out to walk north from the station. We had only gone about half a mile when a big red double decker bus pulled over and stopped beside us (to our amazement!). The driver leaned out of his window and, with a rather puzzled look on his face, asked us where we were going. I suppose our small entourage must have looked a bit strange wandering up a busy London street. Anyway he told us to jump onto his bus as he was going north in the right direction. We took this unusual incident as being a good omen for our future in the big city.

We liked Primrose Hill and the small fairly self-contained "village" of Chalk Farm which was nearby. There was a new housing development on the east side of the hill and when we enquired it seemed there was just one of the new houses left unsold. It was down at the bottom of the recently completed Meadowbank Estate – a perfect small townhouse with 3 storeys and a small garden in the rear. The estate road seemed quiet and safe and we would be just 2 minutes' walk from Primrose Hill. We thought the price (£40,000) was very high but we managed to get a mortgage and soon the house was ours (it's worth £ millions today!).

Family life was "full on" once we moved into the new house. I was kept very busy with my new job, commuting into work in Whitehall every day on my small Honda 90 motorbike. I found I could keep my smart work suit clean and dry by wearing a big heavy traditional riding mac. These riding macs are smart but 100 percent waterproof and they have a wide gusset so you can sit down in the saddle (horse or bike) without getting a wet bum. They also have straps on each side so you can keep the flaps of the coat from blowing away from your legs in the wind. All I had to do was to put on a pair of wellington boots which I could take off and exchange for clean work shoes when I parked my bike under the big Marsham Street offices. I could then step out of my protective clothing as a smart be-suited "mandarin".

After the somewhat claustrophobic life in a small rural village (Embleton/Newton) where everybody knew everybody and you could not go anywhere without being recognised, it was a wonderful release to be living in a big city. At last it seemed possible to escape from all the pre-conceived impressions which dogged relationships in Northumberland. In London nobody was interested in your past or who your parents were – you could be as eccentric or conventional as you liked! Arriving in London we were able to re-invent ourselves – it was a bright new exciting world. We soon made many new friends both with our neighbours and with the bright and interesting fellow civil servants I was working with

Sarah set up a small nursery school, looking after other people's kids as well as our own. We had a big Volvo estate car that we could throw all the children into – plus the dog (and occasionally the cat) – so we would often travel up to Newton after work on a Friday night. In those days the roads were fairly quiet in the evening so we could leave after supper, driving for 5 hours whilst the kids slept and arrive at Newton around midnight. Once we discovered the magic of the newly available stretchy wetsuits, the children would spend a lot of time enjoying the sea. Soon we were enjoying the new sport of windsurfing as well as more conventional sailing and fishing.

Once the two girls started at the French Lycée in Kensington we all had a very early start each morning as they had to be ready to jump on the special Lycée bus at around 7.15am. We certainly "burned the candle at both ends in those days"! Often I would take Rupert up to school in Hampstead on my motorbike before I set off myself for work. The pace was fairly relentless and London life has many other interesting cultural distractions, too.

Very soon we discovered the new French skiing resort of Isola – a very French family resort just north of Nice and always blessed with sunny weather. This was a completely new resort which had been created by an English entrepreneur who had seen how suitable the north-facing valley was from maps. We could rent one of the new smart flats and literally step out of the door onto the slopes – a very useful bonus when you have to fix up skis, boots and sticks for four small people as well as yourselves! The complex also had the great benefit that the flats, restaurants, games rooms and shops were all contained in one big indoor complex. So once you had changed out of your skiing gear there was ample space for kids to run about in the evenings. There was also a pretty good little supermarket so it was easy to buy (to us) exotic food for our meals in the flat. The butcher's department liked nothing better than to find a large chicken for us – all ready to be roasted.

Visits to Isola became a regular feature of our Christmas celebrations. To avoid any danger of jealousies between the two sets of grandparents we soon realised we could excuse ourselves from such potential Christmas pressures by taking a 10-day skiing holiday over Christmas and New Year. The French also had more lavish celebrations – especially the fireworks over the mountains at New Year. After a couple of very stressful trips by air and bus we decided it was altogether easier to make a road trip out of the holiday and drive down (first in our Volvo and then in the converted Mercedes van). Fortunately, the girls' school friend Anique had parents who lived beside Lyons – we often stayed overnight there enjoying wonderful evenings together over the elaborate and very beautiful meals cooked by Anique's mum Monique. It was always a wonderful feeling to drive into the different (and usually much better) weather of Provence once we had passed by Lyons. Then it was a smooth drive on autoroute along the mountainous shore of the Med before starting the long and dramatic ascent up into the Alps above Nice. In those times the mountain road was dramatically dangerous – I remember one occasion when the car was so heavily loaded the brake fluid began to boil on the way down (we had to stop to give it a rest).

As the children got older we moved our skiing up a gear in favour of the bigger mountains of Val D'Isere – again we would usually drive out with all our gear and make an exciting trip out of the journey. This was in the days before the winter Olympics brought great changes to this traditional resort. We had often stayed in the top floor of an old lady's traditional mountain farmhouse where there were still cattle enjoying the shelter in its basement (they helped keep us warm with just a small whiff of manure). After the Olympics the whole place was transformed – angular new buildings, huge motorway flyovers and stainless steel and plastic replaced the old dark weathered wood. Much of its charm had been swept away.

If the snow was one important feature of our family times together then the sea was another. Our regular trips to Newton gave the children ample opportunities to swim, fish and sail – we also had the challenges of learning to play golf! When the children reached teenage years we began to explore the wild nature of ocean sailing first chartering yachts from Ullapool and later from Skye. Of course it was a long drive from London to Ullapool but it was with a wonderful sense of freedom that we set sail, going west as the summer sun set. Our aim was to reach anchor at the Summer Isles, where we would stay our first night at sea. In those days the wildlife was prolific in these waters – hundreds of gannets would be circling and diving like rockets all around our yacht. Dolphins and whales were also often seen. There were no stinking commercial salmon farms in those early days (in the early 80s). After a few days at sea we'd all be going crazy to have a wash in fresh water as the constant exposure to salt made our skins itchy and uncomfortable – finding a mountain waterfall was the perfect answer!

But time rushes on and childhood holidays soon become a thing of the past as children find their own friends and their own excitements, enjoying all the independence which (we hope) a sensible upbringing has given them.

Leaving the Family Business

Once we had established ourselves in the new busy world of London it was absolutely clear that I must get out of the family business and "cut my losses". For better or worse, I had to "cut my own furrow" in life and I needed to realise cash from my share in the family business to do it. Negotiations with the family started slowly and I'm not sure they realised how determined I was to escape!

The legal position concerning my shared tenancy of the farms meant that there was a "trust for sale". So my leaving the business could, as far as the law was concerned, be achieved by my forcing a sale so as to claim my share of the farm's true market value. Obviously nobody wanted to see the farm sold, so I tried to negotiate a fair price with Owen (with our mother and father looking on). Owen was adamant that the Trust would only pay out on the basis of a tenanted value rather than the full market price which could have been achieved with a public sale with vacant possession. Our parents supported him on this – despite the formal legal position.

After the earlier annoyances, this reluctance to pay me my due share really was the last straw – most unreasonable as I thought. I had a life to lead and a family to support so I was not going to be short-changed in my legitimate share of the family assets (which my parents had intended to be shared equally between their 3 children). It was because the extent of the strong feelings and bitterness we felt towards my parents was so intense that we all had to go through the traumatic incident of the returned Christmas presents. My mother was always extremely conscientious and well-organised as far as presents were concerned, whether for Christmas or for birthdays. Each grandchild would have a couple of presents carefully chosen for them, wrapped up, labelled and delivered. In normal times this was all well and good – but these were not normal times. At a time when my mother was providing support for Owen's seriously one-sided decisions about the business and the family Trust, knowing how strongly I opposed the actions which I believed were unfair, it really did seem hypocritical to think we would accept a few presents! When we sent that year's Christmas presents back it was, I think, the first time my mother realised the depths of feeling she had stirred up by her decision to let Owen take charge of the family estate. I guess I will never really understand the complex emotional motives which prompted my mother to take the actions she did. I guess I will never ever know whether it was Owen's own wish to take decisions either without consultation with me or directly against my known wishes – perhaps this came either from my mother or from his wife Maggi. Until leaving Cambridge Owen and I had always got along together fine.

Certainly this family argument was pretty stressful for all concerned but my mother was not going to be deflected from her plans to keep Owen in a key role in Northumberland. No amount of argument or discussion was going to resolve things in a way I regarded as "fair". We commenced a court action to compel Owen to put the farmland on the market. I still have the sale brochure for Newton farm which the courts ordered to be put up for auction in 1978. So Owen was forced to buy back the farmland and a proper market price was established. To us it seemed a tragedy that such an action should have been necessary but logic evidently had no place in this family battle. I did not speak to or see Owen for more than 30 years after all this fuss but I did feel a keen sense of loss as, over the years which followed he sold off almost all the family estate, bit by bit, for cash. It seemed to me such a betrayal of all the values my father had worked for – both with his land and with the Embleton community.

Whitehall – William the "Mandarin"

The very first thing a new civil servant is asked to do is to sign the Official Secrets Act. By doing so he/she joins an exclusive club of those "on the inside". Of course, the reason for having to sign the Act has nothing to do with national security; civil servants are required to keep mum simply to make sure they don't say anything which might embarrass their political masters. Even so, signing the Act is quite a serious business as the penalties for speaking out can be severe.

As an A-grade fast-stream entry, my first job as an Administrative Trainee (AT) would be working for one of the brightest stars in the central road planning unit (General Planning Highways) in the Department of the Environment (DoE). Chris Brearley, my Principal, was a very clever and charming Oxford philosophy graduate in his early 30s. His grasp of detail and his political acumen were tremendous. The quality and speed of his "drafting" was second to none. And, to cap it all, he was a splendid friendly fellow with great conversation and a wonderful sense of humour. The establishment thought very well of Chris and had, accordingly, given him 3 ATs to train and manage. My AT colleagues were John Pearson and Marie Winkler. JP was highly articulate, self-confident and already gave off an air of complete mastery of his subject. MW was calm, self-effacing and extremely effective. Both my AT colleagues appeared to be much more savvy and "street wise" than I – but very soon I learned to play the game.

Our primary work involved dealing with queries and complaints about highways, new roads and prospective by-passes. Usually these came in the form of letters from the public but there were often "red jackets" – letters written personally to our Minister by other MPs – and these had specific deadlines to be met. The content of all our responses might become the subject of high-profile publicity at any moment – so words had to be chosen carefully. This was particularly true when we were required to write speeches for our Minister or provide detailed answers or briefing for questions he might face in Parliament. It was a strange feeling to come from rural Northumberland into this high-pressure world where I had to imagine what a government Minister might want to say in Parliament! My Principal was expert at recasting and revising my (at first) clumsy drafting. After 12 months' practice my style, speed and competence had massively improved. Remember now that this was before the existence of modern word processors. We learned to dictate our speeches, minutes and letters onto magnetic tape which was sent down to the communal typing pool. (Being on good terms with the typists was an essential ingredient of success because this was the only way to get priority work done in time for deadlines.)

The gravity and significance of our work was amplified by the presence of 2 large safes, each with a sophisticated combination lock. All our work papers had to be stored in these safes overnight – for the usual reasons of what was called "national security". Many of our files were marked "Confidential" with a big green cross and each item in the file numbered sequentially so none could be removed without it being noticed. In our various security briefings we were told that it was not the fact that information was stolen that was significant provided you knew it had been stolen. The true danger came when information had been stolen without anyone knowing!

Despite the demanding routine which was necessary to get all 4 children ready for school and then reach my office desk before 9am each day, I thoroughly enjoyed the challenge and the new world of government service. My work colleagues were a varied and stimulating bunch of men and women – young, intelligent, well informed and sometimes eccentric. At least once or twice each week we would find time for a longer pub lunch where personal contacts and trust could be more fully developed. I soon realised that such face-to-face contacts were the best guarantee of trust between different sections and different government departments. In all large organisations each component part inevitably does what it can to protect its own power and reputation – often to the point of not quite telling the full truth. If you knew someone personally (rather than only by written minute or phone conversation) this was always the best way to find out what was really going on. One learned quite quickly that first impressions about the key elements in some happening were almost invariably short of the full truth; questions needed to be asked and all facts double checked with independent sources if possible. If Ministers were given incorrect facts the repercussions could be severe.

During my first year in Highways I was also involved in the wider civil service debate about the future and operation of the newly formed AT (Administration Trainee) scheme. The Civil Service Department was responsible for making sure the scheme was working well and that the new intake of recruits felt confident that their futures were in good hands. I realised that it would be useful if the new AT intake were able to meet each other to compare notes on how they were being trained and treated. I began to canvass opinion and the first person to respond was Liz Cox who also worked in the DoE in a room a few corridors down from me. As soon as we met I knew I had found someone with great energy, common sense and the ability to get things done. Together we launched a campaign to bring the AT group together – and this we did, with help from Susan Scales (a neat young thing from the Civil Service Department). I did not know it then but Liz, now Liz Meek, was to become a life-long friend with whom I have shared many significant moments and many wonderful holidays.

After doing my 12-month stint in Highways I was able to negotiate an arrangement for 3 weeks special leave so I could finish the work on the PhD thesis which I had started at Newcastle University. This was, alas, a very tedious necessity.

Once again I had to plough through all the references and notes. Hundreds of pages needed to be typed up by a professional typing agency – with all the necessary references and appendices. I knew I was taking a risky and radical course because my work challenged the whole idea that economic motives were the primary factor governing farmers' (and villagers') behaviour. This was the main theme of my work. I had been encouraged to take up this challenge because the deficiencies of economics had always been a favourite theme in the talks given by my professor (John Ashton). But talking about such "heresies" was one thing – actually supporting them when they were written into a formal paper was quite another. Nevertheless I was convinced about the importance of my work so I pressed on regardless. Finally the great work was completed and submitted within the deadline. Of course I was scandalised when I found my supervisor – a man of rather limited intelligence – then published much of my work in a paper of his own. But such is the cut-throat world of academic competition. It turned out that the academic establishment did not like my work and I was awarded an MSc rather than the full PhD I had hoped for. Frankly, by this time, I was glad to get rid of the whole business and get on with my challenging and enjoyable civil service career. My time at Newcastle had been fruitful for other reasons as I had been able to finish all my work developing the new layout at Dunstanburgh Golf Course.

My next posting was into local authority finance. The name of our division was Finance Local Authorities (FLA) and we were the lead division in charge of negotiating the annual rate support grant (then about £6,000 million). We had the belligerent local authorities on one side (all wanting more money), the Treasury on the other (trying to protect and limit government expenditure) and our Minister in the middle trying to make himself popular by keeping the council rates down. I found myself promoted to Higher Executive Officer (A) and sitting opposite a hyper-active red-headed torrent of words and activity. This came from my new Principal, Timothy Hornsby. He was super clever, highly articulate and constantly fuelling his nerves on a diet of codeine tablets. Our immediate boss was the smooth urbane Geoffrey Chipperfield and above him the wise and mercurial Under Secretary, Tom Caulcott.

Local authority finance was extremely complicated and extremely high-profile politically. Our Under-Secretary, Tom Caulcott, was exceptionally capable and cunning. He realised very quickly that with my mathematical background I was both quick and imaginative in assessing the many different and complex policy options. Our opposite number in the Treasury was also a very smart cookie, Derek Maughan, who was constantly challenging our complex methodologies. Altogether we had a lot of high-pressure fun. I was able to derive a comprehensive formula linking the different variables so we could calculate the implications of different policy variations very quickly – quicker than the Treasury certainly. Tom was very pleased about this and we did in fact negotiate one of the most generous settlements ever achieved by the Department – much to our Minister's delight.

In the office opposite mine was the young political adviser David Lipsey (now a member of the House of Lords). He had been brought in as a young political hopeful by the Secretary of State but he had no experience of Whitehall and very little comprehension of the complex mechanism of Rate Support Grant. I would often receive sudden visits on the occasions when this young adviser was called up to talk to the Secretary of State – just how did it all work and what should he be saying? Of course I have no doubt the Secretary of State felt much more comfortable taking advice from this very limited (and un-expert) source than from established civil servants. We professional civil servants simply had to "grin and bear it".

I learned a lot about life in the higher civil service from Tom Caulcott during our long evenings working together. There was plenty of time to chat as we had to walk frequently between our offices in Marsham Street and the Treasury in Whitehall. I began to see how people you regarded as friends and colleagues at a junior level gradually became your competitors for senior promotion – and those who were ambitious were frequently not to be trusted. If blame could be avoided and passed to others this was the true skill of those seeking high office! Tom had made enemies in high places and soon left the Department to take up a very lucrative job as Chief Executive of Birmingham City Council. The rest of us battled on.

My Canadian Trip

After just over a year in FLA I, I knew that I would soon receive a new posting. At this time, local authority finances were very much in the news because there was so much concern about rate increases. The government had commissioned a major report to examine different options for financing local government – this was the Layfield Enquiry. Sarah and I had also been chewing over what our future might have in store. Together we came up with a plan that I might be able to use my "hands on" experience in local government finance to good effect and, at the same time, explore the opportunities which Canada might offer for a young family just starting out. I put together a plan, with the support of my bosses, that I might go on a 6-week fact-finding mission to Canada so as to submit a report which would form part of the evidence presented to Layfield. I could carry out such an expedition before my next posting which would likely be to Private Office.

After liaising with Establishments and the various embassies of the Foreign Office which operated in each Canadian Province, I set off with my briefcase in hand and authority to claim all my expenses for travel and accommodation from the government. It was a great trip. Canada had much more sophisticated systems for financing its municipalities (and Provinces) than the UK. They did not, of course, have a lot of historical baggage to contend with so computers were already being used to process the necessary formulae. Toronto was a cold and highly organised metropolitan centre. Ottawa was cold and boring – the centre of Federal Government. Regina in Saskatchewan is flat, very very cold and very very boring. Calgary in Alberta was bubbling with an oil boom, big steaks, and jolly people – great skiing in the Rockies – still very cold. Vancouver in British Columbia was delightful, charming, not so cold and near very beautiful scenery. Skiing at nearby Whistler was my first experience of bottomless powder – like skiing in mid-air but very difficult to get up when you fell. Victoria Island was temperate, rather Scottish and looked very pretty from the seaplane I travelled in. Halifax in Nova Scotia was like a small transplanted Edinburgh – I had the most perfect day of skiing there in crystal-clear blue weather. Montreal was sophisticated, French and very enjoyable – they spoke English to me because I was not American!

I collected lots of data and had many interesting interviews. The Canadians had made their municipal taxation system (based on property taxes as the UK) much more progressive by linking it to each taxpayer's personal circumstances via their income tax code. They also had a system requiring a referendum of the population before any large borrowings were undertaken – this to prevent ambitious politicians buying votes with money from future generations. Canada also had a large federal equalisation programme transferring funds from the rich provinces in the west (BC and Alberta) to the poorer maritime provinces in the east.

When I finished in Canada I visited old neighbours Burt and Ede in Tacoma, Washington State, USA. What a wild and beautiful place is Washington State – mile upon mile of temperate pine forests, buzzing every night with the loud cries of the small tree frogs. Then I took a flight back east to visit the Warriner relatives in Massachusetts before heading home.

Although I had been very impressed with the west coast of Canada we did not, in the event, take the plunge and leave our new (and exciting) life in London. My report was submitted to Layfield but the seeds of the poll tax had evidently already been sown – I had argued very strongly against this because it seemed likely to be very unfair, unprogressive and politically disastrous (as it ultimately proved to be!).

Private Office

As soon as I received a call from the Establishments officer asking me to come to his office for a chat, I knew this would be about my next posting. Everyone's great ambition was to be allocated a post in "Private Office", working directly with a Minister or Permanent Secretary on the red carpeted top floors (15 – 18th) where the office doors were made of heavy walnut. This role of "Private Secretary" is both vital and peculiar. On the one hand, the private secretary acts as the primary channel for information both to and from his boss, serving as the official mouthpiece for instructions issued to the Department. On the other hand, the Private Secretary acts as the eyes and ears of senior Departmental officials who need to have information and understanding about what the Minister and his/her colleagues are thinking. The Private Secretary wants his/her Minister to be successful but, at the same time, has to protect the Department from wild and untenable policies.

When I arrived for my Estabs interview I found a rather fraught Principal waiting for me. He was in serious difficulties because the last 2 candidates he had sent as Private Secretary for Sir Idwal Pugh had both failed to meet his (VERY) high standards and had been summarily sacked. I was, he told me, his last chance to satisfy the needs of this fussy and bad tempered Permanent Secretary. This was a somewhat worrying introduction but within a couple of weeks I found myself facing Sir Idwal Pugh in his plush office high up on the 18th floor. Pugh was a dour Welshman who had a passion for detail and had worked himself up through the Department by sheer hard work and thoroughness. He did not have a sense of humour and there were very strict protocols to be followed. We had the office of the Secretary of State next to ours – nerve centre of the whole Department – and the senior officers I had to deal with on behalf of the Secretary (that's what we called Pugh) were like the powerful robber barons of medieval times, each with their own carefully guarded empires. It was my job to gain the trust and respect of both my boss (the Permanent Secretary) and the Deputy Secretaries and Under-Secretaries that served him.

You can get a good idea of the daily routine from the talk I gave to new recruits in the Civil Service College in January 1976. Here it is.

Peter, my clerical officer, arrives in the office at 8.45am. His first task is to unlock and open our four filing cabinets, take out the "In" and "Out" trays and fish any papers out of the appropriate B/F (Bring Forward) file. (Peter is my Man Friday who knows all the official drivers and can fix all sorts of problems in his own secret ways. It is his job to manage the Secretary's diary and keep all the filing in order.) I arrive in the office at 9am (usually after running up the 18 flights of stairs to work off the likely tensions of the day) – this is about 20 minutes before the Secretary arrives on a normal day. My first task is to check the diary for the day to make sure we have all the necessary briefing papers – papers for the day's meetings are collected and flagged up in folders to be put on the left hand side of the Secretary's desk. Any outstanding briefing must be chased up with senior officers urgently – but this is not usually necessary.

The Secretary arrives with his driver Jim, who then brings him his morning cup of coffee. The first post normally arrives at about the same time. As the Secretary walks through the office door he gives the first orders of the day – he's been thinking about things overnight. The orders come "out of the blue" – perhaps the overnight briefing papers have been deficient in some ways, lunch must be arranged with Mr X, or Mr Y must be located immediately to be spoken to on the phone.

There is a tense moment each morning about 9.30am – will the Secretary decide he wants to dictate letters or minutes before Hilary, our typist, arrives. Hilary is a brilliant shorthand typist (there are no word processors), which is essential because the

Secretary will not tolerate a single typing mistake – she has to scrape off any wrong letters with a razor blade! Normally all goes well and Hilary arrives and begins to work through the post. All papers entering the office are numbered in two categories (classified and unclassified) and these numbers are entered in the appropriate books. Similarly all papers leaving my desk, going into the waste bin, the files or being sent to Ministers or officials are also entered into the books. This is so we always know where papers are – a vital factor in running an effective office.

It is about 9.45am before the numbered and time-stamped post has found its way into my "In" tray. I then begin the job of sorting and examining it – does the Secretary need to see all of it, do any previous papers need to be attached to make sense of a letter or minute, are there any obvious omissions from tables or annexes which the papers claim to have attached, can some questions be passed directly to officials for advice while a copy is simply shown to the Secretary? If papers are passed down to other officials, what sort of instructions should I give them and who else should they be copied to? Perhaps there are some questions or actions which I can simply take myself to save the Secretary's time? I may need to draft minutes or letters of my own, or make phone calls, to try and progress items that are clearly not yet ready for the Secretary to decide on.

Finally the post is ready to be taken in to the Secretary (through the green baize double doors that separate his large office from ours). When I put the post in his "In" tray I also take out his empty coffee cup and any papers he has already put into his "Out" tray. By now it is nearly 10am.

The first meetings of the day normally begin at 10am. The Secretary is either leaving his office for a conference room somewhere or we begin to receive the first of those we have asked to attend the meeting. I make conversation with those who are now waiting in our office. At precisely 10am I check that the Secretary is ready and usher the attendees into his office. I take my seat at the corner of the conference table. I am armed with a supply of any spare papers which might be needed as well as relevant files that I think it wise to have to hand. I have my notebook ready so I can take careful note of points made, decisions reached and who is charged with carrying out those decisions. Generally, after about 45 minutes, the meeting draws to a close and those attending are politely ushered out. By this time there are fresh papers in my "In" tray and I can see that the next meeting is at 11.30am. There are several phone calls I must make; there is the note of the meeting to dictate for Hilary to type up and I must quickly check through the new post which has arrived. On my way out of the meeting I have also picked up more papers from the Secretary's "Out" tray. I have to check through these to see what action, if any, the Secretary has asked for – he will have written instructions on the papers in manuscript. If papers require action they are tossed into my "action" tray, the remainder are stacked in a pile for Peter to deal with and marked by me as "file", "destroy" or "B/F" (bring forward).

The previous paragraphs were written for my talk in 1976. Of course there was more to the job than that. If I am to do my job well it is vital for me to know everything that the Secretary says and does. It is for this reason that the phone system in the office enables me to listen in on all the phone conversations which I put through to the Secretary. Often there may be action to take, errors to correct or relevant files to dig out. If I want a constructive and positive relationship with the powerful barons (Deputy Secretaries and Under-Secretaries) who actually control the Department's affairs I need to show them I will share information. Sometimes I am able to protect them from developing storms. When they learn that they can trust me they, in turn, will share confidences. If all goes well the Private Secretary becomes a "friend" for both the Secretary and his underlings. But there's no doubt it's a tricky tight-rope to walk.

One innovation I introduced proved very effective. I persuaded the Secretary to have regular meetings with some of the bright young "Turks" – Principals who are actually working on the "front line". These are some of the upcoming stars of the future who I know personally from many long lunches. We invite them in, two at each meeting, and this gives the Secretary a chance to question them about what their current policy concerns actually are. This is important because the powerful "barons" who control the work of these Principals have a very natural tendency to conceal problems from the Permanent Secretary. The very fact that they know we are talking to some of their brighter junior staff is an effective antidote to this!

Fun with Sir Dan Pettit

I must recount here a couple of incidents which may give you more insights into the relationship which develops between the Private Secretary and his boss. The first concerns the management of what was then the National Freight Corporation. This had been set up to take a key role in the industrial transport sector following nationalisation in 1947. Its Chief Executive, Sir Dan Pettit, was a larger-than-life character but the Department considered him to be totally incompetent. He was running the Corporation at a loss, which was a constant embarrassment for the Government. Finally the time had come to sack him! I can well remember the somewhat fraught discussion between the Secretary and the embattled Deputy Secretary (Tom Beagley) which led to this somewhat dramatic decision. So I had the task of summoning Sir Dan to the office to receive his marching orders. I think he was certainly smart enough, being very streetwise, to know what was coming. The day duly arrived and Sir Dan appeared with a smile on his face and his black briefcase in his hand. We proceeded together into the inner sanctum of the Secretary's office. My boss was extremely tense – he was not looking forward to what he expected to be a rather stormy meeting. The three of us sat down around the polished conference table. After the usual pleasantries it seemed we were about the get down to brass tacks when, to my astonishment, Sir Dan opened his briefcase and produced a large bottle of champagne. "Sir Idwal" he said, "today happens to be my birthday and what better place to celebrate than with my close friends in the Department." As you can imagine, this completely took the wind out of my boss's sails! "You'd better get 3 glasses, Will" he said. All further discussion of the difficulties faced by NFC was abandoned as we chatted over the champagne. Sir Dan never was sacked and all the problems with NFC continued. This is the reality of how history is made!

Four suppers on the way to Paris

The second incident turned out to be one of the most bizarre days of my life. Sir Idwal had been invited to Paris to give a keynote address to a major international conference of road builders which was being held in one of the fabulous Paris conference centres. We were to be hosted by the British Ambassador and flown out first-class by British Airways, staying just one night in the Ambassador's official residence. I had prepared the papers the day before and reminded Sir Idwal that he needed to bring in his passport. We had already had a fuss and a disappointment when the airport authorities refused to allow Sir Idwal to use the VIP lounge – it appeared he did not quite have the seniority required! So he was a bit grumpy from the start. His other great concern was that we would not under any circumstances accept an invitation to have dinner with the Ambassador (we were due to arrive about 8.30pm). He could not stand the Ambassador's wife because (he said) she fussed on so much and always got his name wrong! He could not bear the thought of having to sit through a tedious couple of hours of polite conversation. I had the job of speaking to the Ambassador and explaining that we would already have eaten before we arrived so there was no need to provide a formal meal.

The day of our departure duly dawned. My clerical officer, Peter, had arranged for the official car to leave the Department around 4pm so we would arrive at Heathrow in time for a flight about 6.30pm. The Secretary asked me to order sandwiches to be made for us to eat just before we left. I checked that the Secretary had remembered his passport – and we proceeded to get on with the morning's business. Around lunchtime I decided I had better check that we had all the correct papers (the speech, names of those present etc.) and, to my horror, found that Sir Idwal had brought the wrong passport – this one was out of date! By this time it was almost 2 o'clock. The Secretary was rather panicking – his wife Maire had evidently put the old passport into his briefcase without realising it was out of date. Yes, he did have an up-to-date passport but it was lying at home 50 miles away down in Kent, where he lived. I told him not to worry; luckily I came to work on an extremely fast BMW motorbike so I would jump on it and go and retrieve the vital document. I had just 2 hours to travel all the way down to Kent and back through south London traffic. It was an exciting trip. Maire duly handed me the passport and I zipped back to the Department. I don't think my boss ever said "thank you" – he just assumed I would fix it as I managed to fix almost anything else!

So our sandwiches duly arrived and I sat down with the Secretary while we munched through them together. Now it was time to get the lift down and get in his official car for our trip to the airport. This part of the trip went without incident but there was soon to be more drama as we were informed that, unfortunately, the BA cabin staff were on strike so there would be no food or drink served during the flight. The Secretary huffed and puffed – he thought this was typical of the useless BA management. We would demand compensation. The appropriate authorities were contacted and "Yes" we could each have a £15 voucher to spend on food and drink in the first class lounge. "Right" said the Secretary, "we'll certainly take full advantage of that and make this incompetent outfit pay for its shortcomings. Off we marched upstairs to sit down for more luxury food and drink. The Secretary was cheered up by "stealing this march" on BA and we boarded the plane in much better spirits. As soon as we had taken off we were very surprised to be offered champagne (free for first class passengers) by the charming cabin staff who, it turned out, were not on strike at all. I was amazed to see my boss stuffing bottle after bottle of champagne miniatures into his brief case – it seemed his lowly Welsh origins had left their mark! We were then offered more luxury small eats which it seemed churlish to decline.

So after 3 evening meals and a good dose of champagne, we finally arrived in Paris. The embassy car picked us up and we swept into Paris in great style – feeling rather pleased with ourselves. The ambassador's residence was GRAND to say the least. But shock horror as we were ushered into the sparkling dining room by smart flunkies to find a splendid dinner spread laid out for us all to enjoy. Sir Idwal simply had to bite his lip as this excess hospitality certainly could not be refused after so much trouble had been invested in its preparation by the ambassador's garrulous wife. We battled through our fourth meal of the evening like dutiful school boys and finally got to bed.

What a day that was! And the final twist in the saga came next morning. I found myself sitting down alone with just the ambassador's wife at the sumptuous breakfast served by the butler. Where was my boss? Suddenly I heard a weak cry from Sir Idwal's room – "Will, Will, would you come here please!" Rather surprised, I went down to the Secretary's room to find him still in his underpants and struggling to unjam the zip on his smart black trousers. No doubt unjamming a senior civil servant's zip is all part of the set of skills required of a Private Secretary – I did it and the rest of the day unfolded without incident.

My New Boss

After about 12 months in my role as Private Secretary it was time for Sir Idwal Pugh to retire. The folk in Establishments asked me if I would be prepared to stay on for a few more months to provide continuity (and guidance) for Sir Peter Baldwin, his replacement. Sir Peter had just been promoted to his first top job and would be coming over from the pinnacle of civil service power, H M Treasury. I find Peter Baldwin to be a most charming and easy going fellow, extremely clever and very committed to "doing things right for the public good". In every way he is a total contrast to Sir Idwal. But he is inexperienced and totally unfamiliar with the role and trappings of power required to run a big government Department. I have the task of 'training" him in what is required. I tell him he will have to get to know the big industrial outfits that build our roads, bridges, cars, buses and houses. He does not like the idea of mucking in with big corporations (like Tarmac and MacAlpine). He receives an invite to go to a slap-up conference organised by the road building industries in an exotic French chateau. I recommend he accepts it – getting to know these people is part of the reality of his new job. At first he refuses – but a couple of months later he realises I am right and changes his mind.

I find myself taking a role more as a personal friend and confidant for Sir Peter than simply having my formal role as Private Secretary. He finds the formalities of power in the big department keep him in a lonely position where he cannot afford to have "friendships" with the Deputy Secretaries and Under-Secretaries he must manage. As a result we often have long talks into the evenings. He confides to me his view that the civil service faces a battle to preserve what he regards as its vital public service ethos. He tells me that there is a silent power struggle going on within the civil service; some civil servants wish to put their own careers, salaries and pensions before the needs of the public service whilst others are determined to maintain a traditional public service ethos. The first group will tailor their advice to remain popular with Ministers whilst the second remain determined to provide objective advice whatever the consequences. He warns me to be aware of this and urges me to use my own public service career to fight for the old values. When the time comes for me to move on when I am promoted to Principal, Sir Peter pulls the necessary "strings" to get me posted to a prestigious job in the Treasury. This is a real "feather in my cap" as a posting to the Treasury is part of the conventional route to the top!

Crosland's Housing Policy Review

Before I can go to the post which has been earmarked for me in the Treasury, I must serve out my first post as Principal managing and co-ordinating the housing policy review set up by our Secretary of State (Tony Crosland). Crosland is one of the more idealistic intellectuals who form part of the Labour Party's cohorts. The dominant group within the Labour party remains rooted in workplace trade unionism. Both the intellectuals and the trade union groups share egalitarian ideals but the relationship between them is often strained – the lofty principles of the academic wing being counteracted by the practical demands of the working classes. One of the most important manifesto commitments of the Labour Party at this time is the priority which is to be given to investment in public housing. This is much cherished by the trade union elements in the party – providing jobs in the building trade and houses for their "needy" constituents. Each month a press release is issued with a great trumpeting of rhetoric announcing that another 30,000-plus new council homes have been built during the month. On the one hand, there are claims that even this is not enough while others worry that the existing housing stock is being managed badly and the maintenance of inner-city housing is being ignored. Perhaps too many council houses are being left vacant? Perhaps the way families are allocated public housing is causing problems, for example of labour mobility? Building all these houses is consuming vast amounts of public expenditure. Crosland believes it's time to review all this.

A great deal of work has already been done before I take up my post. The Department has commissioned a major housing survey managed by the Central Statistical Office (CSO) and costing almost £10 million. I find myself having almost daily dealings with the Department's long-established housing statistician as I try to establish the true facts. How many houses do we actually need? How many are vacant? How does the Department define a single household? What is a sharing household?

The housing statistician is the Department's great guru on all these matters. His office is just 2 doors down from mine. My Under-Secretary is charming and ambitious (a man whose quick mind and silver tongue would take him right to the top as Permanent Secretary). The statistician turns out to be a very tricky character; he's determined to defend some rather dubious numbers and it proves extremely difficult to get straight answers from him. I suspect he is continually massaging his figures to try and justify the current very high level of new-build in the public sector. This is a policy which has been very dear to the hearts of all those who tried to support this key strand of Labour Party policy – particularly to the previous housing Under-Secretary. There are a lot of people who do not want to find that the true statistics do not support the enthusiasm for public house-building. Is the country wasting £ millions building houses we do not really need?

The Housing Statistician has his own special way of defending himself against cross questioning. He does this by appearing miserably afflicted by his stutter. Some officials begin to feel very uneasy about his key role in protecting the figures. He is very definitely a "one man band" with no colleagues we can talk to to discuss or provide further explanations of his conclusions. Suspicions are mounting and we even have a meeting arranged with the Permanent Secretary where even the top man asks me to fix it at a time when this statistician is on leave! I do this with pleasure but, shock horror, when the statistician finds out about the meeting he cancels his leave so he can be present! Generally I begin to sense that the established officers in the Department are most reluctant to face up to the realities I begin to discover in the figures. First, there is a determination to avoid taking the number of vacant homes seriously. The statistics are certainly being bodged to try and obfuscate the whole situation. Second, the glaring management inefficiencies of the local authorities are being heavily played down. These are not things the left-wing Labour people want to hear.

I begin to have less and less confidence in the Department's figures. When I steadily put together my own model of the housing market it seems clear to me that there are many more vacancies than the Department will admit. Even more strange is the information I get when I start to question the good friends I have in the Central Statistical Office (CSO). I am puzzled as to how they have assessed, in the big (very expensive) Housing Survey, how many separate households there are and how many households are sharing. Remember that housing "needs" are based on assessing the number of independent households – many of whom are now said to be sharing accommodation with other households. My pals in CSO say that they deal with this issue simply by asking people living in the same accommodation whether or not they pay for their food separately or whether payments are shared. If they pay separately then they are classed as separate households sharing involuntarily and therefore needing new housing. If they share payments they are considered as one household which already has accommodation. This seems to me to be a pretty hopeless way to assess true housing need on a national scale – there is no evidence whatever obtained to show that people who pay separately for their food actually want or need separate independent homes! It seems to me that the whole project is riddled with uncertainties.

I can now see why our academic and public-spirited Secretary of State (Tony Crosland) has concerns about all the money now being spent on new council house building (mostly on easily accessible greenfield sites while old city centre flats are being left vacant and poorly maintained). Senior department officials are fighting tooth-and-nail to prevent this reality appearing in this housing policy review. I find myself fighting my own internal battle against the Department's statistician and my Under-Secretary. The Under-Secretary is expert at continually finding complex procedural reasons why the full results of the £10 million housing survey cannot yet be published. Even when the Housing Select Committee of Parliament demands to see the survey results my Under Secretary still refuses by finding more clever excuses. I remonstrate with him because I believe this is a disgraceful betrayal of our duty as public servants to provide elected MPs with the facts. Of course my boss is right – the Select Committee has no legal power to obtain the survey results however angry they may become.

In the event it becomes clear that the Prime Minister (Jim Callaghan) and his left-wing buddies don't want Crosland messing up their great "success" in building public sector homes. My boss's political instincts are correct. Crosland is soon moved on by the Prime Minister and is "promoted" to Foreign Secretary; as a result, the whole Housing Policy review conveniently collapses. I have wasted a year … and learned that ambitious civil servants will do whatever they need to do to protect their own position and the position of other senior officials who have backed policies which the facts now show to be wrong. This was altogether an unpleasant business and brought home to me the lessons which Peter Baldwin and Tom Caulcott had warned me about.

HM Treasury

The high ceilings and marble floors of HM Treasury give out a very different vibe compared to the plastic, steel and glass of my previous Marsham Street home. I found myself working to control/manage public expenditure for the whole UK on roads, transport and (of all things) the BBC. My Minister is the Chief Secretary to the Treasury (Joel Barnett) and my ultimate boss in the Treasury is a tough dry old stick called Leo Pliatsky. The Treasury has none of the camaraderie or sociability of the DoE. The Treasury staff seem to take their work more seriously; like nervy policemen we are constantly breathing down the necks of the Departments who we must liaise with. Are they spending their money wisely? Should they spend it differently? Should they spend more or must they spend less? Can we trust what they are telling us? Will we have to force our own views through by tabling questions for the Chief Secretary to put to Cabinet?

My room on the first floor is like a large dusty dark cave although it does have a big window overlooking Parliament Square. The window is covered by a yellowing net curtain which is there to protect me from flying pieces of glass in the event of an IRA explosion! (Remember the country was under constant and unpredictable attack from the IRA at this time.) I learn to use an old-fashioned adding machine without looking at the keys – this is a vital tool in my new job where I have to constantly scrutinise reams of figures. One day I am working in my office when there is indeed a huge explosion outside, followed by the usual sirens and police activity. This is the day on which the IRA blow up one of their enemies, Airey Neave, by putting a bomb in his car parked in the underground car park below the House of Commons.

My work in the Treasury is frustrating and I don't find my superiors have the sparkle and sense of humour I found in DoE. It's lonely work trying to get a grasp on what Departments are up to when you have to do everything at one remove from the realities. You are not even sure you can trust the figures you are being given – certainly not from the Home Office, who clearly want to protect their cherished BBC from any nasty limitations or scrutiny.

My responsibilities in the Treasury included expenditure on roads and public transport (Department of Transport – where I knew plenty of people) and broadcasting (Home Office – where I hardly knew anybody). The Minister I reported to was Joel Barnett, Chief Secretary to the Treasury and therefore responsible for control and allocation of all public spending via decisions in the Cabinet. On the transport side I could see that their Departmental Ministers were constantly seeking to direct spending into the building of new roads, motorways and bypasses. These were nice, high-profile, more or less popular projects where ribbons could be cut and positive press interviews obtained. The big problem for me was that directing expenditure with these priorities left very little money for highway maintenance. From a cost/benefit point of view, spending money on highway maintenance is VERY good value compared to building a new road. If roads can be re-surfaced regularly this preserves the strength of their foundations by preventing ingress of water. If you leave maintenance too late then it costs 5 times as much. Similar arguments apply to the standards set for constructing new roads. When I asked the highway engineers why I hardly ever saw repairs going on on French roads they replied (looking at me as if I were a fool) "well, of course, it's because the French build their roads to last 50 years not 25 years like us!" "OK" I said "so what is the extra cost of these 25 years?" "Oh, about 10 percent".

These revelations by the engineers really shocked me. Needless to say, all my efforts to persuade DoT Ministers to revise their priorities and change the design specification for new roads were a complete failure. Nor could I persuade them to spend money on maintenance rather than new build. The country was wasting tens of £ millions by running its road programme so inefficiently – poor tax-payers, if only they realised! To say this was "frustrating" was an understatement – to say the least. And in my position as a civil servant, the Official Secrets Act meant I was simply unable to say anything in public about it.

I had a similarly disappointing experience when it came to reviewing the level of operating subsidies (again tens of £ millions) paid to the Scottish Office for Caledonian MacBrayne Island ferry services and to the Harland and Wolf shipyards in Northern Ireland. The politicians simply would not allow these very large amounts to be questioned or even examined – the "political" subsidies were a licence to waste public money. No questions could be asked … and, not surprisingly, the various operators and authorities took full advantage of this to pad out their claims.

My first spat with the Home Office involved the raising of the TV licence fee. The BBC wanted more money but the last thing the government needed at a time of rampant inflation was a further increase in the cost of living – especially one which affected the poor more than the rich. When I could not persuade my opposite number in the Home Office to co-operate on this, I put up a paper for the Chief Secretary to take to Cabinet arguing against the increase. Next Thursday I received the "Top Secret" Cabinet minutes at about 6.30pm. The Cabinet had supported the Chief Secretary's refusal to agree the licence increase. Feeling fully vindicated in my arguments with my Home Office contact, I rang him to convey the news that he has lost his battle. "Oh" he says, "did you not hear the BBC 6 o'clock news today. The Home Secretary has already announced the increase!" So here again was another example of real politics – Merlyn Rees had deliberately ignored the Cabinet decision so he could further his own political popularity, simply daring the Prime Minister to sack him!

My next saga with the BBC was what finally brought my career in Whitehall to an end. It all happened just before Christmas in 1979. The Home Secretary was determined to support the BBC in giving the broadcasting Trade Unions large pay increases to avoid a strike which would prevent them showing "The Sound of Music" on Christmas Day. Foolishly the BBC had made a great song and dance about paying £4 million for the rights to show this newly popular Julie Andrews film at Christmas. Remember that during 1979 the Callaghan government was facing aggressive Trade Union demands for pay increases which had ramped inflation up to nearly 20 percent. With difficulty, the government had negotiated a voluntary pay restraint which was barely holding down pay demands – the government's entire credibility was hanging by a thread. Not surprisingly, the broadcasting Unions took their chance when they heard the BBC had already paid the huge sum of £4 million to screen the movie. It was a perfect moment for them to demand a big wage hike in order to actually show the movie. I found my opposite number in the Home Office adamant that his Secretary of State would not accept my refusal to sanction such an increase in wages expenditure. Not only would this increase put the Home Office in breach of the cash limits which were then in place for all public spending but it would also open the flood gates for other Trade Unions to flout the voluntary pay restraint. If this happened the government would not survive.

Once I realised that no agreement was going to be reached I had the job of drafting a paper for the Chief Secretary (Joel Barnett) to take to Cabinet on the next Thursday afternoon. Naturally I had to research all the relevant legislation to find out exactly what powers the government had. It was clear to me that the Home Office had deliberately engineered a situation where their pet sponsored Department was putting a gun to the government's head. Finally I found the legislation I was looking for. The government did have power to control Departmental expenditure in times of emergency where excess expenditure would damage the "National Interest". So here was a power which the Chief Secretary could invoke at one extreme to tell the Home Office he was limiting their expenditure so that they simply would not have the cash they needed to pay the excess wage demands from their Trade Unions. There were, of course, a range of other less draconian policy options but I could see that none of those were going to be effective, given the dogged stance of the Home Office and BBC.

When I had finished drafting my report for the Chief Secretary to put before Cabinet I had to take it directly to Sir Leo Pliatsky. My immediate boss was away on leave and the Under-Secretary was away sick so there was just myself and the Permanent Secretary. Pliatsky was a very tough and outspoken character – often very scary for junior officials. We sat and faced each other knowing that the issues we were dealing with could mean life or death for Jim Callaghan's government. I felt pretty bullish about my recommendation that the Chief Secretary should simply use his emergency powers to make it impossible for the BBC to agree the Unions' pay demands. Pliatsky took one look at this and told me to delete both my recommendation and my reference to the existence of such emergency powers. But, I protested, surely we have a duty as public servants to at least tell Ministers what their full range of policy options might be. "No", he replied, "such a step would be much too controversial – you must remove the references". I continued to protest, reminding him that if the BBC did cave in then the government would almost certainly fall, leaving Mrs Thatcher to take power. "Yes" he said, "that's true, the government may fall but you and I will still be in post (have our jobs)!"

So now, I thought, I can really see how far some senior civil servants are prepared to go to avoid any controversy that might affect their own careers – even to the point of watching the government fall. The BBC did cave in, the Unions got their pay increase, the voluntary pay restraints collapsed, the government fell and Mrs Thatcher took office. I toyed briefly with the prospect of defying the Official Secrets Act and revealing what had happened but the probable hassle and prospect of prison did not appeal. This would have been the first case of a civil servant revealing information that was "in the public interest". As history now shows it was Clive Ponting who "broke the mould" by revealing the true facts about the sinking of the Belgrano in 1984. In the event he was acquitted by the jury despite the judge's direction that it was only the government of the day which could decide what was, or was not, in the public interest. Mrs Thatcher then had the law changed to make this explicit in 1989 – so Ponting's defence (revelation being "in the public interest") no longer exists.

I had no alternative but to resign.

As one important "aside" from the detail of this narrative, those who read this today should remember that during all my time working in Whitehall we (the UK) were under constant threat from IRA terrorism. All public servants were potential targets for such terrorism. We had net blast curtains over our big windows in the Treasury so glass fragments would be safely contained in the event of nearby explosions. We had special government passes to gain entry to government buildings and, of course, we had huge combination-lock safes in all our offices for storing "sensitive" material (mostly stuff which might embarrass our political masters). We were always on the look out for "suspicious" packages which might be bombs or booby traps. My closest experience to IRA bombs was when Airey Neave was blown up in the House of Commons car park. Such were the times we were living in.

New Directions

I could not face the "convenient" dishonesties of senior civil servants – despite the plea by my old boss, Sir Peter Baldwin, that I should fight on for the old values. I did go over and apologise to him, which was a sad moment. But I found the futility of my public service efforts more and more depressing. Anyway, I had other fish to fry as my plans to develop Millbrook as a commercially viable golf course were reaching a critical point. In the event, chance intervened and I found myself, quite unexpectedly, embroiled in managing the fast growing sport of windsurfing when (to my surprise) I was elected Chairman of the National Windsurfer Association a couple of months later. I was also keen to become involved in politics to try and action some of my concerns about management of the environment. Civil service rules had prevented any involvement prior to resigning. I stood as a local authority candidate for the new (and then exciting) SDP – luckily I was not elected (what a waste of my time that would have been!) but I learned (as if I did not know already) that the greatest qualification for any would-be politician was to very much like the sound of their own voices. Later I joined the new Ecology Party, which later became the Green Party – but even these well-

WILL SUTHERLAND

Will Sutherland is aged 36, is married and has four children. After graduating with an MSc in Agricultural Economics from Cambridge, he worked in the Civil Service in Transport, Environment and the Treasury. In 1979 he left Whitehall, and has since developed his own business in leisure services, ranging from the UK Boardsailing Association to golf-course development.

He feels the key issues facing the Council are: to maintain and improve the standard of Camden's existing Housing stock, to fight for more job opportunities within the community, and to keep our streets and parks in good repair. Above all, the spiralling level of the rates must be checked by bringing the Council's runaway expenditure back under control.

He believes the SDP-Liberal Alliance offers the people of Camden an unrivalled selection of candidates, who have the ability, commitment and experience to replace the old political dogmas and infighting with a conscientious cost-effective administration, which will give the whole of Camden a real chance for a fair deal.

meaning folk suffered from the same problem. These people who wanted so much to be "in power" were really the worst sort of people to have such responsibility! More of this later.

At the very least, my time in the civil service had been extremely educational as well as being challenging and mostly fun. I also met some very stimulating, independent minded and able people.

It's amusing now to see the flyer which Camden SDP produced in their efforts to get me elected as a local councillor. I did my bit going around miserably depressed council estates from door to door canvassing. It did not take me long to discover that I was not cut out to be a baby kissing politician!

MY QUEST 3

My seven years working in the inner sanctums of Whitehall opened my eyes to many things.

First and foremost, I saw that modern politicians need to have personalities with a huge "built-in" need for self-promotion and publicity. The tedious, and frequently bitter, struggles for popularity and "power" simply cannot be tolerated unless you have this "need". The best way to persuade a modern politician to go along with your ideas is to promise him/her great opportunities for publicity. I sympathised with the ancient Greeks who felt that those who most wanted "power" were probably the least suitable to exercise it! All those centuries ago, the Greeks had (over 200 years) rejected "populist" democracy, preferring to choose their government representatives by lot.

The second thing I learned is that the politician's search for "power" is largely an illusion. The first thing a civil servant has to do with all newly-elected politicians is to tell them why they cannot fulfil most of their easy manifesto promises. In practice, the real power in this world is held by the big corporations and banks who own the assets and employ the workforce. Then again you also have the power of the large vested interests such as the trade unions and professional associations. Finally there is the influence of important lobby groups and NGOs (Non Government Organisations) who can make political life hell by adverse publicity.

The third thing I discovered is that modern politicians cannot be persuaded in any way to put long-term benefits before short-term expediency. The need to be re-elected trumps all. Tony Crosland's housing policy review had shown how badly inner city public housing was being maintained (Ministers and Local Councillors much preferred to spend money on new-build on green field sites). My own analysis of roads expenditure whilst in the Treasury showed the enormous cost-benefit advantages of spending more on road maintenance or on building roads to a higher specification. But Ministers much preferred the publicity they could get by opening a new stretch of road – as opposed to the complaints they would receive by causing delays through increasing maintenance of existing roads.

The fourth thing I learned was that, at the end of the day, the long-term professional civil servants would invariably moderate their advice to Ministers in ways which would enhance, or at least protect, their own careers. The days of "objective" advice had slipped away with the advent of political advisers (pals of the elected politicians and often would-be politicians themselves) and the careerist ambitions of well paid civil servants.

I had remained very committed to "green" and environmental issues throughout my civil service career but had been unable to find an effective outlet for my concerns through my work. I had kept myself informed about the emerging environmental movement (indeed we had to deal with its manifestations in much of our work with Ministers) but the rules of public office prevented me taking an active part. When I left the civil service I was determined to put this right. I also felt a keen desire to jump onto a public platform and denounce the gross wastefulness and unfairness of many of the existing government policies. I joined the newly formed Social Democratic Party and stood as a local council candidate in the Camden local elections.

I soon found the internal bickering and posturing of the

political people tiresome and unpleasant – both within the SDP and later when I joined the Ecology Party, which became the Green Party. I realised that my "quest" was not going to be served by spending time with these kinds of organisation, dominated as they were by big egos and loud voices.

Chapter 4: The Millbrook Saga

The Millbrook saga is a long one, spanning 27 years from 1975, so I won't go into all of it here. When I left the north for London I had already had the benefit of some funds from the family business. I was already running one successful golf course which had been effectively modernised and transformed (with 10 new holes) by myself and John Carss, the greenkeeper. My dream was to invest some of my family money in buying suitable land to design and build my own golf course – preferably within easy reach of London.

Sarah and I kept our eyes on the land sales advertised by the major property agencies. On one memorable occasion we journeyed up to the Isle of Skye to see 1,000 acres of land near Portree. which already had a 9-hole golf course. It was a wild boggy Scottish hillside which we tramped over for several hours in the mist with our four small kids. The golf course was pretty rudimentary and the land was rough – not really a viable option! What was so wonderful about that trip was the hot baths we all had when back in our small hotel, then a sumptuous meal and a comfy bed – what bliss! The kids had been brilliant throughout – despite the rain and the bogs.

Finally our dream opportunity appeared. Land prices were pretty slack and the Woodward family, a family of traditional farmers, were selling land near Bedford because of family disputes. They had failed to raise the money or the energy to develop the golf course they had planning permission to build on 120 acres of land near Ampthill. This was land on the greensand ridge – hungry, well drained, sandy, barley land just 45 minutes up the M1 from Swiss Cottage – rolling well-drained land perfect for a golf course. At less than £700 per acre and with planning permission already granted, it was ideal. I bought it in 1976. We were not in any rush to develop the land as we did not want to get into debt. We wanted to do all the design, tree planting and construction ourselves – make our own "do-it-yourself" eco-golf course from scratch. It was to be the country's first fully organic golf course.

By this time we already had a family camper van which I had created by putting beds and tables into a long-wheelbase Mercedes 207 van. We could use this as a base over weekends as we got to know our land and begin to stake out a possible layout. This was all great fun for the kids when the weather was fine – we'd take the dog and the cat and all sleep together in the van. We could eat wonderful home-made sausages at the local Chequers pub nearby. The cat would sometimes jump into the van during the night (through an open window) with a young rabbit which would then leap about causing a certain amount of chaos. We were all young, very full of energy and felt we could take on the whole world!

It did not take long to figure out a good, even dramatic, 18-hole layout with two 9-hole loops meeting where the prospective clubhouse would be built. We marked out the planned position of fairways and tree enclosures with bamboo poles, drew a new diagram and submitted the revised layout for planning permission, which was granted. Our first real challenge was controlling the huge number of rabbits that grazed and burrowed all over the sandy land – many coming from the Duke of Bedford's forests which bordered on Millbrook. We had to put up hundreds of yards of rabbit fencing to create tree enclosures for the thousands of trees we planned to plant (most of the land was free of trees save for a few fine elms which would later die in the Dutch elm disease epidemic). The very first stage in building the course was to plant the trees which would delineate the fairways and shape the course. I was able to order these by the thousand, seedlings just two years old, bare rooted – 1plus1's they called them. Each tree cost just a few pence and was about 12 inches high. We could plant hundreds in a day during winter simply by cutting a slot with a spade, pushing in the roots and kicking the slot closed. Planting each tree 3 yards from its neighbour was what was recommended. Once the rabbit fencing (which was time-consuming and expensive) was in place, the tree planting itself was quick and easy. The next vital task was finding, and scything around, each young tree about 3 months later (in late May or early June) when the grass and weeds would otherwise suffocate them. We found that the best technique was to mark each tree with a bamboo stake dipped in red paint – without this the tiny trees were almost impossible to find. Over the years that followed we had many enjoyable days of tree planting on cold winter days with friends from town often coming up to help and enjoy the country air.

I soon found that in practical terms we could only plant about 4,000 trees each year if I was to be able to find time to scythe around each one at the beginning of June – and sometimes once again later in summer if the weather was wet. Eventually we had to surround the entire golf course with rabbit fencing – a tedious, expensive and tiring job. Throughout the entire 27 years of my Millbrook saga I planted more trees every year – amounting up to a total of around 100,000. Of these, far fewer than one in three survive, and many have to be thinned out anyway to allow cheap "nurse" trees to be removed so that the fine specimen trees can flourish. Our first plantings were almost entirely of larch, pine and birch – the so-called pioneer species which can flourish on open land. Later I mixed in giant sequoia, sweet chestnut, oak, beech, walnut, poplar and more. Today there are probably about 35 acres of beautiful big trees which have totally transformed both the landscape and, possibly more important, the climate at Millbrook. Trees provide massive shelter from drying winds as well as pumping out hundreds of gallons of water during every hot summer day – up to 200 gallons a day for a big oak! And, as it grows, each mature tree captures about 20 kg of carbon from the air each year. There are about 600 mature trees to each acre – about 20,000 in all today. – so Millbrook trees are helping remove 400 tons of carbon from the atmosphere each year. I don't feel too bad about driving my car around and sending out about 5 tons of CO_2 each year!

Planting trees was one thing; landscaping greens, tees and bunkers was another. I scanned the adverts for a suitable bulldozer and eventually bought a second-hand 9-ton Fiat 4.5-litre drott. It was an amazing experience learning to drive this powerful beast. The force of its hydraulics was enormous – you could simply lift a whole mature elm tree out of the ground, roots and all. But learning to carve smooth and level surfaces was not so easy. Luckily for me, the soil was super easy to work – light and sandy. In some places there was pure white sand in large quantities just below the surface – no shortage of sand for the bunkers! So I was soon able to carve out the shapes I liked for the 18 greens, replace the topsoil and rotavate ready for seeding. Bunkers, too, were simple to dig out. Later we would have a JCB which made much of this work easier.

We bought a tractor and rotavator and set about preparing what would be the fairways for sowing. But luck was not on our side. 1976 was one of the hottest, driest years ever recorded – all the seed we sowed was wasted as the sun burned down day after day. We had no irrigation at this point. I learned not to sow seed in the spring when the young grass would face a harsh summer of drought and heat but sow in September when the seed would have the whole winter to put roots down deeper before the stress of summer hit.

From the moment I bought the land at Millbrook we became very busy people! Life was fun and we did not want to waste a moment. Of course I was still working full time as a civil servant, getting the kids up for school at 6am each morning so the girls could catch the bus to the Lycée at 7.15am. Then I could take Rupert to school on my motorbike before heading in to work myself. So for many years Millbrook was just an enjoyable but time-consuming hobby for weekends and holidays.

We had all sorts of adventures at Millbrook. The access road was a major headache because the planners had refused to allow access from the main road. Because of this, the previous owners had had to buy several extra parcels of land so access could come in from Millbrook village opposite the pub. This meant crossing the Millbrook river and laying down about half a mile of roadway up to the golf course. I consulted a firm of highway engineers who quoted £40,000 for a suitable bridge and tarmac road. This seemed like an impossible expenditure at such an early stage of the project. But help was soon at hand. Somehow the prospect of building this road had become part of the gossip in the local pub. I was approached out of the blue in the pub by a rough looking fellow who offered to sort out the river crossing and lay substantial foundations for the entire road (from broken brick and builder's rubble). He ran a commercial lorry business and he needed a place where he could dump builders' rubble without paying for commercial disposal. Furthermore he had a pal who worked at the nearby pipeworks who could find 5 huge concrete pipes that had been "rejected because of minor damage" (his figure of speech not mine!). He would need £50 to pay-off his pal. As for the rest, I was doing him a favour as he had more than 500 20-ton loads of broken bricks and rubble to get rid of.

I set to with my bulldozer and chainsaw to cut down the trees that surrounded the river. The kids had a great time swinging in the branches! Late one evening I was working away on my own near the river when I realised my 9-ton bulldozer had sunk into a wet bog! The tracks would not long grip as the underside of the machine was now stuck fast against the ground and still sinking. As the machine began to tip over I had to think fast. Luckily I had bought a very strong length of chain. I quickly tied this around a tree that was still firmly rooted close to the river, tied the other end to my front bucket and used the hydraulics to pull the dozer free.

Once the trees were down, the 5 huge pipes arrived and I pushed them into position with my bulldozer so they would take the flow of the river. All went well and the first few loads of bricks arrived so they could be tipped on top of the pipes to make a neat and secure crossing. The other 500-odd loads followed over the next few weeks until the entire roadway had solid foundations stretching all the way up to the course. The whole project had cost just £50. Later we would find a brilliant local man who laid top quality tarmac (excess from other jobs he was doing) to make a perfect roadway – but that did cost a little more! It just goes to show that you should never be disheartened by the first challenges you meet in any job – with a little patience and some cunning a solution will probably appear!

Ron Mills appears!

So if the roadway and bridge were one miracle, then the arrival of Ron Mills was another! Anyone who has lived in a rural village will know that "gossip" is an important and powerful currency of social exchange. Millbrook village had its pub and the pub drew in its customers from a fairly wide catchment area. Remember that the large and busy conurbation of Luton was only about 15 miles away. So it was not surprising perhaps to expect the news of all our activity to become part of local gossip.

One day when we arrived for one of our frequent weekends of Millbrook activity I found a rough note pinned to a fence post. Basically the note said something on these lines:

"I hear you're going to build a golf course here. That's something I'd really like to do and, if you hire me, I can assure you that you'll never regret it. Signed – Ron Mills (with telephone number)"

I was intrigued by the note because it was clear that whoever had written it had bags of "get up and go" and was at the very least an unusual fellow. I rang the number and explained that we could not pay much, there was no accommodation on the site and that this was going to be a long-term project. I explained that my main requirement was that any employee should be a good mechanic because I already knew from managing Dunstanburgh that keeping machines well maintained and running was really the key to effective running of any good golf course. Ron told me that he was in fact a trained fitter having worked an apprenticeship and then 7 years in various types of garage work – currently working maintaining the heavy machinery at Luton airport. He had no problem with the housing question because he would install his own mobile home and live on the site. I told him that if he could provide one good reference I would take him on. The reference duly arrived and I began a new and extremely productive relationship with Ron and Millbrook which would last without an argument for 27 years.

Ron turned out to be a mechanical and engineering genius – machines, building, electrics, plumbing, digger driving, barman – there was no end to his talents and they were all delivered with calm patience and a sense of humour. Ron was right in his note – I never did regret hiring Ron. Together we built Millbrook and we pretty much enjoyed every minute of it. Ron and his wife Jan stood by me through thick and thin – particularly after Sue's death, when Ron and his family provided a great support for myself and young Hal. Ron had a gift for finding very effective solutions to all sorts of practical problems. The one great lesson I learned from Ron is "Never tackle a job unless you have the right tools to do it". If necessary you have to make the tools yourself! Ron maintained and repaired all my cars and motorbikes. Ron and I built 2 houses and a clubhouse. Ron took on engineering jobs I would have considered absolutely impossible and made them seem easy.

It was very early in my relationship with Ron that I began to appreciate his special qualities. I had damaged the bearings in the gearbox of my bulldozer because I tried to pull a tree stump out by reversing as I pulled the heavy chain. I did this without realising that the reverse gear was simply added to the gear train outside the two massive bearings which took the pressure of normal forward bulldozing. So putting a lot of pressure in reverse gear had twisted the shaft and damaged the bearing. All this happened late in the very hot year of 1976. Millbrook, with sandy soil and no trees to provide shelter, was a roasting hot desert in a continual shimmering heat haze. And there was the Fiat bulldozer, massive but incapacitated as it, too, roasted under the blazing sun. The gear box was buried deep in the bowels of the complex back axle. When Ron finally got the top of the gear box off I could dimly see the gears as they sat in a bath of black oil. There was only a small access panel and I simply could not imagine how Ron was going to take the gearbox to pieces. After a careful examination Ron brought out a heavy hammer and a cold chisel which he was planning to use to unscrew the large threaded ring which kept the bearing together. He could only get access to the bearing by lying flat on his stomach and reaching down into the oil – one hand holding the chisel, the other tapping it steadily with the hammer. Hour after hour the tapping went on. The heat and the discomfort were extreme but Ron was clearly not going to be defeated – if he just kept tapping long enough that bearing would keep turning and eventually come out. And indeed it did – it was not long before the bulldozer was back in action – this time working forwards and not in reverse!

Over the years I was to see Ron's calm patience, imagination and perseverance in action time and time again. You will hear more about the Millbrook saga later.

Windsurfing and Golf

There is no denying that the challenges of Millbrook, the Treasury and the family were full-on and all embracing. Every moment of the day was a busy one; every weekend a race to get things done. Towards the end of 1979 Millbrook was reaching a point where more resources needed to be put in if the scheme was ever to reach fruition. This was certainly another factor leading to my giving up my promising Whitehall career. But windsurfing was also pushing its way into our lives in unexpected ways.

Sarah and I had "discovered" windsurfing when on holiday in the South of France at Antibes in 1972. The sport had been developed by an ambitious American called Hoyle Schweitzer (from ideas already experimented elsewhere). Whatever the true origins of boardsailing, Hoyle Schweitzer was the man who first tried to promote the sport and make a business out of it. He had patented the idea of steering the board by moving the sail where the mast was mounted on a flexible joint. Schweitzer had appointed the Dutch textile manufacturer, Ten Cate, to distribute and market the board in Europe. Later Schweitzer would make an agreement with the shady German ex-car salesman, Fred Ostermann, to produce the Windglider for sale throughout Russia and the Eastern block. The windsurfers we had seen flashing over the waves on the Med in 1972 were the remnants of one of the first promotional regattas in Europe.

WS in training off Newton

As keen sailors with a busy family, we saw immediately that the small size and portability of the windsurfer could enable us to get out sailing quickly without all the hassle of trailers and heavy gear. One person could easily carry the board down to the water or stow it for transport on a car roof rack – and the boards seemed to go pretty fast and offer new opportunities for wave riding and tricks. As soon as we returned to London we tried to find out if anyone was importing the boards into the UK. To our surprise we found the local office of Ten Cate was just about half a mile from our home in Primrose Hill – just north of Swiss Cottage on Finchley Road. We soon met the manager, John Crouch, and bought our first couple of windsurfers.

Once up at Newton we had an entertaining time trying to learn how to sail these new contraptions. No doubt the locals must have thought we were quite crazy as no-one had ever seen anything like this before. After a few hours, many grazed ankles and a good few duckings both Sarah and I slowly got the hang of it and before long we were whizzing across the bay. We soon became real enthusiasts and began to promote the sport in the north east. We bought more new boards and began to give demonstrations which attracted the local press. Our first customers came from what I thought of as an unlikely source – a group of miners from Merton in Co. Durham. This rough looking crew arrived to find out what we were up to and, though we did not know it then, Ray and Monica Terns would become good friends as the sport of windsurfing took off. I was amazed when the gigantic miner, Tommy Terns, peeled off £350 in cash to complete our first sale of a new board! We went on to open the windsurfing school at Newton and Sarah soon became the UK's top instructor.

The Newton Windsurfing School became a magnet for keen windsurfers, not only from Northumberland, but from far and wide. Sarah had great enthusiasm, energy and patience which made her a natural teacher – she also enjoyed meeting new people. On most weekends Newton Haven would be filled with sails – both beginners and experts. We had our dramas when the inexperienced ventured out in gusty off-shore winds. Many is the time I had to race down to the water to man a rescue mission. The Ship Inn did a roaring trade and we made many good friends. All of our four children loved the water, especially when it was rough and the waves came piling in – they would rush to get their wetsuits on to enjoy playing in the surf at high-tide. The big regattas we held at New Year were always popular

– even when it was so cold the water froze on our sails as we tried to wash the sand and salt off them!

For more than 10 years Sarah did a great job running the school and generally promoting the sport all over the country. The whole family could pile into our Volvo estate car and zoom off to exotic venues all over Britain. We also took the family with us on our trips to take part in World or European events abroad – we had a lot of energy in those days! So windsurfing was certainly a major feature of our lives!

The man chosen by Ten Cate to front the development of windsurfing in the UK was an ex-army adventurer called Clive Colenso. Big, strong and cheerful, Clive majored on heavy weather surfing with little time for the mundane pottering about that most of us enjoyed. His favourite venue was an old naval base in Plymouth, Fort Bovisand, where the facilities were spartan to say the least. But we all mucked in down there with our new-fangled wetsuits, tackling wild conditions in wind and rain that would have kept most sailors warm and dry at home. It was very physical, very exciting and we began to develop our triangle-racing skills. At this time, our equipment was too strange for most conventional sailing clubs, who found the whole windsurfing business rather a scary mystery. They regarded the new breed of sailors as some kind of cross between a rough working class crew and a band of carefree (and rule-free!) water loving hippies.

As the years went by and our skills increased, the sport itself began to gather form. World and European championships were held. We went to regular regattas at venues spread all over the UK. In 1977 we went (with the whole family) as part of the UK team to the first World Championships in Sardinia – accompanied by fellow team members German Eslava and his wife Ros Cattliff. In 1978 I went as part of the UK team, again with German Eslava, to the second world championships in Cancun, Mexico. And all this was being done by the pioneering windsurfing fraternity. At this stage Hoyle Schweitzer's patent seemed strong enough to deter would-be competitors. The sailing authorities were still trying to make their minds up about the sport – was it a dreadful nuisance bringing all sorts of riff-raff into their exclusive pastime, or was it the shape of a massive new dimension in popular sailing that would bring sailing to the masses (and big money to sailing clubs!).

I could see from the outset that the low cost, easy portability and low maintenance of the windsurfer should make it a hugely popular recreational activity. With proper organisation and sponsorship it could (and should) end up like golf and tennis as a great mass participation sport where the whole family could enjoy being on the water together. It was unfortunate that the macho approach favoured by its early pioneer, Clive Colenso, was not the most welcoming introduction for your average family! By the time we reached 1979 the sport was already growing fast, the yachting authorities were getting interested and rival producers were challenging Hoyle Schweitzer's dominant position with new unlicensed designs. We gave demonstrations of the sport for the Royal Yachting Association at one of the London reservoirs and they took the first steps to create what would become the RYA Boardsailing Committee.

With support from John Crouch of Ten Cate, we mounted our first attempts to create a National Windsurfing Association and convened the first meeting in our big basement at what was then our London home at 34 Oppidans Road. I think about 30 people came to that meeting and I was chosen as the first Chairman of the new Association.

For all the reasons I've mentioned, windsurfing did grow rapidly. Most of the new sailors had no background in traditional sailing and very few sailing clubs were, at this time, prepared to host our events. Luckily for us, one of our new committee members, Geoff Turner, was a professional computer programmer from Southampton University. With his help and enthusiasm we bought one of the new Apple desktop computers (total memory 256k) and very soon he had devised a neat programme for processing our race results. No longer did somebody have to process 6 or 7 sets of race results by hand to calculate the winning score after however many races had been held. We were now able to produce and print out results within minutes of the final race of the day – even with more than 100 participants. Soon the traditional sailing clubs started to take notice – the new watersport was attracting generous sponsorship from drinks and cigarette companies and large numbers of participants meant correspondingly large bar takings!

So whilst I became more heavily involved in administering windsurfing, Sarah was equally involved in managing development of windsurfing instruction and the windsurfing school which she had started at Newton. At the same time I was now committing much greater investment in Millbrook – putting in irrigation, buying better machinery and building a home for Ron Mills.

More Family matters

Our home at 40 Meadowbank was very practical and comfortable but it was rather small for our growing family. A big old Victorian house came up for sale in the neighbouring Oppidans Road. We decided to buy it and embark on a major programme of expansion and re-building. This proved to be a VERY frustrating enterprise, consuming time and money that could have been much better spent elsewhere. Our young lady architect proved useless and our builders untrustworthy. The whole project was a steep learning curve and extremely exhausting. At one point during the re-building, the house was occupied by squatters! Sarah showed her mettle by moving in herself with the kids when they were out – that gave them a surprise when they came back and they soon found somewhere quieter to squat! Finally the new house was finished – in March 1976 – and we moved in.

The great size of our Oppidans Road house meant that each child now had a room of their own. Sarah and I shared a huge bedroom with ensuite bathroom. We had space for guests, including an au pair girl and a huge basement for games, parties and meetings. With a dog and a cat plus occasional hamsters and rabbits, we made a bustling and busy household. This was all very splendid and grand but little did we know then that tragedy was only about 12 months down the line.

Max's Death and the Divorce – Tragedy in 1977

To put this tragedy and its impact in perspective we need to wind the clock back a bit. Sarah and I had met as energetic, perhaps even wild, teenagers on that stormy wet August day at the end of Seahouses pier. With many common interests and a great love of activity and the outdoors, we immediately became soul mates and soon began to dream about the special family we would have. Sarah's parents were academics and had put the major part of their attention towards their very bright eldest son Peter (who went on to get a first at Cambridge). Because of this Sarah often felt very much that she was an "also ran" and the lack of sufficient appreciation by her parents was sometimes a source of great sorrow to her. When we married and had 4 beautiful children before we were 24, Sarah's mother could not help herself being a great critic. Frequently she reminded Sarah that (like herself) Sarah had thrown away the chance of a wonderful academic career. This was not a kind or helpful thing to do – however well meant. Much later when all the 4 children had been extremely successful through University etc., Sarah's mum, Ruth, apologised for her earlier behaviour. But, at the time, these frequent critical comments did nothing for Sarah's self-esteem. The high expectations of Sarah's mother and the great academic successes of her elder brother Peter had sometimes been a source of tears even when we went out as teenagers together.

For more than 10 years Sarah and I had a wonderfully energetic, happy and productive marriage. Our 4 kids were strong, bright and clever – we tried to treat them respectfully as intelligent fellow humans. This was why they always called us by our first names (and still do today). Our activities were numerous and successful. But there were still some tricky areas! Sarah felt some jealousy, I am sure, of my success in my career as a civil servant (although she was always very supportive of it). She was also frustrated that her own very evident talents were not finding an adequate outlet – teaching in school or running the windsurfing school helped but were not really what she wanted. She wanted more financial independence which I could very well understand – but potentially difficult tax issues prevented me simply gifting assets to her. Perhaps more significantly, since we had been childhood sweethearts, neither of us had any experience of physical relationships with anybody else. We talked quite openly about what this might be like. I don't know to this day whether Sarah explored other options on her many trips away – she certainly had several other male admirers! For myself I did have a brief affair with our neighbour Nada which Sarah knew about – but that was the limit to my exploration.

From 1972 onwards our life in London was busy, very busy. I was a full-time ambitious civil servant going into work in Whitehall every morning on my motorbike after helping get all 4 children off to school. I was running the golf course at Dunstanburgh and we were both becoming very involved in the early development of windsurfing as a sport. Sarah was the chief instructor for the UK and we were running a windsurfing school at Newton. In 1976 we had started our great project – the golf course at Millbrook – we were also committed to major plans for redeveloping an old house in Oppidans Road which gave rise to all sorts of pressures. We often went up to Newton late on Friday and returned for school and work late Sunday. Altogether life was great and we had a huge appetite for it!

In the middle of all this came the disaster of Max's death. Sarah had gone off to Holland for several days to train as the UK super-instructor for windsurfing. She went by ferry in our Mercedes camper van with her good friend Lorraine, who was a single mum with a lovely one-year-old baby (Max). By all accounts they all had a wonderful time. The weather had been good and Sarah was in high spirits when she returned home late in the evening after dropping Lorraine and Max off at their flat under the Post Office tower. Early next morning we received the phone call which would change all our lives. It came from a distraught Lorraine – she had just found Max lying dead from a cot death. For us all, the world suddenly came crashing down – the beautiful baby Max was no more. Lorraine came over to stay with us and there was terrible doom, weeping and grief throughout the big Oppidans Road house. Both Sarah and Lorraine were inconsolable and I had the terrible responsibility of arranging the funeral – Max in his tiny white coffin.

I can still remember the stunned scene as Sarah took the early morning phone call from her good friend Lorraine and we heard the terrible news. The weeping and the misery was intense, particularly during the time Lorraine came to stay with us afterwards for the emotional support she needed at that terrible time. I can remember, too, the anger and the grief. There is really nothing more tragic than to see the small white coffin which you know holds the remains of what was, just a few days before, a bouncing smiling little boy. Sarah loved all babies so this was especially tragic for her after having spent several wonderful sunny days helping look after Max on her trip to Holland.

When I look back now at my London diaries it seems nothing short of amazing that Sarah and I had, thus far, been able to continue at the pace and intensity of all our activities and commitments. With four young children, two houses (300 miles apart), several businesses and a busy social life, every minute of the day was already crammed with action and responsibilities. Little Max's death was an unexpected emotional bombshell that was simply too much to cope with. Sarah and I had already been trying to move our marriage forward so Sarah could have real "ownership" and responsibility for her own business projects – but tax and legal complications had thwarted progress. And we had also been talking about making our marriage more of an "open" marriage. I realised that Sarah had become more and more convinced that I was having affairs with other women (she already knew about my short affair with our neighbour). Denials don't serve much useful purpose against such inner feelings – so the stage was set for a breakdown of some kind. It did not help that we had at that time a beautiful and capable au pair, Suzanne, from Austria.

Sarah must certainly have shared her feelings with her own friends and indeed some of our mutual friends. Somehow it now seems to have become the accepted narrative that William was having numerous affairs with other women hence the tragic divorce. There is very little a man can say to defend himself against such accusations! It's just one word against another in the absence of any proof or admission of guilt. How far Sarah really believed her own accusations I really don't know. At the time our whole emotional world had come crashing down and it was all I (we) could do to "keep the show on the road". There were kids to be fed and taken to school. I had a busy job to attend to and there was a great deal of energy spent on trying to support Lorraine and Sarah, who were at the centre of the storm.

It is true that our au pair (Suzanne) had arrived with us just after the tragedy. I often had a feeling that this was a source of jealousy and possibly suspicion on Sarah's part. I certainly did not have "an affair" with the beautiful Suzanne although we did manage the house and kids together as an effective team during these very difficult times. Suzanne (and her sister Liesi) remained good friends of the family for many years after the divorce.

Max's death seemed brutally hard and unfair – but the "show had to go on" with kids going to school and a household to run. Suzanne and I did all we could to keep things going but Sarah and Lorraine were both suffering total misery and collapse. The final straw came when Sarah came rushing back into the house one evening in floods of tears as she had just started her car only to find that our big black cat had got mangled up in the engine where he had been sleeping.

Whenever there is a sudden death of a loved one it always leaves a big black emotional shadow. Could it have been avoided? Did we do something wrong? Why have the fates picked on us? With the death of Max (and the cat), this black shadow was a crushing blow for us all. I felt powerless to help either Sarah or Lorraine – but somehow I had to go to work and the children had to go to school – some kind of normality had to be preserved. Suddenly life went from being an exciting adventure to something much more dark and threatening – many hidden demons came to the surface and our family began to struggle. I found myself being criticised for not showing enough misery while I was so busy trying (with Suzanne's help) to run the household and also attend to my job. Sarah began to escape into what must have seemed to be a care-free bohemian world of late-night drinking with her artist friends in Camden. Sometimes we hardly saw her for days on end as Suzanne and I battled on. I'm not really sure what Sarah's emotions were at that time – certainly they were complicated and probably included feelings that she could not cope with all her responsibilities (not helped by the criticism from her mother). The fact that Suzanne and I seemed to be managing OK probably just made things even worse!

It soon became clear to me that Sarah's new friend Laurie was now able to provide her with the kind of emotional support that I could not. As an only child from doting parents, Laurie probably also enjoyed the new attention he was getting from Sarah. She, for her part, was swept away by his easy charm and his seemingly expert sympathy for all her problems. I began to think there might be a real danger that she would simply decamp completely and leave me and the children to our own devices. When Sarah did come home we had major rows with all sorts of allegations being thrown in the air in front of the children. There was a great deal of crying and anger. This simply could not go on or the family we both loved so much would be destroyed. We did try marriage guidance but that proved hopeless.

Finally, and with a very heavy heart, I decided I must be the one to leave the home. If I did this it would give Sarah the space she needed to rebuild her confidence and her relationship with the children. I will never forget the evening when I spoke to the children (we sat on the floor in our bathroom) and tried to explain to them what I had decided. And so it was. I left my lovely home and children for a new and very bleak "hand to mouth" existence. I had to find accommodation where I could whilst I tried to keep many balls in the air as well as – somehow – maintain a link to the family. I certainly wept a great deal for loss of what might have been but I was determined to keep some sort of relationship with Sarah and the children whatever the cost. Sarah's brother Peter was a great support and let me stay with him while I tried to find new accommodation.

Sarah did indeed return to Oppidans Road and struggled through her despair into her own new world with her new lover. It may not have been perfect but at least the children had their mother back. The next step was to try and organise a sensible legal separation so we could each run our own affairs. When it came to sorting out the nuts and bolts of our divorce I remembered all the terrible dramas of the divorce of Sarah's brother Peter. His settlement had created a situation where he was called back into Court every few years to review (and increase) his maintenance payments. I instructed my lawyers to do whatever was necessary to make our divorce a final and binding settlement that could not be re-opened. I never doubted that Sarah was very effective in her business dealings and that she was committed to our children's future. Long before our divorce I had wanted to give her control of much of my property so she would have an independent income, but ridiculous tax complications had prevented this. In the end, the divorce allowed me to give property to Sarah without paying tax and it also allowed me to pay all the children's school fees as tax-deductible expenses under a court order. Financially the divorce saved the family well over £100,000. I was pleased to have Millbrook as my main focus as it was close to my base in London. Sarah would take control of all the properties in the north plus the big London house. Sarah proved to be an excellent business person and used her new wealth much more effectively than I ever could have done. Mercifully the divorce settlement was "full and final" and once it was all complete we never had to argue again over what was fair.

After the Separation

After I separated from Sarah I did have one or two brief affairs with other ladies (if that is the right word!). I suppose this is more or less inevitable in the human scheme of things when one is deprived of any physical contact with the opposite sex. Certainly any "free" specimen of decent manhood may be an attractive prospect for a woman looking for a "conquest"! The first happened "out of the blue" when I received a phone call from Susanne's younger sister Liesi. Of course we had met earlier when Susanne was still working with us. Liesi was au pairing in England and said she would like to come and stay with me in London; she was hoping to go to hear jazz at Ronnie Scott's. I suppose Susanne must have given her younger sister a good report about me because we had formed a warm and honest friendship from the moment we first met. Liesi might have been 20 years younger than me but she was entirely mature in her composure and knew what she wanted from life. And what she wanted from me was a loving sexual experience. We spent one lovely night together and parted as good friends. We would keep in touch from time to time for many years afterwards.

My second "affair" began after a work party at the Central Statistical Office where I suddenly saw a pair of attentive eyes watching me across the sea of other party goers. They belonged to Denise, a very successful and smart (in all senses of the word) lady who worked in this Department. We agreed to meet again after the party and I discovered that although Denise had been comfortably married for almost 10 years she had never made love to her husband. How strange is the world? It seemed hard to believe, but evidently she and her husband had been long childhood friends and had fallen into a marriage which both families simply assumed would take place – and so it did. But the two principals had never found a way to move their relationship into one of normal physical intimacy in marriage. Denise was looking for as much safe sexual experience as she could get as one way to prepare herself for the change she wanted in her marriage – she certainly did not want a long -term relationship. We were both intelligent and reasonably level-headed people. She was able to make suitable excuses for spending nights out or weekends away. We had a lot of good times and parted after a year or so on perfectly friendly terms – I hope it did all work out for her. I saw that she rose to a very senior position in her work – as for her marriage, I simply do not know!

My third "affair" happened in 1978 when the teenage girl I had known as Ros Cattliff had separated from her husband German Eslava. Ros and I knew each other well from teenage golfing days and we had windsurfed together many times since then. I had never thought of Ros as a romantic attachment because we had always simply been good friends, each with a (seemingly) happy marriage. But suddenly the vagaries of life had thrown us together again as independent people who shared a love of many of the same outdoor sports. We went skiing together a few times – sometimes with Susanne and Liesi, sometimes alone. It seemed the most natural thing in the world but very soon Ros found a new husband in Claus and I found a new partner in Priscilla. Our short romance petered out but our friendship continued.

Priscilla

As the year 1979 progressed I found myself spending more and more time with my work colleague Priscilla. Very much a career girl, 'Scilla was a great Labour Party supporter and lived in a shared house south of the Thames with her brother Charles. She enjoyed sport and playing poker – we knew many of the same friends and I found her practical common sense and support were a great help in my troubled times. We would spend many happy years together while my four children grew up. It would be hard to find a more sensible, patient and loving person – it's difficult to believe now how easily our mutual trust was broken.

'Scilla – at sea

In many ways Priscilla was a rock that provided the whole family with a dependable foundation. With good grace and generosity she put up with all my sometimes burdensome family commitments and always kept a well-run family home that was open to my children. I had told Priscilla that I would never have more children until my first family was grown up and out of school. (I did not want to repeat the situation my father found himself in.) This she fully accepted since she herself was aiming to follow a successful career in the civil service. In the end, of course, the pressure to have kids did (somehow) get the better of her. To my dismay and amazement she suddenly announced she was pregnant (soon after she had a miscarriage).

I was shocked that our mutual trust had been broken so our relationship came to a sad end in 1987.

It seems that these few short paragraphs do not really do justice to the 8-year-long happy relationship I had with Priscilla. We had run several comfortable and more or less "posh" homes together – first in Hartland Rd, then at 30 Rochester Square, next at the Chapel in Steppingley and finally in the small town house of Bergholt Mews. I hope I provided some support for her in her own civil service career. She certainly helped me weather the various storms that punctuated my efforts to reach a good divorce settlement with Sarah.

I had always told 'Scilla that it would be easy for her to find a good husband so as to have the children she wanted. I certainly did not want to be the cause of her not having kids! After we broke up it did not take her long to do so and I am glad to say she soon had 2 boys to bring up after she married her boss!

1979-83 More Windsurfing
The UKBSA, IBSA plus the IYRU and the IOC

The dominance of Hoyle Schweitzer's patented windsurfer was relatively short-lived. Many profit-hungry competitors soon appeared on the scene and a young British surfer claimed in the Law Courts that he had invented the same system for steering a sail-craft many years previously. In England the most serious challenge to the dominance of the windsurfer came in the form of the "Sea Panther" board produced by the Way family in the Midlands. It soon became clear that a whole range of different types of boards were becoming available on the market – many came from large European manufacturers (Sailboard, Windglider, Bic, etc.).

My initial loyalties to Windsurfer began to fade as the newer makes and designs had more advanced features which gave them greater performance. The numerous "breakaway" designs called themselves "sailboards" in an attempt to distance themselves from the Hoyle Schweitzer monopoly which was based on the "one design" windsurfer. Very soon the competitors to Windsurfer set up their own national association to promote races and look for sponsorship – this was the genesis of the UK Boardsailing Association (UKBSA).

From the very beginning windsurfing was an exciting, dramatic and fast-growing sport which appealed to a whole new class of "sailor". Most of these "sailors" had never had previous experience of sailing or the formalities and complex rules of the 'triangle' racing which had traditionally been the normal form of yachting competition. Not only was the sport relatively cheap to get into but the equipment was light enough to be carried from place to place on a car roof rack – you could even carry 2 or 3 boards on one car. The sport also brought a bonanza to wetsuit manufacturers and the comfort and effectiveness of the wetsuits improved rapidly as a result. Good wetsuits meant that keen windsurfers would continue to enjoy their sport for 12 months in the year.

All these characteristics made windsurfing (used here as a generic term for all boardsailing) an attractive prospect for commercial sponsors who wanted to associate their products with the outdoor sporty excitement of this new sport. Heineken, Carlsberg, Smirnoff, Bacardi, Peter Stuyvesant and several others all "threw their hats into the ring". The traditional sailing establishment looked on with a mixture of jealousy and shock. The governing body of sailing in the UK, the Royal Yachting Association, did not want to be left out of the "party". Several of the leading windsurfers including myself were invited to become part of a new "Boardsailing Committee" chaired by the charming old veteran (a farmer) Robert Lee-Warner. Although I did not trust the motives of the RYA (because I feared they might gobble up the new sport) I did like Robert Lee-Warner. He impressed me at one of our meetings when he told me how he had just found his car had been wheel-clamped by the zealous parking wardens but he had simply taken out the large set of bolt cutters he kept in his car and snipped off the clamp!

My own close involvement in the pioneering development of

windsurfing came about by one of those strange quirks of fate at the Annual General Meeting of the UKBSA in September 1979. I went to the meeting with no intention of taking on any responsibilities for administering the sport. I had already done my stint with the Windsurfer Association. Obviously I was well known within the sport because I had also been a successful competitor, winning the National Championships on a couple of occasions and going with the UK team to both European and World Championship events. There was, it is fair to say, a certain groundswell of tension between the commercially motivated Sea Panther fraternity (the Ways) and the rest of the windsurfing community. So when the AGM reached the point at which the main officers were to be elected we found that the only nomination for Chairman was one of the Ways. Sarah, who was sitting next to me, turned to me saying "we can't let this happen – you had better put your name forward!"

Once again the fates had struck – suddenly I found myself elected to this unpaid but potentially important role. Of course, I was still a mad keen enthusiast for the sport, believing it could become as popular as tennis or golf. And what a great way for "ordinary" people to enjoy sport on the water in a cheap and convenient package! We still had active interest from sponsors in those days so I buckled to and decided to make a go of it. The first thing was to get a proper office set up with a good administrative support. Yes, we had money from sponsors but they, the sponsors, wanted value for money so we could not afford to be slap-dash in our management of the membership or the events. As it turned out, the daughter of our old neighbours in Oppidans Road was looking for work and had all the necessary skills so I asked her if she would like to become part of my paid staff. She accepted and Lesley (Hackett) would be my invaluable "right hand" helper over the next 3 years – we travelled the world together and her tough diplomacy was an essential ingredient to running good events with our somewhat laid-back and anarchic participants.

We ran a busy schedule of large weekend events during every

summer season in the UK but we also were in demand to run international events – such was the legendary effectiveness of our administration. I had Geoff Turner doing the computing and necessary software to work out race results. I had Mike Todd, who was an expert on measurement of board and sail dimensions, to make sure they followed the rules. I had Phil Jones who became an excellent Race Officer on the water to manage the races themselves. As for myself, apart from being an important figurehead and maker of policy, I ran the whole business with strict civil service efficiency. Both the Skippers' meetings and the races started dead on time – it did not take long before our competitors realised that latecomers were losers.

After my experiences running the World Championships at Nahariya in Israel I realised that we were never going to popularise the sport with the wider public and news media unless we changed the traditional way races were run. The rules for sailing races had evolved in different times and for different purposes. The traditional system depended on "protests" being made by competitors who felt that other competitors had broken rules and spoiled their chances of winning. After the races finished there would be a long series of hearings by a Protest Committee to rule on the rightness or wrongness of each protest. The whole business took hours. So when, after the end of the day's races in Israel, the TV reporters asked me who was winning I could only tell them that we would not know the answer until all the protests had been heard. This might take several hours! The TV and news people simply could not believe that all this fuss and bother was necessary.

From this point on, I introduced a completely new system of rule enforcement. We placed referees out on the water on boats near to each of the turning marks and we gave both these, and the Race Officer himself, the authority to call out (by megaphone) the sail numbers of any boards seen breaking the rules (touching marks, colliding with other competitors or being over the line before the start). When your number was called out you had to perform a 720-degree turn before you could continue in the race. I instructed my Race Officer to try and make sure one or two numbers were always called out at the start (for being over the line early) but, if possible, these numbers should not be those of the top sailors. We needed to make a few examples to show we meant business – it worked!

But my new rules proved to be a serious provocation for the traditional sailing authorities. The old traditionalists were also shocked by the jazzy and financially significant sponsorship deals we enjoyed. (Heineken provided free beer for all competitors as well as masses of generous prizes.) As the sport continued to boom in terms of numbers and money, the International Yacht Racing Union were also determined not to be left out – how could they get their hands on all this new money and energy which was coming into what they regarded as "their" sport? I was invited by Nigel Hacking (Secretary of the IYRU – we called him the "mekon" after the sinister villain who had featured in the Eagle comic story of Dan Dare) to become a member of his new Boardsailing Committee. Later this would become a sub-committee of the International Olympic Committee (IOC) as they, too, wanted to bring the popular sport into the Olympics. The IYRU delegated one of their (charming and very wealthy) Danish members, Hajo Fritze, to be my sort of "shadow" and we would get to know each other pretty well as time went by.

My own involvement in the international windsurfing scene was then geared up to a whole new level when some of the leading European competitors and activists asked me to become Executive Secretary of their newly formed International Boardsailing Association (IBSA). This was a paid post and took me all over Europe both to meetings and for running events. One way and another I had some strange experiences. It was always an adventure to set out down the steps of my home in Rochester Square with a rucksack on my back and an airline ticket in my pocket – wondering just what this trip would bring! Two trips in particular I can remember well. The first was to Thailand, the second to Hungary.

I received a call "out of the blue" from a strange entrepreneur called Bert Morsbach. "Would I help him run a windglider event he was organising in Thailand?" It turned out that Bert was manufacturing his own version of the patented Windglider somewhere out in the Far East and he wanted to promote this product with a sponsored event at Pattaya Beach in Thailand. I was invited over to Germany to meet him at one of their big boatshows. I soon got the idea that he was an amusing but tricky customer when it turned out we had no tickets to get into the Boat Show where we would meet his other collaborators. Of course there was heavy security on the entrances. As we walked purposefully towards the turnstiles Bert turned to me and told me to pick up one of the big cardboard boxes which were lying about against a wall. This I did and we both proceeded to walk straight through the security without any questions being asked!

Several months later I found myself looking out of a plane window at the massive white wall of the Himalaya mountains as we jetted towards Bangkok. I bussed down to Pattaya Beach and found the lovely hotel which Bert had booked us into. Sweet-smelling flowers and smiling staff created a magical atmosphere which combined with wonderful food to make a comfortable stay. But the arrangements for the racing were less satisfactory. Pattaya Beach is a busy, noisy place with all sorts of jet skis and motorboats buzzing all over the warm ocean. How were we going to start the race without a very LOUD sound signal – something which both competitors and spectators could not ignore. I asked Bert if we could find any fireworks as we had no starting gun or foghorn. "Oh yes" said Bert "I'll send one of the hotel boys down into town so he can bring back a selection". The boy duly did so and I found myself looking down at a motley selection of strange looking contraptions. We tried a few with little success – not loud enough – but then I spotted one that looked just like the bombs you see in comic strips. It was a round cannon-ball-type device with a menacing looking fuse sticking out of the top. We tied it up with a string stretched between two trees, then lit the fuse and stood well back. There was a huge flash, a mighty explosion and a blue mushroom cloud of smoke curled away into the sky. "That will do fine" I said – so we sent the boy back to buy a good supply for our races next day.

When it came to the races themselves I was managing things from the rickety old ferry boat which served as the race boat. As we moved towards the designated start time Bert became a bit agitated. Once more we tied up our "bomb" with string outside the central cabin and Bert grabbed the matches – he could not wait to get things started. I counted down to the start time and Bert lit the fuse. Once more there was a huge explosion – perfect for all the competitors but Bert himself had been caught in the blast; he'd stayed too close because of all his enthusiasm. His face was black and his white shirt was stained with blood where pieces of the cardboard bomb covering had ripped holes both in the shirt and in his skin! I'm afraid we all had to laugh – what a comedy show! We did finish the series of races but what happened to Bert afterwards I never found out – quite a strange character.

I had another strange experience when the IYRU held one of their important committee meetings in the (then) Russian-controlled Hungarian city of Budapest. We were all booked into the smartest hotel in this very beautiful place. There were no luxury goods of any kind in the shops but neither was there any litter or graffiti – the Communists made sure of that. You have to remember that the US and the Russians were still serious enemies at this time. The Russians had laid on all this hospitality in the hope of upstaging the United States, particularly with regard to the fallout from the Summer Olympics of 1980. The aim of the Russians (and their allies) was to prevent the US Windsurfer being selected as the chosen board for inclusion in the Olympics of 1984. Be that as it may, my own memories are not of the interminable committee meetings but of the beautiful coffee houses and especially of our closing formal dinner.

This dinner took place in a country inn which we were taken to by horse-drawn sledges through the snow. The inn was a fine place with a huge open log fire. What a perfect scene! There were about 20 of us and I found myself sitting next to one of the most beautiful women I have ever seen. She was as intelligent and articulate as she was beautiful. She told me she was originally from Estonia but she had been trained to become a "sleeper" – that is a Russian spy who somehow moves to the West and lives a perfectly normal life for years and years until she/he is called upon to act. In fact, my companion had been at the centre of an international sensation after the 1980 Russian Olympics because she had eloped (escaped – so it seemed) with the young Dutch sailing coach. It turned out that this "escape" had been planned by her handlers. Her job was to marry this young Dutchman and then live what would appear to be a perfectly normal life as she got to know more and more "people that mattered". She told me that she had not found the "freedoms" of the west so great as far as she was concerned. In Russia, she told me, I can walk down any street at night without any fear of either being robbed or pestered by men. "In Holland this is not the case – wherever I walk I find men are always bothering me and I certainly cannot walk about freely at night." Her English was perfect and we had a sparkling evening – I suppose her role as a spy probably faded away after the Berlin Wall came down. I wonder!

As the busy months and years went by, I realised that it really made no sense for me to be doing all this work running windsurfing in the UK with no pay! The sport was growing fast and sponsors were still keen to be involved. The only answer I could come up with was to make myself into an independent agency which the Associations (or anyone else for that matter) could contract to provide services (running regattas, membership, newsletters, sponsorship deals, etc.). The UKBSA were very happy to agree to this because they did not want to lose my services – so I transformed myself into Windsurfing Professional. This way I could try to make a living from further development of the sport.

My vision was to develop the public relations side of windsurfing by making events much more exciting and understandable for the public, news media and spectators. At this time, the traditional sailing authorities still had strong rules preventing any advertising on sails, equipment or persons. This seemed very foolish to me as not only could sails provide a wonderful "billboard" space for displaying adverts; they could also show national flags or even the name of the competitor. I realised we should try to promote a personality cult amongst the leading competitors – so the public could recognise the "good, the bad and the ugly" in a manner of speaking. My first "professional event" was staged with the help of the Tourist Board of the Isle of Man and generous sponsorship from Bacardi. I laid down a set of rules requiring each competitor to have his national flag and name printed on his sail. I asked the organisers to install a high-quality, powerful public-address-system so I could provide a running commentary which would be easily followed by spectators around the seafront. I invited top sailors from Europe and the USA and offered prize money for the winners. With help from the PR department at Bacardi we also had coverage from various international TV crews.

We ran the races under our own rules and effectively set a precedent for many changes which would soon spread to the rest of the sailing world. But at this time the traditionalists were horrified! As for the competitors themselves, they were excited to be racing for money but they were mostly young and "carefree" – it was not easy to get them to "play ball" with the necessary media interviews or to make sure their sails and equipment followed my rules. My efforts to "educate" them to the realities of business sponsorship were largely a failure – race winners would rather go off to the pub to celebrate with their pals than turn up for interviews with irritating TV or radio companies. My attempts to "train" these would-be professionals continued in later events but I don't think I ever really got the message across – or perhaps the racers were not really interested in the money side of things.

As the sport developed, both the major manufacturers and the top competitors steadily began to focus on the attractions of higher performance equipment. This was more sophisticated and more expensive – and most of the new boards were too difficult to handle for straightforward family sailing. This trend was strongly reinforced by the media coverage – photos and film showing off more and more extreme performance. And once the sport had been accepted into the Olympic Games a large part of its activities fell within the remit of the traditional sailing authorities. So there were pressures affecting the sport which came from several different directions. Certainly, the traditional authorities had no positive vision for where things might go – and they certainly had no natural rapport with big commercial sponsors.

Matters were complicated further by the intense competition between the major board manufacturers. The sport had been growing so fast there were many opportunities for profit; this had a very strong attraction for greedy industrialists. Up until now the manufacturers had simply taken the effective administration of their sport as a given. They did not see it as any part of their business to help make sure good events and generous sponsorship continued to benefit the sport. For myself, I could see that the exciting early days were fading and sponsorship was becoming harder to maintain. It seemed most unlikely that I would be able to continue providing the high input of administration solely on the basis of continually increasing levels of sponsorship.

Towards the end of 1982 I began to have talks with the major equipment manufacturers to see how far they might be prepared to underwrite the costs of organising the major events. On their part they were all pretty cagey about this. Nobody wanted to risk even the smallest cut in their profit margins in case their competitors did not follow suit. This was bad news for me. Worse still, I had found the leading race winners continued to be totally uncooperative when I tried to persuade them to turn out to give interviews to news media after I had run a big event at La Torche in Brittany. It seemed that neither the competitors nor the manufacturers would understand that they had to behave differently if they wanted to have any prospect of their sport becoming as big (and well organised) as tennis and golf.

I warned both competitors and manufacturers that I would not go on putting my resources into their sport unless they became more co-operative. The racers needed to be more “professional” and the manufacturers needed to divert some of their profits into administering the sport. When I set off (again) from the UK to run the next big event (“Surfline Sylt” it was called, taking place on the German island of Sylt) I was determined to force the manufacturers to reach a decision one way or another. All the big names were there and I explained once more what I regarded as the only way I could continue to run their sport for them – we needed a small levy to be put on the price of every board so this money could be used to run the sport. When they refused ‘point blank’ I realised my time was up and resigned. Over the next year or so I wound down the office in my home at Rochester Square. My fun (and sometimes frustrating) days in windsurfing were over!

Looking back on all this, I am still very sad that the potential of this great sport has never been realised – and now I don’t believe it ever will. For myself, I enjoyed more than 10 years both as a leading competitor and ultimately as one of the key figures working to develop the sport – both in the UK and internationally. From my early struggles with the heavy teak booms and saggy sail in the sheltered waters of Newton Bay, I ended up winning National Championships, becoming Chairman of both the Windsurfing Association and the UKBSA and finally setting up and managing the International Board Sailing Association. Windsurfing took me to many exotic places: Holland, Mexico, Norway, France, Germany, Italy, Sardinia, Fuerteventura, Israel, Florida, Thailand, Yugoslavia and Greece. My “right hand lady”, Lesley Hackett, came with me to help manage events on most of my travels – her steely charm and clear decisions were a perfect recipe for keeping the (often boisterous) young competitors in line! Unfortunately, in the end, the unimaginative and selfish policies of the traditional yachting authorities combined with the desperate greed of the board manufacturers to ruin the "ordinary man's" access to the sport – what a sorry tale.

German Eslava

My story would not be complete without mention of German (pronounced "Herman") Eslava – Ros's first husband and a native of Colombia. German had been one of Ros Cattliff's students, studying English, and they eventually became husband and wife. They often came to Newton during the 1970s because Ros loved coming to the family bungalow on the dunes and they both became keen windsurfers. Always a somewhat wild and amusing fellow (he came from Spanish-speaking Colombia and spoke English, French, German, Italian with gusto if not with precision!) German came with the UK windsurfing team to the 1978 World Championships in Mexico. This event was held in the then new resort of Cancun in Mexico. German advised those of his immediate friends not to stay in the new 5-star tourist hotel under any circumstances. "They have no idea how to cook western food – you will certainly get serious food poisoning." So we stayed in the local cheap hotel in a nearby town, getting the rickety old public bus service down to the beach each morning. He turned out to be right – all our pals down in the 5-star hotel did indeed become sick as the proverbial dogs whilst we simply had to endure leaking ceilings (in the torrential rainstorms) and 6 kinds of melon for breakfast each day.

German and Ros also came along with us (also in their camper van) to the first Windsurfing World Championships in Sardinia. So one way and another we became good friends – a friendship which continued after Ros and German separated some years later. I spent some time staying with German and his new wife Rosanna when they were living in New Zealand. And it was German who, in a roundabout way, provided the impetus for Ros and I to meet up again in 2013. He was the one who knew of Sarah's hip operations (she also lived in New Zealand) and had told Ros that Sarah might appreciate help. That, in turn, resulted in Ros (who had been a school friend since the age of 9) contacting Sarah and Sarah inviting Ros to stay at Newton over the Christmas when we met again. Such are the strange machinations of fate!

1979–1983

Sarah and I had a few very difficult years trying to sort out our divorce and business affairs. All these negotiations were fraught with complications thrown up by tricky tax laws and the instincts of lawyers to continually find extra causes for argument. Sarah had her own emotional dramas as she hoped to form a long-term relationship with a very capable doctor friend in Newcastle. For one year she took the 3 younger children up to live in Newcastle, evidently wishing to explore this possibility. She left Rupert with me as we did not want to upset his progress at University College School. Eventually in 1981 we reached agreement and so life went on but when the dust had settled I never for one moment regretted my divorce settlement with Sarah – indeed she has turned out to be a reliable friend and a much better business-person than myself!

These were the years where windsurfing (see above), golf (both Millbrook and Dunstanburgh) and the divorce took up most of my time. From 1980 I lived with Priscilla first in Hartland Rd, then Rochester Sq, then at the Chapel in Steppingley and finally in Bergholt Mews.

There are two activities/incidents which deserve a mention during this time.

Skating around Trafalgar Square – July 1981

When we began to live in London I would often take the kids roller skating on what we called the "flowery bridge" (over the main railway line on the way from Chalk Farm to Camden tube station). We could enjoy ourselves there even at night under the street lights – and we all became quite good at skating. London is in fact a pretty good place to roller skate and for many years afterwards I would often put my skates on of a summer evening. My regular trip was to cruise down the pavement towards Camden (from Hartland Road where I lived). I could pick up my favourite ice-cream (blackcurrant and chocolate) from Marine Ices and then free-wheel down the slight incline all the way into Camden. It gave me a great feeling of wellbeing, smiling at the passers-by whilst I licked my ice-cream and kept an eye open to see that my dog Bat was close beside me. From there it was easy to cruise over to Regent's Park, where there would often be other skaters to marvel at (many were very skilful).

I can remember very well my first experience of having a good pair of skates with high quality trucks and big blue cryptonic wheels. They were smooth and fast. I still have the same pair of skates today – the wheels may have cost £50 but they were certainly a wonderful investment! Those skates have done a lot of miles!

Now, when there are great events and happenings afoot in London, the tubes and buses get over-crowded so what better way to get about (and see the fun) than to go on your roller skates. It's quick and easy to get around and your skates make you a good 4 or 5 inches taller – to see over the crowd. I went to Churchill's funeral, Diana and Charles' wedding and Diana's funeral on my roller skates.

It was the wedding of Diana and Charles which gave me the unique (I really do believe it was unique) opportunity to roller-skate around Trafalgar Square, quite alone on a summer spring day and without a single person, car, bike or bus in sight. All the crowds were squeezed into the Mall watching the newly-weds waving on Buckingham Palace balcony so I simply headed off back towards Trafalgar Square. Once away from the crowds there was nobody about, no people, no traffic – quite an eerie quietness. The sun shone down and I could not resist the chance of skating around the great square. Although I was feeling quite elated after this I still had to slog back home all the way uphill along Tottenham Court Road. Suddenly, as I slogged away, I heard the rapid thump thump thump of another roller-skater coming up behind me over the pavement – much faster. A big black man whizzed past me, going backwards, with a smile – it was altogether a strange experience.

Fun with Flexifoil Kites – 1982

My regular motorbike commute into work each day took me down St Martin's Lane and through Trafalgar Square. One of the shops I passed was the strange kite shop which sold all sorts of curious flying devices. I would often pop in there to try and find unusual presents for the kids. One of these presents was a flexi-foil kite which was very new at that time sporting, as it did, a strong flexible carbon-fibre strut and sleek aerodynamics which came into being when the kite inflated itself when rushing through the air. Even in relatively small winds the kite could reach terrific speed, pulling harder and harder on the 2 strings which were used to control it and steer it. In a strong wind, the device fairly whistled across the sky and (I'm sorry to say) sometimes cut down other kites which were less powerful when we flew them at the top of Parliament Hill Fields.

The first flexi-foils were small, about 4 feet across, but they seemed to sell and the makers steadily increased their size. To make things more interesting you could link 3 or 4 kites together on the same pair of strings to create a ladder of kites which (although more cumbersome to steer) could pull with massive power. When the snow came to Millbrook we had a lot of fun with these "power kites" because we could harness them to a big sledge I had made from a pair of old metal skis. Not content with simply being whisked over the snow by the kites, we made a big snow jump and tried, with some success, to whizz over this under kite power. Of course, we all ended up in a big snowy heap but it was, I think, one of the very first attempts to use power kites as a motive force for speed.

Soon after this, one of the most famous early users of a stack of flexi-foils was the sailing tornado catamaran called "Jacob's Ladder". This was one of the more bizarre entrants in the Weymouth speed sailing trials. A 20-foot Tornado racing catamaran was powered by a ladder of 6 large (12 foot wide) flexi-foil kites. It was quite a beast to manage. (In the 1980s we had only just begun to realise that a small windsurfer could sail faster than a £100,000 50-foot catamaran – and hydro-foils had not yet appeared on the sailing scene.) I went down to Weymouth to see what was going on and came across the crew of Jacob's Ladder as they struggled to start their run in a gale-force wind. Both crewmen were extremely tense in their woolly hats and lifejackets. Getting the boat started involved first launching the kites. The kites soared up into the heavens and hovered high above us with their two control-lines humming like violin strings as they were made fast to a stout post which had been driven into the sand. The control lines went on from the post to the catamaran which was pointing out to sea very close to the beach (in just a foot or two of water). The 2 crewmen jumped aboard their craft and then asked their assistant on shore to cut the rope which was holding the control lines fast to the post. The kites leaped upwards and, to everyone's horror, took the entire 20-foot catamaran with them, surging high into the air. One of the crew failed to even get aboard the rapidly rising craft, the other fell from it about 10 feet above the water. The catamaran and its kites continued upwards and outwards. It went up 50 feet into the air and crashed down in pieces about 200 yards out to sea! In those days, the kites only had 2 control-lines so it was impossible to de-power them – it really was a case of "shit or bust" (bust, in this case). Today the modern kite surfers (with 4 control-lines) are probably unaware of the risks taken by early pioneers.

Chapter 5: The Lady Shirley Porter Experience 1983–1986

We now move on to the next big experience of my life, working with, and for, the mercurial and wilful Shirley Porter, Leader of Westminster City Council.

How on earth did I get mixed up with this energetic, abrasive, selfish, rich, cunning Jewish Tesco heiress and all the nonsense of Westminster City Council?

It all started when, soon after leaving the Civil Service, I met another abrasive and dogmatic character called Alex Henney. He wanted to set up a small consultancy with me and another (strange) fellow called Oliver Humphries. It would be called VFM – Value for Money in Local Government – and it would tout for well-paid business with local authorities and the Audit Commission. This was all about hot air and smart suits and ties (bullshit baffles brains) – but, with Mrs Thatcher in Downing Street, quite the flavour of the month so to speak. Over the next 18 months or so, we put together our business pitch in the form of a small leaflet/flyer – which we then circulated around the London local councils. We only had a few responses but one of these was from a (then) junior councillor at Westminster called Shirley Porter (SP). The Council had just had an influx of new-style (shiny suits and slip-on shoes) radical Tory councillors who were now jostling for power with the traditional "old guard" Tories (who were polite and wore neat Tweed suits). She was one of these "new breed" Tories and she wanted our (my) help in finding a way to become the next leader of the Council. Her main fellow "conspirators" were Patricia Kirwan, David Weeks, Barry Legg and Peter Hartley – all keen as mustard to "take power" but relatively inexperienced and all very right-wing.

Our first meeting with SP was in September 1982. Properly suited and with briefcases in hand, we duly turned up first thing in the morning at her office in Radnor Mews. We rang the bell and a very smart “sloanish” voice invited us in BUT we must first remove our shoes. A new pale green carpet had been fitted the week before and NO DIRT must be allowed to get on it. Surprised – this was an unusual request for consultants – we removed our shoes and, feeling rather deflated (suits and bare socks do not really go together), we mounted the stairs. Victoria, SP’s secretary, was on the phone and waved us to sit down on the pale green sofa, which we did. SP was obviously hidden away in her own private office, protected by Victoria. We listened with wonder at one of the strangest conversations I have ever heard. Victoria was evidently speaking (very seriously) with the manager of Harrods. “Had he not realised that the parcel his shop had dispatched to Shirley Porter, a prominent and very wealthy member of London’s Jewish society, should have had a sender’s address. The mysterious parcel which had arrived unexpectedly had been treated as a suspicious item. The police had been called. The parcel had been taken away and X-rayed, revealing a complex web of wires. Naturally the security forces wanted to take no chances and had blown up the parcel! The free beach bag which SP had been looking forward to – it had been one of Harrods’ special offers to its best customers – was destroyed. Would he please make sure another was sent as soon as possible – this time with a proper sender’s address.”

The argument continued for quite a while. Alex and I could not believe our ears! But this was very much typical of many equally strange incidents, as I would discover over the next 3 eventful years.

When we finally faced “the dragon” we found a petite stocky lady with gingery hair, smart clothes and the ultimate commanding manner. She was used to getting her own way and her quick-fire disposition kept everyone on their toes even if it did not always come to sensible conclusions. Clearly she had a burning ambition to be SOMEONE famous. This, I found out later, had a lot to do with the fact that her father (Mr Cohen) had absolutely forbidden either of his two daughters to have anything whatever to do with his business (named after his wife Tess Cohen). SP had built up a pressure-cooker determination to do something about this. For a start she had married Tesco's Chief Executive (Leslie Porter) to get closer to the business – now she wanted to put her own name up in lights as a high-profile politician.

Because SP had bags of energy and bags of money, she became a valued tool for the established Tory hierarchy. Mrs Thatcher was in power – Kenneth Baker was her right-hand man – and they were being dogged in an infuriating way by the successes of their arch-rival Ken Livingstone, who had become leader of the GLC. As Leader of Westminster Council SP saw herself as their great crusader – whatever Red Ken could do as excesses of the left she could outdo in Westminster with excesses of the right. From what I saw and heard, this was a dynamic which Kenneth Baker encouraged even though he knew it could (and did) ultimately destroy SP.

At our first meeting I explained that although sacking council staff was extremely difficult, they (the Council) could make big changes (possibly savings) by "restructuring". By combining smaller departments to make larger ones they could make staff (particularly expensive senior staff) redundant. Naturally the established staff would argue against this, so any new plan would have to be carefully thought through, ideally with the backing of the existing Chief Executive.

SP liked the sound of this. I was invited back (I think Alex H had already found the haughty manner of SP rather disagreeable) to meet her small coterie of the "new-blood" Tory councillors. We had several meetings over the months that followed and I never had any difficulty in getting paid at the agreed rate for my time. Slowly an outline plan was developed and the group asked me to draw up a formal report outlining this (my) plan so that it could be put before the whole Tory group in the run up to their election of a new leader (expected early in 1983). I had already had the opportunity to float some of these ideas with David Witty, the Chief Executive, before finalising the report –

so we knew it was not altogether impractical. David Witty was a workmanlike pragmatic officer of the old school and I felt he could see the "writing on the wall" as the new breed of Tories flexed their muscles. If he did not at least go along with some of their proposals then his job would soon be on the line rather than the jobs of other senior officers!

One radical feature of my new proposal was the idea that important committee chairmen should have their own "Private Secretaries" provided to support them and paid for by the ratepayers. After all, as I pointed out, this was the whole basis on which the Whitehall Mandarins worked – so why not do the same in local government. This was one important way in which the elected councillors could gain much more control and influence over their officers and council policy. Certainly the Leader of the Council should be the first to benefit from such a development. David Witty saw no reason why this should not be done – so the idea of what we called a "policy unit", which would be a resource dedicated to assist the Council Leader, was written into the new plans.

For myself, I was fascinated by the potential challenge of managing, and at least partially controlling, this burgeoning energy which seemed about to sweep into Westminster. I certainly did not agree with the Tory policies which were brutally harsh on the less able and downtrodden. As with all well-trained civil servants, my job was to do what I could to moderate the worst excesses of political zeal which the elected politicians might display. Here was an ideal opportunity to earn a decent salary and see how well I could manage the new brash young Tories of Westminster.

It turned out to be very providential that, whilst I was away at my last (and very controversial) international windsurfing event in Sylt, the new ginger group of Tories had their plans (my plans) accepted and SP had been elected as the new leader of the Council. Two days after I returned from Sylt I raced downstairs in 30 Rochester Square to take a very early morning phone call – it was SP offering me the job as Head of the new Policy Unit at Westminster. I accepted immediately, subject to sorting out details of salary etc with the Chief Executive. Immediately my life was turned upside down by almost constant daily requests to meet up with SP and her pals to progress one thing or another. Meetings might be at 7.30am or 7.30pm. They might take place at very short notice. They might be discussing something completely unfamiliar to me. Once again I was wearing my suit and tie almost every day and my BMW was racing through London traffic either down to Victoria Street (Council offices) or Hyde Park (SP's penthouse flat).

When I took up my post on 26 July 1983 I found myself in a large office on the top floor. To my amazement and great satisfaction I was allocated the tall, young and beautiful (and very efficient) Fiona Allen as my Secretary. She had worked previously in the office of David Witty's second-in-command, David Goad, and I had already been impressed by her common sense and quick thinking. I did not ask to have Fiona posted to me – this was down to David Witty (a very kind decision for which I must be forever grateful). Fiona was in her late twenties and highly proficient in both shorthand and typing, which she taught others in evening classes to earn extra cash. Fiona was a keen horsewoman with all the robustness of character which such activities require – a very calm young lady who was immune to almost all crises and provocations. This was fortunate because the councillors in SP's new ginger group were often extremely unreasonable and abrasive – we were often asked to do the impossible. Fiona would prove to be an invaluable asset to my small team and we kept up our friendship for many years after our paths diverged away from Westminster. Fiona later married a pop musician and ended up living in Australia. We did go through thick and thin together over those 3 Westminster years – I don't remember a single occasion when we had disagreements.

So I now found myself trying to manage SP with all her energies and idiosyncrasies. I wrote all her speeches, provided detailed briefing for all her meetings and composed all her press releases. Virtually every word she uttered came from me. Many of the Tory ginger group's plans and aims were extremely controversial – produced in such a hurry they were "not thought through"! Of course it was quite impossible for me to openly disagree with any of them. It was simply necessary to tell them/her that their ideas were brilliant and that I would take them away and work on them with the relevant Chief Officers. By the time I brought the "ideas" back to them (after the necessary wheeling and dealing with Chief Officers) they had been miraculously mutated into something which might have the same name but a subtly different substance. What the Councillors never realised was that I was able to use their "radical" ideas effectively to "threaten" the Chief Officers with what might happen if they could not come up with some other plan. This would be a plan which I could then present as the polished and fully evolved version of the original idea. I did learn to become extremely skilful in playing one side off against the other without either side really being able to figure out just exactly what I was up to. In this way, Councillors (especially SP) began to feel they could almost "walk on water" because they seemed able to force their ideas on officers so easily. This, as SP would later discover, was a very dangerous mindset to develop.

Just as I had dramas and excitements working for Sir Idwal Pugh so I also had (many more) dramas with SP – who later became infamous as the Lady Porter who had to flee the country to escape massive £ million fines imposed by the Audit Commission. Lady P, as I will call her now, specialised in trying to make important people feel small and insecure. We had many early morning breakfast meetings around the big white marble table in her smart flat. The flat was serviced by a butler, a cook and a personal maid who were employed full time. The old family chauffeur was also an important and very imposing figure – the only person, so far as I know, who Lady P was slightly frightened of. Once or twice he did help us out of difficult situations, some of which would have been uncontrollable without his intervention. It was common knowledge in both the press and City Hall that the chauffeur drove Lady P to City Hall in her big Bentley car but always stopped at least 200 yards away so she could be seen walking into City Hall.

The breakfast meetings were often punctuated by small but unsettling dramas for those unfamiliar with Lady P's little wiles. In the centre of the table there was a large and elaborate silver "Lazy Susan" which could be turned around a central pivot to bring butter, marmalade or whatever within reach. What was not obvious was that the small silver trays carrying the various breakfast foods were not attached to the rotating structure underneath but merely rested on it. Many was the time when a neatly besuited attendee would innocently try to turn the Lazy Susan but instead of turning he or she would simply pull the silver tray from its mounting. I remember one occasion when this resulted in butter, ice and water being thrown over his neighbour – much to Lady P's amusement. Her other favourite visitor's blunder involved the hidden button under the carpet which summoned the butler when pressed by someone's foot. I think it was the (rather pompous) head of the Audit Commission who was roundly ticked off when the Butler appeared for the third or fourth time to ask Lady P what she wanted. She spun round with a furious comment – "would whoever is pressing the button for the butler please stop immediately". Everybody kept their feet very still after that.

Lady P became Lady P not because of her considerable efforts to curry favour by giving enormous donations to charities and trying to support Mrs Thatcher but because her husband (Sir Leslie) received a knighthood for his own large donations and his business acumen. This was certainly a great irritation to her although she never mentioned it. For my own part, I knew the Honours system from my days in Whitehall – Lady P was much too mercurial and controversial to be an easy candidate for an honour.

I spent a lot of time in Lady P's Hyde Park flat and often met Sir Leslie, who would generally be puffing calmly away on his cigar – ignoring the mayhem that might be going on around him. We often shared a mutually raised eyebrow when Lady P was sounding off about some new scandal or injustice. Of course, the flat was almost always occupied by some tradesman or other changing the bathroom or modifying the kitchen or whatever. On one occasion I was with Lady P having tea when her current builder, a large Irishman, appeared from upstairs to consult her. He was met with a barrage of abuse and criticism which went on for about 10 minutes listing all the mistakes and idiotic failures in his hopeless work. He listened without a word. When Lady P had exhausted her repertoire of abuse there was a long silence as she waited for the builder to try to defend himself. She was completely knocked off balance when he simply looked her straight in the eye – "Would you like another cup of tea?" was his response. She did not have a ready answer for that!

On another occasion she asked me to wait downstairs whilst she called her personal maid up to her bedroom. When the maid – a polite well-dressed lady about 50 years old – went up Lady P called for me to come up for a minute. I was puzzled but did as I was asked. When I came into the room the two were facing each other. Lady P put on a very concerned expression on her face and simply asked the woman if she knew where her diamond brooch had gone. To my surprise, the lady replied sharply that she had never been accused of such a thing in all her life, flounced off and said she would be leaving immediately. After the lady rushed out Lady P clapped her hands together and thanked me for being present so she could rid herself of this woman she no longer liked. This was typical of the ruthless and manipulative skill of this tricky woman.

I don't think Lady P was a very clever woman, but she did have a fox-like cunning and was very quick-witted. I was constantly warning Chief Officers not to under-rate her. Of course she would often appear not to understand the complexities of policy in this or that area but then suddenly pick up on a point of detail where an officer might have contradicted something said weeks earlier. Most of the officers were (quite rightly) scared of being made a fool of by her.

In Council meetings, held late in the evenings and open to the public, there was the usual fixed battle between Joe Heggarty, leader of the Labour group, and Lady P for the Conservatives. I had to write Lady P's speeches and prepare all the necessary notes for supplementary questions – all flagged up carefully in marked folders. It was a nerve-wracking business watching the debate and hoping against hope that she would find the right page for the answers. One of her chief critics was Diane Abbot – a stubborn but totally bullet-proof Labour councillor. Amazingly I have watched her go up and up within the Labour hierarchy.

Lady P did have a constant fascination with the idea that new technology would somehow make her life easier. One particularly important area was the telephone system. First I should say that I had the telephone system at her home arranged so I could listen in on all the phone calls, either in or out, through the office's mini-telephone exchange. I knew from my experience in private office in Whitehall just how important it is for a secretary to know exactly what is going on between his/her principal and the outside world. This way misunderstandings can be avoided, the necessary briefing can be prepared, meetings can be set up or relevant officers warned that action may be required. We never had any trouble over this – Lady P trusted me completely to use my own discretion about how I actioned phone calls without her specific authority. Where we did have trouble was with Lady P's constant wish to upgrade this mini-telephone exchange as soon as she saw adverts for the next clever thing. When we finally ended up with BT's all-singing-and-all-dancing ultimate mini-exchange, it was a disaster. Victoria had to input all Lady P's contacts into the memory of this new system and it was supposed to log calls so we had a complete daily record of all numbers called etc. But it never seemed to work. The engineers were called back time and time again – but they found nothing wrong. Lady P became more and more furious; she had spent more than £5,000 on this advanced system but, typical BT, it never worked. Each week we worked our way up the seniority scale of engineers and managers in BT but no-one could fix the problem. Finally Lady P insisted that the Chief Executive of BT himself come with a team of dedicated engineers to see the situation for themselves. We duly received these great men and Lady P told them in no uncertain terms how useless their organisation was and how hopeless their new-fangled gadgets were. The engineers pulled things to pieces for the umpteenth time. The BT Chief Executive conferred with them in tense and confidential words. There was much shaking of heads until Victoria interrupted – "it wouldn't be anything to do with the cleaning lady would it?" There was a long silence with more puzzled looks exchanged. "Why?" "Well", said Victoria "she does come in at 6am every morning and has to plug in the vacuum cleaner." "You don't mean that she may unplug the phone exchange?" came the agonised response. "Well, of course she does. That's how she does the vacuum cleaning!" As so often, there was really a simple answer to all Lady P's problems but nobody had thought of asking whether the new super system was ever unplugged! It worked OK after this revelation.

Once my Policy Unit had become established, the leading Councillors all wanted to benefit from its resources. All the major committee chairmen finally ended up having their own support officers, working under my direction in my office. I hired another personal secretary to help with the growing burden of work – the spirited single mum, Melanie Weldon. She, too, would become a great asset to my team and remains a good friend to the present day.

But the Policy Unit was not without its opponents and critics – not just from the Labour opposition but also within the Council because of jealousies from other officers. Lady P and her ginger group wanted the Council to be even more efficient and aggressive and began to advertise for a new Chief Executive who would embody their ideals. David Witty stepped down gracefully – he was not fired as such (very glad to get out, I should say). The new man was already one of the highest paid Chief Executives in the Country – Mr Rodney Brooke. Clever, urbane and ambitious, Rodney Brooke was delighted to find himself at the centre of things in Westminster. Unlike David Witty he still felt he had the knowledge, the experience and cunning to take on the extreme right-wing Tory councillors.

In Rodney Brooke I knew I had a potential opponent who also, with his new high-profile salary and appointment, had the ear of Lady P. With this new addition she had a new "toy" to explore and to play with. By now she was taking my constant role, as almost her alter ego behind the scenes, for granted. And, like Icarus, she believed she could fly even closer to the sun. Her downfall began when she cooked up the idea, with Rodney Brooke's support, of creating a new post "Head of Administration". This would be something like a Deputy Chief Executive – well paid and part of Rodney Brooke's empire rather than mine. When the new post was advertised it gave me a difficult choice – and here Lady P gave me no clue as to what she expected so I could see my days could well be numbered. If I did not apply then I would certainly find myself in the shadow of yet another "new broom". But if I did apply and fail then my time was definitely over.

In the end I decided to apply for the post but the "die was already cast" and, for whatever reason, Lady P had decided she could manage without me. Needless to say, I did not get the job. I had had 3 crazy challenging but fun years riding the bucking bronco who was Lady P. We had kept the worst of right-wing, radical ideas at bay and I had proved to myself that I could keep on the right side of what could have been a major disaster. The Westminster job had tested every aspect of my resourcefulness – without the speed and convenience of my big BMW bike I could never have been in 2 places at once (a need which was often required as I zoomed between Hyde Park and Victoria Street). When the hard-core Tories decided I was not to get the new job, I knew it was time to go. Fortunately I had already sounded out old Cambridge contacts in the big management consulting firm then known as Arthur Young (it later became Ernst and Young).

The day Lady P no longer took my advice I resigned to take a new job with AY – fortunately at a much higher salary. My plan which attracted their interest at AY was to write a companion book to their big-selling "Manager's Handbook" – it would be called "The Councillor's Handbook". The publishers, Harrop, were interested in marketing the book and I spent the next year working in Rolls House in the City with my bright young assistant Andrea. We did produce a very good book which set out all the "tricks" a councillor needed to know to make sure council officers were doing what was required. Unfortunately, very soon after we finished this work Harrop were bought out by a bigger firm and the book was dropped. It would be interesting to find a copy now!

As far as my relationship with Westminster was concerned, it ceased immediately and I never spoke or had any contact with Lady P again. She was now in the hands of very clever "hostile" forces and it would not be long before they achieved their ambition of destroying her. Several years after I left Westminster I received a call out of the blue asking if I had copies of the old files recording all the decisions and discussions at the Leader's Advisory Sub-Committee (for which I had been secretary). This was the place where I was normally the only council officer present and I prepared the papers and recorded the minutes. LASC was the place where the dominant Tory party ginger group hatched their various cunning (or less cunning) plans. I was told that the files were required so that the Audit Commission could properly investigate the possibility that Lady P had been party to an illegal policy for allocating council housing by giving priority to Tory voters. There was also a big fuss over councillor Peter Hartley's decision to sell off the council cemeteries – for £5 or something similar! As Leader of the Council, Lady P could now be personally liable for misusing ratepayers' money.

As soon as I received the call I knew trouble was brewing. But I certainly was not going to become another player in the hard-ball game which Rodney Brooke was now playing. I said I was sorry but I had no records – what a pity the Council had lost the originals. Losing the records really was a disgraceful stunt to pull but I was not surprised. Lady P's arrogance and frequent unreasonableness had always generated extremely strong feelings amongst her officers. Now it was time for them to get their own back. After all she was also a multi-millionaire so the refund of £20 million or so of public money was really fair enough as far as they were concerned. All I can say about this is that I was with Lady P at every LASC meeting and at the pre- and post-meeting discussions. To my knowledge neither Patricia Kirwan (Chair of Housing who had the idea) nor Peter Hartley (Chairman who decided on sale of the cemeteries) ever discussed their crazy plans with Lady P. But when you live by the sword you almost invariably die by it. Like Icarus, Lady P had flown too close to the sun and crashed in flames. For many years she left the country and made her base in Israel to try and avoid paying her "fine". Eventually she came back and coughed up the money – what a bitter blow that must have been.

As for me, I was well out of it and now earning a much higher salary in "consultancy" – in truth I was wasting my time giving advice to public sector bodies who did not want it. This was all part of efforts by the Audit Commission to make local government more efficient. Other consultancy work was invariably commissioned by senior managers who wanted to find a way of avoiding taking responsibility for difficult decisions. They could do this easily and "keep their noses clean" simply by paying Arthur Young £1,000 a day for my services – what a racket. I now had a smart company car, a pension and more or less a 9-5 job but it did involve a lot of tedious travelling to meet our clients scattered around southern England.

Throughout all this time my work building up Millbrook continued and soon I would be able to work part-time for AY, which gave me much more freedom to push forward with my development of the Millbrook golf course.

Chapter 6: More Family Matters and my time with Sue

By now the tensions caused by my divorce with Sarah had faded away and we reached a new kind of sensible equilibrium. Sarah had already become a keen and proficient business-woman, managing properties in London and Northumberland as well as making a go of the Newton windsurfing school and the holiday cottages. Rupert had left UCS with good exam results and a place to read natural sciences at my old college, St Catharine's, at Cambridge. Ceri and Gael were now both at the Camden School for Girls after making a decision to leave the French Lycée so they could take the A level syllabus more easily. I would often have them visit me in Bergholt Mews during their lunch breaks as the school was just over the road. Later Ceri would decide to study and train for passing her exams at the specialist crammer, Davies, Lang and Dick – she needed good results if she was to achieve her objective of becoming a doctor. Gael would go on to become a boarder at Durham School. Dylan was enjoying water polo and study at the City of London school.

Probably the most interesting event of the year was Rupert's decision to apply for a new and special army scheme which aimed to give a carefully chosen select group of teenagers a year's experience of being an army officer. The candidates for this scheme would have to already have gained a place at University and then pass the officer selection course at Sandhurst. Only a small number would be selected and those would then have to pass successfully through a 6-week crash officer-training course at Sandhurst. I had seen this scheme advertised (in the Times I think) and it seemed a great opportunity for young people with the necessary get-up-and-go to see the world and develop their personal skills. Rupert duly went up to Sandhurst and passed the tests – with special mention because at this time he was an extraordinarily fit and strong young man who had already had many challenging experiences as the eldest child in our busy family. The next step – a very challenging one as it turned out – was to pass through the Sandhurst officer training course. Throughout this course, the young "would-be" officers knew they could be physically attacked at any time (day or night) by a troop of energetic Ghurkha soldiers. At all times they had to be ready to present on parade with clean, ironed shirts and immaculate uniforms – even if they had been up all night wading through mud. A key principle of the training was to take each man to the limit of his/her stamina and strength in the belief that you could never be an effective leader until you had experienced your own frailties.

The army made it clear from the very start that there was absolutely no expectation or intention that these young officers would become regular army officers. When I discussed this at Sandhurst at the dinner given for parents it was explained to me that the army put this (huge) investment into these young people because they knew that those they chose would, sooner or later, become significant people in either business or government. The army needed such people in high places so that there would always be influential people who supported and understood the armed forces.

In fact, Rupert had an amazing spell as a young officer, mostly serving with the Royal Artillery in Germany. Despite his young age he was treated exactly the same as all the other officers – being in charge of a mature group of seasoned soldiers who had to exercise all over Germany with their huge tank-like self-propelled howitzers. He was also lucky enough (as a good skier) to be allocated to be the officer in charge of the regiment's recreational unit which was housed in a comfortable large skiing chalet in Bavaria (I think). Teaching the squaddies to ski and entertaining the landlord's daughters seemed a pretty comfortable posting! He also went on an advanced canoe training exercise in Norway, which involved being thrown off a cliff top strapped in your canoe and falling into roaring rapids in the river below!

Because Rupert was posted abroad most of his army salary was simply paid into his bank account whilst his board and lodging was provided by the army. Better still, he was able to take advantage of very generous tax-free arrangements to buy a smart VW Golf GTI car in Germany. He brought this back to the UK at the end of his service and sold it for a good profit. So, all in all, when Rupert went up to Cambridge he not only had extensive experience of real life but also a large sum of money in the bank. Rupert's experience encouraged Gael to try for the same scheme when it came to her turn to leave school.

1987

From a family perspective the most important event of this year was that Gael met David, the man who would become her husband and father of her three children. Of all our four children Gael had always shown the most amazing quiet stamina and stoicism – whether walking up mountains, enduring rain storms or being lost or injured. Her elder sister Ceri would sometimes complain that nobody understood just how tough Gael was. This was because to all outer appearances Gael appeared very quiet and timid – so much so that her school teachers would express concern about this in her school reports. Sarah and I had no such concerns because we knew that when the going got tough (as it often did with our energetic family) Gael would be the last to give up or complain. We had always wondered how she would ever find a husband who could measure up to these reserves of stamina and steely resolve. As it turned out, David (an officer in the Parachute Regiment) was certainly that man!

Like Rupert, Gael had decided to try for the special army short-service commission scheme for young people with a place at University. Again, like Rupert, she was well equipped both physically and mentally for this challenge – and she already had a place at London University. She, too, passed the officer selection tests but when she returned from taking these tests she told us (with wide-eyed excitement) about the extraordinary young man she had met during the tests. He was tough, big and strong, and had told her about the amazing fierce animals he enjoyed as his pets – Eagle Owls and goodness knows what else. David was going to be a young officer in the elite (and extremely tough) Parachute Regiment. Sarah and I were impressed if a little concerned at the sound of all this! Later that year we would meet David – then a brash young man who did indeed have an extreme physical toughness on the one hand and a limited "army" world view on the other. Here was a man at the top of his young game, super confident and always prepared to express a strong point of view. David was always able to tell us super-dramatic stories of his exploits both inside and outside the army. He had not enjoyed academic work and, from a young age, had made the army his chosen career.

David was a young man who saw the world and all its rights and wrongs in stark black and white. It would be impossible to imagine a human being with more contrasting attitudes and opinions to those held by my dear partner Sue! Both Sue and Sarah were horrified, for slightly different reasons, that Gael might bring such a "trained killer" into our family circle.

Sarah took her responsibilities as a caring mother fairly seriously and launched an all-out attempt to persuade Gael to reconsider her new attachment. She should have realised, of course, that Gael had many of the same forceful personality traits that she had herself. Every ounce of critical talk simply made Gael more determined than ever to stick to her man. And this she duly did (and has done for the last 30-plus years). Finally, in absolute frustration, Sarah kicked Gael out of the family home and told her to go and live with David's family – so she could see what they were really like. The result of this was that Gael that came to live with Sue and me at Millbrook.

ARTHUR YOUNG – February 86 until May 89

My two and a bit years working for Arthur Young (became Ernst and Young) were a useful bridge between full-time work and a new "free" life working to develop Millbrook. I joined AY to try and achieve what I then thought was a useful objective – to write a book which would help people elected into government (primarily local government) manage and direct their officers. I was helped in this by the fact that AY had just had great success with a small black book called "The Manager's Handbook". This book was a best seller to be found in all airport bookshops at the time and the publishers, Harrop, were keen to repeat this success with "The Councillor's Handbook". I also joined AY because the salary was good and I already knew quite a number of the other consultants – either from my time at Cambridge or through the civil service.

Bob Harris, who was the senior partner managing the government side of AY business, was an old contact from Cambridge University – a fellow maths graduate from St Catharine's College. Well organised and well-motivated, Bob was always supportive and certainly believed in the Councillor's Handbook project. But Bob was not very familiar with local government and all its special peculiarities. For this he depended on his right-hand man – Paul Creswell – who was himself an ex-local government officer. Paul was effectively my immediate boss; a bluff and sometimes cynical character. I'm not sure Paul ever really believed in the handbook project which, in one sense, cut across his bread-and-butter work in local authority audit.

The companionship and lively friendships which characterised AY were in sharp contrast to the fairly humdrum and cautious world of local government. This was evident right from the very first week when all the new consultants assembled for a special introductory course at a remote conference centre near the Peak District in Derbyshire. I had taken one of my large flexifoil kites with me for a bit of exercise and entertainment (such kites are common now after the kite surfing boom but were very new in those days). This greatly appealed to a fellow eccentric, Bob Phillips, who had caused some disruption by arriving late on the first day covered in mud and snow. He had decided to walk the last few miles over a route he had planned from a map without realising this took him over wild moorland! Bob was a wizard specialising in the emerging field of Information Technology – he often came to work in skin-tight biking gear and was one of the very bright "geeks" who the senior partners tolerated because of their skills and despite their lack of suits and ties!

There are just two sessions which I still remember from this one-week course out in the moors. The first was entertaining and reasonably useful and relevant. The second turned out to be both instructive and probably "life changing"! In the first we were sorted into various teams – 4 or 5 people in each team – there were about 20-plus people on the course. Our team (which included Bob Phillips) had the challenge of preparing a sales brief to convince a potential client that we were the right people to help them sell a particular design of lawn mower. Our team decided, rather ambitiously as it turned out, to base our presentation primarily upon a video (which we would make) rather than just a written proposal. One of the team was experienced in doing videos and I had a wealth of special knowledge about lawn mowers (from 20 years managing golf courses). We found a strange-looking old coffee machine which the conference centre used as an ornament and this became our new-fangled design for a world-beating mower. We worked frantically late into the night to prepare our report/proposal – the video was scripted and shot and we were ready (just) in time to make our presentation next morning. We were certainly pretty pleased with what we thought would be a brilliantly innovative presentation. We were well aware that the course was not only an introduction but also a clever way of testing the new recruits to see what their true strengths and weaknesses might be.

When our turn came to launch what we imagined would be a

show-stopping performance – I think there were just 20 minutes allocated for each team – we were confounded to discover that the extension leads and adapters we required to operate the video had been removed. Clearly, other teams had their own plans which included the sabotage (by fair means or foul) of other teams' efforts. Of course, this was a useful lesson – consultants aiming to make a presentation did need to make sure all the necessary bits and pieces were going to be available at their potential client's offices. So, in the event, we were stymied and forced to fall back on our limited written material. So we lost our great advantage but the group were kind enough to ask us to show the video after our time slot had gone – they fished out the necessary leads to allow this. We had learned an important lesson – it's not just creativity and imagination which wins business – without the basic practicalities you are not going to get very far. A lesson similar to that which children learn from the nursery story of the tortoise and the hare.

The second session started in a very innocent and low-key way. It was a called a "survival test". Each course participant was handed a set of papers which described a plane crash in the freezing Canadian wilderness. The plane contained a number (12 I think) of items each of which might be useful if the survivors of the crash were to beat the cold and be rescued. These items included such things as matches, warm bedding, foodstuffs, a broken mirror and a burst tyre inner tube – and more which I now forget. The plane was sinking into the lake where it had crashed and the task of each participant in the exercise was to list the 12 items in a priority order so the most important could be collected before the plane sank. We were not allowed to consult others at this stage and were given about 20 minutes to assess the situation and write down our chosen order of priorities. All the sheets listing each of our assessments were then collected by the invigilating team. Nobody knew at this stage what priorities anyone else had listed. At this point, the participants were divided into two teams (about 10 people per team) and each team was allocated a small conference room where they had 3 hours to discuss and review the list of priorities and come up with an agreed team view at the end of the allotted time – or earlier if they could.

No roles or suggested chairmanships were laid down by the survival test organisers – we just had to organise ourselves as best we could. Bear in mind that the members of each team were all experienced business-people, well trained, clever and pretty forceful – otherwise they would not have been recruited by AY. So we had a potential mix of conflicting ideas as each participant worked either to persuade other members of his/her team of the wisdom of his/her initial choices or tried to listen to the arguments of other members of the team which might modify his/her original list. We soon realised that, given the number of forceful characters present, it was not going to be an easy task to reach an agreed conclusion. Different people argued cogently to try and justify their original judgements. Meanwhile each group was being monitored by 2 "examiners", one of whom would be videoing the various interactions within the group.

Working in groups and committees had always been a big feature of my own work both in Whitehall and in Westminster. It was always an enjoyable challenge to see how the dynamics of such groups could be managed and gently channelled into what seemed (to me) the best outcome. So here was a fine opportunity for me to put these skills into practice. First of all, it was necessary to keep one's own position hidden and allow other members of the team to start to express their views. It was hardly ever a good idea to openly contradict a proposal that ran counter to your own priorities – direct opposition would frequently simply harden the determination of the proposer. But over a period of time it should be possible to form soft alliances with others in the group who appeared to share similar priorities to one's own. Gentle humour was the most effective way to undermine those whose views opposed one's own. If there was factual information which I could provide for the group then this could be a powerful influence on their thinking. (I was particularly aware from direct experience at Millbrook that it would be extremely difficult to light a fire using the wet and rotten branches which were likely to be available.)

Slowly but steadily (over 2 hours or more) I was able to build a consensus within the group as to the most likely best order of priorities. We had no personal antagonisms, no harsh words or unresolved disputes. One member of the team remained almost silent throughout the exercise so we never really got the benefit of his views – we'll call him Mr X. Our team reached its "team priority" list before the end of the allotted time. Eleven of us were all delighted with our team result despite the fact that Mr X disagreed with all of the rest of us. We had enjoyed the cut and thrust of the arguments and really felt quite elated with our camaraderie. In fact, most of us remained close friends throughout our time with AY and some for many years thereafter. We presented our team list to the invigilators and enjoyed a nice cup of tea whilst we waited for the feedback and "correct" answer from the organisers.

When all the participants in the course had sat down the organisers were able to rank each person's "strength" as a committee negotiator by comparing individual results with the final team list. We heard first of all that the other team had totally failed to reach any agreed conclusion. In fact, the arguments in that group had become so strong and personal that the invigilators had to stop the exercise before violence broke out. Our group (or "my" group as I felt I should call it), on the other hand, had reached a very friendly, almost unanimous, verdict (Mr X dissenting) well inside the allotted time limit. Even more surprising, my group were astonished to find that their final "team" priority list was almost exactly the same as the list I had handed in before the team session began (10 of the 12 items were the same, I recall). Members of "my" team turned to me with amazement to ask how I had been able to achieve this without them even realising I had a list to defend. The only problem was that the list we (I) had opted for was a totally wrong answer. The correct answer had been prepared by a group of Canadian mounted policemen who had great experience of wilderness survival. I would certainly have led all my team to their deaths! Mr X, on the other hand, who had said so little, had in fact written down a completely correct set of priorities. (In fact, as it turned out, Mr X was sacked from AY a few months later – he was not a good communicator!)

With the exception of Mr X, our team had a good laugh about this conclusion even though it was such a grand failure. We had enjoyed the whole experience and made some lasting friendships. It was a shock for me, of course, to realise that my leadership and persuasion had evidently been disastrously misdirected. Things then got worse (for me) when the examiners told the group that my performance as a "leader" had been one of the most masterful they had ever seen. Video clips were shown as they described a showcase of clever manipulations which I had deployed to channel, bit by bit, the views of other members of the group. This was quite a revelation to me showing, as it did, how cunning and ruthless I had become in trying to get my own way. I vowed from that moment on that I would not again take a "leadership" role in any group because I could not trust myself to be working for the right answer. Many of the behaviours I had learned would now have to be changed – and changed they were. So the exercise really was a profound shock, revealing, as it did, some of the manipulative behaviours I was able to deploy so easily. Even today, more than 30 years later, the lessons of that day in Derbyshire are still very much with me!

Once back at my desk in Rolls House, Fetter Lane, it was time to get moving with the work for the Councillor's Handbook. The layout, patterns of language and general approach would have to try and follow those of the earlier "Manager's Handbook". There were many lessons to be explained. My general mission/objective was, of course, to show elected politicians how their full-time officers/staff were able to hold such a strong hand in protecting their own activities and preferences as opposed to helping politicians achieve stated manifesto policies.

One of the most conspicuous resource gaps in local government has always been the failure of paid officers to provide specific personal support for elected councillors. Most of the Whitehall civil service is, in fact, working directly in this role, writing speeches, issuing press releases and changing laws in order to fulfil (as far as sensibly possible) the wishes of the elected government. All government Ministers have a well-resourced private office connecting them to their departments on the one hand and the public/media on the other. Very few chairmen of local authority committees have anything like this level of support. Full-time officers can easily bamboozle their politicians with legal mumbo-jumbo and over-complex regulations. It's the easiest trick in the book simply to provide elected politicians with so much information and so many meetings to attend that they cannot wade through it all. The sheer pressure of the diary and the in-tray defeat any chance of even remembering what one's elected priorities might have been! The AY "Councillor's Handbook" would strip all this away and provide local politicians with a new template to better arrange their official support and departments.

When the book was finally published, we were pretty pleased with it and began to try and distribute our wisdom into the local government scene. It soon became obvious that we were up against the very feature which the book highlighted, namely the de facto control which full-time experienced government officials hold over busy part-time elected councillors. Naturally the officers (who would be the ones to provide funds and information for buying the book for members) were extremely hostile to our initiatives. It was an uphill task to make the book effective. But, in the event, this was to prove irrelevant as the publishers (Harrop) were almost immediately taken over by a larger firm. The new organisation had no interest in our local government project and so the promotion of our book was stopped.

Elsewhere in AY my "bread and butter" work involved the compulsory management reviews of local government activities which the Audit Commission rules (and government legislation) had introduced. While the accounting arm of AY did the formal audit (for Kent CC and Newham CC) we, on the management consultancy side, carried out a number of reviews in various areas of management (schools, road maintenance, building programmes etc.). So I found myself frequently going down to Newham or even further afield, to Kent (Maidstone). Newham was a strong Labour-run council, totally dominated by councillors who were all members (or even officials) of the National Union of Teachers. At this time, the Labour local authorities were often run by councillors who worked as council employees in neighbouring Labour councils and were active trade unionists. It was a case of "you scratch my back and I'll scratch yours" – a very dubious practice that was most definitely not in the public interest. Newham was a very badly run council with enormous inefficiencies and enormous preference given to jobs for trade union members. I wrote several very critical reports which had to be presented to the council members – but this was, of course, a complete waste of time because nobody in the council was ever going to do anything about it! The senior officers (many of whom were councillors in neighbouring authorities) would simply laugh as I described my findings as they assured me that nothing would be done – except to throw the report into the waste bin as soon as I (AY) left the building.

In Kent, on the other hand, we had a Tory council who enjoyed a comfortable relationship with their officers. Both officers and councillors would pay lip service to our findings and recommendations but, again, very few practical changes were likely to be made. Nobody really wanted to "rock the boat" and the public and press really had neither the interest nor the means to make a fuss about inefficiencies. We simply went through the motions of doing these management reviews without any expectation that our findings would change anything. The whole process was extremely expensive – very time-wasting and tiring for me with all the travelling and interviews which it required. Fact finding was never easy in local government (or corporations) because senior staff (and most of those supporting them) had a strong vested interest in maintaining the status quo. From their point of view almost any change would likely be a change for the worse so they were always very cagey about telling the truth. Right at the end of a one-hour interview we would finish with the usual pleasantries and thanks. I would always finish – sometimes as the interviewee got up to leave – by asking "is there anything else you would like to mention?" This was the only chance I would normally get to hear something of real relevance – "Oh yes, there is just one thing…. The other source of relevant information was usually found by talking to the office cleaners or delivery drivers – they had nothing to lose by telling the truth and many of them would have been working in the business much longer than people working further up the hierarchy.

In practice you could get a good idea about whether a large organisation was well managed by simply looking at the various noticeboards around the premises – and checking to see if all the clocks were running at the correct time. Out-of-date and messy noticeboards and broken clocks were always a sign of bigger problems elsewhere.

Once I moved away from London and up to Millbrook, it became more and more difficult to take the AY job seriously. Anyway my time was increasingly taken up with developing Millbrook and looking after a new baby. At first I was able to drop my full-time job and begin to work as an independent contractor arranging AY work within my own timetable. But this, too, became tiresome and my days of wearing a suit and tie finally came to an end in 1988.

My Time with Sue 1985–89

Some time before 1985 (Liz Meek will remember) I found myself sitting next to a cheery, somewhat quirky, lady at a Christmas lunch with the Meeks at their home in Clapham. This turned out to be Sue Woodward – one of Liz's very oldest friends. They had grown up together as neighbours near Uttoxeter. After lunch Sue and I went out to a cold windswept park and had great fun together flying one of my kites. Sue had a very different take on life to the one I was used to in business and Whitehall. She was working as an occupational therapist with mentally handicapped people and had a burning desire to do good in what seemed to her to be a world moving at speed towards destruction. Perceptive, well-educated and well read, Sue lived and worked in a world radically different from my own. She loved good food and clearly enjoyed the physical battle she had to fly the big kite which we tussled with together with great amusement. We would keep in touch by exchanging letters on several occasions after this first meeting.

In 1985 I decided to visit Sue in her rather miserable little flat where she worked in Buxton. Again we found many things to talk about and she introduced me to the magazine *Resurgence,* which I began to subscribe to. (*Resurgence* had been started by John Papworth, who I would meet later.) The ideas and personalities in Resurgence showed me a new dimension in life and I decided to take this further by setting up a Resurgence Readers' Group in London. I asked the magazine to publish my invitation and I duly met up with a group of fellow Resurgence readers, several of whom would become life-long friends. Alan Senior, Diana Johnson and Christina Matthews were three such people. We began a series of regular meetings in pubs around London where we could discuss our ideas and share information about other events, books or people. Eventually these meetings led me to set up and publish my own 'alternative' magazine 'Ideas for Tomorrow Today", which was designed and each issue laid out by Alan Senior.

I kept in touch with Sue by letter and by phone on and off during 1985 and more so during 1986, when Scilla's desire to have children got the better of her and our relationship came to an end. But at this stage I really had no inkling of any serious romantic attachment – we were good friends with shared common interests and we enjoyed a good night out at the pub or concert together. When it came to the summer of 1986 I was already separating from Scilla so I invited Sue to join me with the kids on what had become our annual sailing holiday off the wild north west coast of Scotland. We had a wonderful time and enjoyed the long evenings, after dropping anchor, by sharing a few glasses of whisky together. I began to realise that our friendship was deepening into something more.

After the sailing holiday together I think we both realised that something more important might be happening. When Sue came up to London for my birthday, we stayed at Bergholt Mews together for the first time and a new era had truly begun.

Sue and Dylan rowing together in Scotland

Dear darling crazy Susan – how wonderful yet how complicated and finally destructive! Who could have known after that lovely Christmas dinner at the Meeks how our careless laughter would ultimately turn to tears? Susan was a very different creature from any of my previous lovers/partners – very alternative, very artistic as well as being very passionate and committed to her own beliefs. Her view of the world, and the large group of alternative friends who came with it, showed me a radically different way of thinking and being. This was mostly refreshing but often puzzling as so much of it contradicted the culture of business and profit in which I had been immersed.

After we had spent that wonderful holiday together sailing off the NW coast of Scotland we began to talk seriously about living together. Sue was somewhat ambivalent about this prospect and tried to warn me that I was taking on a complicated person who had already suffered serious emotional and psychological traumas. She made me read the essay she had written at school as a young teenager after the horrific accidental death of her brother. It was already clear to me that Sue felt completely unloved and betrayed by her parents. Her mother, who had been a youngest child and seemingly very spoilt, seemed to regard her only daughter as competition for the father's attention. Her father had, Sue said, only really been interested in the son who might take over running his farm. This dynamic had resulted in Sue being sent off (very miserable and bitter) to boarding school while her brother remained at home – the "apple of his parents' eyes"! Very shortly after starting her boarding school life, Sue received the terrible news that her only real friend, her brother, had died in a tragic farm accident; he had "drowned" after being sucked down into the moving grain hopper as it emptied.

When all this happened Sue was already feeling great anger and misery because of her newly enforced separation from her dear brother. It is hard to imagine how these feelings must have been amplified by news of the tragedy. Sue never forgave her parents and, of course, they, in their turn, never recovered from the loss of their son – their great hope for the future.

Sue's complicated and bitter feelings towards her parents were amplified almost every time we met them. Her mother never missed an opportunity to criticise her daughter whilst her father was like a profit-driven automaton, determined to extract the maximum yield from his land whatever the long-term cost (this stood against everything Sue believed, sacrificing the health of the Earth for profit). Year after year, their fields were planted with cash crop barley. It seemed that her father's addiction to work had become his only escape from the anger and bitterness caused by his son's death.

When Sue moved down to work in Dorset I would often drive down late on a Friday night to meet up for a pub supper and then we'd often go back to her small home to listen to Carmina Burana – a piece which she loved. Over the weekend we'd go on long cycle rides or walks in the strange Dorset valleys with their many old stone age forts and barrows. On so many things Sue had a completely different take on life to myself. She introduced me to many new books and ideas. Sue's capacity for unrestrained joy was wonderfully infectious – whether racing downhill on our bikes or enjoying a pint of good beer with roast beef and all the trimmings. During such moments the dark shadows which hung about her life seemed very far away.

After Sue had died I found the original typed version of the story which she had written as a young teenager at school. Written in pencil at the end was a brief sentence which simply announced that she (Sue) hoped to join her brother soon! I finally understood then that Sue probably made up her mind to kill herself many years before. The rest of her life, as I later realised, was lived in the shadow of the deception which this inner decision required. Perhaps, in one way, life was simply a gigantic experiment for her with all sorts of experiences to be sought after and (hopefully) enjoyed. We shall never really know.

Very early in our relationship, Sue told me the story of her unnerving experience with an old lady she met on a train journey. In conversation the lady told Sue that she was a "reader of palms" and asked Sue if she would like to have her palm read. Laughing, Sue said "of course" – and showed the lady her open hand. The lady looked at it for several minutes and then became very grave. "What's the matter?" asked Sue. "I won't say" said the lady and quietly gave Sue back her hand. I often wondered, as one strange thing after another took place, just what exactly was this dark kind of "black magic" that seemed to follow Sue in her life. Sue's experience with the palm reader certainly stayed with her for the rest of her life. Deep down she did feel cursed somehow – as the letter she wrote to go with her Will would show when I found it after her death.

Sue was very pleased when she became pregnant – another great adventure. Little Hal was born in Bedford in June 1988 without any complications and a new phase in our lives had begun. Busy summer days passed quickly and life seemed good. But all was not well in Sue's mind.

In January 1989 I already knew that Sue was going through some very difficult inner torments. She began to have great doubts about her abilities as a mother. On two occasions she had "accidents" which might have killed Hal – once dropping him at the top of the stairs, another time letting go of the pram at the top of the hill in front of the Chequers pub. No damage was done but this was a bit scary to say the least! Sue began to seek help and advice from all sorts of health and social workers including the local GP who (I did not know it at the time) prescribed some sort of tranquilisers. Also unknown to me, after our first Christmas together with Hal, Sue had made a Will which was witnessed by Gael but kept secret from me (as I found after Sue's death). Sue had also obviously talked to the young lady GP about her problems but, again, I was never told (because of patient confidentiality)!

This was the text of the letter Sue left with her Will:

"I seem to have become such a changed person – selfish, negative and absent minded. All this in the lap of plenty – with beautiful Millbrook, William, Hal and boundless opportunities to garden, create and thrive.

I seem to be destroying it all – to fulfil my own expectations of myself.

William you've loved me – and for that incredible fact thank you. My emptiness never came up with the bread and cheese as often as was needed.

Hal – I want to release you to the energetic positive world that William occupies. There's so much to learn from him about living. I don't match my words with my actions.

My love for all of you is in there but it's locked away and I'm too confused and lost to find and follow the way to unlock it."

There were several earlier events that seemed to reflect the shadow of this "curse". Soon after Sue and I began living together I was struck down with a serious, and very painful, back injury. This came "out of the blue" to someone who was generally very strong and fit and who had hardly ever been ill in his life before. I was painfully crippled for almost a year. Was this a portent of Sue's seemingly harmful super-natural baggage?

Months later we had another incident – unhappy for me – which I will never forget after the strange ceremony which Sue and I performed over the foundations for the new house we were building together at Millbrook. It was a lovely summer day and we were alone together overlooking the newly dug foundations after the concrete had been poured. We had kept the half-finished bottle of whisky we had enjoyed on that epic Scottish sailing holiday. It seemed opportune to bury this catalyst for our love under the new house we planned to share together. We both took hold of the bottle and then dropped it into the wet concrete and pushed it under. After a contemplative silence I turned to Sue and told her what a great omen this was for our future – she replied (to my surprise) that it felt more like a funeral to her! This might have been a clue to the future but afterwards Sue was very careful to keep her plans well hidden – sharing bits of the story with some but never revealing the whole. I began to realise that I was living with a person whose real self was hidden like the bulk of a huge iceberg underneath the fun and routines of daily life.

Later in 1989 Sue's mood and behaviour did not improve and she was not able to share her true thoughts and feelings with me.

On her birthday in May we went down to stay with good friend Mike Bertele in Salisbury. The spring weather was beautiful. Sue was behaving in a very peculiar way and we spent a long time walking quietly around the graves in the cemetery at Salisbury cathedral. We hardly spoke a word on the long journey home. As we lay together in bed I explained my frustrations at not knowing what was going on in her mind. She simply could not and would not share her feelings with me. I told her that we really had to try and sort things out and suggested that we ask for help from one of my very good Cambridge friends who was an experienced consultant psychiatrist in the NHS. In fact this was the last serious conversation we had.

There was nothing particularly out of the ordinary during the day before Sue killed herself. The weather was fine, the day's routines went by and we snuggled up together in bed to sleep. I woke up early on a fine sunny morning to find Sue had disappeared. There was no note, no clue as to where she might have gone. But I did get a nasty shock when the first thing I saw through my bleary early-morning eyes was the (to me) wicked looking witch's face which seemed to be staring up from Sue's discarded clothes which were on top of a suitcase! I took a photo because this seemed so bizarre – some kind of totem for the "curse" which Sue felt she lived under?

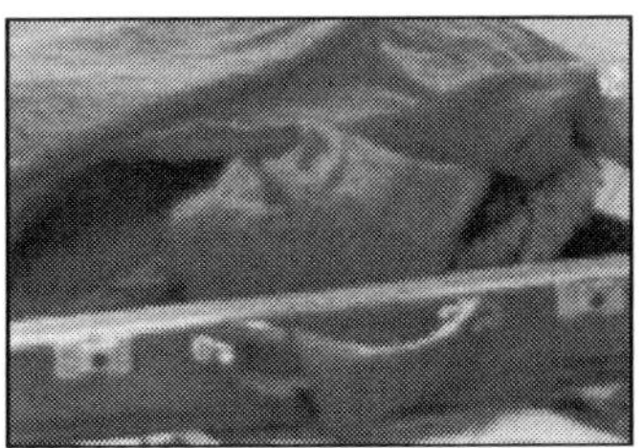

I assumed, because the day was so fine, that Sue might have gone for a long walk in the woods to places we had enjoyed so much together. I set out to search for her but after several hours found no sign. Ron Mills and the other golf course workers also continued the search but found nothing. I began ringing some of her friends as I thought she might have gone off to stay for some reason. Late in the day, still with no news, I rang the local GP, a young lady doctor who I knew Sue had seen several times. It turned out that the doctor had given Sue some pretty powerful drugs in attempts to resolve her depression. Needless to say, Sue, being a somewhat chaotic person, was hopeless at taking such drugs properly and I was unaware of what was going on because neither Sue nor the young doctor would tell me. The doctor immediately told me to ring the police – clearly she knew very well that Sue was a suicide risk. I felt extremely angry to have been kept in the dark about what was going on – the doctor had not told me because of patient confidentiality. Of course neither Gael nor Sue had told me about her making a Will earlier in the year and none of the various social workers had taken me into their confidence.

I realised after Sue killed herself that the strange weekend we had had in Dorset was the scene of Sue's final struggles with herself and her commitment to make an end of her life. I realised that she must have been feeling an enormous pressure because she could sense I was becoming determined to try and discover just what her inner demons were. She had made her plans many months before and knew all along that she must kill herself before Hal was old enough to really know her. It was no wonder she found life, and having a close relationship, such a strain! How far the common problems of post-natal depression and the drugs she did or did not take were really responsible we shall never know. It really was a remarkable achievement for Sue to be able to conceal so much of what was going on in her life and her mind from me while, at the same time, she was sharing some of these concerns with others, whether friends or social workers.

So the local police and fire brigade duly arrived on the scene. Some hours later when the ambitious young senior detective arrived to take charge (from Luton) I realised that he regarded me as a prime murder suspect. This was not pleasant and very scary – there were no witnesses to anything! The police tried to wrong-foot me by arriving unannounced at 4am next morning to search the house – luckily Egon, my dog, alerted me so I was ready for them. In fact, their search was pretty incompetent – they did not look under the hidden trapdoor inside the front door; they did not look for or find Sue's Will and her last note to me (which I only found much later when looking through her papers). Finally her body was found after the irrigation tank had been drained. And, luckily for me, the local PC from Ampthill, who knew us all well, persuaded the slick young detective that it was simply a ridiculous idea to imagine I might have killed Sue.

It only remained for me to go up to the morgue in Bedford and identify the body – a very sad business – and await the hearing in the coroner's court (which would not happen for some months). There was the funeral to arrange and many close friends to speak to and try to comfort. Meantime another potential disaster hit us. Poor little Hal fell extremely ill with measles (which was not diagnosed by the local GP who simply, and very wrongly, prescribed antibiotics). Fortunately Ceri's partner Riaan was a paediatric doctor whose correct diagnosis probably saved Hal's life – Riaan told me that the antibiotics were absolutely the worst thing to give. We must just keep Hal cool so his body could fight through the virus infection – eventually he did and emerged no worse for wear – but it was a worrying time.

I was fortunate to have the help and support of the local Quakers both at the funeral and afterwards. Calm, quiet and sensible – they were wonderful. The aftermath of suicide is full of self-blame and the constant thought of what one might have done to have avoided the catastrophe. Everyone has their own take on the possible reasons. But, in the end, it's hopeless to try and understand what was really going on in the troubled mind of the friend, lover, son or daughter. What is done is done and we'll never ever know the true reasons. It is very tempting to blame yourself and blame others – the emotional scars are deep and painful. Certainly Sue succeeded in one of her chief aims, which was to hit back at her poor parents with a vengeance for the way they had treated her and the way she felt they had let her brother die. In her will she gave them back the little car they had given her.

I certainly felt very angry and very sad that all the bits and pieces which Sue had put in place for her secret plans had been kept secret from me although many other individuals knew about important parts of these plans – particularly the young lady GP doctor in Ampthill. Since this time I have heard other distressed husbands telling similar stories on radio interviews – how their wives (partners) had been sharing their suicidal urges with the local doctors but "patient confidentiality" had prevented these doctors warning the husbands of the situation.

Postscript

Sue had made it clear in her Will that she did not wish to be buried in the family plot which had been purchased by her parents and where her brother's body lay. She wanted her ashes to be scattered at the top of the great mountains of Knoydart – a wild place overlooking the Scottish islands where she had always felt so happy. Rightly or wrongly I decided that I wanted our son Hal to be involved in this important mission so that he might have memories of some kind of closure for his lost mother. So after the cremation I kept Sue's ashes on my office windowsill for the next 4 years.

A month or two after Sue's death I was visited once again by what seemed to be the super-natural events that had shadowed Sue. In the pitch black of a summer's night I was woken by an enormous roaring noise. I leaped out of bed and looked out of my window. Roaring and foaming down the driveway there rushed a six-foot-high wave of brown water! As the torrent crashed away past the house into the trees, I wondered what on earth could have happened. I got up and walked up the steep slope through the trees towards Ron Mills' house and the workshops. There I found the metal sides of the irrigation tank (where Sue had died) had been smashed to pieces – presumably by a lightning strike during the storm which had raged over Millbrook the previous evening. We never rebuilt the tank but dug out a big "swimming pool" higher up the hill and this became the all-important reservoir for our irrigation system.

Thunder and lightning would hit us again 4 years later when I travelled with Hal, Dylan and the Meeks to Scotland on a mission to scatter Sue's ashes. The mountains of Knoydart are on a virtually inaccessible, privately owned peninsula almost opposite to Skye. Access is either by a very long walk or, more easily, by boat. Once again we chartered a yacht from Ardvasar in Skye and made the short trip over to anchor off Knoydart. Taking rucksacks, picnic, survival gear and the ashes, we set off on the long climb. It was a fine day when we started but as we neared the summit (probably a couple of hours later) we were suddenly caught up in a mighty storm. Once again it seemed that the "curse" which followed Sue had somehow caught up with us! Thunder and lightning crashed around us and a wild gale of wind brought hailstones and freezing cold. This reminded me of the storm which had destroyed the tank where Sue died just a few months after the tragedy! With the young Meek children and Hal wrapped up in survival blankets we could go no further. There was a steep slope of perhaps 400 yards leading up to the summit. Dylan had come with us; he raced off into the storm and up to the mountain top where he let the ashes fly out into the storm. It was a dramatic scene as we looked out over the magnificent views to the west. Fifteen minutes later the storm had subsided and we plodded down the mountain knowing that we had finally fulfilled Sue's final wishes.

I will not deny that the months after Sue's death were an extremely testing time of emotional turmoil. Life had to go on – but it was exhausting trying to explain (as best I could) to our many friends what had happened. Everybody seemed to have their own theories as to reasons! On the practical side, I had domestic help from a local girl, Sue Harvey (who had been a witness to Sue's Will) and later from Ceri and Gael's school friend Helen (who would later become Rupert's wife). But running a business and being a new single parent posed quite a challenge. Many friends and all my family did what they could to support me. It did not help that we had to wait until August for the formal Inquest on Sue's death. Here is the report of that Inquest as reported by the local newspaper from 4 August 1989.

TRAGIC MUM DROWNED IN WATER TANK

TRAGIC mother Susan Woodward left her home early one morning, tied a concrete block around her neck and jumped into a nine foot deep water tank.

A Bedford inquest was told that the 37-year-old Millbrook woman had a history of depression which began when her brother died at the age of 14.

By HERALD STAFF

The father of her child, who she lived with, golf club owner William Sutherland said that about four months after the birth of their son in June, 1988, Susan became worried and depressed.

He added that although she had showed signs of depression in the past he became increasingly concerned about her state of mind.

On May 2 this year he awoke at about 6am to find that Susan was not in bed — but he did not think it unusual as she often went for early walks.

During the day he rang friends, her doctor and searched the area but when she had not returned by the evening he informed the police.

Susan's body was recovered next morning from a water tank on Millbrook golf course after an intensive police search.

Pc John Chisholm told the inquest that there was a set of steps nearby which he believed she had used to climb into the tank. A length of cord and pair of scissors were also found nearby.

Pathologist Dr Michael Heath who examined the body said the cause of death was drowning and there was nothing to suggest there had been a struggle involving a third party.

Coroner Malcom Weir, returning a verdict of suicide said there could be no doubt that Susan knew what she was doing and the consequences of her actions.

In the spotlight

RURAL housing problems came under the spotlight at a special seminar hosted by Mid Beds Council at Haynes Village Hall.

Representatives from towns and parishes throughout the district heard speakers from the Department of the Environment and the National Agricultural Centre Rural Trust.

District council chiefs explained their policy of encouraging house building for villagers so giving them a chance to stay in their own communities.

A spokesman told the Herald: "It was stressed that such houses could only be sanctioned to meet local need and could not be accompanied by any speculative development."

The final twist in my superstitions about the super-natural came about one late night several years later (in Ireland) when I decided to talk about Sue's death with my new partner Angela. I did not often dwell on the painful events of 1989 but on this occasion I was sharing my feelings with Angela. We were sitting in the dark in the upstairs front room at Killowen overlooking the great River Barrow just a few hundred yards away. The only lights we could see were the bright navigation lights on the river. No sooner had I begun my reflections when all the lights went out. This was a bit spooky. When we opened the room door we found that our lights, too, had gone out. A major power failure had just taken place – another strange coincidence!

MY QUEST 4

After meeting Sue and her very different circle of friends, my perceptions of the world began to change. I could see more and more clearly that the workings of the conventional world (which I had very much been a part of) were taking the Earth in dangerous and potentially uncomfortable directions. But did I, or anyone else, have the wit and courage to do anything about it? My reflections are summed up well in the poem I wrote in 1987 (with apologies, of course, to William Blake!):

TICK TOCK TYGER
Another letter, an essay, a pinprick in the day.
How many more? Well, who can say?
When and if these words impress, time runs on, come what may.

A play, a film, a talk – they surely stir the pot
but ease the deadly set routine? That they do not.
Another bus, work, shop, perhaps a song or fresh ice cream;
bizarre reflections of man's urban full-employment dream.

But we owe it to ourselves – and to those who will go on
to fight against the numbing grind, the barely hidden con,
the smalltalk, tin thrills and drugs that lubricate and blunt

the slowly moving edge between what is and what we want.

Aha, you say (and you have your right) but what about
those magic shafts of love, of light, of happiness no doubt?
A game, a smile, or a kiss that's thrilling
Can they not bring worth to this parody of living?

These and their like make some better currency of life.
Art, culture, sport, technology replacing strife,
all miracles woven from our talent here on living earth.
They too stand proof against the nightmare curse.

Not quite I think.
Below the superficial wins and losses lies a deeper struggle.
It battles ever onward from primeval cosmic muddle.
All else depends on this ... what was and is.
Pyramid on pyramid and pyramid within pyramid;
Life is living and dying, ready for threshing,
rising and falling with wild intermeshing.

Life that fights entropic rules invented by our brightest fools.
All seeking beauty in the cosmic dance,
this intimate embrace with strange laws of chance.
Time flirts with destiny in a one way street
Embracing unknown future and a past now neat.

Complexity on complexity and challenge upon challenge.
Our human cultures weave and whirl,
playing creation's latest game on earth's green living pearl.
Social and religious threads weave as evolution smiles,
an interwoven quilt for a dance brim-full with guiles.

No peace, no rest, no simple stasis;
life always finds some new and magic races.
Forward, onward, never stopping;
it's not the same as going shopping.

This much we've learned as the years went by.
It all seems simple now.
Our youthful passion and wild growth die
and it's sad to see just how.

Take a breath, survey the scene, keep your senses eagle-keen.
The force of life will not be denied, its urgings never satisfied.
But who knows where its flame will flare
in this harsh game of truth or dare.

Are you one to carry this shimmering torch?
Our tick tock tyger can change its course.
Don't leave historians to decide who's boss
in abstract diversions that argue the toss.

Today, like you, I wonder what to do and how to act.
I hold our tyger by its tail like millions more beside,
"to tweak this tail or leave the sparky beast intact?"
that's what I must decide.

How's your hand on the tyger's tail?
Conscience and inner spirit want to pull,
but pragmatic sense and outright fear combine to let it lull.
One or two small steps may slowly boost resolve
or add excuse for letting bright hopes dissolve,
frozen in an agony of sloth about how and when we cut our cloth.

But will the present look so bright in 20 years from now?
We have to LIVE our lives or drift, if we don't know how.

So how, just how, will efforts rally to the test?
Our friend the Tyger awakened and yet still tamed?
With courage, good humour and resolve – that's best
but much more too:

with thought, perceptive wisdom and not against the grain.
It won't be easy, with progress measured by the pain.

The murderous engines of our consuming need.
They clank and roar in the name of greed.
While politicians prance and prattle
as if they think we're stupid cattle?
Poor people march in dust and pain
while dodging clouds of poison rain.

Mass media fawn and call it heretic
to question smart political rhetoric.
Stored sunlight of a million years
is swallowed cheap, paid in arrears.
This grinding beast takes over lives
and scarce much sanity now survives.

The winners strut as they rip and slash
to mine sweet Earth and make their stash.
We watch. We cringe. We run. We stare.
at this manic genie from Pandora's snare.
Nature smashed by man's destruction
with barren hope of reconstruction.

Machines created to destroy. How we love them, man and boy.
Such fun to play this acquisition game.
Dehumanizing mammon is its other name.
By flame and radiation, by poison and starvation,
All routes to hell without salvation.

Cry: "Stop – our babies, flowers and songs – our joy, it will survive!"
Our Tyger smiles and purrs with grief; however hard we strive
these smash like muslin covered jelly facing Inter City 125.

"No war – please, please, no hunger here about...."
Why waste your words with such a shout

when Tyger's laughing the whole world over
at battles fuelled by greed and power.

"Turn back the clock...." is a joke that's cruel!
Do you think sweet Tyger is a blooming fool.
The thought, dear friends, mocks many years
of human history full of tears.

But watch the sun slide up, the mist, the dew
and hear the birds welcome life anew.
See order, strength and beauty too.
Now just what else can that Tyger do?

Praise God, the Buddha, the Life Force or what you will
Wild Tyger knows FREE WILL is with us still.
Today is real and time ticks on.
Have you the strength to live your song?

Life at Millbrook

For more than 25 years, work and play at Millbrook were a central and sometimes dominant part of my life. In one very real sense Millbrook (beautiful and challenging as it now is) must be the largest "mark" I have left in the sands of time! The opportunity to work and engage with the natural world in a "hands on" and physical way has always been a great source of calm and satisfaction. Perhaps I learned this from my father, for whom work on the farm was almost a religion; perhaps it's just something that's hard wired into my genes.

From the start in 1976 there were two philosophical imperatives for Millbrook: first the golf course should be challenging but fair; second the land, the plants and animals on it should always be managed without poisons or chemicals. We would move the least possible amount of earth in creating the course, using the natural contours as much as possible. We would plant tens of thousands of trees that would, in time, completely change both landscape and climate. As far as we could, we would try to encourage sporting matchplay golf rather than fall into the trap of the remorseless (and difficult) tests required by "medal" golf. The design of the course would require golfers to use their brains as well as their skill and, as far as possible, avoid the rigours of "target" golf. In "target" golf (which has become very prevalent both in the USA and many modern newly designed courses) the golfer is shown a "target" area, usually delineated by bunkers and/or rough, where he should aim to place his shot. If he misses the "target" area (perhaps the green itself) then the hazards will almost certainly ensure that he drops (at least) one shot. There is no graduated punishment here – even being a few inches outside the "target" area will leave you in a bunker and cost you a shot.

On older more traditional and particularly seaside "links" courses, the golfer faces a more subtle and graduated punishment for a misplaced shot. He can see there is an optimal place to put his shot but if he misses this ideal position his next shot will simply be made more challenging. The further away he is from the ideal landing area then the greater the challenge facing him. This challenge may arise from the lie of the land (humps and bumps), the length of the grass (rough or semi-rough), or trees impeding the shot. A wayward shot should also require the golfer to negotiate a more difficult angle of approach into the green. If sand bunkers are to form part of this challenge then they should be of a design which may allow a good player to recoup much of his lost ground (not a deep pot bunker for example). The aim in the design of Millbrook was to use this principle as far as possible rather than relying on the brutal logic of pure "target" golf.

When knowledgeable golfers (often from elite clubs) asked me how I chose the members for my club I always replied that the design of the first hole was what "chose" the members. Why? Well the first hole is not a conventional golf hole! For the player's first shot, the aim is not to hit the greatest distance – quite the contrary, the aim is to place the ball in a sensible position which makes the second shot easiest. It is the second shot which "tests" the player's skill and daring because the first green (a large double green twinned with the 16th) is just over 200 yards away across a deep valley. Of course, the player can "bail out" by just hitting a simple second shot down into the valley, leaving a short but "blind" shot at the green. This requires a critical and, for many, a very challenging decision very early in the round. The true Millbrook enthusiast will enjoy challenges of this kind – others will claim the hole is either unfair or too difficult.

So what is "organic" golf course management?

For anyone running a golf course prior to the Second World War this question would simply be meaningless. At that time (and all times before) there was no great influx or availability of powerful chemicals for pest control, weed control or added fertility. Soon after the war everything changed (for agriculture generally not just golf course management); it seemed that industry could provide a "magical" chemical for every need! Powerful nerve agents would kill worms and leather jackets (the larvae of the daddy longlegs which eat grass roots); selective weedkillers would kill daisies and all broad-leaved weeds; modified output from explosives factories would provide massive boosts of nitrogen, potash and phosphorus to feed the grass.

My own experience as a teenager working on the course at Dunstanburgh gave me first-hand experience of the traditional ways of management. Early every morning, ideally before golfers appeared on the course, I would collect my switch (a long bamboo pole with thin 6 foot fibre glass tip) and my rake from the shed and walk around the south end of the course while Jock Arnott (the other greenkeeper) walked around the north end. Mr Thompson (the head greenkeeper) would start up his magnificent converted lorry to begin mowing the fairways. Our job was to "switch" the greens – sweep them with our long switches – in order to remove the dew (work it into the grass so it did some good rather than evaporating away) but, more important, spread out the worm casts and flick away the "crow pecks" so the greens were clear for play. The "crow pecks" were small bits of turf ripped up by the crows during the night as they picked out and ate the leatherjackets which lived under the surface. The worms were aerating the greens 24 hours each day and their worm casts brought up fine soil to the surface where we effectively brushed it in as a light top dressing. We used our rakes to smooth out every bunker we passed so that over-night marks made by birds, rabbits or dogs would be removed to make the bunkers fit for play.

This was a daily routine. If we found a broadleaved weed in the greens we would simply dig it out by the root with one quick thrust of a sharp penknife – similarly with weeds found in the bunkers. Greens were cut by hand-pushed many-bladed mowers which were set up with the precision of fine Swiss watches – they just purred over the surface sending up a fine mist of cuttings which were blown away (not collected) by the breeze. The idea of irrigating greens with piped water was unheard of until people saw the extraordinary watered greens which the TV showed from America. The seaside greens were all made up of fine dwarf fescue grasses which simply went dormant and brown in summer sun – they soon greened up again when September rains appeared.

The smoothness and fertility of greens was maintained by applying regular small amounts of "top dressing" which we made up ourselves. This was a mixture of fine sieved sandy loam (which we could dig out in large quantities from the hillside of Tom Ha's hill), with dried blood and bonemeal added. We could also buy in dressing made from seaweed. This management regime was a well-tried and effective one used by golf courses over many years until the advent of chemical farming after the war.

These were the techniques and background which I brought to Millbrook from the very beginning. Of course, by this time the use of hand mowing had been overtaken by the very effective 3-reel hydraulic units pioneered by Toro, and golfers were no longer prepared to accept the annoyance of loose cuttings lying on the green. I still enjoyed the early morning patrol with switch and rake, walking through the dew as the sun rose higher and feeling that this simple physical contact with the golf course gave one a good grasp of what jobs needed doing during the day. One of the wisest old farming sayings is that the farmer's boots are the best fertiliser – and there is much to be said for this!

Like my father before me I enjoyed being part of the work-force rather than being a suited figure in an office. Perhaps I would have been a better business person if this had not been the case. I spent many hours doing fencing, planting trees and scything around them in summer as well as doing my share of tractor driving to cut fairways and rough. With Ron Mills on our team the machinery was always well maintained and the cutter blades properly adjusted. The job which was rather less pleasant was checking that the automatic irrigation system was working properly in the heat of summer. This often meant being up for half the night waiting for air to bleed out of the system and looking for faults and leaks. The powerful electric pump was also a sensitive beast because it was vital for it to have a constant supply of water so the rotors did not burn out. The electronic control box was fussy and complicated and the underground wire connectors often seemed to be chewed away by ants and insects – perhaps even mice. Strangely we often found newts living in the underground control boxes.

Generally we had a happy and effective team of green-staff – I remember big Eliot who loved his dragster cars and stocky young Julie who was a stalwart in the local ladies rugby team. I would entertain them all regularly together with Ron for a lunch in my big warm kitchen which I hope gave me a chance to hear their concerns (if they had any) and find solutions.

I cannot leave this section without pointing out, yet again, how great and satisfying has been the planting of all those trees at Millbrook. Readers may express surprise at the idea of regularly planting three or four thousand trees each winter but in fact this is a very easy thing to do. I discovered very early on in my tree planting career that the smaller the tree the quicker it will grow. In those days I could buy 100 2-year-old seedling trees for about £15 to £25. They might be about one foot high with roots of similar length and they came by the thousand bare rooted in big plastic bags. It only took one deep thrust with a spade to make a slit wide enough to drop in the tree roots so it could be kicked closed, and then move 3 yards to the next one. Millbrook soil was light and sandy – very easy to work. I would push in a 3-foot-long bamboo rod beside every tree so that we could find them again in summer to cut away the growth of grass and weeds for the first couple of years. Normally I would do all the planting after Christmas – the trees would have enough time to key in their roots before spring but not so long that winter winds would rock them back and forth to open up the slit where they had been planted. In their first year these tiny trees would grow perhaps 10 cm – it was critically important to scythe around each one in June to provide each with their own sheltered area of micro-climate. In their next year they would grow 20 cm and very soon even more – so after 2 or 3 years there they could look after themselves if they had survived drought and storm (and deer).

Millbrook golfers were initially very dubious about all the tiny trees I was planting and the necessary rabbit-fenced enclosures were a serious nuisance for play. But time would soon change their opinions as the young trees raced upwards – soon at 2 or 3 feet each year. Of course the wealthy neighbouring courses may have spent hundreds of pounds planting 20 foot high standard forest trees but many of these would die and most would be so damaged by transplanting that they would grow barely a few inches each year. Our young trees soon overtook these expensive (and foolish) competitors. Today the Millbrook trees tower over the landscape and those hot dusty early days of shimmering heat above light sandy soil have long since disappeared.

I do remember some quite strange happenings at Millbrook – here are some.

The poplar trees on the 18th! – I had no particular plans to plant trees between the 1st and 18th fairways. I did not want to make either the 18th or the 1st too threatening – especially the drive off the first tee. Some members, I think Reg Manyweathers was one, approached me asking if they could plant some chestnut trees there – they had grown them from conkers. I told them they could but only if they looked after them and fenced them off from the rabbits. I told them that these young deciduous trees were, in my opinion, very unlikely to survive the dry hot summer weather in such an exposed location.

The trees were duly planted and protected in rabbit wire enclosures supported by poplar stakes. Sure enough after the first summer the chestnut trees were blasted and shrivelled up by the wind and heat – despite regular watering by the members. But by a strange quirk of fate, the poplar posts supporting the rabbit wire had taken root (as poplar and willow do). This is why there are now 2 beautiful poplars on the 18th!

The big dead elm on the 5th – There were several large old elms, very beautiful, when Millbrook began but these were all killed after 1976 by Dutch Elm disease. One of them was a feature of the drive on the 5th – early visitors to Millbrook will remember it. We left the hulk of the tree in place even though it was dead and for many years it served to guide the drive on the 5th.

One winter day I had been tidying up some rough woodland beside the 2/14th green. I had a small bonfire going to get rid of the bits and pieces. I left the fire smouldering when I finished for the evening and went home to Lyshott House to have my supper. After supper the wind had got up and I saw sparks and a red glow in the west. When I went up to the course I could not believe my eyes – the entire huge elm was on fire, glowing red hot, showering sparks into the breeze. There was nothing could be done. Next day all that was left was a small heap of white ash – the entire tree had been so dry it had simply self-combusted to nothing.

Hamblett's wobbly walls! – John Hamblett was one of our rather rustic golf members. I always liked his brickwork because it had a nice character rather than being millimetre perfect (like our other bricklayer member, Maurice Brewer). But there were 2 occasions when things did not go to plan. The first day John laid bricks for the front wall of the new clubhouse he brought several other lads along to help. They built the wall up to about 4 feet high at great speed and were very pleased with themselves.

Alas, the next day the whole lot was lying smashed on the ground. It had toppled over – blown over by the wind in the night.

The second happened when I was having a beer with my eldest son Rupert several years after the clubhouse was opened. He was leaning against the south wall (facing the 9th tee) when he suddenly remarked that he thought the entire 12-foot (maybe higher!) wall was moving! We both together gave it a push and, sure enough, the whole wall rocked back a few millimetres. This was pretty scary and when we looked more carefully we found that no wall ties had been put into the wall! It had cracked at the base and might fall over onto happy drinkers at any moment – urgent repairs were needed.

John was always a keen and cheerful worker. Together we worked wonders building Lyshott House, helped by his tireless labourer Dave.

The Kitchen Fire – I was having a beer with Peter Gilbert (Sarah's brother) in the clubhouse one day, sitting in the corner opposite the bar. I was telling him how angry I had been when the planners and fire department had insisted I use very expensive fire resistant varnish to paint the wooden matchboard ceiling. Just as I was telling him what a complete waste of money this had been I saw a huge ball of flame erupt from the fryers in the kitchen. Yes – I kid you not! Don and Wendy were running the bar then. I rushed in grabbed a fire extinguisher and turned it onto the blaze but within seconds the heavy smoke made it impossible to breathe. We had no alternative but to shut the doors and call 999. The fire brigade soon arrived and put out the fire which luckily had been more or less contained in the kitchen.

I think there must be a lesson here – don't tempt fate!

Network for Social Change and our trip to the US in 1988

Let's wind the clock back once again. My relationship with Sue had brought with it a new imperative for me in my search for answers to planetary problems. Sue was much more committed than I to a non-consumer agenda and tried hard to escape from the edicts of a commercial world driven by the desire for money. Her work and her friends all supported this different approach to living – an essentially egalitarian approach where both people and the other life forms on the planet all had an equal chance of fulfilling their lives. Together we had discovered an interesting new grouping made up predominantly of wealthy Quakers – it was called the "Network for Social Change". This was in one sense a "secret" group that did not want to be involved in publicity or lobbying for change. The members of the group wished to remain anonymous but their aim was to make an impact by channelling significant quantities of money (and sometimes personal input) towards worthy causes. If I recall correctly, I believe there was a minimum effective personal wealth requirement of over £1million for those who wished to become members – and each member was expected to contribute at least £2,000 to the Network pool of grant money each year. Sue and I decided to join and become part of what was quite an active and interesting group.

It was during meetings of this Network that I learned much more about "process" (the rules and procedures which govern speaking and behaviour at meetings). The Quakers had their own traditions for working effectively in groups and I felt these were much more "advanced" than the "Robert's Rules" process I had been used to in Whitehall and business. ("Roberts Rules" is the more or less standard set of Standing Orders which business people use, almost without thought, to make their decision – using a dominant Chairman, a published agenda and majority voting.) Quakers relied more upon each individual taking responsibility for making a positive contribution with final decisions being taken by consensus rather than majority vote. They also put great emphasis on listening, which was encouraged by the use of silences. More on this later.

After we became involved in the Network we discovered that they had a sister organisation in the United States called the "Donuts". This was a much larger organisation with a longer history and more of a progressive "New Age" culture than Quaker. Many of its members were the extremely rich heirs to huge industrial fortunes – people who had no need to work and felt a strong responsibility to try and do "good" with their inherited money. Like the Network, the Donuts kept their identity very quiet and almost secret – they had in fact been responsible for the successful founding of Greenpeace and various other important emerging environmental pressure groups. They had even sponsored some left-wing revolutions in Central America! Early in 1988 Sue and I decided we would go to the annual "Donut" meeting in California – it would prove to be an amazing trip.

Long before we encountered the processes of the Network for Social Change and the Donuts, Sue and I had (on Sue's initiative) explored the effects of different rituals or ceremonies on a group of people's thoughts and behaviours. Sue had introduced me to the teachings and writings of an American "white witch" who called herself Starhawk. Starhawk had been an "ordinary" housewife in America who faced the prospect of having a very hazardous toxic waste dump operating very close to her home. She and many other local women had become involved in non-violent civil disobedience as protesters. Many of them were arrested and put into prison. This (very unpleasant) experience made Starhawk (then "just a housewife") think very carefully about better ways of getting their message across. She began to realise that ritual and symbolism could be much more powerful than rhetoric or press releases. And when she began to explore these options further she found herself researching the rituals and processes used by the American Indians. This is how she came to change her name to Starhawk and write a book about her new insights called "Magic, Sex and Politics" (which is a good title, you must admit). In her book Starhawk described some of the rituals and ceremonies she created to explore the power of this new kind of "witchcraft". Most of the established religions have, of course, already taken the use of ritual and ceremony to very sophisticated levels. Starhawk described white witchcraft as a way of using ritual and ceremony to change people's consciousness. Later I would use the lessons from Starhawk to great effect at other large gatherings, particularly the Earth Summit at Rio.

The small group which Sue and I became part of to explore these rituals was called RAIN. One of its key members was a woman called Hilary Bee – she had chosen this name herself when she decided to change from the person she was to the person she wished to be. We had some interesting times trying some of the different processes (rituals) suggested by Starhawk. In fact Hilary went so far as to go to a one-week workshop in the US hosted by a guru who was an American Indian. During this week all the participants were given a chicken which they had to feed and look after – as a way to bring them closer to nature and real life. What none of them knew was that they would be required to kill and eat this chicken on the last day of their course! As you can imagine, this presented a horrific challenge to an intelligent vegetarian idealist from London! I think this experience really did change Hilary's life because she ended up living in New Mexico much closer to nature! Even today I have found that city people, however intelligent and well-meaning they may be, really have no truly deep understanding of what it means to be a top predator species like homo sapiens – killing your own chicken is one quick way to change this.

So it was against this background that Sue and I set off for California early in 1988. We would stop over at David Haenke's in deep Missouri, visit the new Worldwatch Institute in Washington DC and, of course, stay with my relatives, the Warriner families, on the east coast. But our primary mission was to meet the Donuts. We duly arrived at a smart motel-type conference centre in very beautiful gardens (all tended by illegal Mexican immigrant workers!). As always there were working groups set up to deal with different aspects of the Donuts' work. The real point of interest for me was the large meeting they held every evening after supper. It had the very tacky name of "Deep from the Donut Heart" but, despite the tackiness, the meeting used very effective and sophisticated processes. It was the process, which turned out to be extremely powerful, that impressed me. It worked like this.

Anybody was welcome to come along to the meeting which would take place in a large conference room where all the participants could sit on the floor forming a big circle. Those who wished to speak during the meeting were asked to write their name on a piece of paper which would be put into a silver bowl before the meeting began. When the meeting began the participants were invited to choose a number of "facilitators" from within the group. One was called "Witness to the Process" and two others were invited to step forward so as to become "Keepers of the Heart" – they would remain sitting forward slightly inside the circle. The "Keepers of the Heart" were not allowed to contribute or speak unless they were invited to do so by the group. They acted, if you like, as resonators (or even a safety valve) for the feelings within the group. The fact that they could not speak was a constant reminder to others in the group that whatever they said or decided would be enforced upon the Keepers without them having a chance to contribute or complain. The "Keepers" were like the conscience of the group.

Once the formalities had been sorted out, the Witness to the Process reminded the group that each person called to speak would have the floor for just 3 minutes – a bell being rung after 2 minutes and a final bell after 3. The names of speakers would simply be drawn out of the silver bowl at random. I did not, at the time, realise how significant this random choice would be in terms of generating true human interactions rather than speakers being able to prepare a careful speech about their own intended contribution. In most of the meetings I had attended speakers would be invited to speak in turn "around the table" or according to a prepared list of speakers. This enabled each speaker to know when they were going to speak so they could steadily absorb the sense of the meeting and get their contribution ready in their own minds before speaking. With random selection, on the other hand, you never knew who you would be speaking after or what issues you might have to respond to either on behalf of the group or to help the last speaker. This meant the response would be much more spontaneous.

At various times participants making a contribution were invited to bring some article of special significance into the centre of the group. These symbolic objects acted as some kind of emotional anchors for everybody present. They might be something like the first tooth lost by a baby now grown up as a man, a wedding ring from a dead partner, the feather which lay on the ground when two people had first kissed – even a live turtle rescued from a zoo in one case!

The flow of speakers enabled participants to deal with all sorts of emotional roadblocks – either about what had happened (or not happened) earlier during working groups or about deeply personal issues. When the lady beside me had her name drawn from the hat she simply stood up and sang the most beautiful song – it was quite magical – the song, she said, was the song that she had sung on her wedding day. And when people's feelings ran high – as they sometimes did – then the Keepers of the Heart might be called upon to intervene. Again their contributions could be very imaginative – for example, asking the meeting to do "jumping ants" required everybody to get up and roll about on the floor like ants. Acts like this were more effective than words as ways to move the consciousness and emotions of the group into a new place – and it worked.

The maturity of the group was further demonstrated when participants wanted important decisions to be made perhaps about the next day's programme or even more fundamental changes to Donut wider policy. After 3 or 4 people had made contributions – usually setting out the competing options – the Witness to the Process would ask the group if they would accept person A to present the case on one side and person B to present the alternative. So the group simply gave power over to these two representatives who each had the sole responsibility for presenting their side of the argument – this saved a lot of time and hot air. I would see exactly the same level of trust when I worked with the NGO groups at the Rio Earth Summit. The group would not ask for volunteers to step forward to argue the case; the group would itself choose the people they felt would do the best job on the basis of what they already knew about individuals from previous contributions and conversations. Self-selection is, as the Greeks well knew, not the best basis for achieving good solutions. We returned to the UK with many new wisdoms!

Falconry – 1989

Birds of prey came into my life in a somewhat roundabout way. We've already heard how Gael and David met during their entry tests for officer training at Sandhurst. It was clear from that moment that Gael found David's stories about his experiences with fierce Eagle Owls fascinating. Gael had, in any case, always had an extraordinary rapport with animals – and the animals always seemed to know who was boss! So I suppose it was no real surprise when Gael became interested in falconry and, as a result, I learned to fly a small Kestrel (Newt) in March 1989. Later that year Gael (who had by then given up her place at London University) would take up the job of running the birds-of-prey flying displays at Whipsnade Zoo.

With the 100-acre expanse of Millbrook to fly over, we had ample opportunity to develop our skills. A small kestrel like Newt weighs about 8oz but can fly easily against the wildest gale. The instincts and skill of these birds are amazing. Falconry, like equestrianism, is a very old sport so the techniques for training and managing birds of prey have been developed over hundreds if not thousands of years. What magic it must have been in the days before guns and gunpowder to see your trained raptor fly off and catch a nice piece of game for dinner!

William with Peregrine Winston

In many ways, birds of prey have a natural affinity for humans. When they hunt in the wild they will often follow the movement of large animals (including humans) because this can flush out potential prey that would otherwise simply keep hidden. Hawks and falcons are very different characters. There is a strong similarity here to the feline world where leopards are tough street fighters whilst cheetahs are the highly designed lightweight Ferraris of the feline world. In falconry, hawks are the "street fighters" who can wrestle with their prey (which may be running or flying) whilst falcons are precision-engineered high-speed snatchers catching flying birds only. This means falcons are essentially gentle creatures as far as their relationship with humans is concerned. And birds of prey are not (generally) going to peck you with their specialised beak (it's for ripping flesh and feathers) because it is their ferociously sharp talons which they use to kill. A falcon's talons are razor-sharp and may be up to 2cm long – they are powerful too so you don't want to have them slice through your wrist!

Training a bird of prey is an interesting and challenging skill. Today all the birds of prey used in falconry are bred in captivity. This is an absurd and very sad result of "political correctness" combined with total ignorance on the part of lawmakers. In the "old days" falconers would take a couple of chicks from the nest of a wild bird and feed them up until they could fly. Remember here that in the wild only about 1 chick in every 6 ever makes it to hunt by itself! These fully-grown birds would then be allowed – and encouraged – to fly free but fresh food would be put out for them on top of the aviary roof every day. In this way they would get fully fit and learn the ways of the wild outside world – many would also succeed in "making the grade" to become independent hunters on their own. When the falconer wished to train a bird he simply caught it up when it came back to feed – and training could begin. So you can see that traditional falconry used to be a very important way of keeping up the numbers of wild birds.

Today the young birds are reared in an aviary where they cannot see humans – they are fed through a tube in the side of the aviary. This means that when they are picked up at night to be taken off by a new owner they have never seen a human before. The first human they see is their new owner when he/she takes them out of the box they have travelled in. This reminds me of a tense incident when I bought my peregrine falcon Winston. He was calmly resting in a closed cardboard box in the back of my car when we became trapped in a traffic jam on the M25. As the minutes passed I could hear him beginning to rip up the inside of the box – it was going to be a race to get him home before he escaped and crashed around inside the car. Luckily we made it!

So when we get our young bird home (they are about 15 weeks and fully grown) there comes a crucial moment when this beautiful creature sees a human for the first time. All must be calm as the new owner is ready with an open hood. As soon as the box is opened the bird looks around in amazement – no fear I think – and the owner has these few seconds to pop on the hood and pull the draw-string tight with his/her teeth. One mistake or any delay and the bird will panic and begin to duck and dodge – this is a disaster which cannot easily be repaired. Once hooded, the bird remains calm – these creatures are absolutely dependent on their amazing eyesight for any movement or action. It is a kindness to keep them hooded in strange places or when they are being moved about – especially if they are sharp-set (hungry) when they will fly off at anything that looks like food! The idea is to make sure the bird is calm and comfortable when it is first hooded – this way it should always associate being hooded with good feelings.

The intelligence and mental flexibility of different species of raptor varies considerably – almost in inverse proportion to their degree of sophistication in flying. Hawks, particularly Harris Hawks, are extremely intelligent. Like dogs they can figure things out and know who and what is what. Like dogs, they learn to hunt together (unlike other raptors who would simply compete and attack each other). At the other extreme Peregrine Falcons, the ultimate flying machines, have very small but specialised brains and quickly become strictly programmed (inflexible) in their behaviour. One mistake with a Peregrine and you have virtually lost the training challenge because it will be incorrectly programmed from then on. This mentality is, for example, why falconers will, when they show a Peregrine a lure for the first time, tie it to a pheasant feather if they want the falcon to hunt pheasant rather than pigeon.

When you take up falconry there are a lot things you must learn – so going on a formal course at an established falconry centre is a really good idea. You have, for example, to make your own leather jesses (which are the leather straps which go around the falcon's legs and enable you to put the bird on a leash so it cannot fly off). And there are certain standard behaviours which you need to follow, like, for example, teaching your bird to step backwards onto your left-hand glove after you touch the back of its legs when it is on its perch. There is also the vital training which makes sure your bird will jump from the lure (or its prey) onto your glove when you come to pick it up after it has flown. All birds of prey have a very strong instinct to keep their talons firmly embedded in any prey they catch but birds that develop "sticky" feet are very difficult to manage.

If you manage your first challenge well and you can comfortably put a hood on your bird without a fuss then that in itself is a good achievement. The next step is to try and persuade the bird to jump a few inches from its perch to collect food from your gloved hand. If the bird is hungry and all has been calm this should happen fairly easily. And, of course, when you are a bird that can fly there is very little difference in jumping 3 inches to flying 3 feet, and then 30 feet and then 30 yards and then 300 yards. Finally, when it is fully trained and experienced, your bird will spot its food from more than a mile away and come zipping back towards you!

Once the bird is comfortable flying a few feet from its perch to your glove to collect its food you can then begin to train the bird outside using a "creance". A "creance" is a length of light twine wound up in a figure of eight on a stick. You tie the creance to the bird's leash when it takes its first flights outside – just in case it gets spooked by something and ends up flying off into a tree! (A young bird will be very unfit and can only fly short distances.) You wind the "creance" in a figure of eight so that when you let the twine roll off from it there are no twists in the line – if you simply wind it round and round then it will twist when it pulls off the stick and there is a serious risk that your bird will become tangled (a disaster!). If only more parents would realise this trick with the figure of eight winding there would be far fewer tears when young children fly their kites! You will also notice that the large mooring ropes on ships are coiled not in single coils but in figure of eights – for the same reason, so you can pull out rope without twists.

It may seem strange but young birds of prey have to learn to fly! Their first efforts can be clumsy and they get tired very easily. The very large heavy birds, like eagles, actually find it very difficult to fly in still air from a human hand which is only about 3 feet from the ground. A peregrine falcon does not do much better because it has the smallest wings for its weight of any bird (this is so it can fly fast once it gets going). It is no surprise that these falcons and eagles like to nest on cliff edges so they can drop off into space to pick up the speed they need to fly easily. In fact, nature allows for this by giving young birds of prey bigger feathers on their wings than birds which are older. Each year, as your falcon moults out its feathers (they do this once each year), the new feathers are shorter than the previous set (and, in the case of peregrines, much bluer in colour). This means the more experienced birds which have greater flying skills can go faster and faster as each year passes.

So the first time you take your young falcon outside to fly on the creance you will only be expecting it to fly a few yards. Obviously the bird must be hungry or it will not want to fly – birds do not want to waste energy! With experience you can tell very quickly whether or not your bird is hungry (the term is "sharp set") because of its keen and tense behaviour. But all experienced falconers will have a routine of weighing their birds before they fly them – this is so you can double-check how they behave at different weights and have more certainty that they will fly well. On this first occasion you will want to make sure there are no inviting perches within sight which might distract a tired bird – no trees or fence posts! You will also want to make sure that you are flying over cut grass which has no thistles or large docks which might catch the line and bring your bird's flight to an uncomfortable early end!

You take your hooded bird with the creance attached and sit it on a perch. You then take off its hood, when it should be watching you "like a hawk" waiting for sight of food. You can then walk away 5 yards letting out the creance before you covertly take out a small piece of meat (usually a piece of a day-old chick), put it on your glove and show it to the bird. The bird may study this for a few moments before it launches itself off to come and catch it. If all goes well you can lengthen the distance each day until the bird is comfortable flying 20 or 30 yards towards you. Next comes the moment when you no longer tie the bird onto a creance – it will be flying free for the first time. It's vital not to ask the bird to do too much because if it should ever land on the ground or in a nearby tree you will find it very difficult to break this habit in future.

Calmness, careful patience and a steady routine are the vital factors at this stage of a bird's training. Soon you will be able to begin to use the small leather lure (with a piece of meat tied to it) to attract the bird. By swinging the lure you can "tease" the bird to fly faster by keeping the lure just out of its reach for 2 or 3 passes. Again, each day you can increase the number of passes until you feel the bird is becoming fit and strong. Now your falcon is ready to take to the skies on its own and learn to explore wind currents and thermals. All a falcon's instincts drive it to fly higher and higher, knowing that (for a bird) height means power. Very quickly your bird will learn how the local landscape creates updrafts with winds of certain directions. In summer it will pick up warm thermals and circle up and up in them. A peregrine likes nothing better than a full force 8 or 9 gale to really enjoy its flying prowess. In strong winds like this your falcon hardly ever needs to flap its wings because its skill in using wind currents is extreme. Often your bird will enjoy playing with the local rooks, high up above the woods. On a good day your bird may enjoy flying around the area (sometimes a few miles away from you – don't forget they fly at over 60mph and up to 200 plus mph in a dive or stoop). It's always wonderful to see how quickly they spot the lure and a distant peregrine will make a dead straight bee-line for that lure, picking up tremendous speed as it rushes towards you. When your bird is about 50 metres away you must throw the lure high into the air so the bird can snatch it up at full speed – it's a wonderful thing to see.

Generally flying a falcon is a winter activity. This is because your bird will only fly well if it is "sharp set" (hungry). In spring and summer when your bird is moulting out old feathers and growing in new ones it's better to keep it well fed so the new feathers will be firm and blemish-free. You can keep your well-fed bird in an aviary or you can keep it on a perch in your home (I used to keep mine high up in the corner of the kitchen so it could be kept amused by watching what was going on). Generally, as with horses, you must try to take your bird around and about so it experiences all sorts of situations calmly (and well fed) on your glove and without its hood. This way your bird will become used to seeing things like cars, dogs, other people etc, etc. The more experiences it has the less likely it is to get "spooked" and fly off in panic. Many of the old pubs still have rings attached to walls near the bar where people could tie their birds whilst they had a drink.

Hunting other birds with a falcon is an extremely interesting and skilful pastime. Not only do you need a well-trained bird but, even more important, you need a well-trained dog (pointer). Big German Pointers are regarded as ideal for falconry. They are intelligent and calm with an extra-ordinary sense of smell. They are also big enough to bound over rough heather and moorland for mile after mile as they try to find the scent of a game bird. When they do find the scent their natural instinct is to creep very slowly towards the hidden bird, "pointing" towards it with their nose and tail until they get within a few yards. Both dog and bird then freeze as each waits for the other to do something. At this point, the falconer (who may be a mile or more away) will take the hood off his falcon (which he has already trained to hunt for pheasant or grouse) so it can begin to assess the situation. You never "throw" a falcon from your wrist (as you can with a more robust hawk) because, like a cat, it has to make up its own mind how and where it's going to fly. Your bird will sense the wind, looking for hillside or trees that may give it lift, and generally take in the scene. Then, in its own time, it will fly off and begin to search the wind for lift. It has already seen the dog and knows this is where its prey will come from. It circles higher and higher as the falconer walks towards the dog. When the falcon reaches a thousand feet or so the falconer can signal the dog to put up the bird. Immediately the falcon makes its stoop and within seconds its talons should smack into the prey, knocking it out of the sky in a cloud of feathers. Falcon and prey land almost together and the falcon drives in its talons so escape for the stunned prey is impossible. This is a critical point because if the dog has not been properly trained it will also be keen to grab the prey (or even the falcon!). The falconer needs to arrive as quickly as he can to pick up the falcon (which may be tricky if it refuses to release its grip!) and control the excited dog.

I spent many happy hours working with the 3 different falcons I trained. It seems to me that many of those who like to hunt with shotguns could get much greater pleasure from hunting with well-trained birds and dogs. I think it is madness (and poor sport) to shoot dozens of tame pheasants in a day's shooting when you could get much more interest and satisfaction from catching just 2 or 3 game birds in a day's falconry! I would also say that the beautiful white Barn Owl makes a wonderful house pet that you can take for walks just like a dog but it flies rather than runs beside you. Having a bird for a house pet would certainly bring a new dimension into many people's lives.

Also in 1989

We cannot leave 1989 without mention of another significant event – the birth of Ceri's daughter Cecily. Ceri had made a close friendship at the Lycée with a strange boy called Kurt. Strange because he was unconventional in many unusual ways. No doubt his "strangeness" was one reason our very capable daughter found him interesting. Kurt had a very powerful intellect (as well as a powerful physique) – a brilliant musician and keen games (chess and scrabble not rugby or football) player – he had taken and passed great numbers of exams. But his wild head of hair and often abrupt manner set him apart from "normal" people within minutes of a first meeting. Although a big powerful man he showed no interest in sport of any kind and he certainly did not want to become part of the conventional corporate world *under any circumstances.* Kurt would enjoy the drama created when he banged on the roof of any smart Mercedes which was stuck in traffic – often giving the driver some wise crack about the folly of wealth and consumerism.

Rightly or wrongly, I had always encouraged my daughters to have their children as early as possible. Most women do want to have children – that's a pretty hard-wired fact, whatever modern feminists may say. And, provided you are a capable and sensible person, once you have a child you will always make the best arrangements you can to educate and provide for this new young person. For any young parent, grandparents and close friends will invariably become part of the parenting team and the new child is less likely to become a "toy" or a "pet" as happens so often in couples that wait until they have a smart house, a successful career and a good income before re-producing. Anyway it's physically much easier for women to have a child when they are young, fit and not overweight. And when you are young you have more of the energy you need to cope with all the late night feeding and nursing. In fact, time and time again I have seen crazy young teenagers become sensible young mums almost overnight as they find themselves with REAL responsibilities for another small human.

So I was not surprised or annoyed when Ceri told me she was pregnant – with Kurt the father. Ceri was at Edinburgh University studying to become a doctor. She was strong in mind and body with a close group of good friends around her – including her parents and particularly her great friend Susan and her Sutherland grandmother with whom she had travelled around the world. In the event it was not an easy birth. It was a breach birth and poor Cecily had to wear special braces to make sure her hips eventually worked properly. But just as St Andrews University had ultimately shown itself to be so supportive for Sarah when she gave birth to Rupert in her last year, so the Edinburgh University community jumped into action to provide the support Ceri needed. With help from her Granny she was able to buy a flat and she was especially fortunate to have forged a very special friendship with a fellow medic, Susan, who would become a wonderfully supportive part of our family for many years to come. (Tragically Susan died young from cancer after devoting her life as a Doctor trying to keep other people healthy.)

MY QUEST 5

Throughout my time at Westminster and with Arthur Young, I was involved in many direct attempts to improve government decision-making for what I thought of as the public good. Both management and policies in public affairs could be nudged in "good" directions by clever advice and effective manipulation of politicians. At the same time I was taking a much more direct approach to my quest for "right living" in my work, planting trees and creating an organic oasis for plants, birds and insects on my land at Millbrook.

During the late 1980s I began to meet many interesting "alternative" thinkers as I tried to pursue my "quest". John Papworth and his circle of friends was one such person/group. Sue was another important influence. Slowly but surely I began to see that it was a waste of time "blaming" leaders for failing to take good decisions. It was a waste of time protesting and campaigning. The direction in which humanity was heading was simply not within the control of "leaders" because most of what we did was governed by the rules of the institutional systems which made up the foundations of our present civilisation.

With the support of the small Resurgence Group, I decided to direct my quest towards researching and making public the ideas of important alternative thinkers and groups. In 1991 I founded my magazine, Ideas for Tomorrow Today, for this purpose. This took me first to Paris for Ya Wananchi and then to Rio for the first Earth Summit. My experiences at Rio would bring life changing consequences.

John Papworth – 1989

Throughout this year I continued to have more and more contact with John Papworth (JP) and his interesting coterie of friends and associates. We would meet at his large home in St John's Wood where John (an ex-cook in the RAF) would prepare magnificent dinner parties. Scrumptious evening meals would appear amidst clouds of steam from his ovens in the kitchen as the assembled company got to know each other around the large dining room table. The cut and thrust of debate was always fascinating and you never knew who would be there. I had been impressed by JP's book which I think was called "New Politics" and had tracked him down. He was also the man who started the magazine "Resurgence" before handing it over to be run by another of his strange coterie, the Indian mystic Satish Kumar. JP was a most unusual man with unusual talents and a restless energy which he constantly used to upset the status quo and the establishment. He had worked closely with such other radical thinkers as Leopold Kohr, E F Schumacher, Ivan Illich, Teddy Goldsmith, Nicholas Albery and Nicholas Saunders plus, of course, John Seymour. These were all people bursting with ideas; all highly articulate and clamouring for a stage from which to present them.

JP's great passion was what he called 'the Fourth World" – this was the world of small communities and the individual as opposed to the Nation State, big government, corporations and so forth. In this he followed the persuasive teaching of Leopold Kohr (who wrote The Breakdown of Nations) which put forward the idea that small government was better government than big government. Kohr was regarded with saintly status in his homeland of Austria, being awarded their highest honour by the city of Salzburg. His views on the futility of consumerism were summed up by the main ornament in his sitting room which was an old TV set without a screen but simply displaying a bottle of coca-cola!

JP's own life was an interesting story in itself. He never knew his parents and spent all his early life in an orphanage. Despite this, he was able to read widely and developed an amazing memory which enabled him to remember and recite (with great style and delivery) whole plays written by Shaw or Shakespeare. During the Second World War he was drafted into the RAF as a cook and, at the end of the war when he was demobbed, his commanding officer thought he was a very bright chap who should now be given an opportunity to have a proper education. The RAF put JP through London University so he could get a degree – which he duly did. His life then tacked off onto another course entirely as he saw an exciting business opportunity for importing the excellent new French frame tents into the UK. He (and a partner) set up a business importing these tents and soon became very wealthy. When the partnership broke up JP lost a lot of his share to his partner but still had sufficient money to buy his large home in St John's Wood.

With this large house, JP was able to rent out rooms to foreign students who were studying at the University. JP became something of a father figure to many of these students, one of whom came from Zambia and was called Kaunda. Some years later JP would get a call "out of the blue" from this student who had now become President Kaunda of Zambia. In this phone call Kaunda invited JP to become his special personal advisor – which he was very pleased to do. JP spent the next 10 years as Kaunda's right-hand-man in Zambian government. Somewhere along the way JP also became a preacher in the Church of England's hierarchy and proudly showed visitors a picture of himself in his priestly robes walking with the Queen at a ceremony in Zambia.

When he finally returned to England JP was involved in many high-profile acts against the establishment. He loved publicity and was a very articulate speaker. During the time I worked with him his main pre-occupation was publishing his alternative magazine which was called the Fourth World Review. In this context he had forged close links with a number of important alternative thinkers in the United States – particularly Kirkpatrick Sale and David Haenke, who were closely involved in the growing American 'bio-regional movement'. Many of the tenets of the bio-regionalists were very similar to those of the Fourth World movement. I would meet many of these people later.

Those suppers and debates at JP's were a great learning experience for me and I decided to become more directly involved. JP's hope was to hold a big Fourth World Assembly in London in the following year so that international speakers and luminaries could present their radical ideas to a wider audience. But in order to prepare for this it would be important for us to attend the Fourth World Assembly which was being held later in the year in Dallas, Texas. In July we duly boarded flights to Dallas and talked our way through several days of debate at their Assembly. It was certainly an interesting meeting where I learned a lot more about the bio-regional movement and found a new (and very wise) friend in David Haenke from Missouri. Dallas and its environs really resembled a "hell on Earth" – high rise buildings, beggars and vagrants in the streets and all dominated by huge gas guzzling autos rushing hither and thither.

I chiefly remember the meeting for the occasion on which we finished our debates late at night and went out to look for somewhere to eat. As all the decent restaurants were already closed we ended up in a soul-less Macdonald's fast food outlet. We faced plastic furniture, plastic cups, plastic food and mind-less customers. In the midst of all this ultimate cultural squalor JP began to protest and surprised us all by jumping onto a table and beginning to declaim the great speech from Hamlet "To be, or not to be.... He was a brilliant performer and orator and he knew the whole speech perfectly. Those of us with him really did not know what to expect from the assembled crowd of fellow diners. Certainly they had never seen anything like this at MacDonald's before. But, sure enough, a large well-intentioned crowd soon gathered and the whole affair went off to great applause. On another occasion when I took John out for a birthday supper (on his birthday) he repeated a similar performance when he heard the couple at the neighbouring table having a difficult lovers' tiff. This time it was the speech from Romeo – again perfectly delivered to the delight and surprise of the whole restaurant.

One result of all this involvement with JP was that I agreed to organise the 1991 Fourth World Assembly in London. Of course I also got to know JP's family very well – and they were not always entirely supportive of the regular invasions of their dining room by so many outspoken alternative types. JP had met his charming and attractive French wife Marcelle when they were both reporters in Cuba trying to get an interview with Fidel Castro. Castro had evidently taken a fancy to Marcelle, which proved to be a great help in getting the interview! But John was the lucky one able to take Marcelle as his wife. The Papworths had three children, two sons Pierre and John David plus a daughter Marie. Like John, Marcelle was also a wise and alternative thinker but such was the macho pace of debate that she hardly ever had an opportunity to put in a single word. I liked Marcelle very much and felt she was often rather left out of things in these often rumbustious parties. The children did not often participate but I got to know them well in the many private meetings we enjoyed together away from the debating forum around the dinner table.

At the end of the year I began exploring the activities and policies of the Green Party. I got along well with a fellow campaigner, Jane Taylor, who was also involved with the Greens and we later became good friends and fellow activists. I found the Green Party full of just the kind of big egos I had been trying to avoid after my Whitehall and Westminster days – lots of talkers but very few radical thinkers. After my experience with the SDP I could not face wasting more time in empty talk. My only significant contribution was made when Jane Taylor got herself elected onto the Green Party national committee. She asked me if I had any suggestions. One thing I had learned from being involved with Sue in the Quaker dominated Network for Social Change was the importance and power of silence. In our Network meetings the rule was always that there must be one minute of silence between each contribution. At first I thought this a ridiculous and cumbersome idea that would simply prolong meetings needlessly. In fact it proved quite the opposite. Having to pause for that minute made everyone around the table think much more carefully about the contribution they might make – it actually made people LISTEN rather than simply reacting on an emotional level. So I suggested that Jane should propose that the Green Party standing orders for meetings should include a new paragraph giving any member of the Committee a right, once during each meeting, to ask for a minute of silence. This Jane did and the committee accepted the idea even though they found it rather ridiculous.

In the event Jane did have occasion to use this option. It happened when the national committee became deadlocked over the issue of whether or not the party should pay expenses for the leader's travel and subsistence. The then leader was an excellent speaker and some members of the committee felt it would be a good idea to help her so that the she could give more speeches around the country. Others, on the other hand, were appalled that an individual might "make money" out of political work. A heated argument ensued. There was shock when Jane invoked the one minute break clause – almost disbelief that this might change anything, even disbelief that such a clause could actually be part of their standing orders. But Jane referred them to the appropriate section and they duly held their tongues. Strangely at the end of the one minute's silence nobody felt able to continue the arguments and the matter was eventually settled quietly and privately outside of the meeting! I would use this experience later in my work at the Rio Earth Summit.

Paget in 1990

In 1990 Millbrook is now going full blast. The new clubhouse has just opened and I am still a single parent balancing looking after Hal with running the business. I have decided to build a large extension on the west end of Lyshott House so that Gael and David can have a base in England and I can give Gael support whilst David is away soldiering with the Parachute Regiment (often in N. Ireland).

In May I receive a phone call 'out of the blue' from Paget Butler – the beautiful slim young lady with long blonde hair I had met briefly at earlier meetings of the Social Network. She tells me that she has been thinking about me and that she knows how hard it is a year after a suicide when everyone else is simply getting on with their lives while you may still be suffering. She knows this because she experienced something of the same herself when a previous boyfriend had killed himself despite her attempts to "save him". I'm touched by this and arrange to go down to see her at her home in Ashdown forest.

It's a long drive down to Ashdown Forest from Millbrook and the M25 is never the best place to be – even on a powerful motorbike! When I finally arrive at Old Cherry Orchard I find a beautiful large house surrounded by its own forest and grounds. I sound the bell and a few moments later a teenage girl answers the door – she looks very like Paget. As I did not know Paget had any children this is a bit of a surprise – but I am even more surprised to find she actually has 4 more beautiful daughters! I begin to learn more about Paget, her strange life so far and her illustrious (and very wealthy) ancestry. The Butler family were the King's chosen agents during a long history of Britain's occupation of Eire – as such they held the rights to collect taxes (on drink I think). They had castles and became extremely rich. Paget had married early into a stormy marriage, living in Ireland in fairly dire circumstances – we went to visit her old haunts later in our relationship. She was a very "alternative" person – strong minded and sexy she tried to follow the philosophy of Rudolph Steiner. She kept an elegant household full of beautiful things.

I was somewhat bowled over by the sudden onset of this new relationship but it was great for Hal to have a new family to become a part of and I quickly got to know Paget's girls. Slowly and steadily we all got to know each other and enjoyed many good times together.

During 1990 Dylan went to Bristol University and Gael and David got married. The marriage had many elements of drama. Because of the continued antagonisms between Sarah and Gael the bride's family (us) were not invited to the wedding – in fact every effort was made to exclude us. But weddings are a public affair and we went along anyway – we did not wish to miss Gael's big day. David had many of his army chums in attendance and we did feel a certain amount of tension as we sat outside the pub where the official wedding party were enjoying the post wedding speeches and celebrations. It would be quite some time before the emotional bruising caused by this rift was to heal – and even then relations would often follow a roller coaster pattern of good and bad! In the event Gael and David seem to have had a wonderfully successful marriage and have produced 3 fine children who are now each carving a place for themselves in the modern world. Gael became a successful business-woman and (after the children got a bit older) even managed to take a Law degree as a mature student at Oxford.

1991 – Fourth World, Ya Wananchi and "Ideas for Tomorrow Today"

1991 was the year I organised the Fourth World Summit in London and attended the Ya Wananchi conference in Paris. It was also the year I met good friends Rowland and Emily – they lived on Eel Pie island and were closely connected with the UK Green Party (Rowland was their Press Officer). It was the year a Russian architecture student (Gleb) came to live at Millbrook and during which I got mixed up with a strange group of women called the ''Dandelions". The other important people I meet this year are John Seymour plus Angela Ashe (who would later become my wife). In 1991 I also begin to work with Alan Senior to publish my alternative magazine "Ideas for Tomorrow Today".

My magazine contained summaries of books I thought interesting. We reported on significant meetings and protests. We gave information about up and coming meetings and happenings. We tried to summarise the critical world events which had taken place in the 2 months between issues. We provided a platform for innovative thinkers to air their ideas.

The magazine was really aimed at the mainstream rather than simply the "alternative" political thinkers. It steadily built up a reasonable circulation but its purpose was not to make profit but to spread information and provoke thinking about new ideas. Luckily I was able to finance production and distribution of the magazine from the profits of the golf course. I should have been able to claim the initial losses of the magazine against the profits of the main golf course business but (to my great annoyance) the tax authorities ruled against this.

To this day I often wonder whether the major tax investigation which the authorities launched into my business came about because someone somewhere in the security services was worried that a relatively rich ex-civil servant might start "rocking the boat". The tax authorities have enormous and un-

IDEAS FOR TOMORROW TODAY BULLETIN

a bi-monthly bulletin by and for people who are participating in transformation - in their business, their work, and changing their own lives. Presenting news in a wider perspective, networking for a better future, and linking with those on the creative edge of change.

NUMBER 3 FEBRUARY 1992

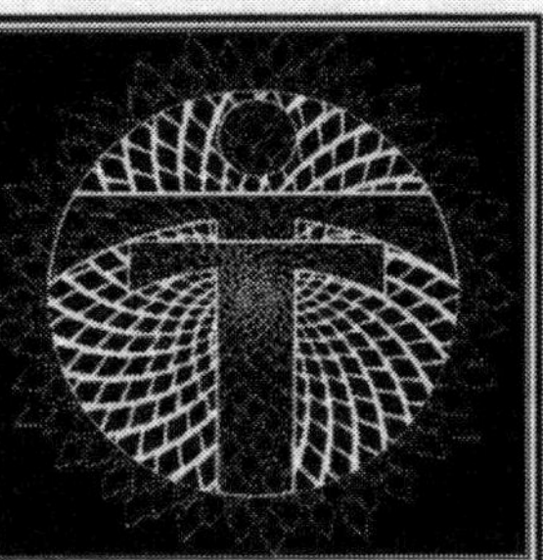

EDITORIAL

Christmas is over and the Bulletin has grown to 8 pages. We are receiving more networking input from those who wish to use our pages to communicate for the future. Many thanks to all our contributors; others please note that 2 pages of the Bulletin are being kept free for YOUR NEWS. The Bulletin has a circulation of over 1000 including all major organisations involved in the transformational movement.

1992 was trumpetted as the year of Europe but not much ever seems to happen. True the acre will be abolished in 1994 and we will have a single currency in 1999. This "gentle" erosion of our sovereignty must be one of the longest seductions ever recorded. Sadly the Europe we are joining has a selfish short-term mentality, taking what it can from the rest of the world and erecting as many barriers as possible to prevent people and trade going the wrong way. Our Bulletin Report from Paris shows just how strongly the rest of the world feels about such greed and isolation.

The dramatic meeting of citizens's groups from around the planet in Paris last December must be one of the most hopeful signs yet that human creativity might bypass greed and exploitation. The massive and unnecessary consumption of resources by northern peoples is rapidly depleting global reserves. Unfortunately people here do not see the results of their shopping sprees because the news media are not interested, corporations conspire to conceal the truth and the innocent who suffer are usually several thousand miles away. Our congratulations to Ethical Consumer Magazine (see Bulletin 2) for trying to explain this to the buying public.

PORTRAIT OF THE DARKEST MONTHS

Statistics for 1991 showed that 48000 UK businesses collapsed, a 65 percent increase on 1990. The Home Secretary was found guilty of contempt of court but refused to resign, meanwhile more police convictions were quashed. An appeal was launched to save the British barn owl from extinction. A consultants' report revealed that the addition of a single digit to our telephone numbers in 1994 is likely to cost £1 billion. 10 kilogrammes of enriched uranium was reported "lost" at Dounreay.

The World Health Organisation predicted annual AIDS deaths at 18 million by the year 2000. The Yugoslavian civil war caused a massive refugee problem. The Soviet Union ceased to exist. There were food riots in Albania, fighting in Georgia and starvation and feuding in Somalia. Algeria saw the beginning of a major Islamic upsurge but the civil war ended in El Salvador. Unemployment in the United States reached 7.1 percent and the World Bank agreed to lend Thailand £32 million to finish the controversial Pak Mool dam. The International Tropical Timber Organisation showed itself to be ineffective as only 7 out of 47 members produced reports required to show how they would achieve sustainable forestry by the year 2000.

On the credit side Christmas saw the first organic chocolate introduced into the UK while New Consumer produced a book "Shopping for a Better World". Students published an alternative careers guide and the Department of the Environment published draft regulations on the release of genetically engineered organisations which were so bad they will have to be totally revised. William Rees Mogg described his vision of a rapidly disintegrating society while Peter Russell eloquently suggested "on TV" that we should treat the Earth more kindly.

The World Bank, G7 and EC nations agreed $250 million for Brazil to assist in forestry conservation. The red cockladed woodpecker stopped tank exercises at Fort Bragg in the USA while the Governor of Idaho vetoed plans to bury 800,000 drums of nuclear waste. Japan finally agreed to stop drift net fishing in line with UN resolutions and the Brazilians announced plans to develop a $5 billion scheme for integrated child support centres. The Dutch government announced they would crack down hard on industrialists to achieve their national environmental plan. And Maurice Strong proposed an independent "Earth Council" to follow on from the UNCED conference in June. The EC agreed a new cohesion fund which will help states comply with regulations, particularly those dealing with nature preservation schemes.

SUBSCRIBE TO THE FUTURE - **IDEAS FOR TOMORROW TODAY BULLETIN**

BASIC: £5.00/YEAR. SUSTAINING: £10.00/YEAR - FOR 6 ISSUES

TO 'IDEAS FOR TOMORROW TODAY' - 31 BELLEVUE ROAD, EALING, W13 8DF

regulated power to destroy a person's business. In my case they began by refusing to accept the income figures in my tax returns for the golf course – they claimed that I must be taking huge sums in cash which were never declared. They demanded that I prove I had not taken this money! To attempt this I was required to identify and list every pound I had spent (on meals, presents, holidays, taxis, etc.) over the previous 2 years. This was a major and very time-consuming task at a difficult time when I was wrestling with the responsibilities of being a single parent. It was also extremely expensive as I needed to engage the services of expensive professional accountants to assist me in my battle with the Revenue.

It took about 6 months of work and several stressful meetings with the Tax Inspectors in Bedford before the issues were finally resolved. It cost me thousands of pounds and countless wasted hours of work before the investigation was completed to the tax people's satisfaction. They eventually decided to drop their case on condition that I re-paid all the money I had claimed as tax relief against the losses incurred in setting up Ideas for Tomorrow Today. This was a serious blow to my efforts to continue to develop the magazine as I could no longer subsidise this work from my larger golf business. Reluctantly (and feeling very bitter against the tax people) I decided I could no longer afford to keep the magazine going. The tax authorities had destroyed my business without any evidence whatsoever of malpractice or dishonesty on my part – they had cost me thousands of pounds in accountant's fees and dozens of hours of wasted labour. No compensation was offered (not even an apology) when they failed to justify their suspicions. This whole miserable experience was a stark lesson on the dangerous power of unaccountable state authorities.

Throughout 1991 I am very involved with Paget and her family while the rest of my family get on with their lives without much drama. I am also becoming much more committed to "saving the world" because I feel very determined to follow up all the ideals which Sue held so dear. Paget is very much supporting me in this although she is much more interested in the "micro-level" – how individual people relate to each other – rather than the "macro-level" which interests me (the world of politics and cultural institutions). There is a lot of "to-ing and fro-ing" between Millbrook and Cherry Orchard (a tiring and tedious journey around the M25). I am still flying my Lanner falcon Tor.

Fourth World Assembly 1991

This took place in London during the summer. Although I was the "official" organiser this was a task fraught with challenges because of the many strong personalities involved. A decision made one day could be overturned on the next. The intended format of the Assembly would follow a similar pattern to that of the Summit we had attended in Dallas. There would be key speakers giving a series of talks during every day. There would be smaller working groups who would go away and hold private meetings to bring back their "deep thoughts" to share with the rest of the conference. I had arranged for a number of international "stars" to come over, paying for their flights and accommodation. These included John Seymour, Elisabet Sahtouris, Kirkpatrick Sale, David Haenke and Judith Plant. The greatest problem with the Assembly was the tendency for all discussion to be dominated by the "big egos" who liked the sound of their own voices. These individuals were very difficult to manage and fundamentally they were not interested in hearing what other people had to say – their mission was to impress their own ideas onto everybody else. They would take it very badly to be told to cut short their speeches and interventions.

In my own working group I suggested we agree on what "process" we would use before we even began to talk about important issues. I suggested we use what I called the "talking leaves" method since we were meeting on a tree lined lawn in Regents Park. Every member of our group would pick up 5 leaves and each time they made a contribution or spoke they were required to put one leaf into the centre of the circle. When they had no leaves left then they could make no further contribution until everybody else had used up their own leaves – or there was a unanimous wish within the group to hear their contribution. This worked much better – more ideas, happier participants. But in the main hall the problems of controlling the "egos" remained – and, sadly, John Papworth, for all his wit and wisdom, was one of the worst offenders (a fact his children knew well). Things got so bad in the main hall as speakers jostled for time on the floor that a group of us got together and made a "black comedy" video skit to show just how crazy this "ego war" had become.

It was a relief to me when the Assembly finally came to a close. The whole affair had been an exhausting exercise in self-control and I'm not sure anyone emerged any the wiser for all the fine words that had been spoken. For the most part, speakers spent their time on the rostrum exhorting others (both governments, corporations and individuals) to change the way they did things. It was only John Seymour who suggested that we ourselves should make changes for the better in our own lives. In this, John was echoing the words of one of his great "heroes" – an American called Wendell Berry. You can get a flavour of why both John and I find Wendell Berry's wisdoms such a "breath of fresh air" by reading the extract from one of his books below…

WORD AND FLESH – WENDELL BERRY

"As you like it – "I can live no longer by thinking." Orlando.

Every movement has its thinkers with their jargon. Environmentalists have "planetary" concerns but these concerns contain an abstract anxiety that is desperate and useless exactly to the extent that it is abstract. ***These heroes of abstraction keep galloping in on their white horses to save the planet – but they are falling off in the grandstand.***

Though we have serious problems nearly everywhere on the planet, we have no problem that can accurately be described as planetary. And short of the total annihilation of the human race, there is certainly no planetary solution.

That will'o-the-wisp, the larger scale solution to a large scale problem which is so dear to governments, universities and corporations serves mostly to distract people from the small, private problems that they may in fact have the power to solve. In fact the problems are our lives! In the developed countries the large problems exist because all of us are living either partly wrong or almost entirely wrong lives.

The economics of our communities and households are wrong. The only answers are to be found in culture and character. To fail to see this is to go on dividing the world into guilty producers and innocent consumers. Unfortunately we have failed to produce new examples of good home and community economies and we have nearly completed the destruction of the examples we once had.

The problem is not how to care for the planet but how to care for the millions of human and natural neighbourhoods and each of their millions of parcels of land. Only love can bring intelligence out of our institutions and organisations. Love cannot live by thinking, yet to put flesh on its purpose it must think.

The religion and the environmentalism of the highly industrialised countries are at bottom a sham because they make it their business to fight against something they do not really wish to destroy. We all live by robbing nature but our standards of living demand that this robbery shall continue. We must achieve the character and acquire the skills to live much poorer than we do. We must waste less, we must do more for ourselves and for each other. It is either that or continue merely to talk about changes that we are inviting catastrophe to make.

We have become a nation of fantasists, believing apparently in the infinite availability of resources. We believe that democratic freedom can be preserved by people ignorant of the history of democracy and indifferent to the responsibilities of freedom. Our leaders are oblivious to the realities of our time – just like previous leaders. In fact we are involved in a war against the world, against our freedom (from dependence), and indeed against our existence. We have forgotten that Nature is necessarily part of all of our enterprises and that she imposes conditions of her own."

The words of Wendell Berry and John Seymour (written in the 1970s) seemed to me the only sensible and constructive wisdom I had picked up from the entire conference. I had already met John Seymour and his partner Angela Ashe at John Papworth's in the run-up to the conference and I had immediately been struck by his good humour and common sense and her pert competence. Angela and John were already living a more or less self-sufficient life in Ireland and I determined then to go and see for myself how they did this. So, in this sense alone, the London Fourth World Assembly changed my own life – changes which would ultimately produce two talented children in Roisin and Liam.

The "Dandelions" and Gometra

Just how did I meet the "Dandelions"? I really cannot remember but I suspect it was through Paget, who I was visiting frequently down at Forest Row. Who were they? Three interesting ladies who had a mission to create a new type of community where the dominant values of consumerism would be replaced by creativity, art and "right living". Somehow they had borrowed money to buy a big old house in a secluded wooded estate down in deepest Cornwall and they were promoting creative and artistic retreats there. The place was a strange mixture between a hotel, a monastery and an artist's commune. Their expectation and hope was that the pattern of living they were trying to develop would spread like the seeds of the dandelion blown hither and thither in the wind. Being unconventional and forceful characters, they were able to attract and arrange for interesting performers and events to take place at their remote headquarters in the rambling old house at Hazelwood. The house was a mixture of an "intentional community" and a hotel catering for (mostly) wealthy alternative "New Age" types. Some of the inmates seemed to be almost prisoners within this community and I never did find out just how and why they were there. Mysteriously the ladies who worked in the kitchen, cleaned the place and made the beds were never invited to participate in the cultural events. They seemed to live in "servants' quarters" somewhere and they certainly lived under the spell of the forceful trio of ladies who called themselves the "Dandelions". Whether there were some complex lesbian relationships involved I never did find out.

You have to remember that at this time my own personal life was still in quite an unstable state. Sue's death had ripped away any kind of stable contentment as I battled to keep all the various "balls in the air" – looking after Hal, running the golf course, dealing with my wider family, exploring and working with alternative politics, producing my magazine IfTT, and finding time to have a relationship with Paget and her large family. By now the golf course at Millbrook was running along smoothly as a going concern and I was seriously thinking of selling up. My first four children were grown up now and I no longer needed my huge house at Lyshott. I did not know if my relationship with Paget was going to last. Sarah seemed very keen for me to set up business near her again down in Bordeaux and we looked at various beautiful estates which I might have bought down there. (In fact I would have done so if I had been able to find a decent accountant in the UK who could advise on the various French tax implications.) I wondered about the possibility of some kind of communal living which would provide a supportive emotional platform for myself and Hal. Taking time to visit (and enjoy) the events at Hazelwood was one exploration of such possibilities.

One of the other possible avenues I explored involved making contact with Helen Abel's (Rupert's wife) family in Camden and their group of idealistic friends. The Abels are an idealistic and egalitarian family and we had many long discussions about ways to create a "better" society. In the event both the Abels and the Dandelions (and Paget) would become embroiled (yes, I think that is the right word) in another potential project of mine. This revolved around Gometra – an interesting 1,000acre island off the north tip of Mull in Scotland.

After the inspiration, if that is the right word, of John Seymour and Wendell Berry and the frustrations of the Fourth World Assembly I decided to explore possibilities of setting up a self-sufficient community on my own. Ideally this would be on an island which was fairly inaccessible so that we would have some security in the event of a breakdown in civilisation. During this time we not only had the shadow of nuclear war but also the very real (as it seemed then) possibility of the oil running out. The market price of golf courses was very high at this time – it was just before a busy boom began in golf course building – and I could sell Millbrook and use the cash to buy an island and set up my own "model" community. I discussed the details this plan with the Abels and Paget and the Dandelions.

Later in the year, I took a trip up to visit Gometra with Ron Mills so we could assess together the practical possibility of taking on this new "grand" project. Most of the island was wild heather and moorland which had become over-run with deer after an abortive attempt to set up a commercial deer farm had failed. There was a fine large house, a deep lagoon for a harbour and a couple of hundred acres of good land which could be farmed. With Ron as a right-hand man, we could make our own electricity, build new accommodation and get the good land back into food production. I spoke to the owners and agreed a price for a sale but then, to my surprise, I found that others in the group of people I had been sharing my plans with had secretly made their own contact with the owners – in effect competing covertly against me! Paget and the Dandelions had come up with some kind of plan of their own without telling me. And in London I had rather confrontational meetings with the group involving the Abels.

This kind of "duplicity" came as a nasty shock and made me both sad and cross. It was a serious blow to my relationship with Paget and I realised that my ideas and the ideas of the Abels were not really on the same wavelength. I quickly abandoned the project and realised that the idealistic dream of working "in community" was just that. My feelings were further strengthened by reading the results of some comprehensive research which had been conducted by a Dutch NGO into the success and problems of a large number of different "intentional communities" throughout the world. I think only 2 or 3 out of several hundred had actually been successful over the long term and these were invariably dominated by some kind of powerful leadership – either an individual (who might own the property) or a small group. Almost all were destroyed by arguments over management of money and sexual relations. So it was time to think again!
My focus returned to Millbrook.

This is the home I built at Lyshott House.

This is the great valley showing clubhouse (on left), Ron Mills' home and Lyshott House in the wood. These are all buildings built by Ron and myself!

Here is a joyful photo of my mother nursing baby Hal – taken at around the same time.

Chapter 7: The Rio Earth Summit and the Strange Magic of Paget's Amethysts

How the Alternative Treaties were written in 1992

By a strange set of happenings and circumstance during June 1992, I found myself editing, co-ordinating and finally publishing the Alternative Treaties from Rio. This is the first time this mysterious story has been published! You can find the text of the Alternative Treaties at:
https://www.earthsummit2002.org/toolkits/women/ngo-doku/ngo-conf/ngoearth2-2.html

Here is an example of the massive cluster of Paget's amethysts which played a crucial part in this story. But the story begins a couple of years before Rio when I began the publication of my small bi-monthly magazine called "Ideas for Tomorrow Today!"

Ya Wananchi – in Paris 1991

The aim of "Ideas for Tomorrow Today" was to provide the established business community with sensible objective information and analysis about alternative political thinking and especially the work of important environmental NGOs. The NGO environmental movement had grown from very small beginnings in the early 1970s to become important influential players on the national scene. At first nobody in the "establishment" really took protest organisations like Greenpeace or Friends of the Earth seriously. They might tie themselves to trees or throw bags of flour at politicians and business leaders but they were still fringe activists with relatively few resources. People in business and government did not really know much about the thinking of the "weirdos" with the beards, rucksacks and sandals.

I thought that some of the "alternative" thinking was important and that these new ecological radicals might have important lessons for us all to learn. This was the mission of my magazine: to provide summary analysis of ideas, books, speeches and meetings which I thought might be significant. By doing this in a few pages every couple of months I hoped to find an audience in the mainstream and break down the barriers of prejudice and ignorance. I had seen for myself when I worked in Whitehall how Ministers had simply failed to grasp the importance of the new environmental NGOs (particularly Friends of the Earth). They failed to realise that these annoying "hippies" actually represented a powerful emerging public concern about the environment. In the end, after a lot of battles and legal hassle, the government was forced to radically change the way it planned the construction of new roads. People demanded much more consultation and a complex Public Inquiry system was developed.

In order the produce the magazine I made it my business to get to know a wide circle of activists, read their writings and go to their meetings. I became great friends with Rowland (and Emily) Morgan who was chief press officer for the Green Party. My friend Jane Taylor was also very involved with the Green Party and the small group who had the idea of creating the newspaper "Positive News". (Jane was also a great supporter of my idea for a non-political RHINO party – to enable people to vote "NO" – she persuaded me to buy the Rhino picture in Ludlow so I would never forget our commitment to this idea.) So, one way or another, I not only heard about the French government's initiative to hold a global conference of NGOs in Paris but I was also able to get a journalist's pass to attend.

So what was all this about? Already in 1991 the news media were beginning to take interest in what would be the first Earth Summit to be hosted by the United Nations in Rio during 1992. This had come about as a result of a more or less secret initiative by a leading Swiss businessman (Schmidt Heine) who had co-ordinated the interests (and money) of a powerful group of 40 international corporations. The corporate world was becoming concerned about growing public pressures for businesses to be regulated to protect the environment. This pressure seemed likely to become manifest in different ways in different countries – and a complex set of different rules would place a serious obstacle in the way of global trading. If the United Nations could be persuaded to bring countries together then some of the major environmental issues could be dealt with in a co-ordinated system of global treaties. The problem was that the United Nations had no money – very few of its member states actually paid their annual due, leaving the United States picking up most of the bill. Schmidt Heine was good friends with Maurice Strong, one of the senior UN officials, and together they hatched a plan to host an Earth Summit which would be financed by the consortium of the 40 corporations co-ordinated by Schmidt Heine. So the plan for a Rio Earth Summit in 1992 was launched and negotiators began the long process of gearing themselves up to present their various countries' cases.

All this was fine and good but, as so often in the past, the French government did not like a situation where the United States appeared to be taking a dominant role in directing global affairs. So the French came up with a plan to "muddy the waters" by sponsoring and energising the emerging global NGO movements in order to create some kind of "counterweight" to what they saw as a US initiative. In order to do this, the French commissioned a "tame" African NGO and gave them money and resources to organise and invite NGOs from all over the world to a special global conference of NGOs to be held in Paris in the year (1991) before Rio. The organisers were instructed to choose leading NGOs in each country in such a way that the number of representatives would reflect the population of that country (as opposed, for example, to the size of its economy). All representatives attending the Paris conference would have their air fares and expenses paid for by the French government.

In total about 5,000 representatives of the global NGO community descended on Paris and gathered in a huge conference centre to debate what they saw as key issues for Rio. Lots of Press and Media were in attendance – including myself for IfTT.

The name of the conference – Ya Wananchi – is a Swahili expression meaning "Brothers of the Earth". Generally there was a strong feeling of optimism and excitement running through the various delegations. For the very first time in the history of Earth it seemed possible that the ordinary people of the Earth could make an important input into the policy deliberations of their governments. Certainly the sea of brown, black, yellow and white faces gathered in the huge conference room made a big impression. But events did not get off to a very auspicious beginning. The very first issue raised had nothing to do with saving the environment. Instead, we were subjected to several long and bad-tempered tirades from the 3 or 4 people who represented the United States. They were furious to find themselves in such a minority position amidst the thousands of brown, black, and yellow faces. "Did the organisers not realise that it was a travesty of sense and justice to reduce the role of such a dominant economic power as the US to what seemed like merely a token appearance?"

The French organisers had scored a bull's-eye here right at the outset by showing the US just how unrepresentative their country was of the true pattern of citizenship throughout the

Earth. Various other delegates attempted to persuade the US people to accept the fairness and the reality of their situation but to no avail – the argument persisted for what seemed like hours. Finally a very young (teenage) girl from one of the South American countries (it could well have been Venezuela) took the stage. She ticked off the US delegates who, she said, had shown a disgraceful lack of appreciation for the true reasons the NGOs were gathered together. All this childish argument was simply wasting valuable time which should be better spent discussing the real environmental issues facing the Earth. The meeting finally began to focus on more relevant issues.

I met some interesting people at the conference. It took me some time and research to discover just how all this had come about, who had initiated it and who had paid for it? Once again, dear reader, you have to remember that even in 1991 the use of email and the internet was still at a relatively undeveloped stage. One person who was convinced that the power of the internet to bring people together was going to be central to future social developments was an American computer wizard called Robert Pollard. I found him tapping away on his little black Apple Mac computer and soon got into an interesting conversation about the future. I did not know then that a year later I would find myself working with, and paying for, Robert to come to live at Millbrook as together we followed up, co-ordinated and finally published the Alternative Treaties from Rio.

The main upshot and result of the Ya Wananchi conference was that various organisations of the international NGOs got together to form working groups. The aim of these groups was to prepare policy papers which could be brought to the Rio summit in the following year with the intention of showing what were key policy objectives for the Earth as seen by the world's NGOs. In all, I think there were policy groups set up for more than 30 policy areas – such as air, water, women, money, trade, etc, etc. Although I did not know it then I would meet all these groups in Rio in the following year.

The Bio-regional Conference in Texas

Before we get to Rio I have to tell the tale of my visit to the biennial bioregional conference in Texas. We have already met the eccentric wise old bird David Haenke. He had been involved from the beginnings of the bio-regional movement and had been very enthusiastic about its philosophies. David was a man of determined high principles – he had no possessions or wealth of his own – just a battered old white Ford car. He lived very cheaply by "house sitting" for richer friends – and he tried to grow much of his own food. David would not use any toilet that was flushed into a modern sewage system. He believed that the flush toilet was a perfect metaphor for everything that was wrong with the way humans were now living. We took expensive clean water, pumped it at great cost into people's homes, then used it to flush away what we call "waste" which contained vital plant nutrients. To cap it all, the "waste" had then to be pumped to a processing plant where the nitrogen-rich run-off went into rivers and lakes. Finally the stinking contaminated sludge was often dumped on good farmland. Not only were these nutrients lost to the soil but they soon became serious pollution as they fuelled algae and other undesirable growth in lakes, rivers and seas. The fossil fuel energy required to pump away, process and then dump sewage was yet another source of carbon pollution as well as a waste of scarce resources. David felt that those who were happy to use these flush toilets showed a total disregard for their own responsibilities and an unjustified trust that somewhere someone else would deal responsibly with the problem. I suppose it's a similar mindset to those dog owners who throw their used doggy shitbags under bushes – assuming somebody sometime will surely deal with this problem!

Note – David always took a small spade with him on his travels so that he could find a suitable piece of earth to nourish with his human waste. I remember him telling me how he had had to go to Central Park in New York after being invited there to address a committee of the United Nations. So he dug the necessary hole in a quiet secluded sport and did his business without any problems!

David Haenke had told me about the ideas of the bio-regionalists which had also been promoted by the writer Kirk-patrick Sale. (Bio-regionalists believed that the fundamental geographical areas of government must follow natural boundaries – particularly watersheds. This was vital if communities were to be able to control their own living environment.) I was interested in learning more about the bio-regionalists and their way of doing things so I paid my conference dues and bought my plane ticket for Texas. The biennial conference was being held in a vacant summer camp – wooden houses set in a pretty valley. Each person arriving was given two badges – one with a species of tree on it, the other with some species of animal. We were told that the tree badge would allocate us into relatively large groups whose aim was to discuss and formulate ideas on specific major policy issues (trade, money, arms, etc.). The animal badge would put each of us into a much smaller group – just 5-6 persons – so we could express and explore personal and emotional issues. Different time slots were set each day for these groups to meet – and there was a large communal noticeboard where anybody could post announcements or adverts.

Each morning the conference held a general assembly to which everyone was invited. This took place in the open air within a large cliff-lined natural arena. We all (perhaps 300 people) stood in a circle while the organisers made announcements and then invited anyone who wished to say or discuss anything to step forward into the circle and make their contribution.

The general assembly worked very well. Cooking groups were self-selected to prepare the day's communal meals. Baby-sitting arrangements were made. A group asked for volunteers to perform a play. Another group was arranging a barn dance. And so it went on – and the community created and self-organised itself in a remarkably efficient way. The day's business then proceeded and we met in our various groups. These too worked well. It was perfectly possible to change the major topic group you were in once the groups had established themselves.

The small inter-personal groups also worked well – if you had the patience to sit calmly and attentively to listen to various stressed ladies talking about all the faults of their mothers!

The conference was marred by angry and unresolved clashes with and between two fringe groups – the permaculturists on the one hand and the rainbow people on the other. The rainbow people dressed, as their title implies, in bright colourful clothing and their philosophy was aligned with that of anarchists and radical hippies. The rainbow people objected strongly to having any structure and were more interested in getting drunk and being generally selfish and destructive. They were, if you like, the casualties of wage slavery, the nation state and consumerism. The permaculture people, on the other hand, behaved like religious fanatics or fascists. Time and time again they were determined to force everyone to adopt the comprehensive text-book answers they had learned on their permaculture courses – no debate was permitted or necessary; all the rules had been laid down by their guru, Bill Mollison. (I don't think the author of permaculture, Bill Mollison, would have been very happy about this but the effect of the "chain letter" teaching system he had promoted seemed to bring about this dogmatic result.)

Once again – as at the Network for Social Change and the Donuts – I learned a lot about how groups can learn to work effectively together. I also made an exciting romantic attachment to an Australian professor – Ariel. This was a lady who was smart, clever and forceful with a keen passion to save the environment and stop resource exploitation by the greedy corporations of the world. We would meet again when I stayed in her flat in New York, and once more at Rio.

The Rio Earth Summit and the Alternative Treaties 1992!

The Rio Earth Summit marked a major watershed in my life's story. My first feelings about the Summit were entirely negative – I thought it seemed likely to be yet another talking shop where men and women in smart suits worked up one compromise or another to avoid making much change to the status quo. Rio was also a very long way away from Millbrook – it was not the kind of trip you could make in a weekend. Altogether I felt that my going there would be a crazy waste of time and money – there were more important things to be done at home. But some of my friends took the opposite point of view. In their view, Rio was a unique event in the Earth's history with the possibility of actually making progress on important environmental issues. I had the background and the interest in these issues so surely I must go!

Eventually it was my friend Jane Taylor who told me "you must go to Rio…." I began to make tentative enquiries about flights and accommodation. To my surprise it turned out that the Brazilian grandmother of my daughter Ceri's best friend Isabel lived in a small apartment very close to the conference head-quarters. She did have a tiny back room which I could camp down in without any problems. So this was duly arranged and I booked my flights.

Bear in mind that I had no idea what was going to happen, who I might meet or what I might do there. True, I had met one or two of the key NGO people at the Ya Wananchi event in Paris but I did not know if they would be there or how things would be organised. It was (is) a long flight to Rio and the plane fills with steam when the doors are finally opened to a hot humid Brazilian afternoon. I find the Granny's flat and get to know cheerful noisy Brazilians! That's all fine so I head off to find the "office" for the so-called Alternative Summit which is being organised by global NGOs in the big public park next to the beach. The park has been rented by a local entrepreneur who has sold off hundreds of show stands for individual NGOs to promote their activities – all the usual suspects are there and it is a big, hot and dusty scene. As a quid pro quo the NGO organisers have also arranged more than 30 large tents kitted out with seating so that each of the various Alternative Treaty conference groups has a space where debate and policy development can take place. In each conference tent there are microphones plus sets of earphones so that each contribution can be simultaneously translated into one of the 4 major colonial languages – English, French, Portuguese and Spanish. It's an amazing logistic feat to have all this infrastructure ready and in place in time for the conference. How it was all done I never found out – some wealthy benefactors must certainly have been involved.

One mysterious and perhaps magical feature of my trip to Rio was the huge crystal stone I was asked to take with me by Paget on our final supper in Forest Row just before I left. We were enjoying supper together around her beautiful table with the daughters and a generally positive atmosphere. In the centre of Paget's dining table there was always this huge volcanic crystal stone – it must have been at least 18 inches long and 12 inches wide – very impressive. Suddenly Paget turned to me, picked up the big chunk of crystals and gave it to me. Very composed, she said "This came from Rio and you must take this back to Rio. You will know what to do with it when you get there!" I protested that I could not possibly take such an important family ornament on what seemed like a 'wild goosechase' mission to Rio. Anyway, the large heavy crystal would take up almost all my baggage allowance. But Paget was adamant – so early next day I found myself lugging a heavy bag into Gatwick airport with absolutely no idea why or what I was supposed to do with the huge crystal inside it.

So here I was in hot noisy Rio (dance music blasting out all the warm night long through open windows) with the crystal in my bag under the bed and no idea what I was going to be doing over the next few days. I had been sitting next to an important lady from the Quaker movement during my flight over and she had been lamenting how the Quakers were no longer in the vanguard of protest against the ecological vandalism which now ravaged the Earth. Gone were the days of front-line protests such as those against atomic war. And so it was at the Alternative Summit; none of the Quakers nor the conventional religions had a visible presence except for the Bahai. I knew nothing about the Bahai. They had many well-dressed attendants and a "peace centre" where anyone could go to relax and meditate in calm surroundings. The Bahai were there, they said, to help facilitate good accord and positive debate – often there would be one or two Bahai people in each of the 30 or so separate large conference tents. (There was one tent for each of the Treaty groups.)

I spent my time exploring the numerous NGO stands which filled the extensive public park beside the beach. I tried to find out what organisations were doing and attended two or three of the more important debates in the various Treaty tents. The entire scene was hot, busy and dusty. The park spread over about 4 or 5 acres and was the centre of "alternative" conference activity for probably 10,000 people from virtually every country on Earth. Naturally there was a multiplicity of languages and a wonderful variety of clothing. Relatively rich people from the NGOs of western industrialised countries wore cheap T shirts, shorts and sandals. People from "poorer" countries wore smarter clothes to befit this great event. The most beautifully dressed were tribal peoples, whether from Africa or the Americas, whose wonderful embroidered hand-made clothes would have been completely unaffordable for those of us (rich?) from the west. So the cost and quality of people's clothing was in inverse relationship to their conventional "wealth" – a rather interesting fact!

The other very striking feature (to me at any rate) of the Rio Earth Summit was the clothing and working environment of the "official" delegates – including the representatives of the big "corporate" western NGOs. These people wore dark business suits – with shirts and ties for the men. Of course, all of their working environment was fully air conditioned – both in their official cars and in their hotels and conference centres. Their clothing was totally unsuitable for the hot, humid climate of Rio. In fact, they had cut themselves off from any contact whatever with the real world around them. This was, of course, a perfect match for the "make believe" world of infinite resources which our dominant consumer cultures (especially economists) believe can be exploited indefinitely by an all-powerful human species. I realised then that the "business suit" is a uniform which evidently gives man the "right to plunder!"

In the Alternative Treaty tents themselves I was very struck by the unwritten and very civilised formalities which were observed quite naturally in all of the debates. Generally there was no time limit set on the length of each contribution. There was an absolute rule that nobody should interrupt another speaker. Furthermore the delays inherent in simultaneous translation provided time for people to understand more clearly what the previous speaker had actually been saying before they attempted any response. Of course, there were arguments and forceful debate – sometimes to the point of personality battles which were not helpful to progressing arguments. I had learned from my work with RAIN, the writings of Star Hawk and the experiences of Donuts and Bio-regionalists that ritual and ceremony could be more powerful than argument. I took to carrying about with me a number of small smooth stones which I had found on the beach. When delegates sometimes became locked in arguments which had become very emotionally charged, I took it upon myself to come forward to the dais and place one of the small stones on it. I would then bow to the "contestants" and begin to return to my seat. Invariably either one or other of the participants would ask what the stone was there for? I would simply reply that it was a magic stone which would help them resolve the arguments which had, until then, seemed insurmountable. Usually there was then some huffing and puffing – sighs of "ridiculous!" or "nonsense" but invariably the argument ended and discussion moved on. The stone and its intervention simply broke the emotional tensions.

I suppose my unconventional behaviour did attract some attention – this strange man with the stones! Of course, nobody knew then that I had an even larger stone under my bed nearby! But I still had no idea how and when Paget's big crystal would find its purpose.

Every morning at around 9am the Alternative Treaties delegates would gather in plenary assembly – in a very large conference auditorium which was actually a distance away from the tented park. Several hundred people would gather each day to hear the news, venues for planned demonstrations, times of information talks and anything else anybody thought useful. Slides with information and announcements would be projected large onto screens as delegates with something to say queued at 3 separate microphones to take their turns. Again this was an impressive example of "good" human behaviour – generally people waited their turn to make sensible and brief statements. If it was necessary or useful to respond to some contribution then the assembly simply left this to be the responsibility of the following speaker (who may have been planning to speak about something completely different). I was particularly impressed after hearing a tragic and passionate speech from a native Brazilian whose land and village had been taken away by a large and aggressive corporation with the connivance of the Brazilian government. He urged delegates to join them to make a violent protest, blocking roads and smashing government buildings. The whole gathering became tense with emotion. I wondered what would happen next. The speaker next in line was a small and fragile looking Indian lady who had been hoping to speak about tree planting in the Himalayas. After the passionate tale we had all just heard, I wondered what she would do. In the event she was brilliant – extremely sympathetic on the one hand but cautioning her "brother" to take great care in case their demonstration collapsed into violence, losing them public support and putting them in the wrong just as the corporation and government had been in the wrong. It was heart-warming to see how humans could behave in such an unselfish, responsible and responsive way.

As the days went by there was one issue which kept coming up in the morning plenary session without any resolution. This was the tricky question of whether the global NGO movement should now accept a formal invitation to have seats allocated to NGOs within the United Nations. Some delegates, particularly those from the US, said this would be a one-off opportunity for NGOs to assert their right to be part of the collection of government representatives who could really make changes in global policies. Others, particularly those from Malaysia, saw the invitation as a plot to wrap up the often uncomfortable campaigning of NGOs in smart suits and comfortable rhetoric. They felt the outcome would simply bury NGO concerns within the carefully orchestrated corridors of power. After four abortive days of inconclusive debate the Plenary Assembly decided that this important but controversial issue should be passed on for decision to a group of 12 delegates – 2 to be chosen by each of the 6 continental areas of the Earth. This was agreed. Each continental region held its own meetings every night so that evening each would choose its 2 representatives and these 12 would then meet in a special conference tent in two days' time. Whatever conclusion the 12 reached would be accepted as binding on the global NGO movement.

I was impressed that, yet again, the assembly seemed to have found a positive way to handle a very tricky question. Strong feelings had already been expressed by many delegates – some even imagining that the entire proposal was simply a plot by the American CIA to bring NGOs within the conventional fold. That evening when I attended the meeting of the European region there were about 30 people present – a few I had already met at earlier gatherings in Europe, either at Paris or at ANPED (an Association of large European NGOs that had met in Rome). There was a fairly brief discussion of the controversial UN proposal (the group strongly opposed accepting the UN invitation) and then the question arose as to who would be the 2 chosen representatives from Europe. Although I had hardly spoken, several of the leading personalities immediately turned to me to ask if I would be prepared to be one of the European representatives. They said they had liked both what I had said and the way I had said it. I protested that they hardly knew me – no, they said but we know enough and we are sure you will do a good job. (We were all of the view that accepting the UN invitation would end the powerful independent role which NGOs now held outside the formal mechanisms of government. Many of us had already seen how the delegates from the big, established NGOs were already wearing their suits and ties within the air-conditioned corporate sponsored conference spaces – seduced by the trappings of power.)

So there it was – I began to think how I would make an impact on the forthcoming "crunch" debate with the other 11 representatives.

Sure enough, Paget's big crystal was my answer. On the day of the big debate I put the glittering crystal into my bag and lugged it with me to the tent where the debate would take place. It was a bright hot day, the tent crowded with spectators and TV crews. How were things going to unfold? Nobody knew I had the big crystal in my bag under my seat but I had to choose my moment carefully so that revealing the crystal would make the greatest impact – there would only be one chance. As I expected, the debate dragged on with the US delegates slugging it out with those from Malaysia. Even after an hour or so, no consensus had been reached. Finally I decided that the moment had come when I would make my (dramatic) contribution. I rose from my seat, taking the big crystal from my bag and walked forward into the centre of the small circle as everyone gazed on in amazement. Slowly I put the crystal in the centre and returned to my seat. The TV cameras loved it – the other delegates were puzzled as to what would happen next. I sat down and made my small speech just saying that when the molecules came together to make those beautiful crystals nobody told them what to do – they just knew what to do. We would be wrong to give up our independence by becoming part of the formal machinery of governments that we did not believe in. This intervention immediately brought the debate to an end as a big majority of the delegates agreed to refuse the invitation. The 'magic' crystal had indeed found a use in a way that I could never have imagined – perhaps Paget had some intuition or instinct that I did not know of. It was one of the strangest experiences of my life.

For reasons I do not to this day understand, I felt I should keep the story of my intervention in the history of the global NGO movement a secret. Somehow the strange 'magic' of that crystal had to be protected so it could never again simply become an expensive trinket on a wealthy family's sideboard. I told nobody what had happened – not for more than 15 years – and it's a strange story to look back on with all the "if's" and "maybe's" which might have prevented it ever happening. Quietly and alone, I put the crystal back into my bag and walked slowly down to the Rio harbour where I knew the Greenpeace boat was moored. There was nobody about when I took the crystal out and threw it far out into the Rio harbour beside the Greenpeace ship. As far as I know, it must still be there today – a silent witness to what had been a monumental day. It felt very strange to have found myself acting as a "tool" for the fates on that unique day in Rio when all the peoples of the Earth had come together for the first time to talk about a viable future.

So by now after a week in the heat of Rio, I had gone from being an anonymous nobody to somebody who everybody in the Alternative Treaty camp talked about in the whispered corridors of gossip. "The man with the stones!" As the days available for finishing the Alternative Treaties work ran out, it became clear that the NGOs would not be able to finish their work at Rio. So what could be done? I had already met Robert Pollard (my contact from Ya Wananchi); he was still beavering away again at his computers in Rio. I discussed with him the possibility of us two working together to help the NGOs complete their work after Rio had ended. Surely we could do this via email and regular liaison with all the groups involved. He was excited by this. I agreed to provide him with board and lodging at my home on the golf course where I now had a big office and plenty of spare bedrooms. We went together to see the movers and shakers in the NGO co-ordinating office and they were happy to say 'just do it!". So we did. Robert took up residence in Millbrook and used his computer enthusiasm and energy to keep in touch with (and chase when necessary) over 170 different NGOs all over the world. For the next 12 months we worked together on this ambitious project – he did the chasing and communicating, I did the editing and policy feedback. Eventually we had all the Treaties agreed and completed. We circulated the electronic version to all our NGO contributors but I also had a thousand copies printed at my own expense. Despite their strongly opposing views, it is strange to see that the United Nations has now accepted the validity of these Alternative Treaties from 1992 and posted copies on their official website.

Altogether the Rio experience had unfolded like some pre-scripted storybook saga. It was truly extraordinary that my strong initial misgivings had eventually led to my taking such a central role in the whole Alternative Rio scene. I had met many wonderful people – especially those from places where even the most basic necessities of life were extremely hard to find – water and fuel for example. I had seen that the air-conditioned world of suits and ties was a world of profit and corporate power which had become totally disconnected from the real world. For the most part, our elected governments simply pandered to this "make believe" world of apparently infinite resources in their attempts to boost consumerism and employment. I had seen that it was the people (tribal and indigenous) who had least in terms of modern resources who held their heads up highest and wore the most beautifully handmade clothes. I had been sad to see the run-down cheap sweaty T shirts and shorts worn by most of the western NGO delegates – as if they were apologising for their very existence. I resolved in my own mind that I could never again "preach" to others as to what they should or should not do unless I could myself move towards a lifestyle more in harmony with the natural world. Many of the other westerners I had met at Rio felt exactly the same – and they too would make huge changes in their lifestyles. It was this imperative which led me to Ireland to join John Seymour and Angela Ashe on their (more or less) self-sufficient smallholding.

Post-script to Rio

5 years after Rio the French again took steps to try and "throw dust" in the face of the United States. As with Ya Wananchi in 1991, the French provided a big NGO (this time Dutch) with funds to organise a 5-year follow-up to Rio that would bring together NGOs from all over the world. Clearly, the hope was that such a meeting would lead to a global outcry about the lack of progress being made. Once again the aim was to irritate the US!

About 2 weeks before the follow-up conference was scheduled to take place (in Copenhagen) I received a phone call "out of the blue" from the Dutch NGO responsible for arranging the event. I was told that the NGO now found itself in great difficulty because it turned out that the French would only provide the necessary funds on condition that each representative received a printed copy of the Alternative Treaties! So the question was – could I provide 500 copies and get them to Copenhagen within 10 days?

I very much wanted to support the Conference so told the organisers that I would do my best to produce the Treaties. Of course it would not be cheap – each printed Treaty would cost about £2.50 to produce at such short notice and I would need to be reimbursed for my fuel and ferry expenses (4 ferry trips – Ireland/UK and UK/Holland). I sent them my invoice and made my arrangements to rush over to the UK, get the Treaties printed and then take the big boxes to Denmark in my small van.

Everything did work out and I finally arrived in Copenhagen where the organisers met me with sighs of relief. The Treaties were duly distributed and the conference got under way.

This was a very different event to the Alternative Rio Summit because it was only attended by delegates from the larger NGOs. True, they had arrived from all over the Earth and they did represent many thousands of their members but there were none of the smaller NGOs and certainly no tribal or ethnic peoples. All the delegates were professional salaried staff from what had become large corporate NGOs – the "bleeding heart" organisations as I had come to call them. Of course, such organisations raise huge sums in charitable donations as they promote their work through dramatic advertising and skilful fund raising. But generally the idealists who founded them have long since retired or moved on leaving hard-nosed business people in charge.

I found myself extremely depressed by the attitudes I found when talking to the delegates. They were certainly interested in whether their fellow delegates had better salaries, retirement packages and working conditions than their own. And had they been able to fly business class? But none of them seemed keen to "rock the boat" by being controversial. Many of the journalists I talked to felt exactly the same as I did – the event was a complete "damp squib". Then, to cap it all, the Dutch NGO organisers did not make the payment which had been promised to me – they simply wound themselves up and disappeared leaving me several thousand pounds out of pocket. It was not a good experience.

Also in 1992

It was a busy and significant year. I met John and Angela several times both in England and Ireland – they even came to stay at Millbrook. I went on a 3-week trip out to New Zealand with Hal, Jan Mills and Luke (Ron's eldest boy) – catching up with Rupert and family and seeing all the usual tourist sights. Later in the year I finally broke up with Paget and broke my arm falling off my bike when taking Hal to school. Millbrook was a busy place and a thriving business. We had many happy times there but my first family was growing up fast and all would soon be heading off in new directions. I did not know it then but my big house at Millbrook (Lyshott House) would soon become an empty shell. This is a picture of the family as it was then.

Dylan, Ceri, Rupert with Hal, Helen, James, Gael, baby Georgina, David, Cecily

MY QUEST 6

My experiences at Rio made me see that the "suits" (corporate, government and NGO) who ran the world were doing so largely for their own purposes and from a standpoint where they had effectively cut themselves off from the real natural world. For them, the "natural world" was simply a ready (and apparently) unlimited source (out there somewhere) of useful resources which technology would always be able to convert into consumer goods. The growing number of reasonably well-off western environmental protesters were a relatively small group of angry, shabby, slightly guilty individuals who could be "bought off" fairly easily by talk of sustainability and one or two global treaties dealing with key concerns. In between was the huge mass of the world's population, struggling to survive the exploitation of their countries by greedy corporations, on the one hand, and their own desire to adopt western consumer lifestyles on the other.

My quest for solutions to the global problems found an outlet in my work to edit and finally publish the Alternative Treaties. These seemed to me at least an expression of a different set of more life-enhancing values which a large number of ordinary people on the Earth would prefer to live by. But, in themselves, the Alternative Treaties provided no mechanisms which could either encourage or put into effect a transition from one world to another. In looking for such a mechanism I was inspired by both John Seymour, Wendell Berry and to some extent by Paget and the Dandelions. The answer began with the realisation that "we are the problem and we are the solution". If each individual was able to take even small steps towards more "right living" then the challenges of living the good life on a healthy planet could begin to be solved. This realisation provided the genesis of self-sufficiency and my move to live and work with John Seymour in Ireland.

Chapter 8: The School for Self-sufficiency 1993

This is the view of the great river Barrow from my upstairs office at Killowen. Together with John, Angela, Hal, Roisin and Liam, we had many wonderful times there.

A few months after I first met John and Angela, I found myself astride my trusty BMW motorbike heading west towards the boat at Fishguard. I had telephoned Angela to say I would be along to see them by the end of the day. It was just 9am in the morning. Angela (who was later to become my wife) says she turned to John and told him that Will Sutherland had said he would be coming that evening but frankly she doubted whether he would make it! She was very nearly right as I had several missed turns along the narrow Irish boreens, one of which took me deep into one of the neighbour's manure heaps. As my heavily laden motorcycle crawled deeper into the black mire I had no alternative but to keep moving – the question was whether the slurry would get deeper or finally slope up towards dry land! Fate was on my side or my story might have been very different.

When I finally arrived at Killowen, Angela rustled us up a lovely supper. A large ham was brought in from the storeroom and generous slices were cut; fresh eggs and mushrooms were fried and served with thick slices of home-made brown bread and butter. It was all washed down with large mugs of home brewed beer. John and I talked away in front of an open fire in the tiny wood panelled living room which they called the "snug" because it was so small. We sat late into the night discussing their plans to start the School and I heard more of their story.

John had retired from farming in 1980 when he sold his farm to his children in Wales. He had got into terrible debt and was unable to buy another home because of these debts. Luckily he had heard from a friend that there was a small cottage in Ireland which he could rent for £10 per week. This sounded perfect as a rural idyll in which to devote time to writing. It was then he asked Angela if she would like to go along with him. Angela was one of the young students who had been working at the Welsh farm.

They had arrived at Killowen on a dark autumn night to find there was no running water, no electricity and, worse still, the cottage had a leaky roof and a fine rats' nest above the front door! From the outset Angela insisted that the place was sorted out properly – it was extremely hard work carrying all the water up from the spring down by the river. They started immediately to clear the garden which was a mass of briars, brambles and rocks. Although the rent of £10 per week did not seem much, Angela told John he must get it reduced to £5 and this was duly agreed. At long last a breath of financial good sense had been brought to bear on the Seymour lifestyle.

Before long, hard work had turned the cottage into a clean and comfortable home where John was able to concentrate on his writing. They called this remote cottage at Killowen "Davitt cottage" as a tribute to Michael Davitt who was probably one of the world's most successful cultural engineers. Davitt was the brains and inspiration behind the Irish Land League which came to prominence in the late 19th century. Although Davitt began his nationalist campaign as a committed Fenian he later realised that violence could achieve nothing but more violence. Born in 1845, he and his family were evicted from their home when he was four years old – like many of their fellow Irish they left Ireland for Liverpool. Davitt worked in factories as a child but lost his arm in a machine accident. Providentially this led to him being properly educated thanks to support from a local philanthropist. The wider vision which this provided, together with his long experience in British prisons, made him see that there were other ways to fight against imperialism by use of civil action and the formal mechanisms of democratic government. Davitt raised large sums of money by travelling widely and promoting his ideas in talks and articles. Eventually the Land League (which was fronted by Charles Parnell who later led the 1916 Easter uprising) had enough funds to enable the workers on Colonel Boycott's estate to down tools. Boycott was ruined and forced to leave Ireland – this is where the term "boycott" originated. This, and the idea that non-violent action could achieve progress, was really the beginning of the end for colonial rule in Ireland. Throughout his life, Davitt campaigned for non-violent action to progress his egalitarian and liberal ideas. Davitt was the first person to realise how colonial rule could be undermined, and ultimately destroyed, by withdrawing support from the system rather than fighting against it. Ghandi would use a similar approach in his struggle against British rule in India.

Whilst at Killowen John wrote 15 of his books as well as making a major series of environmental films for the BBC. These documentaries were broadcast at the very beginning of environmental awareness amongst the public and they took John and Angela all over the world with BBC film crews. Later John and Angela would spend 2 years travelling the length and breadth of Britain and Ireland giving talks to promote John's books and ideas. It was during this time on the road that John and Angela realized that just talking about better ways of living was not enough. What people needed were practical examples of good home and community economies and so the seeds were sown for what was to become the School for Self Sufficiency.

After 10 years of hard work John and Angela had cleared off many of the debts but they were still not in a position to raise enough cash to get a school started. A proper cowshed would have to be built, a cow purchased and there would need to be more tools and a rotavator. I was able to give them the financial assistance they needed and I very much enjoyed my occasional visits to help get the project off the ground. As time went by and John's great strength began to fade with age I was able to give more of my own time to making the project a success. It was amazing how people from all over the world seemed to find out about the school and miraculously make their way to find us at the bottom righthand corner of Ireland.

Eventually I became increasingly frustrated by the rigorous and exam-obsessed education system in England. It did not seem a good place for an active young boy like Hal to be. I decided to move to Ireland and Angela and I became a couple (later we married). From 1993 onwards John, Angela and I worked together running the school.

Sadly John is with us no more but his work certainly lives on, not just in his books and writing but also in the continued work at the School for Self Sufficiency. The sales of *The New Complete Book of Self Sufficiency* continue to increase each year and Dorling Kindersley still take the trouble to keep new editions up to date. Although John is not here himself, his spirit imbues everything we do on our self-sufficiency courses. We had many good times together in our Killowen family – the sketch below was done by one of our (talented) Italian WWOOFers! (Willing Workers on Organic Farms is a wonderful "organisation" which operates websites in almost every country of the world offering willing volunteers the chance to work with many different types of "hosts", all of whom run organic farms of some kind.)

1993

My records and diaries for 1993 are skimpy. It was the year I made a definitive decision to throw in my lot with John and Angela in Ireland so I gradually began to spend more time there and they frequently came to Millbrook. Gleb was still staying at Millbrook – as an impoverished architectural student from Moscow he was unable to afford accommodation in London. I failed to buy a possible estate for development as a golf course in France and dropped the idea of selling Millbrook. Throughout the year I worked on the Alternative Treaties with Robert Pollard. We pressed on with all the routine maintenance and improvements at Millbrook and Hal attended the Waverley primary school in Flitwick near Millbrook.

Visits to Ireland

My trips back and forth to Ireland became more frequent. It was inspiring to talk and get to know John and Angela. Not only had John written the definitive book on self-sufficiency (what some might call "right living") but he had also, with Angela and Herve Giradet, made what was probably the very first serious BBC documentary about man's often disastrous impact on the environment. The film was made in Iraq and was called "Far from Paradise". John had trained in agriculture as a young man before leaving England to spend many years (before the outbreak of the Second World War) working in Africa, first as an itinerant vet and later as a copper miner and finally a fisherman. John had great energy and an enquiring mind so he was constantly reading and talking to the interesting people he made it his business to meet. He had also served for many years as a professional soldier, first in the Italian war in Ethiopia and then for the entire Burma campaign fighting with African soldiers against the Japanese. He very seldom talked about his wartime experiences but fighting the Japanese had clearly been a brutal experience. His troops were all black Africans and spoke Swahili. They fought through thick jungle with no tents and all supplies dropped by air. Conserving ammunition was key so his greatest challenge was to train his men not to shoot until the enemy were so close they could not miss. The worst feature of the war for John was the fact that no Japanese would ever surrender. During all the years of the campaign they were unable to take a single prisoner. Every wounded or captured Japanese soldier kept one grenade ready primed hidden under his jacket. Their aim was to kill the enemy and themselves as soon as anyone came close enough. They held an absolute belief that it was dishonourable to surrender. The consequence was that each wounded or cornered enemy soldier had to be shot dead from a safe distance. John did not find this easy for, as he said, these were just ordinary farmers or fishermen caught up following their orders in a battle which was outside their control.

John was not what anyone would call a good "businessman"! He had never really settled down after his wartime experiences – any money he had he would spend immediately – preferably on champagne at the Ritz! He told us he would never have survived the war if it had not been for the wind-up gramophone he had carried with him throughout the jungle campaign. He had taken 6 classical recordings with him and it was only by playing these during quieter moments that the horrors of the situation could be put in perspective by the civilising influence of musical genius. After the war he decided he could never take a conventional job. He soon found a way to earn some cash by setting off overland to India and writing a book about it – "The Hard Way to India". On his return he lived in an old trolley bus before he joined Bob Roberts (the famous folk ballad singer) crewing an old Thames sailing barge taking coastal cargoes around Britain and Holland.

Finally he met his Australian wife Sally and they soon had a family (3 daughters). Eventually she persuaded him to leave the peripatetic life of the sea and move to a dilapidated old cottage in Suffolk. There they had to learn from scratch how to grow food and rear animals for themselves. Sally was a gifted artist and potter. Together they wrote the (now famous) book "The Fat of the Land", which is a very personal and amusing tale of all their successes and failures. John would go on to write many more books, several of them guide-books, as a way of earning some cash. Later John and Sally would put together the first book of self-sufficiency ("Self Sufficiency") where all the diagrams and illustrations were (beautifully) drawn by Sally. As always, John's text was direct, opinionated and practical. This original version was published by Faber and is now a collector's item.

John and Sally struggled on because they had little money – John made extra cash by working as a reporter for the BBC (hence his later work on the TV documentary "Far from Paradise"). He also wrote a number of very successful guide-books about different areas of Britain. It must have been a helter-skelter roller coaster life because John was a great adventurer and performer. He needed excitement and he needed singing, music and dancing. He loved the hurly burly of the country or dockside pub with its great melting pot of interesting folk. Time and routine had no meaning for him. I found from my own experience (especially when John could no longer drive himself as his eyesight faded) that going out to the pub with John was always a potentially exciting experience. Who would we meet? Where would we end up? Would we get back the same day? His stamina and capacity for wine, women and song was what we might now call "mega"! John was the ultimate party man – never frightened of dancing on the table – and Ireland was definitely the right place for him to be.

In 1964 John had moved with Sally to a much larger farm at Fachongle in Wales. This became a meeting place for many important and influential radical thinkers of the time. Remember that the world was just beginning to adjust to the new realities of the industrial consumer age after publication of Rachel Carson's book "Silent Spring". John's visitors included Leopold Kohr ("The Breakdown of Nations"), John Papworth

("Resurgence"), Fritz Schumacher ("Small is Beautiful") and Ivan Illich ("Deschooling Society"). Taken together, the writings and speeches produced by this group had a profound impact on the development of alternative political thinking long before the green pressure Groups and official Green parties took the stage.

The big change in John's life came when two young men who worked in the London publishing business decided they had a new and potentially very profitable idea. They realised that money could be made by publishing a very lavishly designed book *provided its content did not date and it could be reprinted again and again without change or redesign.* Of course, as is often the case with new ideas, all their contemporaries believed they were crazy. Their names would later become household words – Dorling and Kindersley! John's book was one of two they chose to use in this (then) risky venture. They bought the publishing rights from Faber and work began with many artists and designers – all working with John over many months (and at great expense) to produce the book that would make their fortune. Perhaps they were lucky to have John on their team but they clearly had great intuition and an instinct for what would sell. John always had the great gift as a writer to make the reader feel they were talking to a real person with real opinions (good or bad). His content always included a good selection of personal anecdotes which brought the content to life. Of course, as I discovered later, many of these anecdotes were in the nature of the parables written in the Bible – some were even made up stories which provided a human context for transmitting useful information.

"The Complete Book of Self Sufficiency" was published in 1976 and D/K "hit the jackpot". Sales were booming and the money came pouring in. No doubt the sales were boosted by the popularity of the BBC's new series "The Good Life"! But in many ways it seemed that the surplus of new money simply made John's life more chaotic with more parties, more hippies and more unwise adventures. This all came to a crunch in 1981 when John "escaped" from all his complicated personal and financial troubles at Fachongle and left with young Angela Ashe as his only companion to make a new life in Ireland. John was a youthful 67 and Angela was still a teenager but she was tough, intelligent and extremely resourceful. Despite their difference in years, they were a devoted couple who loved each other like father and daughter. Fortunately for John, Angela was the only person I ever met who could keep him under some sort of control. This "control" applied particularly to money – the way it was earned and the way it was spent.

Angela was the seventh child (her twin sadly died at birth) of a staunchly Republican Irish family from Birmingham. As a young teenager she had "escaped' her stormy and troubled family to stay with her elder brother who had become part of the wild hippie set at Fachongle. Finding that life at the farm suited her better than Birmingham she stayed there and soon became a "person to be reckoned with" as she took on the important daily work of the dairy. She was the one who would end up supporting John when he needed it.

Under Angela's watchful eye, they were able to eke out a living as they steadily improved the old run-down cottage at Killowen. The site and the views are magical – overlooking the great sweep of the River Barrow and sheltered on the north side by a grove of magnificent beech trees. But Killowen is remote – accessed down a long (often muddy) farm lane and with no immediate neighbours. On my visits I always found Angela and John to be great hosts (Angela is a wonderful cook and housekeeper) and their simple lifestyle had its own great sophistication and attraction. But the first time I filled the kettle to make tea in the morning I was roundly ticked off for putting in too much water – why waste expensive electricity? I soon discovered that they were living hand-to-mouth as far as money was concerned.

The situation at Killowen was not a comfortable one for me, coming, as I did, from a wealthy farming background and owning a 7-bedroom mansion on my 100-acre Bedfordshire golf course. So what was to be done? Over songs and whisky in front of a roaring fire in the small Killowen "snug", we chewed over the possibilities for making a "self-sufficiency school". Already John and Angela frequently received visitors who wished to "meet the great man" – perhaps there might be some way to turn this interest into money? We talked about the type of courses we could do so visitors could actually pay to experience the satisfaction of a different (non-consumer) way of living and actually learn some of the skills set out in the "Complete Book". I very much wanted to help John and Angela so as to make this idea come to fruition. The whole potential project fitted with my own determination to find new directions after my experiences at Rio. I wondered what it might take to really get this idea started. John was adamant that any real smallholding must have a cow and a dairy but they did not have the money to build a new cowshed/dairy. So here I saw my opportunity and I offered to make a gift to them of £5,000 so the necessary work could be done. Angela was very nervous about this but I made it clear that I would make no conditions and there would be no strings attached. I would be happy to see the project succeed. And so the School for Self Sufficiency began.

Once the cowshed was built some research was needed to find a suitable house cow. As it happened Peter Goggin, who ran the little hardware shop in New Ross, wanted to give up his cow at that time so Polly soon found a new home at Killowen. She was a wonderful cow, producing great calves and copious supplies of milk. It was a very sad day when we had to have her put down many years later when she was 28 years old. Her udders, already large, had stretched over the years and when they were almost touching the ground she constantly got them torn and ripped by thorns and wire. It was becoming impossible for her to suckle or be milked. Each evening we brought Polly in with her calf so they could be separated but close to each other in the cowshed overnight before milking in the morning. Once milked, both animals could return to our small riverside field together.

As John became older and I spent more time in Ireland I began to help run the courses. I learned to make baskets from the local basket maker, Irene, and I learned from John how to make the "lectures" entertaining as well as informative. We soon found that running these courses involved much more than simply telling people how to grow food, lay blocks, or make baskets, beer and bread. It was mostly successful (in conventional terms) professional people that wanted to come on courses. They wanted to change their lives but most were not yet quite sure how. Many hours were spent talking about very personal questions as well as what could be done to "rescue" humanity from greed and consumerism. We met many fine people and made many good friends. The courses also provided an important source of income.

Tarantella

In Ireland I could not resist buying the rotting hulk of a very old National 18 racing dinghy which had been built (very beautifully) in 1939. She had been left to rot in somebody's back garden so rain water had collected in her stern and almost all of the oak ribs had rotted away. She still had her original cotton sails and measurement certificate and must, in her day, have been a very fast and sophisticated craft. Her owner had taken her to the local boatyard and there she was lying on the floor waiting to be fixed. The boatyard told me that it would have cost far too much in time and labour to replace the ribs etc, so she was now up for sale – her original name was Tarantella. I offered 500 euros for her – and this was accepted. We took her back to Killowen on her trailer and I built the roof and walls of what would become our future conservatory around her so we could work on her throughout the winter. We wanted to repair her properly using copper nails and roves – a job requiring two people, one inside the boat with the heavy rove punch, the other underneath with a big lump hammer to hold against the end of the copper nail. This old-fashioned system meant that the ribs could be fitted extremely tightly to the clinker planking which was still in very good condition. (Copper nails are used because they do not rust and the copper they release into the wood prevents rot and decay. The nails are square so they don't split the timber. The nail is tapped through a hole which has been made with a gimlet – a sharp spike which parts the fibres of the wood without cutting them. The roves are small copper disks with a hole in the centre that fits over the protruding length of nail.)

We had to cut 3 inches off all the planking at the stern to remove the rotten sections and we had to buy tropical hardwood to rebuild the transom. The new oak ribs had to be made from American oak which had the necessary straight grain which permitted steaming and bending without the thin ribs splitting. It was a challenging job to soak the oak ribs in boiling water, passing them to and fro until they were sufficiently hot to be pliable. They then had to be rushed to the boat, squeezed into place while they were still very hot then holes had to be forced through them with a sharp gimlet (not drilled which would weaken the wood) so that the copper nails could be passed through from the underneath. Copper nails and the rove punch make a very tight fastening – the excess length of copper nail above the rove can then be snipped off leaving a very neat strong finish.

It took several months to finish this job before we finally took her down to the beach at Duncannon and dropped her off in shallow sea water. We were depressed to find she leaked more like a basket than a boat – but we knew the old planking would take some time to "take up". Slowly the sea water would soak into the old wood making it expand tight against the nails and roves. Sure enough when she had been in the water for 24 hours back in the river at Killowen she was completely watertight – a wonderful transformation. We had many happy sailing excursions in her sometimes down to the Hook and other times up to St Mullins. We learned to have great respect for the power of the river Barrow as well as the great sweeping current generated by the tide. When we finally bought a small 4 horsepower outboard we could explore the river with much more freedom.

Here she is – in lovely fully repaired form

By the end of this year I had formed a great love for Ireland and the slower more civilised way of life that still persisted there. We enjoyed wonderful late-night music sessions at local pubs – particularly Colfer's pub run by the Murphy brothers over at Bannow. The talent and creative zip of the musicians and singers was of a different kind altogether from anything I had experienced in England. Angela and John were both great singers themselves and would often give a turn as we sat around the dining table.

I was still a single parent at this time as far as young Hal was concerned and I was not happy with the way in which grading and exams were increasingly dominating the English schooling system. I could already see that Ireland had a lot to offer and I could also see that John (at almost 80 years old) was not getting any younger. Angela and I were now lovers and this was something John was very pleased about because he had always known that Angela must make her own life for herself with some suitable younger man. We all got along well and enjoyed many good times together. As far as I was concerned, a new world was opening up and I was able to leave the day to day hassles of running a golf course and the sad memories of life with Sue far away over the sea in England. John was like a cheery grandfather for Hal and would tell him wonderful stories as Hal sat on his knee by the fire in the Killowen snug. Every winter night once the clock passed 6 pm John would get out the whisky bottle as the "sun was over the yard arm" and light the fire in the snug while Angela and/or I prepared supper.

There was a wonderful postscript to our Tarantella story. There is, in Ireland, a very active Class Association for modern National 18 dinghies. The latest boats are super-fast racing machines, long enough to cope effectively with the often choppy wide waters around Ireland. They have 2 trapezes and ultra-light hulls. I contacted the Class Secretary because I thought it would be interesting to take our restored boat to one of the regular race meetings. His response was to suggest that I write a short story for the Class magazine – about how we had discovered and restored the boat. This I duly did – including a photo. Several weeks later I received an email "out of the blue" from a gentleman in the UK. He told me how excited he was to see this story. This was because he was sitting beside his grand-father who had been one of the shipwrights who originally built Tarantella before the Second World War. I sent him some more photos which he was delighted to have.

1994

Life during the year continued to involve frequent trips back-wards and forwards between Millbrook and Killowen. During the summer we held our first proper course in self-sufficiency at Killowen so this was the beginning of what became a regular seasonal business. John was still reasonably fit at this time and we had a fully operational dairy making pounds of cheese, butter and cream plus the usual pigs and chickens, of course. We had decided that I would build a small extension on the west end of the cottage to include an office, a spare bedroom and shower room and a properly designed composting toilet.

1995 – Some Significant Deaths

We continued the routine of regular travel between Millbrook and Killowen. John Papworth's lovely wife Marcelle died of cancer. We visited her in hospital to say "goodbye" just a day or two before she died. Then we were able to give her a natural burial on a plot of woodland owned by the family in the west country – we dug her grave ourselves and it was altogether a memorable, sad but cathartic occasion. All this came about because of the initiative which had been taken by our friend Nicholas Albery in setting up the Natural Death Centre. We often met Nicholas at the wonderful supper parties given by John Papworth. A charming unconventional man, he always had a twinkle in his eye and a radical idea up his sleeve. (He also set up the Institute for Social Inventions which gave a prize each year to the best new social invention.) Nicholas's German wife Josefine was a dark and formidable creature who we all tried to avoid (fortunately supper parties were not "her thing").

Nicholas believed that the English (and westerners in general) were hopelessly in denial about death. Mostly they wanted to pretend it did not exist or simply would not happen to them. And when it did happen the ritual was so impersonal and automatic that it was virtually meaningless. His demure and seemingly humourless wife fully supported Nicholas's initiative and together they set up the Natural Death Centre. Each year the Centre would organise a National Day of Death where enlightened undertakers and coffin makers could show their wares. Each year the Centre awarded a prize for the best organised "death" (funeral) of the year. Bio-degradable coffins were strongly advised and, if possible, the bereaved were encouraged to dig the grave and bury their loved one themselves – even on their own property.

One other unconventional idea proposed by the Centre was that each person should be encouraged to have a professionally made video which would convey messages and memories to their loved ones when played at their funeral. To help with this the Centre had prepared a specific guidance document which might help people make such a video. Nicholas wished to have a trial session using this guidance document and it was arranged that a professional video maker would call at their flat and Josefine would make a suitable trial video using the guidance. When the time came Josefine fell ill so Nicholas took her place – and the video was duly shot. A couple of weeks later, to everyone's horror, Nicholas himself was killed whilst sitting in the passenger seat of his mother's car as she drove from the driveway into the path of an oncoming car. (Nicholas himself did not drive or own a car as he believed cars were evil.) So tragically those of us who went to Nicholas's funeral saw and heard him talking to us "from beyond the grave" – it was a sympathetic and moving experience.

Later in 1995 Hal's grandfather – the sole remaining Woodward – also died and, to our surprise, we were contacted by his lawyers in Uttoxeter to be told that his entire estate had been left with them in trust for Hal – to be used for his education and future welfare. This was an unexpected bonus and, despite resistance from the lawyers, I was able to arrange for the trust to buy a small flat in London as an investment and "pied a terre" in the UK. This proved to be a good decision as the rest of the money in stocks and shares was steadily drained away with school fees and other educational expenditures.

Also in 1995

In July I arranged to drive out on my BMW to meet up with Angela and John, who were in Austria trying to help local village people find employment in providing activity summer holidays (in the slack time between skiing seasons). The Austrians had been impressed by our initiative in starting the self-sufficiency school and wanted to learn more about our methods and experience. The villages were already experimenting with growing flax and making their own linen, which was then made into (very expensive and beautiful) clothing. They also had a business making cedar roofing shingles which are a very effective and common way to cover roofs in Austria. It was a charming experience to work with these "well grounded" people as well as being impressive to see how they were able to keep their mountainous village communities alive. Angela and I then drove south through the Alps to Italy and back home through France.

In October Rupert and Helen got married – by this time Rupert already had his PhD and had a new job working for the key government science agency in New Zealand.

1996

This is the year Hal moves schooling from Flitwick in Bedford to Campile in Ireland. SS courses continue in Ireland. Hal, Angela and I have a very good skiing holiday with Rupert Morris in the Peter Pan hotel in Chamonix. Dylan goes off teaching in China. We finish the house extension at Killowen and Hal moves into his new room in October. My aunt Doreen's husband, Les, dies on the day they publish their book called "Unexpected Deaths in Suffolk" – a research project based on old parish records.

Angela's Temper

Late in 1996 I have my first truly frightening late-night episode trying to calm and manage a violent temper tantrum from Angela. I remember one visiting journalist describing Angela as a cross between Attila the Hun and Margaret Thatcher – definitely someone you wanted to be "on your side". I knew, of course, that this unbridled fierceness was a strength as well as a weakness in the types of family situation which Angela had evidently faced during her early years in Birmingham. It was also a huge asset when trying to manage John and his many rowdy (and potentially destructive) drinking pals. Nobody would cross Angela except by mistake – especially as she would often threaten to call in her big brothers to dish out suitably nasty additional punishment.

Angela had certainly had a complicated and often stormy upbringing. I am no expert on the complexities of individual personalities and I never really was able to understand, let alone manage, her dangerous outbursts of temper. In her public persona Angela was invariably polite, well-spoken and perfectly turned out – even cleaning the underneath of her shoes! For the most part she had learned to control her demons. But when the demons struck – as they seemed to do perhaps 3 or 4 times each year – you had better watch out because anything might happen. Angela's grasp of the emotional complexities of the human world were (and no doubt "are") orders of magnitude greater than mine. But her general level of trust in other people and their motives was paper-thin so that the slightest signs could provoke massive (and often inappropriate) retaliation. As the years went by, her lack of trust in me and her (completely incorrect) suspicions that I was unfaithful to her, got worse and worse – as this story will show.

Hal in Ireland

Once in Ireland young Hal was faced with a completely new set of values and behaviours. No more rigours of testing and exams and no more constant comparisons between your toys and theirs. Primary school at Horeswood was a relaxed affair where prowess at hurling was much more important than the type of car driven by your parents (Ireland had not yet launched into its disastrous journey to become the Celtic Tiger – fuelled by easy EU credit). The so-called Gaelic sports of Ireland have a tremendous significance because all attempts by the English to ban them during colonial times failed. Indeed the GAA (the

Gaelic Athletic Association) became the stalking horse for rebellion against colonial rule. The rules of the GAA put a total ban on anyone who was seen either attending or playing in one of the "British" games – like football, rugby or cricket. Such a "traitor" would be debarred from GAA membership for life! These rules have been relaxed today but their influence is strong and this is why it is amazing that the Irish do so well at these "banned" sports now.

In County Wexford it is the Gaelic sport hurling that has become almost a religion. Every young boy starts playing with his first hurley stick almost as soon as he can walk. Fathers and sons can be seen whacking the schlitter (the hard leather hurley ball) backwards and forward on the big beach at Duncannon almost every day of the week. Hurling is a fast and extremely athletic game where a good eye for a fast-moving ball is essential. Many Irish villages will have (somewhere just outside the housing) a big high wall which the local lads (and it is mostly lads) can use to hit the ball against with their hurleys; so for hour after hour they practice their hand-eye co-ordination. Hal was already blessed with fast legs and a good eye for a ball and took to hurling with great enthusiasm. He became a star of the local village team and people even talked about him possibly becoming the first Englishman to play for Wexford.

Hal also enjoyed playing his flute and soon got into the spirit of the Irish who love performance of all kinds. We would often go to "sessions" at the various pubs nearby (I think New Ross had about 95 pubs then!) where great "craic" was to be had. There was no restriction on kids being in pubs at this time so even the late summer evenings (it's light until 11 o'clock in Ireland on a summer evening) we'd all be enjoying the songs and music. These were great family occasions.

After Horeswood, Hal would go on to become a boarder at the very friendly and very liberal Quaker school of Newtown in Waterford. Sport and music (especially singing) formed a very important part of school life and Hal would make many good life-long friends from amongst his school pals. I think it is fair to say that Hal was a pretty lively pupil – not, perhaps, as focussed and disciplined as he might have been as far as the academic side of work was concerned. But he was a great sportsman – particularly hockey and athletics – and became a talented singer as part of the school's prize-winning Chamber Choir. I remember his music teacher grumbling that Hal was rather a disruptive influence on her class so I suggested she ask him to sing the solos. Fair play to her, she took this risk and sure enough Hal became one of her star soloists – even going on to pass an audition for the select All Ireland Chamber Choir.

Music

One great debt I owe to my time in Ireland is the pleasure I now get from playing music on my 'cello. This is how all that came about. Obviously in Ireland we frequently went to powerful lively music sessions in the local pubs – Ireland is famous for these. I saw how important music, poetry and song are throughout all society and activity in Ireland. At almost any dinner party, every guest would be expected to make some contribution to the merriment – and it was normally a solo contribution. Children learned music and dance from a very young age to take part in the competitions – and those who became "All Ireland Champions" found fame on the same sort of scale as professional footballers! The Welsh have similar features in their culture as do the Scots but somehow the English lost most of theirs in the hard years of Cromwell and the Puritans.

It constantly amazed and impressed me to see how easily the folk musicians and singers played all their music from memory – often for hour after hour late into the night. I had learned to play the 'cello and piano at school but strictly "from the black notes" – the very idea of playing by ear or even from memory just seemed to be an impossible dream. I could already see that the ambience and culture of the Irish music session was entirely different from the rather military culture of classical music training in England. Irish players had a pint of Guinness (usually) beside them and a smile on their faces – any newcomer was welcomed in with an invitation to share whatever tune or recitation they might have to offer! It was the trying and taking part that mattered rather than just the accuracy of the notes or rendition (up to a point anyway). This was very different from what I had found when I ever played a wrong note in England – players and conductors seemed to take this as almost a personal insult – "how dare anyone play a wrong note!". So here in Ireland there seemed to be a much more positive attitude – certainly much more friendly and less intimidating than what I had experienced in England. Several times people who found I could read a musical score were amazed that I no longer played – to them it seemed crazy because very few of the folk musicians could read written music notation – musical notation was a black art as far as they were concerned.

There is certainly a strange cultural divide between folk and classical music. There is a very strong tradition in folk music that all tunes should be learned "by ear" either in a session or, more often now, from a specially made recording. The argument is that you cannot get the folk rhythm and authentic interpretation just by reading from the black notes. This produces a strange (and unsatisfactory in my view) compromise in the teaching of folk music where if the tune is written down at all it is written using the names of the notes (A, B, C, etc) rather than in conventional musical notation. This is cumbersome to say the least and creates a difficult barrier for those wishing to learn to read conventional music scores later in life.

What finally tipped the scales on music for me was reading an article in the New Scientist magazine which summarised the results of a big research project looking at the link between practice and musical performance. These results seemed to contradict the story I had always been told (by parents and English musicians) that either you had musical talent or you did not. If you did not have the talent then you might as well give up. What the study found was that of all the thousands of music students questioned not a single one who was now regarded as excellent had done less than 10,000 hours of practice. There was no magical short-cut to becoming a good musician. They concluded that anyone who was prepared to spend 10,000 hours practising would indeed become a good musician (that's about 3 hours each day for 10 years!). This also tied in with what I had been told by experienced music teachers – that it normally took about 10 years of constant playing for a person to reach a grade 8 standard.

So against this background I "took the plunge" and decided I would now make 10 minutes each day free to play my 'cello. And, more than that, I would try to learn some tunes WITHOUT using any written notes. This was indeed a long voyage of discovery and rediscovery and, luckily for me, I had the support and backing of Angela and John as I began my hesitant beginnings. Angela also decided to take recorder lessons so we were at least exploring new musical things together. I stuck to my plan and, for better or worse, took my 'cello up every day and gave it 10 minutes (usually a few more, of course!). It was hard going at first but I stumbled on and after a few weeks I could almost play one simple tune – without using the notes. Somehow, miraculously, it steadily became easier. After a year or so I could play a few tunes rather shakily but I was at least convinced that the New Scientist researchers had been right. My brain was adjusting and what had at first seemed impossible was at least now possible – if still difficult.

When I had learned just a few simple tunes I decided it was time to brave my other "hang-up", which was a fear of playing in public. Nobody wants to become a source of ridicule or to look like a fool in front of people you know. My answer to this was to jump in our old van and travel 20 miles or so to a strange town where I would not be known – there I could make a fool of myself without serious consequence. So this I did – very nervously I must admit. But, on the whole my audiences were surprised and generally supportive to see this strange old chap trying to play some traditional Irish music on a 'cello. Good for the Irish! This all proved positive. The next step was to brave some of the local sessions where, once again, I found the musicians supportive if mildly amused.

By the end of the next year I would be brave enough to try my hand playing major classical works with the Wexford Sinfonia. Here again the other musicians were supportive of a new relatively inexperienced player. Olwen, the first 'cellist, paired me up with Anne Mcleod, who was as patient a person as she was excellent as a musician. A great new world had opened up for me. It was just as exciting to wait for the conductor's baton to come down at the beginning of a great symphony played in a beautiful cathedral as it had been to be waiting to drive off in some important golf match. To all those who had the patience to help me I am eternally grateful – and to anyone reading this who may feel they have no musical talent, believe me, you are wrong. Music is a gift we all have – all it takes is practice, self-belief and some friendly support and you, too, can play. I'm not shy about my music now and I can play a hundred tunes I never thought I could – it's true magic.

Having re-learned to play the 'cello I was keen to encourage other "mature" adults to re-discover the music-making they may have left behind at school. I began to give private individual lessons to a number of keen would-be players – in fact they learned surprisingly quickly because they were all highly motivated to do so. One lady was so taken with my lovely old 'cello that she wanted to buy it from me – which she did. I then had the challenging and tricky job of finding a new 'cello for myself. Choosing a new instrument, one that you may well spend the rest of your life with, is not a quick or easy task! I visited numerous music shops – in Oxford, Bristol and, finally London. It had been my expectation that London would be the most expensive but this did not prove to be the case and I found the options at Quiviers in Mortimer Street very interesting. When you want to buy an instrument you give the shop some idea of your budget and the kind of thing you are looking for. They then dig out 5 or 6 instruments they think may fit the bill – and you spend a couple of hours in their practice room trying each one. Some are easy to play but weak in sound, others more demanding but stronger; some have good high notes, others strong low notes … and so it goes on. After 2 hours I really could find none that really stood out but then I saw a strangely coloured (purple) 'cello hanging on the wall of the practice room. I thought I'd just give that a try. "Wow" – it was fantastic, bright, strong, resonant and easy to play. I rushed downstairs to ask the shop whether it was for sale. "Yes – it was – but for £28,000". I nearly fell over at that point but the salesman was quick to tell me that he did have another similar 'cello from the same workshop (in Chicago) – perhaps I'd like to try that one? It was £20,000 cheaper but I liked it as a good strong instrument – very pretty and made by a Polish luthier (called Jan Bobak – he's now quite famous). And here it is …

My Bobak 'cello

1997 – Sale of Lyshott House and dealings with David Clay

Hal is now going to school in Ireland and we are much more based there. Self-sufficiency courses continue and we spend a fair bit of time getting to know people involved in environmental groups in Ireland. John, Angela, Hal and I continue to work pretty well as a family "team" although Angela and I have another scary fight in February. By now I have paid off John's mortgage on the cottage at Killowen and the courses are running along well. We have a regular stream of WWOOFers – usually young people from almost any country in the world – mostly great people. Generally we prefer couples and ask them to stay for more than 2 weeks so we don't waste time simply training them. At my mother's suggestion we had bought a large second-hand mobile home which we installed at the top of the garden to provide simple but comfortable accommodation.

In April this year I have a strange experience on a sudden quick trip to London. I have seen an advert that Nigel Kennedy will be playing a special solo violin concert in the Festival Hall. This is a concert to mark his return to public performance after a long lay-off. The first half of the concert will be unaccompanied Bach, the second part a tribute to Bob Marley. I book my ticket by phone and head off across the Irish sea to pick up my motorbike at Millbrook. After whizzing down to town and parking my bike outside the Festival Hall I am just putting my jacket and helmet into the cloakroom when I hear my name shouted from the other end of the foyer. By a most strange coincidence it is my old Cambridge pal Les Hales, who has just flown over from Hong Kong with his wife Rosetta to go to the same concert. Even more strange, we find that we have bought tickets in the same row within 2 seats of each other! He from Hong Kong, me from Ireland, and our seats just two apart – we sit together in the event and enjoy a great virtuoso performance.

In summer we put Lyshott House up for sale as my first

family have now "spread their wings" and we can use the money better elsewhere. This all goes through OK and we decide to rent a place in Woburn Sands to ensure we have a base near Millbrook. Later in the year I finally pluck up the courage to join the Wexford Sinfonia and learn to establish myself as a competent orchestral player. During June I become determined to move on from Millbrook by putting it up for sale. We have no decent offers as this is a time when several new golf courses have been built nearby – rather saturating the market. In frustration, I decide to take up an offer to meet a special consultant, David Clay, who says he has a clever scheme to raise a large capital sum by rebranding Millbrook as a new smarter course, Lyshott Heath, and selling special memberships through extensive advertising and smart brochures. Although I am dubious about the scheme I eventually decide to go ahead as I am keen to move on after losing nearly half my club members to a newly formed "members' club" set up with the aid and assistance of my former (and very good) club secretary (who has left and taken my membership records with her!). David Clay's scheme required me to pay him a large monthly retainer. The scheme struggles on – only partially successful until several years later a new group of members (again assisted by the club manager) stage another coup so they can finally buy the course in 2002.

In October Angela, Hal and I make a good holiday trip to go skiing in the US with Ben and Bonna – we enjoyed the trip.

1998

Routine business continues in Ireland – again we run courses. Dylan gets his "blue" playing golf for Cambridge University in the Varsity match against Oxford. He's at my old college in Cambridge now after applying to do a PhD on the financing of the Chinese motor industry. This all came about after his great experiences teaching English in China, which enabled him to become proficient in Chinese. Naturally Cambridge were keen to be involved in understanding the extraordinary transformation of the Chinese economy. At Millbrook, Derek Cooke starts as the new course manager (it's now rebranded as Lyshott Heath). John Seymour's eyesight begins to fail – he's 84 years old now and can no longer drive – I have the job now of driving him as necessary. Roisin is born by Caesarean section in Waterford – Angela is almost killed by a cold blood transfusion. We buy a second-hand wooden traditional Cornish Crabber sailing boat and take it over to Ireland – it's a great boat and we will have many good times sailing in it on the Shannon and up the river Barrow. SS courses continue. Harry is born to Rupert and Helen in New Zealand.

1999

This is the year when we are heavily involved in direct action protests against construction of a waste incinerator near Campile and the planting of genetically engineered sugar beet by Monsanto near Duncannon.

Early in the year all local residents around Campile receive a smart shiny leaflet inviting us to a presentation in the village hall – this would be a chance to hear about a new proposal to build a modern waste incinerator on the site of the old power station. We duly went along to the meeting, which was well attended. The presentation was slick and the presenters were suave smartly dressed (well paid!) folk from the city. We were assured that the incinerator would operate at very high temperatures so that all plastic by-products would be safely destroyed and, in any case, the gas discharges would be continually monitored. And, of course, local jobs would also be provided. (Ireland was struggling to find a rational waste disposal policy at the time – particularly for Dublin – and most of the waste would be coming from that city.) Not surprisingly, the local people were very suspicious – it all seemed too good to be true and we knew that elsewhere in Europe incinerators had been banned because of the dangers of atmospheric pollution. The question and answer session did not go well for the presenters and the meeting broke up in some disarray.

Speaking with local people afterwards, I said I felt that some sort of direct action was necessary if we wanted to make sure politicians understood our concerns – simply writing letters or making speeches would not do. I suggested we make an anti-incinerator logo (a smoking factory within a black circle with a diagonal line through it) and fix posters with the logo on roadsides all over the area. A group of tough looking local lads thought this was a great idea – no need to worry they would do it and they'd fix stencilled logos on plywood backing high on every lamppost they could find. They lived virtually underneath the power station chimneys and they were not going to sit back and let these city smoothies do as they pleased.

Within days we found the lads' logo signs all over Wexford – they had certainly done their stuff and it made a big impression. The sheer number of signs all along the main road from Rosslare towards Waterford was making all the tourists ask what was going on. And local media had a field day showing the scale of the protest. It certainly did have a big impact and local politicians soon began to take up the protest. The government and the promoters of the scheme quickly backed down.

The sugar beet drama marked the beginning of efforts by Monsanto to increase the sale of their most profitable product – the non-selective weedkiller "Roundup". Wexford is Ireland's major sugar-beet growing area – it has most sun! By genetically modifying sugar-beet plants so they became tolerant to Roundup, farmers would be able to control all weeds simply by spraying the entire crop with the weedkiller. We believed that experience showed that any unknown man-made genetic species could create totally unforeseeable problems if it was introduced into the natural ecological environment. The dynamic nature of complex interactions between natural species and their environment could (as it had many times in the past) lead to dramatic problems. Why would anyone allow or encourage such risks simply so a big international company could make larger profits? It all seemed both risky and unnecessary – and anyway we suspected that the weeds themselves would quickly become resistant (as they have done!).

We soon found ourselves at meetings with groups of concerned young people and students from Dublin. Monsanto hired their own specialist security firms to monitor the new experimental crops and photograph protestors. With all the hustle and bustle, everybody in New Ross knew of the protests and the reasons why. John became the figurehead and "leader" of the protests. We found great support generally for the case against Monsanto although nobody wanted to upset the local farmer who had been paid a good sum to carry out the planting. A great get-together was arranged for protestors to meet in the village of Duncannon near to the affected fields. On the morning of the action day I was woken early on a very wet morning by a knock on the door. Outside I found a very wet friend from the pub, big Richie. Over his shoulder he had a sack. "I have them" he said and showed me the smashed remains of hundreds of beet plants. He had wasted no time in helping out the protestors and had spent most of that dark wet night destroying a large part of the crop. This was a prelude to a day of action where John, with the young protestors, would rampage through the fields destroying any remaining plants. 7 were arrested and later taken to court in New Ross in what became an internationally well-known event – the trial of the Arthurstown Seven! In the event great speeches were made – but the judge took a very lenient view and was very critical of the overbearing attitude of Monsanto. John found himself being interviewed by TV crews from as far afield as Australia and the USA – it was not the kind of publicity Monsanto wanted! They did try to plant more beet in the following year but we destroyed that as well by spraying with a conventional weedkiller. Monsanto gave up after that.

At home in Killowen life moved along. Roisin was growing up quickly and in April Liam was born – also in Waterford hospital. It was a happy time with two young babies to keep us busy. In the Autumn I was the one to accompany John on yet another trip to Salzburg, where we would be the celebrity speakers at a major meeting of mountain village Lord Mayors. The Salzburg local government had always had a very strong desire to keep village life alive in the mountains and valleys around the town. To provide advice and inspiration to support this policy the town had originally awarded one of its top honours to the Austrian academic and writer Leopold Kohr. Kohr had always written forcefully about his belief that humans behave differently (better) if they live in small communities rather than in huge faceless cities. His writings and thinking had been very influential on both John Seymour and John Papworth and they had all known each other well. Kohr was "famous" for his disgust at consumerism – the TV he had in his living room had no screen and certainly no electronics; inside the empty space where the screen should have been was an empty bottle of coca-cola! After Kohr died the city of Salzburg decided to appoint John Seymour to fill his place as a man providing celebrity inspiration. John, too, was awarded the city's top honour and we were treated like royalty – staying in the best hotel and going to the finest restaurants and concerts. Later we would be taxied out to the mountains each day to take part in the bi-annual conference of village mayors. It was quite an inspiration to see how progressive the mayors were in trying to find imaginative solutions to provide local employment and activity.

The primary aim of the mayors' conference was to reinforce the state's policies for keeping diverse economic activities going so as to provide employment in the mountain villages all year around. Many villages already had a good winter income from the accommodation they provided for skiing. Our job was to inspire and re-assure the mayors about the sense and effectiveness of the state's continuing efforts to keep people living and working in the mountain areas. New ways had to be found of keeping remote communities viable as the way of life they provided was very special.

It was an interesting trip. Strange to arrive from the muddy lane of Killowen to be treated like royalty in the sophisticated bright lights and beautiful buildings of Salzburg. I had taken my 'cello with me – partly to pass the time and partly to show the Austrians how folk music formed such a vibrant part of rural life in Ireland. To my surprise, the organisers of the trip laid on a special concert at which I was to be the sole performer – it was not quite the arrangement I had been expecting (perhaps an informal session in the bar!). So everything was arranged with rows of chairs set up in the big hotel conference room and I did my best to put on a decent show! They took it all very seriously.

Back at Killowen we began work on clearing the ground for the foundations of a new large extension which would provide a big sitting room and a large "master" bedroom. Soon after work began, the digger driver uncovered a massive boulder which seemed to form part of the base of the rear house walls. Bear in mind that these old cottage walls were simply made from rubble and boulders filled in with mud and lime, then made waterproof by a good coating of plaster on the outside – there were no foundations. We all scratched our heads wondering whether or not to risk dislodging the huge boulder. The digger driver just left it there until he had finished all the other work excavating the site. Finally a decision had to be made – should he move the boulder or not? The driver took a big hammer from his cab and gave the boulder a mighty smack while he felt its surface and listened to the response. It seemed to ring out fairly well – not being damped by being fixed into the wall. Carefully he pushed it away (it was too heavy even for the big digger to lift) – and the house remained standing! Finally he could push and roll it away into a corner of the garden. We were now clear to start the building work.

Back at Millbrook I was still hoping that David Clay's ambitious scheme would produce results but the bank was getting increasingly hostile and the rebranding of Millbrook was not going as fast as we'd hoped.

2000

In January the Wexford Sinfonia played Beethoven's 4th piano concerto with the up and coming young Irish pianist Finghin Collins. His grasp of the piece (he was just 23 years old at the time) was amazing but we had a strange incident before our concert at the lovely old church in Graignamanor. It had been a bright winter day and we rehearsed all afternoon without problems – after all the church had huge vertical plane glass windows. But as evening fell we found ourselves virtually playing in the dark – this was long before the days of LED music lamps! Doom and gloom, it seemed that nobody had checked to see if the internal church lighting was working properly – and it certainly was not. But it was no easy job to fix new bulbs because the lighting was about 35 feet up above us in the church ceiling. Huge ladders had to be brought out and a great kerfuffle ensued as to whether we would get the lighting fixed in time before the audience appeared. There's certainly a lesson to be learned although now we all carry our small LED music-stand lights with us.

In February Angela and I decided we'd make a major trip to USA and New Zealand. We would visit Ben again in Annapolis and go on to see Rupert and Helen in New Zealand. We packed the young kids onto the plane and off we went. It was a good trip – and great to enjoy the warm summer sun in New Zealand, where we hired a car with air conditioning and enjoyed the great scenery and wonderful food. We came back via Los Angeles, where we stayed in a comfortable hotel recommended to us by the Air New Zealand cabin staff. We were most impressed by the facilities provided in New Zealand for those with young children – a complete contrast from Britain and the US. We came back to Europe in March.

In April we had drama aplenty after John went a bit crazy with the fire in the snug by piling paper and wood on until the flames became extreme. All this happened late on a Sunday evening while I was blissfully unaware at an orchestral rehearsal half an hour away in Wexford. Obviously the chimney then caught fire and the fire broke out through loose bricks in the chimney. This set the roof beams on fire and smoke very nearly suffocated the two young children who were sleeping in their bunks upstairs. The drama was relayed to me when I was enjoying a drink in the pub at Wexford around 10.30pm after finishing our rehearsal. The barmaid came over and to my great surprise informed me that Angela was on the phone and I needed to take the call immediately. It was a shock to be told that the house was on fire, but the kids were safe and the fire brigade now had the whole thing under control. I raced home to find a calm but chaotic scene – the roof was wrecked and the kids' room unusable. Fortunately for us, all was well insured and in fact we ended up with a completely new bathroom and a new roof – so, in the end, the fire turned out to be a blessing in disguise!

We had further dramas with the house later in the summer when all the sewerage became blocked. I soon cleared the sewerage pipes around the house but still could not find the blockage. When we looked into the large concrete cesspit which had been installed as a new fixture about 10 years previously (before I moved to Ireland) we discovered the liquid was just clear water. No sewage had ever reached the tank! The blockage must be somewhere between the tank and the house (about 30 metres away). Eventually I found there was another inspection cover which had been hidden under the wood in our big woodshed. When we lifted that cover we found there was a large inspection chamber – about 4 feet long, 4 feet deep and 18 inches wide. This was completely filled with beautiful black soil and all the healthy manure worms that went with it. Somehow this inspection chamber had served to take and process all the sewage produced by the cottage over the previous 10 years! It was a dramatic demonstration of the power of nature – worms in this case – and how "waste" is dealt with effectively by the natural world.

When we examined the pipework leading to the main septic

tank, we found that the builders who installed it had broken the pipe when they were building the tank. Instead of taking it all out and replacing it they had simply thrown some old plastic bags on top of the broken pipe and backfilled with earth. No doubt they imagined nobody would ever discover the break!

By now Hal was already boarding at Newtown School in Waterford. Newtown is a very old-established Quaker school with an excellent record in sport as well as academia and music. Hal would make many good friends there and we found the school's whole approach extremely constructive. The school's strongest resource was its music department, run by a very gifted lady who stood no nonsense and produced a series of wonderful singers and musicians. When she complained in Hal's report that he messed about too much in her classes I suggested to her that she might try making him sing the lead solos. She did just that and I have no doubt that the disciplined structure and encouragement she provided in the school's prize-winning Chamber Choir were exactly the training Hal needed.

Throughout 2000 I continued my building work on the new house extension – a big job which involved laying more than 3,000 blocks as well as building a strong slate roof. John was still able to help despite his age, by bringing up blocks so I could lay them. This building work would continue throughout the year. The other initiative I started this year was a plan to revise and extend John's original "Complete Book of Self Sufficiency". By now we had introduced quite a few new and useful features into the curriculum of our regular self-sufficiency courses – basket making, scything and block laying, for example. We could include these and more, as well as re-organise the structure of the book to make it easier to use. It also seemed sensible to take the chance whilst John was still very much alive and could continue to be associated with his original work. I worked out a proposed new structure and composed a large quantity of new text which we sent to David Lamb and Christopher Davies at DK in London. The new book would be substantially bigger (by about 100 pages) than the original and a considerable quantity of new artwork would also be needed – it was a major project. Fortunately DK gave the idea a favourable reception – remembering that the original book had been the foundation of their great success.

At Millbrook I continued to work with David Clay and to liaise with the senior managers at the bank. We took a tenancy of a house in Woburn Sands so as to have a sensible base to work from near the course.

MY QUEST 7

By living a more or less self-sufficient life at Killowen, I began to see much more clearly that it was not just the sympathetic management of one's local soil community (trees, animals, plants etc.) that mattered. Just as important was the non-material lifestyle that went with this. In our work with students and volunteers we could show (and they could take part in) a different kind of lifestyle which was not based on having more and more flashy goods or access to a dream world of Hollywood escapism. Beautiful meals, poetry, art, music, games, walks, friendship and good conversation – were all part of a different set of values to be enjoyed, surrounded by handmade artefacts suitable for "slow" living in unspoiled natural surroundings.

We saw it as our mission to share our lifestyle with as many people as we sensibly could. We did this by taking volunteers to live with us and help us – about 30 each year and mostly young energetic people – and by running our courses – again for about 30 people each year. We often had the news media calling around to make stories about our unusual way of life.

This was the reason I decided to pursue my "quest" by expanding and re-writing John Seymour's original Complete Book of Self Sufficiency. It took a little persuasion to get Dorling and Kindersley to take on the new version but finally they were "on board" and the new edition was eventually published. Thousands of copies of the New Complete Book in many languages are bought every year by interested people all over the world. The Book and the self-sufficiency website continue (in 2019) to provide education and inspiration for many thousands of people as well as bringing new students on my courses. I am greatly indebted to Ariane and Tom who came to Craster, Northumberland, in 2018, for all their help in updating and redesigning the self-sufficiency website (www.self-sufficiency.net).

New Complete Book

Chapter 9: Early Work on the New Complete Book, 2001

Early in the year we had a very positive response from David Lamb in London. He then invited us over to meet him and Christopher Davies for more detailed discussion of my proposal for a new expanded version. David and Christopher had been involved from the very first with the original Complete Book and were very positive about my proposals. They could now use clever new computer software to colour in all the original illustrations and a new team of artists and editors would be put together to get the new book together. I would be spending a lot of time with the new editors over the next 18 months. Unfortunately this proved to be a very stressful exercise where the designers pulled all the strings and did everything they could to make sure I got the blame for any delays. This was infuriating but probably quite normal in a modern profit-hungry business. Typically the editor/designers would send over perhaps a dozen pages of newly designed layout, pictures but no text, and ask me to fill in the necessary text boxes with exactly the correct number of words to fit the box. This, in itself, is not an easy task but they would also impose very tight deadlines – often of just a few days. Worse still, I was never allowed to meet the artists who were preparing the new artwork and illustrations (for reasons I never discovered – expense most likely). As a result, quite a few of the illustrations were factually incorrect (some still are as DK have consistently refused to amend them).

But one way or another, we were able to press on and steadily put the new book together. The editing team came out to Ireland and we commissioned our own artwork, too. We were also able to include important new chapters, including one on "Making the Break". John was even allowed to include reference to the "Merchants of Greed" in his new introduction! John, of course, was now too old and his eyesight too poor to make any other contribution to this new revised edition but he was happy to let me get on with it all. What is slightly irksome is that John's daughter Anne has never once said "thank you" to me for my work and initiative in getting the Complete Book revised, re-organised, extended and re-published. She, of course, is now the major recipient of the valuable stream of royalties which my work has produced – and she had no part whatsoever in producing the book. It is really quite extraordinary to see that her website makes absolutely no mention of the enormous role Angela and I played in giving her father a great 10 years of comfortable and worry-free life after sorting out all his financial troubles. Not only did I provide the cash to get the self-sufficiency courses going but I also paid off his mortgage and persuaded Dorling Kindersley to re-publish the New Complete Book. The royalties are of the order of £10,000 each year (I receive just 30 percent). It's a strange world because I'm sure Anne has no reason whatever to make an argument with me! Funny old life – but no doubt Anne had a pretty stressful childhood which has left its mark. I have no doubt that John, the wild explorer, must have been quite a nightmare to live with for his young family all those years ago.

2002 – The End of Millbrook

By the middle of 2001 the situation at Millbrook (now Lyshott Heath) had finally resolved itself as a ginger group of the members conceived a plan to purchase the course for the members. This was a scheme they cooked up during an annual exotic golf holiday they all took together in Thailand along with my new manager Derek Cooke. It was certainly a well organised "plot" and whether they were all masons or members of the rotary, there was a lot of secret action behind the scenes. The club "ginger group" had found a wealthy backer who, it seemed, was ready to put up the bulk of the money and let the club run the course themselves whilst it was simply a very long-term investment for him. This whole scheme came to a climax in 2002 when my bank foreclosed on my overdraft without any warning and the course was forced "into administration". The bank appointed a very expensive major firm of accountants to oversee the sale. These accountants charged me £20,000 for a single phone call in which they told me they were very happy for me to go on running the business whilst I negotiated a sensible sale (around £1 million) with the club ginger group and its wealthy supporter. This I was eventually able to do and when all the legal formalities were finally completed, the sale went through.

At one and the same time, it was a relief to leave all the day-to-day hassle of Millbrook, tax collectors and banks behind me. On the other, it was sad to see all my work taken over by the golf club members who would, I imagined, now proceed to cut down trees, fill in bunkers and generally make the course much less challenging. The members would, of course, do everything they could to remove the covenants I had put in place to try and ensure the land remained fully organic as it always had since I started work on it in 1976. Because of potential complications over possible claims for compensation from disgruntled Lyshott Heath members, my lawyers advised me to keep well clear of the business in the years immediately following the take-over. I was, in any case, not keen to witness the changes the members were likely to make.

The Fates step in – 14 years later

We had better jump forward now to revisit this story because things did not turn out in any way that I could have expected. By 2014 I had returned to Northumberland to help my 99-year-old mother manage her affairs and one day, out of the blue, I received a message from the Embleton golf club to say that a Duncan Steele had visited and was asking after me. Now I knew Duncan very well from old Millbrook days. Duncan's father, Terry Steele, had been one of my very first members and had always supported my work – even my most unpopular actions. Terry was a self-made businessman (in some sort of scrap metal business, I think). With a deep gruff voice and slow speech, Terry loved Millbrook and, as they say, "cut his own furrow" through life. His support and love for the place was often a great help in boosting my own resolve when things were not going well. Terry had been the first person to buy one of my original life memberships (for just £1,000) and he was always chuckling when he told other members what a bargain he had made!

Terry had just one son, Duncan, who often accompanied him to Millbrook even from quite a young age. As a young lad I've no doubt that Duncan was very much doted upon by his parents so it was not surprising perhaps that his efforts at golf often brought on some stormy outburst of temper and frustration. But Duncan was mad keen on golf and slowly but surely he began to master his demons. I would like to think I had a steadying influence as we played many games of golf together. Certainly I do believe I passed on some of my own golfing philosophy to Duncan. But I did not think Duncan had great academic or business ambitions, nor did I think I would ever see Duncan again after I passed the course to the members. So I wondered what this mysterious call had been about!

One way or another Duncan and I exchanged telephone numbers and I discovered, to my great surprise, that Duncan had now become Head Greenkeeper at Millbrook. We made an appointment to play golf together at Dunstanburgh and Duncan told me that he and his wife, Donna, were now living in Ron Mills' old house (that Ron and I had built together). They were managing the course together with an energetic young course manager and Duncan was absolutely committed to keeping Millbrook's character just as it had been when he was a boy. So the following year I plucked up the courage to visit Millbrook – still not quite knowing what I might expect to find. Ros and I were already in the south in our camper van so I planned to visit late on a summer evening when I hoped to be able to look around without having to meet any of my old "friends or enemies"! We parked the van well away from the course so as not to attract attention and walked up the driveway – the fine avenue of walnut trees still lined the drive towards the Chequers pub.

The fates had other surprises in store for us! We had not walked more than 100 yards when a car came down the road towards us. It stopped and the window wound down to reveal one of the Freeman twins with a big smile on his face – "Good evening , Mr Sutherland". He actually seemed pleased to see me as we exchanged a few pleasantries as if the 14 years since our last meeting had never happened. Chris and Bob Freeman had also been very early members to join Millbrook – they were identical twins but one had a moustache and the other did not!

We continued up the drive towards the clubhouse and it was amazing to see how the trees had grown to be ENORMOUS. The landscape had changed completely – very beautiful in the evening sunshine and totally transformed by the forest of trees. As we walked over the 9th fairway we saw a buggy racing towards us. It stopped beside us and Donna jumped out with a big smile on her face, warm greetings and big hugs. She was filling in divots after coming home from work and of course we must pull up our campervan into their driveway and spend the night. We continued our walk. Far from making the course easier, the trees now closed in the fairways making every hole even more challenging. I was surprised to see the row of walnut trees I had planted along the Woburn Road now standing 30 feet tall – they had always struggled in the shade of the big hedge but now the walnuts had won. Each of the dozen or so giant sequoias was now about 20 feet high; sweet chestnuts, oak, cedar and maple were all doing well. And all had grown much bigger than I could have expected.

When we had a chance to talk to Duncan and Donna it was fully evident that they loved Millbrook and the idea of Millbrook just as I had. By some cosmic process, the (sometimes grumpy) young boy I had played golf with so many years ago had now become the mature and committed guardian of the dream I had had myself all those years ago. Somehow the fates had been kind. As I write this in 2019, I could not wish the place to be in better hands.

Also in 2002

With dear old Nulla and building sand

I found myself nipping backwards and forwards to the UK throughout this year – partly to sort out the Millbrook sale and partly to liaise with Dorling Kindersley about the New Complete Book. We continued with SS courses at Killowen and had the usual crop of WWOOFers. We went skiing again at Isola. For the most part, life at Killowen was good. Roisin and Liam thrived as they helped in the garden and enjoyed the joys of rural life.

In the early part of the year Angela became very depressed and we had several nasty violent scenes which were very upsetting. To this day I don't know the reasons for all this. Certainly we were having increasing challenges managing

John's health, which was now going downhill – eyesight and hearing both going and various uncomfortable operations in hospital. To make things worse, John had (as many old people do) started to complain to others about our "failure" to look after him properly. This was particularly upsetting when he made these (unjustified) complaints to his daughter Anne in Wales.

When the golf course was finally sold I bought a house in Waterford for Angela and we resolved to take the children over there so they could attend the Gaelic speaking school nearby. By this time my tax affairs were being dealt with in Ireland and I was still not sure if I would be subject to heavy capital gains tax or legal challenge in the UK. So putting the new house in Angela's name seemed like a good idea. She simply kept the house when we finally separated so it provided useful financial resources for bringing up the children.

This year sees the New Complete Book finally completed and published. The year also sees us purchase a long-wheelbase green VW panel van which we take over to the UK to be converted into a camper van by a small firm who are agents for Reimo in Kent (they are a very big and successful firm now!). We call our camper van the "Skylark" and she went on to serve us/me faithfully for 15 years and 250,000 miles – a very satisfactory outcome.

2003

This is our first year without the golf course to worry about. We now have our city house over in Waterford and will live there much of the time so we can take the kids to the Irish speaking (Gaelic) school there. We continue with SS courses and WWOOFers. We go to Nice and skiing at Isola again. We go to Brittany to visit Angela's cousin Louise and her family. Angela and I have more nasty rows – again the cause remains a mystery to me but I know that Angela has at this time a very suspicious nature, always imagining people are plotting against her and imagining I am having affairs with other women.

We meet John's strange and very academic theological friend Edward Echelin. He is trying everything he can to find words in Christ's teachings which may encourage the established churches to be more outspoken about environmental problems. He is also a passionate opponent of the patenting of life forms and all types of genetic engineering. He's an interesting man to talk to and some weeks after his visit to Killowen we receive a small envelope through the post. It's from Edward and contains a very small (smaller than my thumb) piece of a bramble root. The accompanying letter tells us that he has stolen this small cutting from a commercial plant breeding station. He wants to prevent them being able to patent the plant so asks us to plant the cutting and spread the bramble as far and wide as we can! I duly find a vacant area in the garden and pop in the tiny root. It is not long before the plant is huge and rampant, growing new shoots at least 10 feet long every year which bury their ends in the ground and sprout new roots. It is truly a plant with "attitude" because it is covered in massive sharp thorns but it does produce huge tasty blackberries. These berries are about 4 times the size of wild blackberries which makes it easy to pick 10 pounds in a few minutes to make another gallon of excellent red wine (just like fresh Beaujolais!).

Over in the UK the big fateful occurrence is the sudden death of Ruth and Cecil Gilbert (Sarah's parents) in a car crash near Alnwick. It seemed that fate had taken a hand in resolving what might have become a very sad situation if one of this happily married couple had died before the other. As it was, we were told that both had died almost instantly as their small Citroen Deux-Chevaux was hit head-on by a large bus. The bus driver said he had been misled by a flashing indicator (because the Citroen had just pulled off the dual carriageway) and drove straight out into the main road when he should have stopped at the major junction. It was a tragic end to two long and productive lives. The joint funeral in Newcastle was a very sad occasion.

We continue to sail the Crabber over on the Shannon. I

continued to play concerts regularly with the Wexford Sinfonia.

In September both Roisin and Liam are injured at school by kids throwing rocks about on a nearby building site – this is not satisfactory and is one factor making us decide to educate the children at home. This is our legal right under the Irish constitution. We join the Irish Home Education Network (HEN) and soon become active members.

Ceri flies over to Ireland because she has concerns about the way Hal is being treated (both at home and at school) – we have various difficult meetings.

During 2003 we were troubled by unpleasant and unfounded arguments over John's care with the rest of his family. It seems to be a common occurrence where old people begin to lose their sense of proportion and begin to feel grumpy and sorry for themselves, often blaming those who care for them. The allegations and innuendo became so bad I wrote this open letter – sent to John's children – but it serves as a record of the true facts. Especially the financial support I provided for John (and Angela) in the early days.

3 May 2003

It is clear from the insults and accusations that have been flying around over the past few weeks that there are a great many misunderstandings about the financial relations between John, Angela and myself. There are a number of facts that I should like to make clear:

1. When John and Angela moved over to Killowen in October 1980 they were in an extremely precarious financial position.
John had a £20,000 debt to the Midland Bank on which he had to pay not just interest but also a life policy of £54 per month.
John had £15,000 capital gains tax to pay on the sale of the farm.
John had to pay a weekly sum of £67 to his ex-wife Francis.
John was having to pay Bristol accountants £3-4,000 each year to do his accounts.

2. At the start I believe John and Angela rented Killowen for £5 per week. The place was damp, full of rats and virtually without furniture. There was no running water or electricity and the only furniture they had was rotten old stuff left behind by the previous occupants and some old plastic chairs given by Paddy Burke. This was an extremely arduous situation for Angela but she coped with it and worked through it.

3. It was 3 years later that Angela and John managed to persuade the local bank manager to give them a 100 percent mortgage.

4. Angela eventually sorted out the English capital gains tax problem and persuaded John to give up his Bristol Accountants. But their problems were far from over for John was then given incorrect advice by Dublin accountants to the effect that he would not have to pay Irish tax because he was a writer. In fact only works of fiction are exempt and so John received a formal tax demand for £87,000 in 1992. Despite the fact that they both had to work very hard to pay off these debts they never ever had any money only borrowings and debts.

5. In this desperate financial situation John bought Dreolin – a boat which was virtually never used. Meanwhile Angela was still having to deal with constant hassle over money with tax men and bailiffs threatening to remove goods or take the house.

6. So when I first visited at Killowen John was facing demands for £87,000 Irish tax as well as having large outstanding mortgage debts on the house. His royalties at the time were very small and Angela was in the process of persuading him to set up the School for Self Sufficiency as a money earning business after years of slogging around England selling books. It was not a situation where the Bank would lend any more money, and all seemed desperate.

7. I had a great admiration for John's work so I decided to become involved and with Angela's help (she is a very practical and intelligent woman) I managed to pay off the tax debt and also lend them sufficient money to get the school started (a cowshed had to be built etc.) I also bought a half share in the boat to ease their cash crisis.

8. *There were still difficulties with paying the bank mortgage and, as my relationship with John and Angela developed, I decided to pay off the balance of the mortgage so that the Bank would have no further lien on the property. John was then able to go ahead with his longstanding wish that the house should belong to Angela so that her security and tenure would no longer be at risk. I believe John also altered his Will at this point so that his children would receive all the royalties from his writings rather than a half share going to Angela. I should say that I have absolutely no financial interest in Killowen whatever even though I have put a huge amount of work into improving the place.*
9. *All of the recent improvements, new furniture and extensions to the house were financed by a wedding present made to Angela by my mother. There is in fact very little left at Killowen which actually belongs to John because over the last few years he has been steadily giving things away.*
10. *None of this has been easy for me as I had serious problems with my own business in England which was going bankrupt. But I continued to believe in John's work and took on the task up updating "The Forgotten Arts and Crafts" for Dorling and Kindersley. After this had been done successfully we were able to negotiate a deal to extend and update "The Complete Book" and as John was ill and unable to work on it I spent most of last year producing the new book. The royalties from these books should bring John some income over the years to come.*
11. *John is an independent and forceful character and it has not always been easy to help him with his illnesses and his work but it has been a source of much pleasure to me to see him being able to spend money on himself, his trips and his family as a result of what I have been able to do to sort out the financial situation. I must emphasise that for the last 10 years all of John's royalties and pensions have been available to him to do what he liked with as Angela and I have been paying the*

living expense at Killowen. So I find it amazing that people keep implying that John has very little money to live on. Since his debts were cleared John has been spending his royalties and pension lavishly – for example:109 Euros for one meal with Jane, paying off Rhiannon's debts and giving her his cash card, taking other people out for expensive meals, his trip to Australia which cost him thousands, over £2,000 for a new hearing aid, £2,000 for his reading machine and so on. It has been good to see John being able to do this but ridiculous to hear people implying he is virtually penniless. At present I know John has £6,000 in his bank account in England plus his regular pension.

12. *The last few years have been extremely hard for Angela who has stood by John more or less single-handed, visiting him every day in hospital and trying to get him to take proper treatment for his eyes, his teeth, his back passage, his prostate, his strokes and his bladder. As you know, John was wetting his bed every night for almost a year before the crisis last summer. And all this has been going on at a time when Angela has had to deal with the trauma of her own mother's major stroke – having to fit in lengthy and tiring visits to Birmingham to take care of her.*
13. *Angela and John decided many years ago to reprint "The Fat of the Land" so together they set up Metanioa Press with a 100 percent loan. Angela and John undertook a huge publicity campaign to get this to work and eventually they paid off the loan and the book began to bring in a small amount of money. Without consulting Angela, John sold the American rights to some hillbilly for £350, he also sold the Norwegian rights without consultation. Angela was horrified by this and that is why she bought the English rights of the book which she now owns.*
14. *On several occasions Angela and I have offered to buy John a caravan so that he could stay in Wales more easily. Kate had previously refused to sell John back any land and later Anne said she could have no more caravans on her property. So the*

idea was dropped. Anne has now agreed with John to build a room onto her place which John would pay for. John is now at last in a position to do so because Angela and I have paid off all his debts.

15. *It is very good for John that his children are now able to make the time and the space to look after him in his old age but we are confused about what is going on now. John explained to us before he left for Wales that he wished to keep his base in Ireland so it is a big surprise to find that he has evidently changed his mind about this and now wants to move from Killowen permanently.*
16. *In view of all I have done for John without any expectation of recovering my money or receiving anything for the time and effort involved in helping him over the past 10 years, I am now extremely saddened and angered by all the implied criticism and resentment expressed by his children to Angela and myself. This does not create a climate for co-operation or renegotiating agreements that have already been made.*

It is very sad that the long, productive and loving relationship between Angela and John should now be spoiled by unnecessary allegations and unfounded suspicions. We have all done our best to live with and help John. None of us can claim to be perfect but we should at least be prepared to acknowledge this simple fact.

I hope you will all give this some careful thought and that in this way the destructive cycle of argument and counter-argument may be broken.

2004

John has finally moved over to live with his daughter Anne in Wales. On the one hand we are sorry to see him go but on the other we are fed up with the stress of constant criticism. John has become his own worst enemy as far as that is concerned. Like many old people, his mind is not always clear and he cannot help grumbling about the trial and tribulations of existence. We have had some very exhausting experiences trying to deal with his growing health problems and his blindness.

We go skiing again at Isola after Christmas at Killowen. I have more scary stormy rows with Angela.

Hal and Luke are involved in a serious car crash when Luke (who has no driving licence or permission) takes his mum's car on a mad midnight joy ride! Nobody is hurt but it's a bit of a shock.

We continue to run SS courses. We sail our Crabber on the Shannon. We go to Birmingham for the wedding of Angela's niece Carla. We go to Embleton to see my Mum (MS). I meet Tim Brooke, the architect, to discuss plans for developing the building site which I own to the south of Manor Cottage. I also discuss the sale of Manor Cottage itself with the estate agents, George White. MS, Doreen and cousin Diana come over to Ireland to spend some pleasant days at Killowen.

Jock Colquhoun, an old St Catharine's friend, dies of liver cancer. We rent out the Waterford house because we are now educating the children at home in Killowen.

We go over to see John in Wales, where he is very sick and barely able to speak. On our way back to Killowen we hear John has died so we turn around and head straight back to Wales for his burial and funeral. We dig his grave ourselves (with many friends to help) and bury him on his old farm. Later we will arrange a big public memorial service for John in the Star of the Sea church near Duncannon. We put up a fine gravestone as a memorial to him on the plot he bought for himself in the graveyard overlooking the sea. This is the poem he wanted on his memorial stone:

We are the music-makers,
And we are the dreamers of dreams,
Wandering by lone sea-breakers,
And sitting by desolate streams.
World-losers and world-forsakers,
Upon whom the pale moon gleams;
Yet we are the movers and shakers,
Of the world forever, it seems.

With wonderful deathless ditties
We build up the world's great cities,
And out of a fabulous story
We fashion an empire's glory:
One man with a dream, at pleasure,
Shall go forth and conquer a crown;
And three with a new song's measure
Can trample an empire down.

We, in the ages lying
In the buried past of the earth,
Built Nineveh with our sighing,
And Babel itself with our mirth;
And o'erthrew them with prophesying
To the old of the new world's worth;
For each age is a dream that is dying,
Or one that is coming to birth.

I sell Manor Cottage and buy a small new house in New Ross as an investment. I will work to do this house up over the next months before selling it again at a small profit.

In December my father's brother Gordon dies in Berwick aged 97 – we go to his funeral.

2005

After Christmas at Killowen we all fly to Nice for another holiday in the sun. We hire an apartment from Pierre Vacances, who seem good – at least you know what you are getting!

When we return we meet Wilco, who is a small wiry Dutchman. He lives in Spain with his German wife Heike and their 2 kids and they are “professional” house-sitters who own nothing but what they can put in their old VW estate car. Wilco had written to us earlier asking if he could bring his family to stay and work with us for 12 months so his children could learn English. We soon found Wilco was a brilliant linguist himself – speaking Dutch, German, Spanish, French, English and Russian – all fluently. He was also very hard working (when he needed to be) and a passionate disciple of forest archery. Heike and Wilco followed the simplest possible lifestyle as we discovered when they did indeed come over to live in our mobile home 6 months later. We found them to be extraordinary, resourceful people. Heike had been a champion athlete for the East Germans and was a tall slim powerful woman – she quickly established herself as a local community activist, running athletic training for the local kids and many other things at the local school. Their two boys were also of the Midwich cuckoo variety – blond, energetic and intelligent. Their eldest, Florian, was in his early teens and the finest looking boy you could imagine – like some angel with beautiful long blond hair down to his shoulders. He became school friends with another very striking boy – a tall black Rastafarian – and they made a most unusual pair as they walked through New Ross. As far as we could tell the family lived on some sort of small pension with Wilco taking on well-paid hard-labouring jobs (shovelling sand or cement) when they needed more cash. They kept themselves to themselves and were a great help.

In February I make a formal declaration that my residence for tax purposes began in Ireland in 2003. This is accepted and I get my RSI number (like a National Insurance number). My accountant confirms that I will receive no more UK tax returns – which is very beneficial since the capital gains tax laws in Ireland are much more generous and simple to apply compared to those of the UK.

I continue with my work to upgrade the new house I have bought in New Ross (laying floor tiles and putting in a kitchen). In March we all fly over to Embleton to see Ben and Bonna. We also make regular visits to Birmingham, where Angela's mother is now confined to a care-home after a nasty stroke which nearly killed her – she cannot speak and cannot move any part of one side of her body. It is a very distressing situation where she will live on for many years of agony and discomfort – unable to communicate and often in great pain.

At Killowen I continue to work on finishing off the new barn – laying a nice wooden floor and buying good quality slates for the roof. The barn will be a great asset as extra accommodation, teaching space and an excellent workshop. As always we continue to run the SS courses. Hal continues at Newtown school – singing solos now with the prize winning Chamber Choir, which makes a special trip to Prague. Later Hal will fly to the US to spend a couple of weeks with Ben and Bonna. Hal also experiences a crazy few weeks working as a building labourer for Angela's wild brother Jimmy in Wales.

The new barn at Killowen

In Waterford we find new tenants for the house at 56 Williamstown Park and in New Ross I finish and sell the house at 6 Orchard Close. During August we take a quick trip over to the UK to have a look at a possible larger sailing boat to buy – the Southerly 105 called *Masquerade*. Later in the year I will buy her and commission repair work before I sail her over to Ireland with the help of the previous owner, Peter. We put our dear old Cornish Crabber up for sale – she has been a wonderful boat but is rather too small now to take our more grown-up family. Eventually Dara Malloy, our friend from the Arran Islands, decides to buy her and we make arrangements to meet up with him on the Shannon, where his old Volvo has to strain every muscle to pull the 3.5 ton boat up on its trailer.

During 2005 we also buy a very smart fast 22-foot motor boat which we cannot resist when we see her on a trip down to Cornwall. We hope we may be able to use her for quicker trips to Waterford by river. We call her *Saoirse* – freedom – and take her back to Killowen behind the VW camper van. In fact we eventually find the stress and noise too much – and it's not easy to keep her safely moored on our tidal quay because the huge wash from passing cargo ships is likely to smash her against the stone. This is disappointing but we are forced to sell her to a wealthy Dublin lawyer.

In November we rent a small cottage for a week on the Arran islands – a fine week walking and exploring the amazing Bronze Age forts and the ancient Celtic shrines. We have some nice times with Dara and his family (who also home-educate their children as well as being great followers of the original Celtic Christianity).

2006

Work continues improving the property at Killowen and, with great help from Heike, we lay a big concrete driveway and parking area for improved access (without mud!). In January I fly over to Southampton to meet the yacht surveyor at Northshore – the survey of *Masquerade* is not too bad but quite a bit of (expensive) work will need to be done.

At the end of January we go over to the UK for the funeral of my mother's sister, Doreen. after her tragic death caused by a hospital accident. I also begin preparations for my Mum's 90th birthday, which we plan to hold at my grandfather, Sir Arthur's, former home, the Mansion House in Newcastle. I fly to Newcastle to discuss arrangements with the manager – the date is booked.

Once again we go over to the west to spend some time on the Arran Islands. In March we will again go skiing with Pierre Vacances in Isola. In April I finish off the balcony and concrete steps for the new barn – it's looking very good. In May we take a long caravan trip up to stay in the beautiful landscape of Donegal. Then it's time to fly to the UK for the 90th birthday party in Newcastle.

Granny at 95

Chapter 10: Granny's 90th Birthday Party

In June 2006 Granny (my Mum) would reach the great age of 90 years. I had decided that something special should be arranged to mark the occasion and my first "port of call" was Thurso House – now the "Mansion House". When I phoned the manager he was delighted to hear the family wanted to use the house for a big party – special terms were arranged, menus chosen, and seating organised. Invitations were duly dispatched to all the various branches of the family, dispersed as they were around Britain and the world.

Here is the attendance list for that wonderful 90th party:

2 JUNE PARTY 2006 – ATTENDANCE

Ben, Bonna, Lesley plus her parents, Gene and June	6
Owen, Jan, David and Jane plus Jonathan	5
Cousins Jo and Dil	2
Cousin Di and son Jack	2
Diana's son Tom, Rachel plus 2 kids	4
Ceri, Riaan, Cecily, Louis, Ralph, James, Georgina and Harriet	8
Dylan and Helen	2
William, Angela, Roisin, Liam, Hal, Philomena (A's sister)	6
Ian Sutherland and Ginny	2
John Sutherland plus Heather	2
Michael Sutherland plus partner	2
Mum (Peggy)	1

The whole affair went off well on a beautifully sunny day. The younger kids enjoyed themselves playing in the garden whilst the adults talked away and re-connected themselves with all the family news. Owen and I each made short speeches in rhyming form and my Mum was in very good spirits – really things could not have gone better. It was strange for me to revisit Thurso House after such a long time – seeing that the Council had left much of the upstairs rooms unchanged. My grandfather's bedroom was just as he had left it – his exercise bike still waiting for a new user! I wondered what the Queen must have thought when she stayed in the house!

There was a strange postscript to this great day when I was telephoned by the Newcastle police some weeks later. Evidently there had been some trickery or embezzlement involving the manager and staff. I was asked to provide a copy of the party invoice, which I did. We heard no more about it!

Masquerade sails to Ireland

Later in June it's time for me to go over to Northshore once again to pick up *Masquerade* and sail her back to Ireland. All the work has been done and the engine given a thorough maintenance overhaul (so they say) and we watch with some trepidation as the big mobile crane takes her slowly down to the quayside. I meet Peter (a very nice man who was the previous owner) as he has very kindly offered to help me crew the boat on its first trip for me (last trip for him) over to Waterford. We bring our kit on board and prepare to leave but when we actually start the engine and check that the cooling water is flowing properly we find a problem – very little cooling water seems to be flowing through. The engineers are called down and a new impeller is fitted in case this is the problem – but there is still not much improvement. The engine temperature seems to fluctuate although it does not seem to reach dangerous levels. We are assured that this is probably just a feature of the Southerly's engine – it does not put through much water and anyway water collects in the anti-siphon sump then blows out in a big rush. After a couple of hours delay whilst all this is investigated we finally motor off down the Solent.

It was a fine, calm night as we motored smoothly along the south coast. Our plan was to keep on down the coast until we could pull in to Falmouth to pick up a mooring and have a break. All this went smoothly – with occasional worries about the water temperature. We moored out in Falmouth harbour and rowed our tender in to have a nice dinner at a local pub. We would press on again early next morning after checking the weather forecast for our crossing of the Irish sea.

Masquerade at anchor near the Scilly Isles

Next day we had a firm south westerly breeze and headed off down towards Land's End – it's a forbidding point of rock with a threatening looking lighthouse. As night fell the wind began to pick up and we had to shorten sail. The waves became very steep and irregular (they are often like this in the shallow Irish sea when wind and tide are against each other). Life became rather uncomfortable and the automatic steering gear could no longer cope with the irregular wave patterns. Peter became very sea sick and was completely incapacitated. I shortened sail again as the wind reached gale force – we were crashing through the seas now, close-hauled on the port tack. It was great to see how the stiff, strong boat coped easily with the storm and I had no fears whatever of anything breaking.

The Southerly is an 8-ton yacht with a massive steel keel-plate and extremely strong rigging – perfectly at home in a gale. So I was left on my own, manning the helm full-time and bashing on through the storm. Just after midnight the storm cleared and I was amazed to see the boat surrounded by hundreds of small porpoises – it was somehow a re-assuring feeling not to be quite alone in the big black ocean. Soon the gale picked up again and we battered on through the rough dark night. It was a welcome sight to see the lights of the Hook as dawn broke – it had been a long night at the wheel and poor Peter was completely exhausted. But Masquerade had coped without problems and by lunchtime we were motoring sedately up the river Suir towards the marina at Waterford. After we tied up the boat, Angela picked us up and we enjoyed a fine supper back at Killowen before collapsing into a well-earned sleep.

Heike and Wilco left us later in June. We continued to run the SS courses and also took a long trip in *Masquerade* along the south Irish coast to Dungarvan and Cork. There was some wonderful sailing – a good trip. We left the boat moored in Nelson's pool at Crosshaven. We would have several more good sailing trips during the summer.

Home Education

In October Hal went up to University at Trinity in Dublin to begin a new chapter in his life. At Killowen we continued to take an active part in the running of the Home Education Network – with all the inevitable personality politics such organisations involve. There was continued debate in Ireland about how home education should be regulated – if indeed it should be regulated at all. As far as we were concerned, we had found the children's primary-school experience very unsatisfactory – no more than a babysitting service where the bright children became bored and the slow children got left behind whilst the teacher tried to control the 2 or 3 troublesome kids that came from disturbed homes. Children between the ages of 6 and 12 have an enormous range of capabilities and interests – girls tending to be much more academically interested than boys. With 30-plus kids in each class, conventional school can be a very unsettling experience – putting many kids off education altogether. We had Roisin, who was extremely capable, organised and conscientious – excellent at reading and writing at a very young age and very grown up in her whole outlook. She found primary school tiresome and boring when she wanted to get on with reading and finding out about the world. Liam, on the other hand, had little interest in academic learning at this stage because he was interested in how things worked.

With home education both children learned a lot about life from all the riding they could do up at our local stables run by the wise old Irishman Paddy. Paddy had years of experience teaching people to ride and he knew exactly which horses each child could cope with – gradually taking them into more challenging situations. We might worry about teenagers riding motorbikes but for some reason we never worried about our young offspring racing around the countryside on huge horses! You can do this in Ireland in a way you cannot in England.

Another big advantage of home education is the opportunities it provides for making music. We had bought a lovely old Schiedmayer piano at a second-hand piano shop in Birmingham and this was always available for the kids. Roisin had a violin and Liam a 'cello and it was easy for me to give the kids a basic grounding in reading music and finding the right notes on their instruments. We had many debates with professional music teachers who played in the Wexford Sinfonia about the best way to teach music. The traditional folk players were always adamant, of course, that all their music must be learned by ear from other good players – in this way the rhythms and interpretation would always be in line with tradition. All traditional tunes were played from memory. The "old school" classical teachers adopted a more military style of teaching – always from the notes and never from memory or by ear. The new school of Suzuki classical teachers taught everything "by ear" using CDs. So what was the best approach?

Playing in pub sessions I had found many of the traditional players keen to try and learn to play "from the notes" but later in life most found this extremely difficult because their brains were so conditioned to doing things differently. For many of these excellent musicians, these difficulties were a great sadness because they could see a whole huge world of music out there which they did not have easy access to. The classical orchestral players, on the other hand, were generally very frustrated that they were unable to join in sessions or play by ear – probably not more than 1in 10 could do this because their brains were so well conditioned to playing from the score. Those who became classical players via the Suzuki system also had to make a difficult transition at some point (usually in the teenage years) to learning to play from the black notes. I decided that learning to play "from the black notes" was the best compromise but I tried not to link black notes with the names of notes. Instead I simply showed the children where to put their fingers (on violin or 'cello) to play each note. I felt this would ensure a more direct link between the mark on the paper and the note being played. On the classical musical tradition in France exactly the opposite is true – they use the sol, fa system where each written note is first recognised in sol, fa and then this is the name of the note to be played.

One way or another, the children always had musical instruments close at hand and in tune so they could play as often as they liked. They picked things up very quickly and we soon found them a good piano teacher who also ran a small string group. This young teacher, Andrea, was a great advocate of learning music theory. This worried me at first because I had always found the theory both dry, difficult and boring. But I soon realised that the big advantage of theory is that you can get it 100 percent right – and it gives you a deeper perspective of the music you are playing. Roisin in particular seemed to really enjoy learning theory – as she would prove later with amazingly high marks in her theory exams. Later I was able to bring back a lovely Celtic harp from France (as a payment for house-sitting which I did for a friend in a big fancy chateau) and this, too, became part of the family musical activity.

I am often asked how we spend our time and what we do in our "smallholder's life" at Killowen. Most days are different, of course, because of weather, accident or unexpected visit. But the short summary of a typical day which I posted for subscribers to my website may give you at least a flavour of a typical day's routine. The children, of course, kept themselves busy in the company of the various animals on the smallholding.

A SMALLHOLDER'S DIARY – MAY 2007

Our smallholding day begins as soon as I open our big oak front door. Bran, our golden lab, meets me with a lick and the three cats, Corky, Reiltin and Ginger, meow hopefully for their morning milk. I slip on my steel-toe-capped rubber Birkenstocks and set off with the pig and chicken food. We use rolled barley and dried milk powder as a basic diet, made up into a mash by soaking it with a kettle of boiling water. The curlews are whistling down on the river Barrow as I walk up the garden and I can hear the two young pigs working themselves up for breakfast. We give the pigs all the substandard garden produce and weeds throughout the summer – what a great way to boost the compost heap and get some fine bacon as a bonus.

I leave some barley in the bucket for the chickens as I will be keeping them in for another hour just to discourage laying-out secretly in the orchard. Meanwhile there is the greenhouse to check. My midnight slug patrols have been yielding a frighteningly large quantity of multi-coloured slugs; these hungry pests seem unable to resist the lure of dry dog food which I put out in a plastic tub. They are then easily destroyed – but even so it is wise to check underneath any pots for rogue slugs which have escaped the midnight purge. The young tomatoes look fine and we won't have to water today. I keep a couple of full watering cans in the greenhouse so the water can warm up.

Angela has home-cured bacon on for breakfast and fried the frozen field mushrooms we saved from last autumn. Our two kids are already tucking into their hot porridge and honey. There is nothing like a proper bacon breakfast to get the day started. We have just eaten the last of our home-made brown bread so it is time to put on another batch. The kids help me mix up the flour so I can knead it and put the dough to rise before we all go out to collect the eggs and feed the chickens. The children love to collect the eggs. They also love to collect the post from our distant post-box on the smallholding gate – it seems to be one of the highlights of their day.

The weather is fine so my next job is to look over the new seedbeds to see what hoeing can be done. It's best to hoe in the morning. If you do this the hot sun has all day to dry out uprooted weeds. If you mark new sowing very accurately with straight lines between pegs then you can hoe between rows without danger. I like to hoe before the weeds even appear. Remember you can save quite a bit of cash if you make pegs from your own bamboo. Bamboo either grows like a voracious weed or not at all. I planted three clumps and only one has taken but it now threatens to engulf the orchard – the chickens love it and I have to cut it back seriously every year when I am scything. The carrots have just started to show so they are a priority for weeding – slugs seem to have a particular love of carrot seedlings and can demolish the lot in a bad year. For lunch we eat the newly-baked bread with cheese, pumpkin soup and a mug of our homemade beer. With lunch over, we all do our usual hour of music – Angela sings, I play the 'cello, Roisin plays the violin and Liam the piano. We teach our children at home and music is a large part of our daily routine. Soon it is time to gear myself up to fix strong supports for the young runner beans.

We always prepare for runner beans by digging a big trench after Christmas. We fill the bottom with rotted manure and backfill before driving in treated posts to make two rows. The posts mark the prepared area and provide a secure foundation for the raised poles and string supports which I am now about to put on. It always amazes me how much string you need. Last year I had been lucky enough to spot a trail of blue bailer twine along the road after a silage wrapper had caught up on a fence. We stopped the car and made the best of the farmer's misfortune by winding in about half a mile of good string! It takes a couple of hours to thread this around a frame made of roofing battens. Finally we have a dramatic piece of garden architecture strong enough to support the vigorous beans and survive the summer gales.

Late in the afternoon the southerly breeze wafts out the smell of roast pork which is sizzling in the Stanley range. This has to be a signal to start the evening chores; I put the chickens to bed, feed the pigs and make up the feeds for tomorrow before I kick off my boots and take a well-earned shower. Our evening meal is the highlight of another busy day and a chance to enjoy our produce at its best – pork, spuds and sugar snap peas from the deep freeze, followed by stewed plums with hot chocolate custard. It's very special when we sit around our table like this eating our own home grown food. It confirms our direct connections to the natural world and makes what we do seem so worthwhile.

This is a view of the Killowen cottage (Davitt Cottage) looking south towards the river Barrow in the distance. You can see the two big compost bins, the walnut trees and the red cover over our Cornish Crabber beside the house extension. I built on this extension to provide extra space – this involved laying over 3,000 blocks!

BRITTANY – 2007/2008

We had visited Louise (Angela's niece) and her husband Laurent several times in Brittany. These visits had been pleasant although we always found Laurent a rather mysterious and somewhat distant figure. Laurent worked in his father's business selling marine equipment, often to the French navy. In the evenings after supper he would tend to sit by himself with a glass of wine in what seemed like a brooding mood. The situation was not improved when his father sold the business and he found himself working for new bosses. Louise was very kind but always seemed to be rather "under the thumb" of moody Laurent. Their two girls played comfortably enough with Roisin and Liam.

By the year 2007 Louise and Laurent had built themselves a fine new house in the small village of Rosnoen. The house was high up on top of a hill with wonderful views over the river Aulne, which was about half a mile below. Louise had 2 daughters and the eldest, Morgane, was about the same age as Roisin. The children went to school at the village primary school which was close by in the centre of the village.

At this time we were educating the children at home and it seemed like a good idea to try and arrange for them to go to the same school as Louise's children. This could be a great opportunity for them to be immersed in a different culture and learn (easily as we thought) a new language. With this aim in mind, we began to make plans to leave Killowen for the year and make a home in Brittany near to Louise and Laurent.

In preparation for our move, I sailed our boat, *Masquerade*, over to Brittany in the middle of the year. As crew I found a willing volunteer in our musician friend Eddie – who was often a taxi driver when he needed to earn some money. Eddie is a brave and good-natured fellow but he had never sailed before. We chose a good spell of weather where the wind was likely to be in the north – a free wind all the way down to Brittany. In the event this was not an ideal decision because we had uncomfortable following seas all the way – waves too big for the self-steering gear to work properly so we had to man the helm continuously. To add to our difficulties, the light in the compass binnacle failed – it was a bit of a pain trying to steer and hold a torch as the yacht twisted and turned on the waves. Poor Eddie was very sea-sick but still soldiered on – he was a great companion as we pressed on alone through the night under the stars. In the black of night a school of busy little porpoises raced past us. They were very close and made wonderful sparkling vapour trails of phosphorescence in the water as they passed.

As morning dawned what a joy it was to find a calm anchorage in a clear sandy bay just opposite St Mary's on the Scillies. At lunchtime the beer and pub grub tasted magnificent. After a calm night and a good sleep, we pressed on early next morning down towards the rugged island of Ouessant and finally the great harbour of Brest. Brest is a busy naval port and you have to watch out for fast moving naval vessels as you cross the big inner sea, the Rade de Brest, towards the river Aulne. It's a 4 or 5 hour trip up the river then to find a tidal mooring. Finally we were glad to simply navigate into a large tidal pool below the house of Louise and Laurent – *Masquerade* (with her lifting keel) would sit on the mud there most of the time when it was not high water. We moored her fore and aft with anchors and jumped into our tender to make the shore. A hot meal was waiting for us and very pleasant it was. After a couple of days' rest we took the ferry back to Ireland, leaving *Masquerade* on her mud bank.

Back in Ireland there were courses to run and arrangements to be made for house-sitters who would be able to look after the dogs, cats, garden and chickens whilst we were away for 9 months. We already had considerable experience in finding such people either via the WWOOF website or HelpX. The latter seemed most likely to produce results and we duly placed the advert below:

Comments: Couple wanted from October 2007 to spring 2008,

to look after smallholding while owners are away. Our smallholding lies in a beautiful setting on the banks of the river Barrow. For the last 12 years we have been running courses in the art of self-sufficiency and we are trying to take some time away. At this time there will only be dogs, and cats to feed and the garden and greenhouse to look after. Accommodation is in a mobile home with 2 bedrooms, shower, toilet, kitchen and living room. There is also a converted barn loft with kitchen, double sleeping loft and living room. We are 6 miles from New Ross and applicants would need to have their own transport as there is no public transport. We are sorry but we cannot accommodate pets.

For a long time (it seemed) our advert produced no response. We had been planning to take the children to Brittany in time for them to start school in Rosnoen at the beginning of the school year. But eventually the fates were to shine on us for, just before we were due to leave, we received an email from an Irish couple who were working in Outer Mongolia! Yes – it's true! It seemed amazing that our request could have reached Mongolia let alone found an Irish couple needing a convenient and cheap place to live back in Ireland. It turned out that our invitation was exactly the type of thing they had been looking for. Their plans (helping Buddhist monks teach vegetable growing to the locals) had had to be radically changed because the husband's father had suddenly become very ill and was not expected to live much longer. The couple who were in their mid-forties had sold their business and their house in Ireland a few years before so they could travel the world. They had been prompted to do this after the shock sudden death of the husband's brother. So we found ourselves in a win-win situation – they duly turned up and were very happy to house-sit as we had asked. They were an interesting and conscientious couple, very self-contained and well informed. It seemed that they had been running their own successful business in Ireland for about 20 years when suddenly they were brought up short when his brother died. Did they really want to continue as "slaves" to their business until retirement beckoned? "No" – so they sold up everything (house and business) and became free agents to travel the world – doing good where they could. When we returned to Killowen they continued on their travels and we kept in touch for many years after – often being surprised to receive news from other far flung corners of the globe.

The next challenge which hit our plans happened whilst I was in a hurry to mow the lawn before a thunderstorm arrived. Running with the grass-collecting bucket, I missed my footing on the concrete garden steps and "crack" my leg gave way. It was certainly very painful but I did not at the time realise the leg was broken. In fact I went on for the next couple of days hobbling around but eventually decided I had better go and see my good friend and doctor, Doctor Paul, in Waterford. He took one look at my leg and sent me straight off to the hospital for an X-ray. Sure enough, the small bone was broken and I found myself being given a pair of crutches and sent on to see the osteopath consultant. The consultant was a gruff Asian man who told me that I must report straight back to the hospital early the following morning so he could operate and put a metal pin to mend the break. This I refused to do! I had seen the X-ray, which showed the two parts of the bone to be well aligned but about 2 or 3 millimetres apart. I had already read a number of research articles in New Scientist magazine about the wonderful way bone grows. The most important conclusion from this research was the need to make sure the bone continued to be subject to gentle load stresses as it healed. Bone grows in response to the small electric fields which are generated by piezo electric effects within the bone itself. Without these fields bone will simply grow in a shapeless mass.

I checked a few more references on the internet and Dr Paul consulted a pal of his who had experience in sporting injuries. The hospital consultant had told me my leg would never heal properly without an operation and that if I went without I would always suffer from pain. I decided to take my chance since I had already had two broken arms, each of which had healed perfectly despite more dire warnings from the hospital doctors in England. I held my ground and with a lot of head shaking was finally sent to the department where they put on the plasters. To my surprise I found the fellow dealing with my case was a chap I already knew well from music sessions. He had a good laugh at my accident, telling me just how often he had to deal with these sorts of stupid injury and how lucky I was to have broken a bone and not the tendon on the other side of my leg. The upshot of all this was that we had to delay our departure to Brittany for a week and poor Angela had to do all the driving whilst I recuperated. In fact my leg healed well. (Three weeks later when we were enjoying warm sunny autumn weather in Brittany I decided to cut off the plaster myself with big garden pruners. My leg was getting sweaty and smelly in the heat and I wanted to put more gentle pressure on the healing bones. It was a bit tender at first but a couple of weeks later it had pretty well sorted itself out and I certainly have had no adverse effects of any kind!)

So finally we were on the ferry over to Cherbourg and our Brittany adventure was under way. The countryside, settlement pattern and scenery in Finisterre (around Brest) reminded me very much of Northumberland. It was obvious that people did not choose to live in Brittany to become rich! The houses were built to withstand stormy gales and the people were all very formal and polite. Most of the cars were old and the pace of life was slow. The Celtic or Irish influence was very strong – a matter of great pride for every village. There was a strong tradition of local music and dancing where each village had its own set of elaborately embroidered dresses (each village with its own patterns and colours) which were provided for the children of the village to perform in the great summer dance festivals. Like most of France, Brittany is strongly socialist and egalitarian. Religious teaching is absolutely forbidden in schools. Each village is run by its own Mairie, where the executive mayor holds office for 6 years between elections. The Mairie is an ever-present force in village life. We found, for example, that in every village and small town the teaching of classical music is managed, subsidised and controlled by the Mairie. The big ice rink in Brest was provided and subsidised by the Mairie. The University Community orchestra was organised and supported financially by the Mairie (on condition it gave performances in poor and remote areas each year as directed by the Mairie). This wonderful, energetic and talented orchestra would play a big part in my own Brittany experience.

I found out about the orchestra almost by accident. When in Brest I wanted to get information about musical activities in the area so found my way to a dusty back street where one of the music shops was situated. I asked the chap behind the counter if he knew of any amateur music-making in the town. "Oh yes" he replied "you should contact Jean Phillipe at the University. He will love to see you." With some trepidation, this I duly did. It was a short conversation – "Yes – just come along next Monday evening. In such and such a conference room at the University you will find us. Everybody is welcome!" Next Monday I put my 'cello in the van and headed, rather nervously, into Brest to try and find the right place. It was not too difficult to find because I soon saw there were many people swarming about with their instruments – some old, many young. I introduced myself to the conductor, the great Jean Phillipe himself, who was bustling about with great energy and activity. With a quick shake of the hand he simply motioned me to take a vacant seat in the 'cello section. All communication was in rapid-fire French – both the conversations and the musical directions. I found myself sitting next to a young woman (Elizabeth) who I found later was a doctor in one of Brest's prisons! But really nobody of the 60 or 70 players who were present took any notice of me. The music was on the stand and in two minutes we were playing. What a brilliant set-up. Many of the players were music students at the University. Jean Phillippe conducted the orchestra as part of his University job. All the music and hire of the halls etc. was paid for by the Mairie – we musicians simply played for free. Better still, Jean Phillippe had infectious enthusiasm and a great sense of romance and tact in managing his disparate group of players. As a conductor he was never judgemental although he often directed players having difficulties to practise "a la maison" – so next week they'd play the section more fluently.

I had many wonderful experiences and performances with this orchestra. There was little time for chit chat during rehearsals but we always had a big party to let our hair down and unwind after major performances – crepes and cider being the great Breton favourites. The orchestra practised for 3 hours every Monday evening and played a concert with new material about every 6 weeks. We often travelled far and wide to give concerts in other parts of the region. Playing the great Saint-Saëns C major organ symphony in Quimper cathedral was a particularly memorable experience. One challenge which always faced me each Monday evening was how many of the lovely 'cello-playing girls I might have to kiss! Kissing is absolutely THE polite thing to do when you meet a woman you know in Brittany. Women, even the very pretty ones, expect to be kissed and can be quite offended if you fail in this department (on each cheek of course). It was sometimes more tactful to arrive just a little bit late so everyone was in position, making the kissing impossible. I noticed that Benoit, the first 'cellist, almost always arrived late and I wonder to this day whether all the kissing was a reason! Once I got used to the kissing it seemed a very nice and natural thing to do – certainly the friendly touching of cheeks "broke the ice" and definitely made relationships warmer. I made great friends in the orchestra and eventually graduated to be asked to be first 'cellist on quite a few (nerve wracking) occasions – you cannot afford to lose your place or lose count of rests when you are in the "hot" seat!

In hindsight now, I can see that our Brittany experience was a turning point in my marriage to Angela. We did have some wonderful times there – with beautiful scenery, beaches and sea; plus great food and drink – but ultimately the kids' experience in school was uncomfortable and our relationship with Louise and

Laurent became frosty and even hostile. Roisin and Liam were very brave and composed going to a school with strange people and a foreign language. Sadly it turned out that far from Morgane being a supportive friend, she took the chance to "enjoy herself" by teasing Roisin and Liam and generally trying to make their school life hell. We had no way of predicting this outcome but we soon found that Morgane virtually ran Louise's household, using sulks and temper to get whatever she wanted. She evidently did not like having Roisin as a competitor for attention. Roisin, for her part, was simply devastated by the lack of trust in her friendship and the lies that other kids told the teacher.

Not surprisingly, Angela became extremely angry about all this and tried to persuade Louise to stop Morgane's unpleasant behaviour. Of course, the whole episode was a challenging learning experience for the kids – one which Roisin (as a girl) was much more sensitive to than Liam. Liam, it seemed, had already created quite a reputation for himself in his own (very) quiet way. First of all, he was an extraordinarily good long-distance-runner and so could run the other kids off-their-feet in the playground. Second, he was already very experienced in water as we had spent a lot of time swimming; so when it came to the school's termly outing to the local swimming pool he had amazed the teachers with his fortitude. One of the "tests" the kids had to do was to hold their heads under water for a few moments. In Liam's case, moments stretched to minutes until the teachers got worried he might be drowning but of course he came up with his gentle smile. Third, because when a boy kept punching him in the side (below the height of the desks so the teacher could not see) Liam quietly held the sharp point of a compass so that the next punch produced a howl of pain from his attacker. Together, these performances gave him his own protected space.

The situation with Morgane continued to deteriorate as neither Louise nor Laurent was either willing or able to control their eldest daughter. This was extremely unfair on Roisin.

Eventually Angela drew herself up into a great rage and became determined to put a stop to the troubles by yet another argument with Louise. I strongly cautioned her against this because I knew from personal experience that the likely outcome would be violent. In the event I could not stop the confrontation which did indeed become violent as Angela physically attacked Louise. This marked a turning point not just in our affairs in Brittany but also in my own situation with Angela. Louise was devastated by the attack, both sad and very angry. She confided in me that others in the family had already known Angela could act in this way and she let no time pass before she told the rest of the family what had happened – very much putting Angela in the wrong.

Up until this time I had never found any support from anyone when I told my stories of violence and threats from Angela's temper. Over the past few years I had been warned by Angela that if I did not behave as she wanted she would get her two (very tough) brothers to beat me up. I knew the brothers were quite capable of doing just this – or worse – so I had often been faced with very difficult decisions. Now at last I had another member of the Ashe family on my side and this finally opened the opportunity for me to follow my own courses of action with much less fear of serious reprisals from the family. Later in the summer I would use the new situation to confront Angela and force our (already struggling) relationship into a new (and as it turned out – terminal) phase.

Our time in Brittany was leading up to Christmas now and we had decided to return to Ireland to check things and celebrate the end of the year at Killowen. This is the Christmas doggerel which I sent out that year – it gives a good flavour of how we spent our time!

THE SUTHERLANDS IN BRITTANY

Kergonnec Izella, Rosnoen, Bretagne, France 29590

The night it is dark and the moon it shines thin
It's freezing rock hard and it's France that we're in
The logs they are chene but the fire is just great
Our two kids sleep soundly but we're still up late
Bright days fairly rush by as Noel presses in
Can we get the job done by the teeth of our skin?

I remember it well when the sun shone in spring
Digging and weeding with a zest and a zing
Then the rains came and soaked us so we prayed to Al Gore
Global warming or what, he says we must expect more
No boating or camping in grey sodden skies
While the barbecue's rusty and the slugs reach great size

But our new concrete driveway defeated the mud
And we cut grass and gardened whenever we could
The soft fruits were brilliant, the strawberries great
Made jam, pies and jelly and enjoyed what we ate
Ran courses, made sausages, scythed hay and brewed beer
Wove baskets and fed chickens with never a tear

We sold our dear Crabber to friends in the west
Lough Derg's her new home and it's all for the best
Sailed the big boat to Brittany in a northerly gale
Brave Eddie my crew can tell you the tale
We stopped at the Scillies for rest and a pint
Then on around Ouessant both seasick and faint

The Concise Book came out in the middle of June
After blood sweat and tears not a moment too soon
We do what we can to make D and K rich
And help the folk in the towns the rat race unhitch
But our website is weak and broad band is out
Dear Eircom are useless and not worth a shout

As August went on we made plans for France
For the kids to attend school there while we had the chance
The beauty of Brittany it quite took our fancy
Though finding good house sitters was going to be chancy
But lo and behold our message got through
To Peter and Liz in Mongolia – it's true

Just days before leaving my leg it got broke
So the best of good plans was changed at a stroke
But the sun went on shining and we arrived a week late
Lived on in our caravan three weeks from that date
'til a house we did find in a sweet sheltered nook
Paying rent to the Perots by hook or by crook.

Now the New Year's upon us – 2008
The days getting longer and we just can't wait
Bon chance to you all and three cheers for the French
Their drains may be funny but we don't mind the stench!

WS

March 2008

In March we had a great shock when the news came from Annapolis that my brother Ben was dying of acute leukaemia. At first Ben thought he had just caught a bad cold but within 24 hours this had become serious pneumonia. When he was rushed into hospital tests soon showed that his immune system had completely collapsed, white blood cells destroyed by acute leukaemia. Crash treatment was required if he was to have any chance but 24 hours later he was dead. By the time we had even tried to sort out airfares and practicalities it was too late. This was the message we sent.

A MESSAGE FROM WILLIAM AND OWEN

We send this message as time and distance prevent our being present on this saddest of all sad occasions.

Our brother Ben was – as you all know – an unusual man. While we kicked balls around and ran about on the school playing fields he was working away in a dark basement with a screwdriver and soldering iron. Just what he did was always something of a mystery. But while we worried about passing exams, Ben never had any doubts that his own special talents would find a place in the modern world. He was right, of course; he usually was!

Today we join you, with our Mother Peggy, in remembering Ben. We are together at Embleton, where Ben spent his childhood. We shall visit the places where Ben flew his first radio-controlled plane, where we played hide-and-seek amongst the sand dunes, where we hunted pigeons with our bows and arrows. We shall look at the bedroom where as a child Ben made his own unique photo-electric alarm clock. We shall walk across the golf course to Dunstanburgh Castle, where Ben often flew his radio-controlled gliders. The wind will blow and the waves rush in and we shall remember Ben.

As time went by, we watched Ben build the skills and experience which would ultimately enable him to prepare his beautiful boat Flying Angel for her journey to a new life in the United States. As the old saying goes – the rest is history!

Of course, we remember, too, the kindness and good temper which Ben always showed when playing host both to us and to the many nephews and nieces who occasionally had cause to visit his fine home and family in Annapolis. Ben and Bonna made a busy bustling family whose visits across the Atlantic were always very special for us. Ben will be greatly missed. Despite the thousands of miles that lie between us, we feel as close to you today as we shall ever be in our shared grief for Ben.

Ben's family on this side of the Atlantic would all like to be remembered with you today. William and Angela, Liam, Roisin,

Hal, Dylan, Gael, Ceri, Rupert and Sarah. Owen and Jan, Jane and Jonathan and Maggi and, most of all, our mother Peggy. We send our love and our deepest sorrow to our American friends and loved ones.

Troubles in Brittany

In March we finally decided that the kids' experience at the local Rosnoen school was not really working out – there were simply too many tensions. In a small close-knit village community the pressures from such tensions can become extreme – so it was back to home education once more. We continued to enjoy the cycling, horse riding and music with frequent swimming at the nice pool in Morgat and ice skating most Sundays on the ice rink at Brest. Roisin was preparing with the local "circle celtique" for the big Breton dance festival, where all the local villages send dance teams to compete in the middle of June. Our tenancy at Kergonnec would soon come to an end but we also needed to get back to Ireland to sort out our next pair of house-sitters.

Kergonnec Neighbours

As we leave Kergonnec for Ireland the situation with our neighbour, M. Derien, becomes stranger. He is old and very poorly. Left on his own, the visits from his son seem to be getting much less frequent. There is one visitor – some sort of social worker we assume – who seems to call each day. But the mystery is that M. Derien no longer seems able to use his car. How he gets food we do not know but we have become his port of last resort as a source of cigarettes and wine. He drinks at least one bottle each day. We do not know whether he has been stopped from driving by his doctor or his relatives. But he pops up looking over his gate regularly to replenish his wine supplies. So far the medical authorities have not remonstrated with us for supplying this essential but perhaps dangerous commodity.

April

The saga with M. Derien finally came to a crisis when his son knocks on our door just as we were about to have supper. He was polite but direct – Had we "fait des courses" (done the shopping) for M. Derien? Mais Oui – est-ce qu'il y a une probleme? Alas, the old man had to be taken to hospital in emergency as he is on serious medication which cannot be combined with smoke and drink. He has been forbidden to use his car for medical reasons. This now explains why we were finding numerous empty packs of Gitane cigarettes under our caravan and why our dear neighbours Mac and Judy had been retrieving empty wine bottles from the bottom of their garden! My morning exchange with M. Derien next day was not a happy one as his son was on the receiving end of many a Merde and other curses. Poor old fellow.

The Confrontation of 13 June

By now the weather was rapidly improving and when our tenancy at Kergonnec came to an end we simply moved to stay on *Masquerade* which was moored above the tidal lock in the beautiful little village of Port Launay. Liam could practise his roller blading on the street and we could all cycle along the tow path a mile or so into Chateaulin.

It was from this base that our final actions in Brittany took place and it was here that I made my first concerted attempt to confront Angela's (as it seemed to me) unreasonable controlling behaviour. It happened this way. Roisin's dance group was building up to take part in the summer competition while I was practising the 'cello for the Brest orchestra's final summer concert. Unfortunately the orchestra's concert was scheduled to take place on Angela's birthday but it would all happen in the small church 20 miles off-shore on the pretty island of Ouessant. Each year the orchestra was committed to perform for this wild remote island community as part of its financial deal whereby the Mairie in Brest provided support which was conditional on taking music to remote communities.

Ouessant is a wild but beautiful place so I suggested we might all head off there and hire a cottage so both the concert and Angela's birthday party could be celebrated. At first this seemed like a great idea and I started to research possible options but it soon became clear that A was determined to stop me playing in the concert. This put me in a very difficult position because Jean Phillippe, our conductor, had asked me to be the first 'cellist along with Elizabeth since all the other 'cellists had firm prior commitments which prevented them taking the 24-hour trip to Ouessant. The orchestra needed at least 2 'cellos to function and play its concert. Of course I knew it would be A's birthday on the day of the concert but I was sure we could either celebrate it on a different day or rent a cottage and celebrate together at the concert on Ouessant. As things turned out A simply refused to compromise in any way – it was up to me to choose either the orchestra or the marriage!

A great set-piece confrontation took place in front of the children. This time I thought A was being totally unreasonable – I knew that Roisin had to be in Chateaulin on the day after the Ouessant concert but this was easily possible if we took the early morning ferry back from Ouessant (in fact I did take this ferry and get back in time to watch the dancing). So I "took my life in my hands" and decided I had no option but to stop the argument, defy Angela and jump in the van and race off to try (at this already late stage) to try and catch the ferry to Ouessant. The passage below describes my Ouessant trip but the longer term "fall out" from this impasse would finally bring our marriage to an end.

Ouessant Weekend – June 2008

The French expressway to Brest is a welcome sight for those who are late for the ferry! Going around the north of Brest through the traffic lights and dodging the occasional Saturday cyclist was testing whilst searching for the essential signpost to Le Conquet. After Brest the road narrows but it is only about 20 mins to the little holiday ferryport. Everybody said that parking would be a nightmare and they were right. Most of the little town is yellow-lined and pedestrianised; the ferry car park was stuffed full. Already a large gaggle of passengers pressed around the ferry gangway with only 10 mins to go until departure.

Elizabeth and Julia raced over to the van to collect my baggage and the ’cello. Amazingly, Jean Phillippe seemed to be organized and cheerful as he gave me my ticket. The challenge now was to park the van and get back in time to catch the boat. Up the narrow one-way-street we went but not a place was to be seen. In desperation I chose a piece of wide paving where I could park without obstructing the road even if it was on a yellow line in the ‘blue’ zone. Putting my faith in our Irish number plates I pulled over, locked up and ran back to the boat where the last passengers were just getting on.

The rocky outline of the Ouessant group of islands dotted the blue horizon as we swirled away from the quay. The breeze cooled the sun with the speed of the boat. Rather like the ferry to Skye but slightly smaller and no cars. A grizzled double bass player wished me good afternoon in English and we carried on a patchy conversation in French above the roar of the diesel engine. First stop was the little port of Molene – not much to see, just a small island village and about 20 boats moored in the shelter of the harbour. We pressed on, passing numerous shoal markers along a forbidding stretch of sea, dotted with huge lighthouses. Not for nothing does Ouessant have the French lighthouse museum. We saw divers getting ready to explore the many wrecks which apparently litter the area – mostly from the war apparently.

Ouessant itself presents a towering rocky face on its sheltered eastern side and the harbour is tight within the cliffs with little sign of habitation. The island is bigger than it looks from the sea. There were well over 50 cars parked around the ferryport and the usual gathering of taxis and bike hire cash desks. I changed the time of my ticket for the early Sunday sailing and immediately found the island to be a relaxed and friendly place. The 50 or so members of the orchestra waited in a slightly tense gaggle whilst the double basses, timpani and harp were craned off the ferry in a steel container and the old bus carried its first load of passengers off to the village. Ten mins later it was our turn. People pondered their arrangements for accommodation. The "chef" repeated the arrangements – we would sort out accommodation after dropping off all the instruments at the église, the repetition (rehearsal) would start at 5 and afterwards we would return to the camp site for an al fresco supper. The concert would start at 9pm and afterwards there would be drinks at the Mairie.

The church was old, cool and rather battered-looking. Instruments were laid out and we walked the half mile or so back to the municipal camping. This was neat and grassy, with 8-foot hedges making 50-metre-square enclosures. The Mairie had pitched 4 large tents for us, blue and purple, each with 12 bunks. People chose their spots without regard to sex or age – snoring seemed to be the only concern. Some had brought their own tents and chose cosy spots round about to pitch them.

It was about a 10-minute walk to the church and we bumbled down there in small groups as 5 o'clock drew closer. Arriving at the church we found George's "4 winds" group hard at work practising the pieces they were going to play on Sunday morning. Plastic seats and music stands were already in place for the orchestra and we duly did our tuning and roisining and whatever in the vestry before taking our places for the final repetition.

We began with the Mozart bassoon concerto where the bass line mostly bounces along like a rhythm section. The church resonated like a great stone bell so the chef asked us to play very staccato – it would be better, of course, when the place was full of people. Playing Mozart on a sunny summer's day is always refreshing and very clean somehow. The notes all gently stitch together like a small mountain stream. Next came the much heavier trombone concerto – lots of notes (in E flat) – and thick chords in great contrast to what had come before. But the trombones did sound good in the church as they bellowed out the rather martial theme. Finally we got to Peter and the Wolf, which we were playing for about the fourth time – but this time with only 3 'cellos and no Benoit or Anne. It is a fairly challenging piece because of the entries, difficult notes and the changes in tempo. The 'cellos have several tricky moments but we did not do too badly. To round off the rehearsal, the chef took out his violin and played through a fantastic virtuoso Bach duet with his 'student' Awami (who is a huge black fellow with dreadlocks) playing the viola (brilliantly well) – it was worth coming just to hear that piece alone.

With our instruments packed away again in the vestry we trotted back up the road to the campsite for supper. A great variety of home-made food had been brought – very nice pizzas, pies and salads – plenty of beer, wine and the ever-present Breton cider – then a luscious choice of sticky desserts which all the French adore. It was a good very welcome meal as most of us had not had any lunch because of the rush to catch the ferry. But it was soon time to put on our performing clothes and plod back to the church in the gathering twilight. By now the various lighthouses were swishing their great beams over the islands, and business in the several restaurants was in full swing with happy looking visitors. Once the church was settled, with about half its benches filled, we were surprised (and pleased) to hear that Nolwen (who normally just takes the photos) was going to start proceedings by giving a short harp recital. The harp sounded perfect in the church, playing what sounded like old Celtic airs, the final one being accompanied by the first flautist – very ethereal. She started playing the Celtic harp when she was 7 years old and said that there were a couple of people who taught the harp in and around Brest.

Then it was our turn to file on and do our stuff. We did not do too badly although Elizabeth did knock over our music stand when turning over at one critical point in the trombone concerto – but we soon got back on track. After the final piece and applause the chef and Awami performed their duet once again – even better than before. The church emptied, the instruments were packed away in the vestry which would be locked for the night and we all duly trotted off to find the Mairie and the promised drinks. It was fairly black-dark by this time and the navigation lights blinked and flashed all around whilst the searchlight beams of the lighthouse swept constantly across the island. Antoine from the orchestra chatted away to me – he spoke excellent English after spending a year studying in Finland. A considerable amount of wine and beer was consumed. It was a fine evening to be drinking on the patio and everyone seemed in good humour. Around half past midnight things drew to a close and the company wandered back into town – some to their digs in B & B, other to the campsite. My little group with Antoine, one of the timp players and a couple of the violinists (student doctors as it turned out) was diverted into the local pub where there was a lively music session going on and I enjoyed a very good pint of the local Breton beer.

This was the first time I had seen a rollicking session with everyone singing old Breton songs to the accompaniment of 3 squeezeboxes and a couple of whistles. There were several ex-pat types enjoying themselves and a mighty fine time was had by all. Alas, at 1am the pub stopped serving and we found ourselves out in the street walking back to the campsite – fairly tired by this time. I was expecting everyone else to be tucked up in bed. But quite the contrary: the whole company was waiting at the campsite gates, fully togged up in warm clothes and walking gear for what I was told was the annual pilgrimage to the Celtic cross overlooking the Atlantic. We plodded off into the night, carrying with us plentiful supplies of beer. After walking for about 25 minutes we left the village and came down into a large field overlooking the sea. A tall old stone cross could be seen silhouetted against the horizon – this was to be our goal. We encamped around the cross – in four groups, one for each side of the stone base. More fizzy beer was consumed in the atmosphere of an end-of-term feast. More Breton songs were sung – louder and louder as the night drew on. Eventually fatigue and constantly speaking French got the better of me and I joined the flautist from 4 winds to walk back to camp. Others were going off to the beach; it was half past 3 in the morning and the dawn was already breaking. It was good to see the young folk going wild and having the energy to stay up all night. I collapsed into my sleeping bag in a quiet pitch-black tent which seemed to be almost empty. It was freezing cold and damp as I shivered my way to the morning whilst various revellers tripped in and out of the communal sleeping quarters with or without girlfriends and boyfriends. At 8am I got up to shave, wash and have a snack before the bus left at 20 past 9. To my amazement almost everyone was already up and about and had had breakfast despite the long night – they can certainly get up in the morning, these Bretons! One croissant and a hot chocolate later I was picking up my 'cello from the vestry and hurrying to get on the bus.

After dumping our bags at the base of the pier, we sat on the top of the sea wall to look out for the ferry. It duly surged into the tiny port which was a focus of activity in what must be a daily ritual for the island – there are 2 ferries to Le Coquet each day and one to Brest. The journeys take one and two hours respectively. Our attention was caught by a dolphin that was pottering about in the harbour. He was evidently waiting for us to leave because as soon as the ferry got up to full speed we saw him chasing up behind us. With hardly a flick of his tail he followed us for fully half an hour. He surfaced to breathe about every 45 seconds and seemed to swim about 20 feet away from the boat and about 6 feet deep. The water was completely clear and we could seem him easily just as he must have been able to see us. The boat was travelling at about 20 knots but it seemed very easy for him to keep up – quite amazing. He went off to play with the other boats when we berthed at Molene. He must have been full of energy because he was pushing and pulling one sailing boat about by using its anchor chain. The sailors seemed to be rather surprised by this as they goggled down at him from their foredeck. Quite a playful dolphin.

Half an hour later we were saying our goodbyes at Le Coquet and I was preparing myself to find the van locked up or with penalty stickers on the windscreen. But my fears were groundless – there she was waiting for me to load up and take to the expressway once more en route for a day of Breton dancing. Soon I was back in Chateaulin in time to see Roisin perform – the family gave me a frosty reception.

So back to Killowen

After the sad dramas before Ouessant, our time in Brittany did not have long to run. Soon we would be back in Killowen looking after the animals, running courses and managing the garden. By now we were heavily involved in the affairs of Ireland's growing Home Education Network and I wrote this piece for them which really sums up our Breton experience.

Quite how we ended up sending our two home-schoolers, Roisin and Liam (10 and 9), to a French primary school I am not sure. But do it we did and it certainly proved to be a most interesting 7 months in ways we could not have imagined before we took the plunge. No doubt the children will tell us more of their true feelings about the whole thing when they are grown up but we are certainly happy to share our experience with other members of HEN.

The first thing we realized as we tried to understand our local culture is that Brittany and France are very definitely NOT the same thing. The Bretons regard themselves as an autonomous and very Celtic people, flying their own flag and speaking their own language (which is virtually identical to Welsh, by the way). Every village has a Celtic Circle which meets at least once each week and there are lessons in Breton dancing and music every weekend for the children. These lead up to the great festivals which take place during the summer as well as being a springboard for regular Fez Noz (party) evenings. These are a sort of Breton version of the Scottish Ceilidh but with cider and pancakes taking the place of whisky and haggis.

The next thing we discovered was the huge importance of the village Mairie (the elected Mayor and his team), who have a smart office in the centre of every French town and village. There are no counties in France – just 10,000 mayors who are under the control of the national prefecture which runs the large Departments for the central Government. If you want to find out anything that is going on in a village or town then you head straight for the Mairie and, if they cannot answer, go on to the Tourist Office. The Mairie runs the schools and will decide if your child can join. The Mairie keeps records of every club and association – you can choose from dozens ranging from dancing, through Judo, to tennis, football, rowing, boules, swimming, riding, walking, surfing ... and so on and so on. Everyone runs courses for children at very reasonable prices and the facilities (indoor sports halls, music rooms, etc.) are excellent. Almost all villages/towns have a Maison pour Tous where staff will give you details of dozens of courses on offer (from learning welding, computing, foreign languages etc). Often there is internet access and meeting rooms too. Then there will also be a Salle Polyvalent (room for all things, rather like a smart big Parish Hall) – this is where the Celtic Circle will meet, the school puts on their "spectacles", and the local clubs have evening activities all subsidized by the Mairie.

You don't live in Brittany if you want to be rich so the people of Finisterre tend to be an easy going bunch. They are very formal on first meeting but solid friends once they begin to know you. Of course, the 2-hour lunch break from 12 midday to at least 2 pm is ABSOLUTELY a central part of Breton life – many small cafes offer 12-euro 3-course lunches (including wine), and most of the big supermarkets do good lunches for less than 10 euro. Everywhere you go you will see the black and white

Breton flag – black and white like the Cornish flag in England – so again the old shared Celtic history is revealed. With so many mysterious groups of standing stones, Brittany has many Druids and you are never far away from deep spiritual echoes of the past. This is nowhere more evident than in the wish of the people to dance. You can dance in a Breton pub without any licence (as required in the UK) and I found several pubs where young people (including tourists) would dance communally to live music late into the night. Breton dancing is basically communal dancing similar in some ways to Greek circle dancing – where everybody gets to meet and join hands with everybody else at some stage.

Postscript

I did not know it then but (as you will see) I would find myself spending much more enjoyable time working in Brittany in the years that followed. This came about because of my friendship with Nick and Nicky Dann who lived near the big river at Rosnoen and whose kids went to the local school with ours. Nick was an interesting character – very smart and very enterprising. His wife Nicky was a wonderful mum and a great cook – we enjoyed many great family meals in their home together. Nick had developed great skill as a "professional" gambler and spent many hours each day on his computer as he calculated odds and worked out sophisticated mathematical algorithms. He was quite prepared to lose thousands of pounds in an afternoon in the knowledge that if he persisted day after day he must, on the basis of his statistical algorithms, eventually "hit the jackpot". This he evidently did and when he did he would invest the winnings in property which he then developed with help from me and other local tradesmen. It seemed to be a winning formula – if a rather stressful way of making a living!

2009-2010

The 2 years which followed my fateful trip to Ouessant rank in awfulness with the 3 other periods when my life seemed crushed against impossible problems. The first happened in 1953 when I was sent away to school at Mowden Hall. The second ran from 1976 until my divorce was finally settled with Sarah in 1981. The third period covered the time immediately before and after Sue killed herself in 1989.

My relationship with Angela (for 15 years or so) was wonderful in many ways. Angela was (and no doubt still "is") a very intelligent and resourceful person, a wonderful cook and a great source of common sense. But, and it is a big "but", she is somehow a prisoner of her troubled early family life and this seems to lead to occasions of violent temper. I soon learned that even very small incidents can spark a violent reaction which is completely out of proportion to some imagined provocation. Many, many times I tried to persuade Angela to take some counselling or guidance which might help us avoid these dangerous flare-ups which often resulted in her launching physical attacks. It is, I can tell you, pretty scary to be attacked either without warning or during the night when you are asleep! The only remedy is to try and keep your own temper and hold off the assailant as best you can until the flare-up abates.

There is little point in cataloguing all the various incidents which led up to my finally leaving Killowen in 2010. For several years before 2008 there had been 3 or 4 very scary incidents each year – usually involving "out of control" violence late at night. On many occasions Angela took angry fits of jealousy when I was out with other groups of friends. Of course, she accused me of having affairs (which I certainly never did) and there were frequent arguments and scenes in front of the children. Many times I had to escape out into the night to try to figure out what to do next. You have to remember that Angela came from a staunchly Irish family with close connections with the IRA. Her 3 brothers were extremely tough characters. I normally got along OK with the brothers despite my being a rich property-owning English "toff" but I certainly had no doubt that Angela's threats that the "brothers would get me" were very real.

Several strands came together to create a situation where I could and must leave. Angela would frequently accuse me of causing all the problems because (she said) I had "narcissistic personality disorder" (NPD). When I looked this up and listened to various videos from those who had been involved with this disorder one thing struck me very strongly. There was a clear and specific message "if there is violence you must report it". Before I read this advice I had, like many other men, been careful to keep Angela's violent attacks a secret within the family. But the advice was so adamant that, with some trepidation, I decided to go to a private counsellor in Waterford. It was a relief to share my worries with someone independent and experienced. Her feedback (I would not call it advice) was not very re-assuring and I began to realise I would have to find a way to escape the situation. But this was a very tough prospect – leaving 2 lovely young children and a beautiful home – not to mention the fact of Angela's threats of reprisals from her brothers.

In order to force some resolution, I decided to try and get myself referred to a consultant psychiatrist and to make sure that Angela knew I was doing so. I went to the local GP and explained my situation. Much to my surprise, he was extremely helpful and, after cross-questioning me thoroughly over 15 minutes, he warned me that things were unlikely to get any better. "You have left relationships before" he said "and I'm sure you can manage to do so again". He referred me to the local psychiatrist and when the referral letter arrived at Killowen, I was able to show it to Angela as I thought this would show her that we were in a serious situation. I spent an hour being interviewed by the psychiatrist and, after a certain amount of laughter, he assured me that I was perfectly normal.

I realised, of course, that the fights and arguments we had in front of the children were very damaging as well as unpleasant. So pressures were building up constantly for some solution to be found. The occasion when Angela had attacked Louise in Brittany had provided me with at least one member of the Ashe family who would understand my situation. At last, I had some kind of strong ally within the Ashe family who could support my stories of physical attacks. I realised that this would make any reprisals from "the brothers" much less likely.

Life at Killowen was now becoming very frosty and tense almost reaching breaking point. I decided to move out to sleep in the barn (quite comfortable but inconvenient) for greater safety after I was stabbed through the cheek with a sharp pencil in a row with Angela. It was becoming increasingly difficult to run courses because Angela's behaviour was so unpredictable and potentially hostile. By this time I had reported my concerns to the local social workers, who were extremely level headed and sympathetic. They told me that they knew that just as many men as women suffer domestic violence but very few men indeed are prepared to admit it. In my own case I found that Angela was easily able to convince our friends that the entire problem was my fault. Even some of my best golfing pals simply refused to believe my story. But I was warned by one friend about the situation which had happened with his brother who had also been having violent clashes with his wife. One afternoon this brother had been sitting in his armchair calmly minding his own business when the wife had burst into the sitting room. She was talking to a friend on her mobile phone and, as she came into the room, she began to shout and scream that she was being attacked, banging the mantelpiece and breaking ornaments. Unknown to her, her husband, who was still sitting in his chair, had videoed the whole performance on his mobile phone. He did not tell her this at the time. She reported him to the police, calling her friend to give evidence about the violence from over-hearing her phone call. The matter went all the way to court, at which point the husband revealed the video and played it to the magistrate thus saving himself and putting his wife in the dock.

So I was well aware that, in these domestic situations where it is one word against another, the police and the courts will almost invariably side with the woman. I remember another story told me by a GP friend who had been called to comfort a woman who claimed to have been assaulted. He spent half an hour trying to comfort this tearful lady. When the police finally arrived he was shocked to see them arrest the lady who, it seems, they knew very well had been attacking and provoking her husband over many previous months.

I could see no easy way out of my stressful and unhappy situation – a situation that was dragging the whole family into unproductive misery. The social workers had told me I must always keep an escape package ready in a safe place outside the house, with spare car keys, money and credit cards plus spare clothes. This I did. It seems angry women are expert at hiding the car keys and/or your wallet so you can be trapped!

Two events came together "out of the blue" to resolve my dilemma. For the last self-sufficiency course I ran at Killowen I had hired a local cottage to provide accommodation for the students – 2 ladies and an energetic man from Spain. The cottage was available for an extra day after the course finished and the 2 girls had gone away to visit Galway. I decided I would stay in the pleasant cottage with the Spanish guy as it was more comfortable than the barn at Killowen. At around 6am next morning I was woken by Angela, who burst into the cottage. She rushed into the room where I was sleeping, shouting that she knew I was having an affair with one of the students. She then grabbed my computer and threw it down the stairs. I followed her to try and retrieve the computer because (as she knew) it contained all my writing, addresses and so forth. I tried to wrestle the computer from her while she was shouting that she was being attacked. Fortunately for me, the Spanish student witnessed the whole drama. Angela's allegations about my supposed affair were complete nonsense (unfortunately for Angela, the girls were away anyway). So her plan to catch me out had backfired badly. I went straight down to the Garda station in New Ross with the Spanish guy as a witness and we made joint statements describing the violent attack which had taken place. At last I had some independent evidence on record of my true situation. What a relief it was to know that it would now be much more difficult for Angela to fabricate a case putting the blame on me for violence or sexual molestation.

My second piece of good fortune came about when I returned to Killowen from a trip checking and cleaning *Masquerade* in Brittany during May 2009. I had bought wine and presents for Angela and the kids but the disembarkation from the ferry at Rosslare was severely delayed by some sort of elaborate customs checks. As a result I arrived home much later than expected and found Angela furious at my explanations – quite what she believed I had been up to I cannot imagine! She demanded that I come outside so she could talk to me – but I knew this was very likely to lead to more violence. Fortunately for me, just at that moment one of our friends arrived unexpectedly at the front door. When Angela went to meet her I realised my opportunity had come to escape because the camper van was ready waiting outside with all my clothes, wallet and equipment from France. I could slip away without the kind of threats I had received before – that she would burn the house down, lie down in front of the car or kill the children if I left (for example). I left quickly and quietly with a heavy heart. I drove miserably off to camp at Bannow – a beautiful remote spot by the sea where we had played and picnicked so many times before. My phone was flat and the rain poured down as I rested and paused for a couple of days in the campervan to reflect on the new situation. It was a miserable time.

There was one sad twist to this tale. Very sadly I had to miss seeing Roisin perform on one of her big dance nights. Although I did not know it (because my phone battery was flat) Angela had texted to invite me to come to this important event. Here the fates had conspired against us and, as has been said many times, it's a pity that there's no way a sender can know if a text has actually been received (we have What's App now of course!).

But there was also a positive twist. All my problems in Ireland – particularly Angela's determination that I should not have any meaningful contact with other members of my extended family – had made me (with some trepidation) begin to make first efforts at re-establishing my friendship (and love) for Sarah. I also had four elder children (and some grandchildren) that Angela would never let me see. Sarah was now divorced from Laurie and by a strange quirk of fate, we met once more during May at the wedding anniversary celebrations of our mutual old friends the Danzigers. We both had a sparkle in our eye and a gladness in our hearts as we spent the night together in one of the guest rooms at St Catharine's in Cambridge – it's not so often one gets to renew a love affair after more than 30 years apart!

Sadly there was no going back on my decision to leave Killowen and my two lovely Irish children. I never had the slightest doubt that Angela would be a good mother to them. I had already seen how her big sister Eileen had passionately devoted herself to making a big success of her son's life. I could see that Angela had serious (almost obsessive) determination to give our children all the opportunities she had missed herself within her own dysfunctional family. What had become a destructive co-dependency between us had now been ended and it would not be long before all Angela's intelligence and practical resourcefulness re-asserted itself. I was glad to have been able (over 15 years) to build up and extend the house and out-buildings and we had had many wonderful times together. I had already given Angela the new house we had bought in Waterford, so I knew she should not be short of resources. It was very sad that Angela had done so much to deliberately try to turn the two children against me – but far better that they loved and trusted their mother than my trying to fight against this.

With one or two niggles and fusses we soon got our divorce sorted out. My mother was very sad to lose contact with the two

Irish children because she had very much enjoyed their frequent visits. They did try to keep in touch with her, writing regularly to tell her (and me, I suppose) of their (very successful) progress. My mother, for her part, felt she should support their education so they could attend Newtown school (which had been so good for Hal) and, later, go to the Keats Academy to prepare for taking the important leaving certificate (where both obtained excellent results). It seems, by all accounts, that our experiment with home schooling has produced two strong, capable and intelligent young people who will, no doubt, make their mark on the world as all my other children already have! One day perhaps they will be able to understand better the way our lives unfolded. One day perhaps they will get to know their other equally capable and intelligent half-siblings. One day perhaps they will feel able to meet their father again and we shall celebrate the way things have turned out! Who knows?

2010 – Life moves on

My fortunate escape from troubles in Ireland left me with only the possessions I was able to take away in my VW camper van. I had my tools, my 'cello, my computer and 2 filing cabinets of past papers. I had my state and civil service pension to live on plus some (limited) royalties from sales of the "Complete Book" together with a small income from running SS courses. I had no place to live and no clear idea of what I should do next. Fortunately I did have plenty of options as regards places to live. It is a big help being good at fixing things and doing practical work! Nick and Nicky (in Brittany) were always keen to let me stay in one of their properties in return for doing work. My mum was always glad to have me to stay. Sarah, of course, had numerous properties (in England, France and New Zealand). I had my lovely yacht (moored in Port Launay, Brittany) and Ceri would also appreciate my help at some point.

The main focus of my life moved to France, where I would be able to run my SS courses at Sarah's lovely old Bordeaux farm house. This I did for the next 3 years. It worked very well. Sarah is a wonderful hostess and we both thoroughly enjoyed the stimulating company of students from all over the world. In many ways her gites and big old house were ideal but, as so often in life, there were complications. First of all, the climate and weather in Bordeaux is not at all easy for growing temperate vegetables. Second, and most annoying, Sarah was continually battling with her ex-husband Laurie over complicated, unresolved issues from their divorce. These involved ownership and use of the Bordeaux properties and I could see no easy end to the uncertainties. I was also becoming concerned about the situation of my mother who, now in her late 90s, was beginning to find it difficult to manage on her own.

Sarah and I start our new relationship

Chapter 11: Life moves on in France with Sarah

My Strange Romance with Estie

Life, as we know, has many strange twists and turns. This was one of them.

Whilst I was running the SS courses at St Leger I received a request "out of the blue" to take on a lady from South Africa as a volunteer. She had left South Africa for complicated personal reasons to come to Europe with her young son Luke. She said she had always wanted to meet and work with me. There had been, as I later discovered, difficult and unresolved problems with her divorce from a rich (Belgian, I think) husband. Because of all the complications it seemed Estie had very little money and was surviving by working as a WWOOFer.

I did not know what to expect as I met Estie and Luke from the train in La Reole. But here they were: a robust, good-looking young woman and a cheerful young man – both with big smiles and not much luggage. Strong shoes, practical clothes and no make-up! Sarah welcomed them generously, as she always did, and found them space to stay in one of the old gites.

Both Estie and Luke proved to be good and cheerful workers. They already had a good deal of experience and had done training courses with the permaculture people. We found we shared many concerns about the way the modern world was going and I certainly admired Estie's principled rejection of consumerism.

I had imagined that, like most volunteers, Estie and Luke would stay for 2 or 3 weeks and then move on but it soon became apparent that they had no such plans. Estie was trying to sort out problems with her property back in South Africa and there were still outstanding issues with her divorced husband. Other than this, they were "free agents" in Europe. I already had plans of my own to return to Brittany to work with Nick

Dann on his strange old mill property. We were all getting along well and I found both Estie's physical presence and her mysterious past very intriguing. I asked her if she would like to come up to Brittany with me so we could continue to work together over the winter. After some reflection, this she agreed to do. Without much ado we soon became lovers and a very wonderful and passionate affair it was.

You will, dear reader, get some insight (and perhaps inspiration) from the feelings which I expressed in a poem written to Estie as I sat by the fire alone in the old Mill in November 2010. As it turned out our love and passions burned out 2 years later just as mysteriously as they had arisen.

My Love

Half way around the world my love has come to me
With sunshine and music this tryst was meant to be
Ancient hearths with bright log fires and candles soft
Our guides to explore twin souls under feathered cloth

Marching over grass with grit and hope on autumn days
Before long tasty evenings in amber caves of feasting
And afterwards touching and laughing in new ways
As the owls whispered while the dark earth was turning

This strange thread of deeper magic can burn you like a flame
Where the doors of trust and belief are opened still
And the boundaries of pleasure and pain explored again
As the flashing urge of life regains its power to thrill

Today she is calm and warm with early morning smiles
Soft and strong her body smooth like pearl and ivory
Her lips like softest down can change the world by kissing
Her hands so clever firm and kind reflect the strength that's in her mind

Like yarn tight woven our lives can be a mighty rope
Soft spoken warriors in a long march fuelled by heart and hope
To change the world by stealth without the need for wealth
And face the odds and go beyond the brittleness of dreams

And now the snow is falling and she is far away
But her spirit sits besides me and warms up every day
Her thoughts and fierce encouragement inhabit all I say
This sweet wild force from Africa – I hope she's come to stay.

What more is there to say about this strange romantic interlude? You may wonder what Sarah (and the rest of the family) made of it all. I think that Sarah (we all lived together in Bordeaux, you must remember) found the whole affair as surprising as I did. We had no fights, tensions or arguments that I was aware of, and no dangerous flashes of jealousy as might certainly have happened in the past. I suppose we are all getting older and wiser. Sarah probably looked on with some amusement to see my infatuation with this new person in our lives.

After all the ups and downs which Sarah and I had been through I don't suppose she thought my sudden romance with Estie could change our great friendship. There was more mystery, however, when Estie met Riaan and Ceri (we house-sat for them in their big French house for a while). Quite naturally Estie and Riaan spoke together in Afrikaans, which was both of their first languages. It turned out that Riaan had been at school in South Africa with Estie's sister! Here again I never "got to the bottom" of the relationship and what it showed about Estie's past life because all their conversation was in Afrikaans.

Whilst Estie was away on one of her mysterious trips I was away helping Nick at his old (very lovely) old water mill in Brittany. For myself, I found both the countryside, sea and culture of Brittany wonderfully refreshing. Even the Irish music (at Quimper and Locronan) reached levels of greatness I could hardly believe. You may get a flavour of this from this contemporaneous account of one trip to Quimper.

THE SESSION – *Reflections from November 2010 in Brittany*

You will find Irish music in every corner of the Earth. Somehow its artistry, passion and wildness bear witness to a more vibrant culture than what sometimes seems like our constipated Hollywood sham. The tinsel and plastic consumer world of Hollywood escapism has little to show for it except destruction. Soon after midnight when the pub doors are shut and the lights turned down it does seem possible to touch a deeper vein of the human spirit. No one wrote this music down – it has flowed down through the generations and the centuries – and survived every form of persecution. And when this music begins to flow it's hard to keep still, although – sadly – the dancers are often hard to find!

Friday night's omens were not altogether good. "The Session" web site covers the world and connects the faithful to their passion but the entry for Quimper (An Poitin by the station on Friday nights) was seven years out of date! But few sessions worth the name are announced either in print or neon lights. The night was black dark at 9pm when I left the Bodrezal Mill and headed south and east on the 35-min drive to Quimper. Leaving the motorway you quickly move into sight of the great twin towers of Quimper cathedral, turn left and left again until you are running parallel to the river and soon the station comes into sight. TGVs wait quietly in shadow for their customers. You park and walk through neon-tinged drizzle towards the pub. A few idle Saturday night punters stare at your 'cello bag and you wonder what they are thinking.

The pub is bustle and banter – a log fire in the corner and pretty girls behind the bar. No music at this stage. I ask when and if the music will start. "Vers dix heures normalement" is the casual answer. I buy a pression beer and sit at a vacant table trying to beat "the kid" at chess on my iPhone. The "kid" is graded "novice" but trounces me each time with amusing ease. Soon I notice groups of customers going up the backstairs

– hmmm strange, maybe the session will be up there although last time (3 years ago) it was by the door. More folk go upstairs, a jaunty fellow with a peaked cap like my own, goes up with his round black bowron case. Aha – I buy another beer. This time I ask for the local brew whose name I now remember – it's Coren and a very nice traditional draught bitter (and it's a pint) drawn by hand pump. Excellent.

It's time to brave the stairs and find out what's going on. Amazingly the pub stretches on and on upstairs – old wood and heavy bar stools. There are instruments around the high table on the left away from the bar and microphones festooned from the ceiling above. (This is a common and sensible device for piping the live music into the bar instead of glitzy muzak.) There is a group of cheerful folk who I take to be musicians chatting and laughing at the bar. I sip my drink and make conversation to a rather overweight middle-aged man with a grey moustache and a red anorak. Is he a musician? He mumbles a half-hearted "no" but I suspect differently. But he is not part of the "in" set.

Suddenly there is a move to take all the music downstairs – there are not enough punters in the bar. We tread downstairs and begin to set ourselves up beside the door. I ask if I can join in – "of course", and hardly an eyebrow is raised. But before we can play a note more musicians arrive and we are directed to go back upstairs. To my horror I realize I have forgotten to bring my wooden spike-holder and there is a beautifully smooth hardwood floor. I find a crack under the table and sufficient room to bow. There is a whistle player on my right, a lady flautist, a youngish male flautist beside her and then a wizened looking guitarist back in the corner. He has a dark-haired, well-groomed man in his 30s next to him playing the pipes and a flute. Then another flute beside an elderly smiling banjo player. There's a lady flute player beside him with a fine silver necklace and then young Killian from County Clare, who is a flute playing student on an Erasmus year. Beside and behind him are two wild-looking bowron players – one with long black hair and dark animal eyes, the other roundish with short cropped hair and the peaked cap. Next to me I have two fiddle players and sitting down at the next table there's a black-bearded man playing a banjo.

Instruments are sorted out and there is some finicky tuning going on. But in a few moments the black-bearded banjo player launches the first set. He plays 8 bars on his own before the powerhouse erupts with a vigour and pace that is always surprising – makes the hairs stand up on the back of your neck. The bar is full now – mostly with young people – and the craic is certainly mighty. The two dark-haired lads either side of the guitarist are a powerhouse of excellence – the general standard is world-class as they rip out reel after reel. There are occasional jigs thrown in for good measure. Everyone of them seems capable of leading on their own but the men in the corner have really got their teeth into the scene.

At this stage the banter is all in French and it's hard to tell who is who. After about an hour, the black-bearded fellow comes and asks me if I'm drinking Coren. He's Irish, called Peter, and he runs the bar. From now on it's drinks on the house and plenty of them. The lady next to me, an excellent fiddle player, is Rowana. She is Australian and knows Shane (the other Australian fiddle player I met 3 years ago) – she is taking over from Shane in her group as Shane is having another baby. There is quite a lot of interest in the 'cello now. One of the punters tells me there is a session Thursday nights in Locronan, where another 'cellist plays! That sounds interesting as Locronan is beautiful. Peter asks if he can have a go on the 'cello. I explain that I'm a classical 'cellist who enjoys sessions and plays O'Carolan and a good few slow airs. He says he is looking forward to hearing some later.

There's a short break and change-around in the seating. I'm now next to Silvia – the prettiest 40 something or other fiddle player. She lived in Ireland 20 plus years ago and also plays very well. She has a go at the 'cello, too. I think some of the men are rather interested in Silvia as I detect just the tiniest hint of jealousy from the whistle player on my left. But how all the relationships work here is still a closed book.

The bell rings for "time" – to my surprise I see it is already 1am. We stop playing and I am not quite sure what will happen next. The pipe player is told to shut up when he launches another tune. I assume it must be all over and start to collect my things. Then Rowana tells me that the real session will only start when all the punters have gone and Peter has shut the blinds. The dark-haired lady from downstairs at the bar now joins us – wild she certainly is. She is Eilish – the barman's feisty Irish wife, in her fifties – and she plays a mean fiddle as well as the bones. The session now winds itself up into an increasing frenzy – people take it in turns to lead or play their party pieces. In a lull Silvia asks me to play and I become the focus of a dozen interested pairs of eyes. I play "the Boy with the Black hair" to general amazement. Eilish certainly loves it and asks for another – so I have finally broken the ice. At the next break I am swept away by Eilish, who is clearly a force to be reckoned with – kisses and hugs and I can stay with them anytime if I don't feel like driving home. She left Ireland 8 years ago, fleeing the Celtic Tiger and says they at least try to keep some civilization going here in Quimper. Peter chats away too, saying I should stay as they have another house. It seems they have quite a house party after each session – because of drink drive and all that. By now they are all speaking English – and drinking pints of Guinness – little bits of something like the real Ireland scattered all over the world. They do not have time for consumerism or politics around this table.

By now it's after 3am and I'm rather tiring of the piper's constant wild reels – a few hornpipes or polkas would make a change! Time to go. By now my moustachioed fatman has got out his mouthorgan and played a few jigs – he's a perfectly competent musician but does not altogether get full support from the session. My suspicions were correct. I pack my things and Peter lets me out the back door into the rain. On the motorway home it turns to snow and finally it's nice to get back to have a shower and wash off some of the nicotine smell as they smoked like chimneys in there. Just after 4am I'm tucked up warm. What an amazing night ... and they do this every week!

Another Irish Interlude

Because of complications with her visa and residency in Europe, Estie decided she would try to gain entry to Britain by moving to Ireland. I decided to join her there. Here is the little old Rose Cottage Estie and I rented for 3 months together in the wilds of Donegal.

The cottage facilities were basic to say the least. The only source of heat and hot water was the turf fire (we had ample supplies of turf included with the rent). I was hoping to be able to find time to continue my writing but it turned out to be far from easy to find personal space in such a small and primitive cottage. We continued to find ourselves bogged down in debate about how Estie could resolve her financial and personal problems. Clearly there were serious outstanding issues with her ex-husband. One night as we finished another frustrating conversation on this topic, Estie remarked to me how many of her problems would be solved if her (relatively elderly) ex-husband were to die. The very next day, again seemingly out of the blue, Estie received a message to say her husband had indeed died that very night! In fact Estie, to my surprise, was very distraught by this news. I felt that the new situation had somehow undermined the simple loving relationship we had had – all very strange and mysterious.

Later I would "rescue" Estie and Luke from Ireland as their time there ran out and visa problems forced them to leave. The only way for them to return to France now would be for me to collect them and bring them back in *Masquerade* – so customs checks and immigration would be avoided. I set off to sail single-handed from Brest to Kinsale. The direct route, via the Scilly Islands, is nearly 400 miles. *Masquerade* is a strong, well-kitted-out yacht with self-steering gear, a good GPS system and a roller-reefing mainsail which all make single-handed sailing relatively straightforward. The weather forecast was good so I passed out of the lock at Port Launay and headed west. It's a wonderful experience sailing alone through the night 100 miles from the nearest land. The skies are dark so the stars are bright and the shooting stars often make a fine display – sometimes bright green or red. On a strong boat you feel quite safe and at one with the Earth. The main concerns are fishing boats which have right of way and seem to turn here and there without warning as they chase their prey, and large container ships which appear rapidly over the horizon at 20 knots plus. You never know if any of these fellow travellers have seen your small yacht or not!

I found a sheltered anchorage near Port Mary in the Scillies and stopped for a rest. Next day I continued – still with a good weather forecast – for the final leg across the Irish Sea. Now the Irish Sea is an uncomfortable place to be when wind is against tide as the sea is relatively shallow so waves are often short and steep. As I sailed into the night, the wind steadily began to freshen. This was totally unforeseen in the weather forecast and the biggest gusts always seemed to come when Beethoven's rousing music was playing out from my stereo! I was furious that the weather had tricked me like this and became more and more furious as the wind continued to increase to a full gale. Huge white-breaking wavetops were rushing towards me in the black darkness. It was too rough to use the self-steering gear. I could only jam the wheel as best I could whilst I tried to reef in the big foresail – I had already wound in most of the mainsail. The yacht is throwing me about like the worst of fairground rides as I try to winch in the straining foresail. Alas, my grip on the sheet slips and the gale rips the rope from my hand. The foresail flies out in the gale flapping with a noise like machine gun fire. Before I can do anything the foresail has wrapped itself several times around the forestay so all attempts at controlling it or winding it in are gone. I realise I must start the engine to give myself any control of the situation. Thank goodness it starts and I have no option but to run before the storm as the wind howls through the rigging and the big white-wave crests rush up behind me. At least, the situation is under control now and I must just wait, still cursing the weather forecast, until dawn comes and the storm abates.

Time passes slowly in these moments as one reflects on a successful (!) escape from disaster. The dawn does indeed come some four or five hours later – and the storm abates. But I am still left with the problem of getting the foresail sorted out. I cannot use the roller reefing and I cannot climb up the forestay where the sail is all twisted up. Certainly I cannot sail on with the sail as it is. After some thought, the penny finally drops. I could unravel the sail by turning the boat around so the wind itself will hold the bit of the sail that's showing in position whilst the boat turns around it. I turn the boat through 360 degrees and "yes" the foresail looks less tangled. I continue to keep turning the boat round and round until the sail miraculously flies free. I can winch it in now and continue my journey. I finally arrive at Kinsale on a fine sunny afternoon – I have rung Estie and Luke in advance and they meet me on the quay. We have a glad re-union and after a blissful rest over-night we set sail again for Brittany.

Estie and Luke have never sailed before so this trip is quite an experience for them! We set off with a fine brisk breeze, the sun beaming down, the spray flying and Masquerade battling along at near her top speed of about 7 knots. It seems wonderful to me but Estie and Luke are almost dying of fear and sea-sickness. They disappear below in total misery and this remains their condition throughout the entire trip – they hated it! As we neared the Scilly Isles, the wind turned against us and we had no option but to motor the last 20 miles – and very uncomfortable it was, bashing into a stiff head sea. We anchored safely in the main harbour at Port Mary but, shock/horror, when we tried to move the yacht next day (following instructions from the harbour master) the engine would not start. We had been lucky the previous day to make it all the way because, as it turned out, the rough passage had disturbed all the sediment in the fuel tank and blocked the fuel filters. I was confined to battling away in the smelly bilges of *Masquerade* in order to screw off the fuel filter which I then took to the small engineering boatyard on shore near our anchorage. I showed the filter to the charming engineer who ran the place and he proceeded to disappear for about 20 minutes whilst he looked through all the various fuel filters he kept in stock. Eventually he returned with one he thought might fit. So it was back to the boat and the bilges for me. Did it fit? No, it did not. Next day I was back again to the garage/boatyard. The engineer who ran the place was away but his side-kick in the office was there. He asked me what my problem was. When I told him I needed a new filter for my Bukh diesel he took down a thick reference book which listed thousands of oil filters. In 2 minutes he found the correct reference for my engine, picked up the phone and spoke to the helicopter office – could they collect an X,Y,Z filter on their daily flight tomorrow. Yes they could – so if I came back at 2pm tomorrow the filter would be waiting for me. Indeed it was and I thanked my lucky stars for the wizard who had sorted things out. I soon fitted the filter and we proceeded on to Brest. What a joy it is for any mariner when the big lighthouses on Ouessant show their beams on the distant horizon – it's a rocky shore that must be well avoided but at least you know you're on the right course for Brest.

Back in Brittany Estie and Luke were getting itchy feet to get back to Italy, where they had grand plans to work with an alternative community and put into practice all their permaculture know-how. First, however, they had things to sort out in Holland and Belgium and I realised that our romance had come to an end. We kept in touch for some time after I had dropped them off for the next stage in their life saga. Eventually they did get to their dream community in Italy and I hope very much it turned out well for them. We had wonderful times and I'm pleased that at least I taught young Luke to play the violin – he must be a wizard at it by now!

I continued for a time to work for Nick in Brittany and live at the old Bodrezal Mill. I had good times there and some excellent wwoofers. Meeting these open-minded, gutsy and energetic (mostly) young people is always a refreshing experience. We have good times together and I hope I may be able to pass some experience and wisdom to help them on their own journeys. Jess was one great girl, strong and independent. I persuaded her to take out her flute again and we had a lot of fun playing duets together. Kathleen was another – a strong minded American girl who had already travelled widely. At first she seemed a typically brash American but slowly we came to trust each other. I hope I gave her the inspiration and a new confidence to seek new directions in her life as she had evidently had some very disappointing relationships with men. This is the poem I wrote for her when she left.

Brave Kathleen

No one knows where you have been,
the smells and sights that you have seen.
Demeanour calm just like a queen,
that's the face of brave Kathleen
But now the time has come to stop,
to find a man and set up shop.
To use your strength and make things grow
with all the skills you've come to know.
To trust in life and its strange force,
let nature run its own sweet course.
To laugh at those who would pour scorn
and smile each day to greet the morn.
To love your man, bring out his best,
let patient care meet every test.
Your pretty face will do the trick,
your smile, your song will make things tick.
You'll surely change the Earth for good
and do the things you know you should.
I thank you now and wish you well.
Will we meet again? No-one can tell!

I still keep in touch with Kathleen from time to time. In fact she did find a good loving man very soon after she went back to the States and from all I hear they are very happy together with music playing a big part in their lives. I hope my advice and support may have helped her in this.

The Ocean talks in Whispers

After my strange romance with Estie fizzled out, I spent a somewhat unsettled time living between Bordeaux, Brittany and staying with my Mum in Northumberland. It was a time of very mixed feelings – sadness, of course, on leaving my home and children in Ireland but satisfaction, too, in re-building my important relationships with Sarah and my older children. Sarah continued to be a brilliant and enthusiastic host for my annual summer series of self-sufficiency courses. I continued to enjoy my time working for Nick on the old Mill at Bodrezal. One New Year's eve I will not forget found me (in 2011) watching the traditional drunken celebrations taking place on the beach at Low Newton. It was a clear night and I did not myself have much to celebrate at this time. Seeing the revellers singing and drinking (as I watched on from the top of the hill) I could not help the build-up of some kind of anger – this "doggerel" was the result.

THE OCEAN TALKS IN WHISPERS

The ocean talks in whispers as it runs upon the sand
While humans laugh and drink and curse but do not understand
That forces far beyond their ken are working hand in hand
With larger shapes of destiny whose future's not been planned

A match that's small and tiny bright can light the midnight fire
while stars look down and children watch as flames burn higher, higher
Another cosmic milestone come and gone – My God it could be dire
That pile of sticks with New Year tricks could be a funeral pyre

For the Earth in all her majesty is not a gentle place
She's not obliged to break her back to house the human race

We've covered her with shit and smoke, a positive disgrace
One day she'll get her own back so just you watch this space

"I told you so" the Walrus said and shed a bitter tear
We've lost the plot, I don't know what will come about next year
It won't be good, it won't be wise for there is no wisdom here
The only way to treat these clowns is to scare them stiff with fear

"Jeepers friend" I heard her say "is this the blooming end?"
The fuel's all gone, the soil's to pot, we're going round the bend
Money's scarce, our jobs are rot and it's too late to pretend
That humans rule a world they've done nothing but offend

Yet creeping through the cracks of doom a tiny voice speaks out
It's not too late you stupid pigs to turn the ship about.
With seeing eyes and red raw souls you can save the Earth you love
So use your brains and DO NOT WAIT for orders from above.

Back to England in 2013 – "Granny's" final years

Ceri, who was now living with her family near Embleton, had been doing great work helping her Granny despite being extremely busy herself with her career as a doctor and bringing up her two young children, Ralph and Louis. She had rented a huge (cold) old house at Little Houghton near Embleton and it seemed to make sense for me to move in with them so I could be closer to my Mum as well as help with Ceri's children (as she and Riaan pursued their busy careers). One big plus for me was the chance to re-instate the lovely old vegetable garden and greenhouse at Little Houghton – this I did and it was a great success. So far as I know the new occupiers employ a professional gardener to keep the garden going – it had a wonderfully tasty grape vine in the greenhouse which produced lots of lovely fruit after I rebuilt the greenhouse!

The Little Houghton Mansion

We always had quite a party when Hal came up from London and his energy multiplied that which already flowed from Louis and Ralph. Here they are together digging on the Embleton beach together with Dylan's kids, Gustav and Eddie!

Hal and the boys enjoying the beach

The focus of my life now moved steadily towards giving my mother the support she needed to enjoy the last years of her life. Ceri decided she wanted to have her own space in the house at Little Houghton so I moved in with my mother. This enabled me to get a much better idea of how her faculties were slowly deteriorating – despite the fact that in day-to-day contact and conversation all seemed the same as usual. When Ceri moved to Newcastle to be closer to her work, the question arose as to what might happen to Eunice, who had come back with them from South Africa to help look after Louis and Ralph. One obvious solution might be for Eunice to become a caring companion for my mother. This seemed a very acceptable idea for all the parties involved so Eunice moved into the Smithy and remained my mother's faithful and kind companion/carer until she died in 2018.

Eunice and "Granny"

Throughout 2013 I spent a lot of time trying to help Ceri with her problems at work. Clearly, Ceri thought that many of the hospital practices were potentially dangerous and she felt bullied by both managers and colleagues who wished to stop her "whistle blowing". Many letters, emails and meetings flowed back and forth as the parties involved tried to resolve the various issues. In the event Ceri was given extended leave but there is no doubt it was a very stressful time. As it turned out, things would also become much more stressful closer to home when

Ceri and I found ourselves in bitter conflict over the care of my mother in the year which followed. Even now I don't understand the true reasons for all these difficulties and arguments. Of course, Ceri had spent a lot of time with my Mum and wanted to make sure she was being well looked after. No doubt it was difficult for her to accept that it would be impossible for her to play a big role in this now she was living in Newcastle. For better or worse I now had to do the best I could to sort out my Mum's affairs, keep her finances in order and make sure she got out and about as much as possible. We chatted about old times, played cards and enjoyed making tasty meals together. Trips to the ice cream van on Seahouses pier were a special favourite – Mum really loved her 99s!! Soon my new relationship with Ros would provide my Mum with another caring and supportive companion.

My Early Dalliance with Cyber Currency

My activities at Little Houghton left me with some time to keep up to date with developments in the wider world (as I have always tried to do). One of my sources of entertainment and news was (and still is) the regular 30-minute youtube videos (released by Russia Today) featuring the zippy US commentator Max Keiser (and his partner Stacey). In one of these I picked up his reference to the completely new concept of crypto currency – Bitcoin had recently crept into the news. As a one-time graduate in mathematics I immediately took up the challenge of trying to find out how all this worked – it seemed a miraculously clever idea and had very mysterious origins. It was not difficult to find the bitcoin "White Paper" which had been released into the internet a couple of years earlier by its anonymous creator (Satoshi Nakamoto) and I found its logic very powerful.

The aim of the White Paper was to create an unbreakable way to transfer value from one person to another over the internet WITHOUT the need for a "trusted third party". Of course, we are all very used to using Paypal or a Bank credit card to buy things we want via the internet but this is very different from paying for something with real cash. We can pay with cash without using a bank or a credit card. Satoshi wanted something that would work like "cash" but be usable over the internet. Satoshi also wanted something that was completely independent of the fiat money created by the conventional state-sponsored banking system. In fact he included the text of the headline in the Times newspaper (3 January 2009) in the code for his first block of bitcoins because it referred to the breakdown of the banking system after 2008. Clearly one of his objectives was to provide "ordinary" people with something more trustworthy than the evidently unstable fractional reserve (state-backed) banking system. He wanted to create something that was like digital "gold".

For a long time I had also believed that the so-called "fiat" money was creating serious problems for the world. Why? Two reasons really.

First, the "fiat" element means the money is not backed by anything concrete (like gold or silver) and this means the amounts in circulation can be changed very easily (either by banks or governments) – states can do this to create inflation (make people spend more quickly) or even finance wars (by raising more debt to buy arms).

Second, the "fiat" currency (which now dominates trade on Earth) is almost all (99 percent) created by banks as interest-bearing debt – this means someone somewhere has to pay the interest. Interest can only be paid if more money is continually created to enable the supply of money to increase. Effectively the system cannot operate unless there is economic growth – this is a major factor encouraging exploitation of the Earth as well as inflation. Without these factors, the current fiat money system would be like a snake eating its tail. It goes without saying that inflation, wars and economic growth are all very bad for the Earth.

At first I was somewhat baffled by the terminology of the block chain, the hash function and what was meant by a distributed ledger. It was relatively simple to understand the use of private and public keys which would protect each owner's digital "wallet" from being used by any third party – this was pretty much the same as the logic of the old fashioned "tally sticks" (used to record debts for many centuries in the past). It seemed a very clever idea that any individual could be rewarded for using their computer(s) to both record and confirm each block of transactions (every 10 minutes) on the distributed ledger. Whoever won the race to do this would receive a number of bitcoins as a reward. This is the process known as "mining". So long as the "miners" can make a profit they will continue to provide the large number of independent computers and computing resources required to make the block chain work and process transactions.

The term "mining" is perhaps rather misleading. "Mining" is in fact the computing activity that is needed to maintain and secure the block chain – making sure all new transactions have been confirmed within the next block of the block chain. At any one time, thousands of independent computers (nodes) are trying to find the "magic number" (the nonce) which will lock the most recent transactions in the block chain. It took me a little while to realise that a bitcoin was just a number which was allocated to a digital wallet. This is no different from the digital number which your bank keeps for you. But whereas you simply have to trust your bank to honour its obligation, your bitcoin is protected because it is saved in the block-chain on thousands of independent computers. Obviously both the number and the digital wallet were simply recorded on computers as strings of 1s and 0s. The algorithm invented by Satoshi was designed so the difficulty of finding the "nonce" would always be adjusted to ensure that each block of these linked digital numbers would be confirmed (locked) every 10 minutes.

The "nonce" is the number which, when added to the other 1s and 0s in the block, would produce an alphanumeric code with a certain number of 0s at the beginning when the appropriate "hash" function was applied to the whole block. Computer programmers had been using "hash" functions for many years as a simple way to make sure a large volume of software code had been copied correctly. The "hash" function was a simple set of mathematical operations which would run through the whole ordered mass of code within the block and, at the end, produce a unique alphanumeric code of just 64 characters. Even the smallest change in the sequence of numbers would produce a completely different code.

Many people seem very confused as to why numbers in the bitcoin blockchain should have any value whatever! But history shows us that any article which cannot be easily made or duplicated and which does not rot or decay can become "money". Wampum shells (with a hole bored in them), buck-skins, cigarettes and, of course, gold and silver coins have all been used as "money". The electronic numbers which make "fiat" bank money are trusted only because we believe the banks that create and hold them can be trusted (a fact which history certainly throws some doubt on!) Note that the value of state-backed "fiat" money is (to some extent) enforced by the state when it requires us (by force if necessary) to pay taxes. This "fiat" money is one kind of money which is defined as "legal tender". Imperial powers have always used the "straight jacket" of legal tender in the tax systems they have imposed to dominate their colonies. The banks which create and hold "fiat" currency are required by the State to supply details of every individual account so that income taxes can be collected effectively. In this sense, the banks are "agents" for central government.

The numbers which are held on the block chain as "bitcoin" cannot be duplicated; they cost considerable amounts of money (at present about £5,000 in electricity for each bitcoin) because of the energy required to operate the block chain and, of course, they do not rot or disappear unless a majority of several thousand independent computers is hacked or destroyed. The first recorded instance of someone using bitcoin to buy a real object was the (now famous) purchase of a pizza for 10,000 bitcoins in New York on 22 May 2010. This date is known as

"Bitcoin Pizza Day".

Once I had done some basic research, I saw that bitcoin really did have the potential to become the equivalent of "digital gold". The total quantity would always be limited (by the structure of the algorithm) and its value would be set by the market independent of state manipulation. What's more it could be transferred electronically between individuals much more easily than gold or silver, and more cheaply than bank money. Bitcoin was very definitely a deflationary currency (because the total amount was fixed) so its value must tend to rise as its use increased. Note that deflationary currencies tend to encourage people to spend more slowly (because the price of goods will be less next week) and this is one way to discourage the economic growth which is destroying the Earth. (Governments, of course, are terrified of deflation precisely because it puts a serious brake on "growth" and they need "growth" to maintain employment, support consumerism and win elections.)

So it was not long before I realised that cyber currencies had the possibility to become a global money system with the potential to reduce the power of the nation state (which would not be able – easily – to collect cyber currencies as taxation or manipulate their value to affect economies). I bought a few bitcoins late in 2012 when the price was still below £10. I told quite a few friends about my excitement over this development but Sarah was the only one who asked me to buy any for her – she spent £150 to buy just over 7 bitcoins early in 2013. Like me, she did pretty well as the value soon began to rocket upwards (reaching $20,000 in December 2017).

But all was not well in the "bitcoin garden". This first generation cyber currency had no management structure of any kind, no marketing arm and no decision-making protocols. This led to much acrimonious debate about the best block size – various elements split away. Worse still, the original protocols and algorithms which had created bitcoin could not be upgraded to cater for the huge increase in the numbers of transactions. (Bitcoin can only process a maximum of about 7 transactions per second – at least 1,000 times slower than competitors such as Visa.) Worse still, the continual upgrading of computing power (as miners competed to find the next "nonce") required more and more electricity to be used to confirm each block. This latter was, if you like, an inevitable computing "arms race" which the inventor had not foreseen (today in 2019 the huge amount of electricity required means bitcoin can only be mined in areas where the price of power is cheap (for example China and Iceland). There are now more than 1,000 different (newer) cyber-currencies competing in this emerging market place – many have much more sophisticated protocols than bitcoin.

One new cyber-currency which struck me as particularly innovative and clever was Dash. Invented by the genius of Evan Duffield and promoted by the wonderfully smart and articulate Amanda B Johnston – Dash had a management structure and vision which impressed me. I sold my remaining bitcoin early in 2017 and bought Dash instead. Dash was trading at £14.44 when I bought 26 in January. Unusually for me I was so impressed by Dash that I wrote to many of my golfing friends suggesting they might take a speculative investment of two or three hundred pounds in Dash just to learn about the cyber currency market. To this day I'm not sure if any took up my suggestion but in fact the value of Dash had risen to £360 by September and to £1,400 (briefly) in December – not a bad rate of return at 10,000 percent in less than a year! Dash is still trading at over $80 as I write but the big bitcoin crunch adjustment is still to come and the continuing development work at Dash is moving towards the really exciting prospect of "Evolution" which should be as easy to use as conventional currencies.

Throughout the development of cyber currencies the attitude of state governments has been rather confused. There have been (and are) many scams in the cyber space and I have seen very few articles or commentaries which show any detailed understanding of what's going on. China has seen the greatest surge of large bitcoin mining rigs partly because there are places in China where electricity is very cheap and partly because cyber currencies offer the possibility of moving money abroad without government control. Short of shutting the internet down completely, it is not going to be easy for governments to control or regulate what is going on.

What is clear to me is that nothing in the cyber space will settle down properly until bitcoin has collapsed. For the moment I am hanging on to my Dash. There can be no doubt that the appearance and development of cyber currencies is one of the most remarkable (and unexpected) results of humanity's love affair with the computer. It certainly has the potential to reduce the power of the nation state – how and when this will come about, it is impossible to say.

Facebook's "Libra"

I cannot leave this topic without talking about Mr Suckerberg's (my nick name) new proposal for Facebook to launch a "corporate" digital currency. With potentially 2 billion users and enormous technical resources, this new initiative could have enormous implications. As I write (in autumn 2019) Facebook has just published a "White Paper" which sets out its vision for its new corporate currency called "Libra".

Now Facebook has joined the crypto race
Keen as mustard to take its place
Pegged to fiat currencies at global rates
To challenge banks and Nation States

Suckerberg's keen to get much bigger
That's the plan he's trying to figure
Launch the "Libra", take on the world
We'll soon see his scheme unfurled

But creeping tyranny is in the wings
Waiting its chance to do bad things
When digital currency replaces cash

It's human freedom they'll surely smash

This is not a move to make one glad
The "Libra" will very likely make us sad
This is not a thing one should endorse
When corporate greed is the driving force

I don't suppose you need me to tell you that there is a great deal of difference between money and cash! We glibly use the term money as a "cover-all" expression for all the different types of money we may use – bank money, Apple Pay, Paypal, coins and notes – and perhaps even crypto-currencies. But we understand very well that "cash" is what we might call "free" money. Once we have those coins and notes in our pocket (or under our bed) no government or corporation can really stop us from using them (or not using them) however we please. Every tradesman is likely to have two prices for each job – one for "digital" bank money (recorded by the state via the banking system) and another (cheaper) price for cash which the state may find it difficult to lay its hands on. As we shall see, the best crypto-currencies are also "free" money just like cash only easier to use on the internet or for transfer over long distances between countries.

Digital money is money that exists only as 1s and 0s within the memory of a computer – you cannot hold digital money in your hand as coins or notes. With the important exception of crypto-currencies, all digital money has to be "held in trust" on the computers of some external agency. Usually this is bank regulated, and at least partially controlled, by some national government.. The integrity of crypto-currencies, on the other hand, does not depend on "trust" but on the power of the blockchain and the privacy of cryptographically protected private keys.

Facebook has a vision for "Libra" as a new-style corporate-created digital money. This has big implications both for banks, for governments and for you and me. If we wish to live in a "free" world then it's vital we have at least some money (at present cash and crypto) which is outside the control of state and corporation. Any move to a cashless society is a recipe for tyranny – when even your ability to buy food may be cut off on one pretext or another by an over-arching power. China, with its comprehensive system of social credit scoring, is already well on the way to being such a society.

The Facebook White Paper is a long and turgid document and its vision may well be heavily modified before Libra becomes a reality (possibly next year). So far Libra has hardly even made front page news. After all, most modern mass media journalists are lazy beggars who are not keen to research challenging subjects – easier to write about lying politicians or sex mad soap opera stars. But, make no mistake, this mega-corporate vision is likely to have significant consequences – not just for the slow-witted traditional banks but also for governments as well as you and me. Where Facebook has started, others may follow – particularly Amazon and Google.

As is its custom, Facebook has made great play of its supposed good intentions in launching this new corporate money. It says it will bring cheap banking to the millions who at present have no access. The value of Facebook money (the Libra) will be guaranteed by being based on a basket of well-established fiat currencies (e.g. the dollar, the pound, the euro etc.). When you buy Libra for fiat money (whether dollars, pounds, or other) then your money will be exchanged for Libra and then held in a central bank account in Switzerland. The whole process will be managed by a large consortium of well-established "validators" (such as Visa, Paypal, Facebook, Mastercard, Coinbase, Uber, etc, etc. – there are more than 30 although some have already pulled out). The "validators" will maintain records on a blockchain and take profits from investing the fiat money which they receive from purchasers of Libra. Once you have your Libra then you can spend it, save it or send it with a user friendly App designed by Facebook. You can even run your business with it, though how far Facebook will co-operate with state tax authorities remains unclear!

Oh yes – and Facebook promise they will never use your financial dealings to give them extra information to combine with your Facebook profile. They are good at making promises!

You will find an excellent exposition about all this on youtube www.youtube.com/watch?v=7S6506vkth4 by Andreas Antonopolous. I can thoroughly recommend you find 30 minutes to listen to what he has to say. In summary Antonopolous believes that the "free" money we need if we are to live in a "free" society should satisfy 5 conditions. It should be:

- **Open** – Anyone should be able to use it in any way they want
- **Borderless** – It should work in the same way in every and any country on Earth
- **Neutral** – There should be no control on how you use it – what you buy or who you send it to
- **Immutable** – neither its value nor the way it works should be under the control of any outside power whether state or corporate
- **Auditable and Transparent** – the way it works should always be open to inspection

Most of the emerging crypto-currencies meet all these requirements as do the major world currencies when they are in the form of coin or notes such as the Euro or Dollar. In fact over thousands of years gold and silver have always been the safest form of "free" money.

Clearly the new Facebook currency fails on the first four conditions – we don't yet know about the fifth. So nobody can claim that the Libra is a true crypto-currency. It will have a Committee of the great and the good managing it, an office and a Chief Executive (in Geneva). This means that state controls will prevent it being used in "rogue" states such as Iran or any others that the US does not like. "Libra" will certainly not be allowed to operate in China or Russia. It also means Facebook will almost certainly have to provide national governments with all the information they need to levy taxes. And, at the end of the day, we only have Facebook's promises that they will not misuse the new personal information their currency will provide.

In short, the Libra is anything but a "free" currency. It is part of a direct and calculated move (by both corporations and nation states) towards a "cashless" society where they have greater control over the masses and there will be no "free" money. No doubt with 2 billion potential users the Libra will also pose a serious threat to the traditional forms of monetary control used by nation states to "manage" their economies. Those holding Libra rather than bank money will be outside state control – although we don't yet know if the Libra management in Geneva will have its own wider economic objectives! The Libra certainly has the potential to destroy the retail banking sector just as iTunes and the internet destroyed the old established music industry.

A new Garden at Christon Bank

Going back to my plans in Northumberland, I now faced the question of how and where to run my SS courses in 2014. Bordeaux was too complicated and too remote and Little Houghton was no longer an option under new occupants. Fortunately Peter Gilbert (Sarah's brother) was now considering bringing the old, walled kitchen garden at Christon Bank back into use. Diggers had been brought in to remove the self-sown trees and the garden itself was now ready to weed and cultivate. This prospect was a dream come true for me because the wonderfully productive layout and micro-climate generated by the Victorian walled garden was a magical thing to behold. There are, in fact, very few properly-run walled gardens to be found anywhere in Britain – we have become almost totally dependent on large-scale industrial agriculture. So Ros and I set to work to dig and weed; paths had to be laid and a new greenhouse built. Indeed some of this work could be done by the students themselves as soon as courses began in 2014.

Early days preparing the east facing section

We start digging and weeding

The garden newly paved

Grandchildren Gus and Eddie enjoying some harvesting

Chapter 12: A New Life with Ros, 2013

Once again, over the fun and games of Christmas 2013, the twists and turns of fate brought new surprises into my life. Sarah and the family were convening for general family celebrations at Low Newton and one of the visitors turned out to be my old friend and sometime romantic partner (from 1978) Ros. She had come over from Germany (as she often did at Christmas) after her first husband (German – who had been in touch with Sarah in New Zealand) had suggested that she should see if Sarah needed help after her various hip operations. We found ourselves staying together in Heather Cairns' tiny old cottage in the Square. It was wintry and cold and we had already caught up with each other's news and the state of our "love-lives" (non-existent in Ros's case partly because Claus was now beginning to suffer dementia and non-existent in mine because Estie had long since disappeared from the scene). It was not long before we were cuddled up together to keep warm and revive the old romance we had had so long ago. Such are the chances and vagaries of life – sometimes painful and sometimes wonderful.

Bitter Arguments about "Granny"

The care and management of elderly relatives is well known to be fraught with challenges. All sorts of tricky judgements have to be made about the "mental competence" of individuals who were once supremely able to handle their own affairs. The old people themselves are often prone to fits of depression and anger as their capabilities begin to fail them – both physically and mentally. Of course everyone involved wants to do their best to make their loved one's last years (or months) as good as they can be. But different people have different ideas and even the professionals (who don't have the experience of day to day living) cannot be trusted to make the best decisions. And it is often difficult to avoid jealousies or misunderstandings about money – the "root of all evil". How will money be spent and how will it be divided up in the final reckoning?

The Family enjoys a Christmas feast at Newton

All these factors seemed to combine to produce a cocktail of bad feelings and argument about the care of my mother after a dramatic and unexpected intervention by Ceri during September 2014. This was very sad and very exhausting for those of us directly involved in Granny's day-to-day care. But, in the event, it did not (luckily) significantly affect the well-being of Granny herself. We were lucky to have a committed team of Eunice, Ros, myself, Judy Turnbull, Marjorie and even Alison (the hairdresser) who worked together (with occasional inputs from doctors and social workers) to keep Granny going for as long as possible. Judy, a local neighbour who had known our family for many years, frequently brought home-cooked lunches and a cheerful face to the Smithy. Marjorie (who I called the "white tornado") came by regularly (as she had done for many years) to do a whistle-stop clean-up, wash and iron the sheets and (sometimes) re-decorate a room she felt looked too shabby! Always cheerful, always busy, Marjorie brought instant good cheer into the house as well as keeping us all up to date on local gossip. The Friday morning weekly hair-do and Alison's cheerful chatting with Granny also helped keep her spirits up and invariably put her in the mood for a lunch outing – often to the friendly company of Lisa and Nicole at the Fishing Boat Inn (Boulmer).

Granny, Ros and Eunice enjoying Howick Gardens

The 100th Birthday

My Mum's 100th birthday turned out to be a great success – with a big party for family, friends and the whole village followed by an excellent supper for the wider family. Several months before the party my Mum had wanted to meet and talk through her funeral plans with one of my good friends – a humanist celebrant, Rupert Morris. Although she wanted the funeral to be in the Embleton Church so that villagers would feel comfortable, she was also keen to include a humanist element which Rupert could provide. During the long discussion over supper Rupert suddenly remarked – "why wait until your funeral to celebrate the wonderful life you have had helping the village in so many ways. Why don't I come up to your 100th birthday so we can celebrate all these achievements whilst you are still alive!" And so it was arranged. Rupert would give one speech (as well as being "master of ceremonies"), Heather Cairns would give another and Jill Mills, (the baby who brought my mother up to Northumberland from London before the Second World War) would give another.

The big day came and we were mightily impressed by the efficiency of the local caterers (Mick Holland) and the helpfulness of Adam Moody, who provided wine and drink (sale or return) from the village shop. A general invitation had been circulated throughout the village so we knew that we could expect about 120 people to attend. The Creighton Hall was all a hustle and bustle as Ros and I returned to the Smithy to collect my mother for the great event. The whole thing had been my Mum's wish in the first place but now, to our horror, she had lost her nerve and was refusing to come. What could be done? We had more than 100 people waiting! I raced back to the Hall to tell Rupert what was going on – so he had the tricky task of keeping the assembled company cheerful whilst we tried to resolve the impasse. I had the idea that taking Marjorie and Judy back to the Smithy might give us a better chance of getting the "star of the show" to make an appearance. And so it proved to be – the two ladies made it clear that they were not going to take "no" for an answer and almost physically swept Granny along to the party!

Cutting the cake with Judy Turnbull clapping!

From then on everything fell into place. Margaret and Andy Watchorn sang "Where have you been all the day, Bill Boy" – one of my Mum's favourite songs. Rupert and Heather made excellent speeches and, by a miracle, Jill Mills (now over 80) appeared just at the right moment to make her contribution. She was interviewed on stage by Rupert about her time with Granny – and they had an interesting dialogue with Granny which everyone could hear. The big cake was cut to great applause and Granny enjoyed chatting with her grandchildren and others who came to sit with her. After two hours or so Granny was able to retreat once more to the peace and quiet of the Smithy as the party continued.

Owen, Granny, William and Jill Mills (the "baby")

Granny's Death and Funeral

Almost 2 years later, at the end, her death was as she had wished it – at home and without a fuss. There had been no warning or signs of illness on the previous day. We had enjoyed one of our usual outings to find ice cream on the Seahouses pier. But early next morning I would receive a shocked phone call from Eunice and I immediately rushed over to Embleton to see what had happened. There was poor Granny, lying dead on the bathroom floor. We covered her up and waited for the police and ambulance services to arrive. We had already contacted Alistair Turner's, the Alnwick Funeral directors, to handle the funeral and they soon came along to remove the body. It was a very stressful time especially for poor Eunice – although she must have known that this day would soon come. We made the necessary phone calls to inform all family and friends what had happened and began to turn our minds to the funeral arrangements.

The Funeral

Saying final goodbyes to one's close relatives is never an easy process. We were fortunate that the local vicar, Alison, and my humanist friend, Rupert, were able to work comfortably and effectively together to conduct a simple service in Embleton Church. Rupert was able to chronicle the major events in my Mum's life and pay tribute to all the important public roles she had taken in village and county life. Hal recited his very moving "poem" expressing his joyful childhood memories of visits to the Smithy and I gave my own recollections of early family life at Dunstan Steads.

Hal's "Poem"

I am five years old, and my granny lives in Northumberland. It is a long drive but I am happy and excited to make the journey. I make a little nest in the backseat of the car with my sleeping bag. I know that once I finally fall asleep, when I wake up I will be at the old smithy. I will be at granny's house.

In the morning granny greets me with a big bright smile and a gentle hug. Honey the dog is wagging her tail by the kitchen table, and gives me a familiar kiss with her wet nose. I am really looking forward to finishing my breakfast so I can go and play.

Granny has an amazing selection of toys. The collection has been pruned and honed by the laws of natural selection, survival of the fittest.

I sit on the cosy carpeted floor playing. Rainbows of light swirl on the living room walls as sunshine spills through the glass prisms hanging by the window.

On top of the television there are lots of handbells of different shapes and sizes. Chunky bells that give a jarring clang, and pretty bells shaped like well-dressed ladies that tinkle politely.

I ring every single one with curious enthusiasm and vigour. I want to test out all the different sounds. Granny is patient and kind and does not mind the incessant ringing. She is happy to see my interest and the joy in my face. Later we go for a walk on the beach. I am working on a shell collection and granny is helping me find the most beautiful ones. She keeps her eyes peeled and calls me over every now and then to show me what she's found.

In the evening granny does jigsaw puzzles with hundreds and hundreds of pieces. I am in awe of how she can give order to such chaos. She always gets them done. She teaches me how to play patience and solitaire. It feels good being in her company. It is calm and peaceful.

I love smiling at my granny. Because when I smile she smiles back and her whole face lights up. It makes me feel even happier. I will always remember how she smiled with her eyes.

I am almost thirty years old,

And my granny lives in Northumberland. She isn't around anymore but she lives on through her family, her kind deeds, and the memories she created. Memories forever free from any anger or unkindness. Memories full of smiles, full of sweet acts of generosity.

My granny lives in Northumberland.

And now Northumberland is home for me too.

My Own Recollections which I gave at the Funeral

My brothers and I grew up in a very well organised household. The clocks ran on time, the meals ran on time – a cooked lunch at 12 and tea (with bread and jam plus cakes) at half past 4. Willie and Elsie Train would arrive promptly at 9 every morning: one to discuss what produce to bring up from the vegetable garden, the other to start the morning cleaning. Ron Cox, the farm manager, would be in the office to sort out the day's farm work with my father.

It was a household where raised voices, bad tempers and argument were almost unknown. It was a place where swearing never took place – an occasional "dash it" perhaps. It was a place where alcohol and tobacco were dark and toxic substances only used by the posh and the foolish. Pubs were mysterious places which probably fostered betting and adultery.

My mother – Lady Sutherland – "Peggy" to most and "Granny" to many – was an intelligent and well organised person (as many of you know!). But her background was dramatically different to that of my father. Her parents, Bert and Elsie, were a joyful couple, always singing and whistling. Life there seemed to revolve around games and sports of all kinds – Bert was a central figure in the village life of Chalfont St Giles, active in the bowling club, being a hockey umpire, compering the local dances and always ready to buy us a delicious ice-cream.

My father's family, on the other hand, was dominated by the short and very stern figure of the aged Sir Arthur Munro Sutherland – past Lord Mayor of Newcastle, ex Lord Lieutenant of the County and major philanthropist. His household (either in Thurso House or Hethpool) was run on almost military lines by the Scottish butler Wallace and his wife Mrs Wallace. His Rolls Royce cars had the number plates AMS1, 2 and 3 (now taken by the TV reality star Alan Sugar!) When we visited we were scrubbed and polished (both our shoes and our faces) and it was a case of "children being seen but not heard"!

So – you may wonder – what was it that enabled the young

nanny from East Ham to co-exist so successfully with Ivan, son of the rich philanthropist from Newcastle? The answer is, I think, a simple one – both families were staunch Methodists. And the common thread of Methodism (as I discovered much later in life) is public service – a duty to serve the community. Methodists, like Quakers, can be very rich but the privileges of riches bring with them an overriding responsibility to serve.

As far as I know, my mother never went to church and my father frequently argued forcefully with the vicar about the church's doctrine of original sin – which he believed was quite mistaken! But both had a strong belief in their duty to serve the community. In my father's case, this was manifest in his careful stewardship of his land and those who lived and worked upon it. "Profit" was a dirty word to my father – any excess should be, and was, spent on improving the farm – planting trees (such as those around the Embleton cricket pitch), building houses for his workers, improving roadways and maintaining drains and fences. My father fought – yes that is the right word – to stop commercial development – car parks, ice-cream parlours and amusements – which would destroy Embleton's beaches and duneland. In my mother's case, this duty was manifest in her many public activities which you will see listed in the Order of Service. (Some of this even rubbed off on me as I spent more than 10 years working in Whitehall trying to keep the ambitions of short-term egotistical politicians under control!)

As I have said, my mother was a very well organised person. When I came back to Embleton to help her 5 years ago, I found a folder in her green filing cabinet with the heading "DEATH". Inside were the documents which form the Order of Service you have in front of you today. I had never seen the "Creed" which Gael is about to read to you. But its content really sums up many of the things I have just been talking about.

Before the creed I would like to share with you some of the sayings my mother would often repeat to us as children:

First the simple one – "More haste – less speed"; then – "No use crying over spilt milk!" and sometimes on the way home in the car – "My goodness there's enough blue sky to make a pair of Dutchman's trousers!"

Finally one that probably sums up my mother's chief strength:

"Patience is a virtue; virtue is a grace and those that do possess it need not a pretty face."

Granny's gravestone at Spitalford Cemetery outside Embleton

HER CREED – read by Gael

I would be true for there are those that trust me
I would be pure for there are those who care
I would be strong for there is much to suffer
I would be brave for there is much to dare
I would be friend to all: both the foe and the friendless
I would be giving and forget the gift
I would be humble for I know my weakness
I would look up and live, and love and lift....

Peggy's Many Years of Community Service

Farmer's Wife
Parish Councillor
Alnwick District Councillor
Northumberland County Councillor
President of the Embleton Women's Institute
Magistrate
School Governor
Board member of visitors for Acklington Prison
Past President of Northumberland Community Council
Member of Creighton Hall Committee
Member of Northumberland Family Practitioners Committee
Seahouses Harbour Commissioner
Past President and Treasurer of Children's Christmas Tea
Past President of North Sunderland Lifeboat Ladies Guild
Past President of Northumberland National Association of Local Councils
Organiser of Embleton Meals on Wheels and Luncheon Club
Handbell ringer
Bridge Player
Skilled Embroiderer
Yoga Participant
Mother, Grandmother and Great Grandmother

Postscript

I don't suppose that any of us will ever truly understand the powerful emotions involved in all the heated family arguments which took place about my mother's care. My mother had been quite clear that she wanted Owen and myself to take care of her financial affairs. Several years before she had completed all the formalities so that Owen and myself had power of attorney. When I began to study her files I was horrified to find Granny's legal affairs were in a terrible mess. Her former lawyers had lost the deeds of the Smithy many years before (evidently by leaving them in a taxi!). Nothing had been done to remedy this! So we had an urgent and major hassle instructing Granny's new lawyers, Hay and Kilner, to help us obtain a satisfactory possessory title whilst Granny was still alive and competent. Next I found, on a careful reading of her Will, that the lawyers had also created a totally unfair and unwanted situation whereby the structure of her life-insurance policies and the terms of her Will would, unless amended, produce a grossly distorted distribution of her estate to her grandchildren. Once again we were able to sort this out whilst Granny was still alive and well.

It was a relief when the estate was wound up after her death to see that, with very competent help from Alice Clewes at the lawyers Hay and Kilner, all the monies were distributed as fairly as was possible. We staged a successful funeral – partly conventional, partly humanist – as she wanted. And, sad though the day was, a "good time" was had by all. Sorting out her gravestone turned out to be a pleasure thanks to the tact, imagination and artistic skill of Ken Common at Bart Endean in Morpeth. So Granny is forever accompanied by her beloved dog Rosie and, at the bottom of the stone, some daffodils – a touching idea of the stone mason when he learned that she could, when requested, recite the whole of Wordsworth's poem "The Daffodils". As far as her estate was concerned, we were able to arrange for Owen's son, Jonathan, to buy the Smithy. This was very much in accord with my mother's wishes and fortunately Jonathan was able to raise the necessary money and process the formalities. So the Sutherlands keep a foothold in Embleton, the grandchildren received their shares in Granny's estate and life moves on.

A New Life for Eunice

Once again we were fortunate that the fates had taken a hand in the difficult transition which Eunice must face once her caring duties for Granny were over. In the months prior to her death my Mum had enjoyed getting out of the house for day care 2 or 3 days each week at the friendly local care-home in Rennington. Szilvia, the manager, was quite happy for Eunice to accompany my Mum and become in effect a part-time professional carer (she had lots of experience but, at that time, no formal qualifications). So when my Mum died Eunice was, with an enthusiastic welcome from the care-home, to become a full-time carer. She had the car which was given to her by my Mum and we soon found a nice one-bedroom flat for her in Alnwick.

My Golfing Connections

Ever since my golfing days at Cambridge University there have been many close friendships and good times I have enjoyed because of golf. In my short book "Deep Golf" I speculate that one reason for this is the inescapable fact that playing golf reveals many facets of human personality which would otherwise be buried in the disciplines of social convention. People who play golf together share a certain strange intimacy. Their mutual carousing, banter and affections are all the greater as a result. Fortunately the majority of golfers are able to laugh at each other's human frailties which are in fact such an important part of being human. The game does produce a unique camaraderie.

There have been three separate golfing groups which I have enjoyed and been a part of for more than 50 years. The "Old

Stymies" are an enthusiastic and wide-spread group of ex-Cambridge University golfers (mostly from the second team – the Stymies – who enjoyed playing the game more than winning!). The Old Leysian golfers are another cheerful band of golfing enthusiasts (all old boys of my school) and their teams (of which I have often been a part) play in big national public school events – notably the Halford Hewitt and the Grafton Morrish. (Old Leysians are very nice people whose charm and good manners often get in the way of winning.) Finally there is the Times Editorial Golfing Society (TEGS) which meets at least twice each year and brings together a well-briefed and well connected set of (now) ex-journalists. (TEGS golfers enjoy the cut and thrust of entertaining debate which produces many flashes of wit and wisdom.)

The Old Stymies group is large and its membership includes many who have become important figures in the wider world of golf – members of the Royal and Ancient and senior club members (many ex-Captains) of the county's most iconic clubs (such as Royal St George's, Royal Wimbledon, Royal West Norfolk, Royal Worlingon and so on). One sub-set of the Old Stymies is the "select" group of my vintage (1966 and 1967) which Jeremy Garnett brings together every year at his old cottage in South Creake (near Brancaster in Norfolk). We have been making the pilgrimage to this November event for almost 50 years now. The wonderful club room in the Brancaster (Royal West Norfolk) clubhouse is almost a "home from home" for many of us. It's almost akin to some desert watering hole where you can always be sure to meet unexpected old friends in most comfortable surroundings.

Jeremy's cottage has been the scene of many a fine evening. As the years have passed the time for bed has steadily crept forward – the old days of late drinking and tense games of "Jenga" have passed too. But somehow there is great comfort in seeing that the fine old clock on the kitchen wall came to a stop many years ago – attempts to fix it have failed. The clock gave me inspiration for the following doggerel … which may sum up some of the emotions we all feel about the great tradition of Garnett's Norfolk weekends. For many years a special feature of the weekend has been a dramatic (and sometimes dangerous) display of fireworks – initiated by myself many years ago and manfully continued by Garnett.

BRANCASTER WEEKEND

Nothing ever changes, all is just the same
The sea, the turf and the challenge of the "game"
The beer is good on Friday night
The breakfast's huge, a sumptuous bite

Then it's into cars to dash away
The weather's fine, hulloo, hallay
We see the links from on the hill
The clubhouse, marshes, lie there still

Head down, stay calm, we're on the tee
The game is on, let's wait and see
If golfing gods will have their way
With luck we'll have a winning day

The snake and camel are always there
They're not too fussy who they snare
The units wandering from us to them
We win but quickly give them back again

Sunday lunch comes all too soon
The table's set – knife, fork and spoon
We say goodbyes and thank our host
It's hard to choose what we liked most

As time moves on through cosmic space
We did our best to enjoy the race
The weekend's gone, we enjoyed the game
Nothing ever changes, all is just the same

NOTE – The snake and the camel are strange terms which are part of a complex system of golfing side bets – small 10p bets which spice up the game (always foursomes matchplay golf). All are explained in my book "Deep Golf".

The Old Leysian Golfers get together in a regular annual programme of events. Teams are selected for the "prestigious" Halford Hewitt and Grafton Morrish events. These old public school events must bring together a huge number of influential businessmen – movers and shakers of the corporate world. 64 of the leading English and Scottish schools take part – so there are 640 competitors plus many followers-on. The car parks (at Royal St George's and at Deal) are always full of the expensive motor car "toys" these wealthy men enjoy – Bentleys, Ferraris, Porsches and so forth. The standard of golf is extremely high, accompanied, as always, by plenty of eating and drinking.

TEGS are a different kettle of fish entirely. In 1983, or was it in 84, I was telephoned "out of the blue" by my old Cambridge golfing pal Tim Dickson. He was then a journalist for the Financial Times and had just become involved with a group of fellow Times journalists who wanted to use their affiliation to this leading newspaper to gain access to exclusive golf courses. It seemed that the group was made up of members with widely differing golfing skills (some bordering on virtually useless!); they needed at least one other decent golfer to make sure they did not make complete fools of themselves on the first tee! Was I interested? They needed someone (like me) to make up the numbers for golf at Brancaster and Hunstanton (two of my favourite courses). Of course, I was pleased to go along.

Tim has made it his life's work to foster and encourage the traditional culture of golf which places 2-ball matchplay far above the grinding and testing tedium of strokeplay. He has done this by tirelessly playing his part as a member of several leading traditional clubs – Royal Wimbledon, Royal St George's and Luffness being among them. This involves many years of tedious but important work on the Committees which run these clubs. Tim has already been honoured by his peers who have elected him as their Captain (for a year) both at Royal Wimbledon and now (2020) Royal St George's, where he will be presiding over the world's most important golfing event – the British Open. To his great credit Tim has also created his own golfing publication – the Golf Quarterly – which he edits and publishes. This brings a regular dose of good sense and right-thinking to many golf clubs throughout the country. I have a lot to thank Tim for because it was he who wrote the first positive article about my development of the Millbrook course (back in 1976). His glowing report in the Financial Times gave me the green light I needed to ensure my bank manager was fully supportive of the project!

As far as the TEGS group is concerned, journalists tend to be well-informed, somewhat rebellious, extremely articulate and not short of native wit. We have had a lot of fun and considerable sums of money often changed hands either over the late night poker table or in the energetic betting which took place before competition. Golfing standards were variable and unpredictable to say the least, and various handicapping systems were introduced to try and "level the playing field". There is a lot of good natured argument spanning sport, politics and philosophy in general at these meetings. The general ethos of TEGS is summed up in my doggerel below!

The golfers of TEGS love their wine
Their wit and their play are sublime
And they make the odd bet
Which they often regret
'cos their golf fails them time after time

Three cheers for the golfers of TEGS
Playing golf after bacon and eggs
What a splendid young bunch
They drink fine wine at lunch

it's no wonder they lose their tee pegs

The TEGS golfer's a man who loves sport
But he don't always do what he ought
Carousing and drinking
when he could have been thinking
how to swing the new club he just bought

A TEGS man may often three putt
Though the last one's no more than a foot
Such a twitch here and there
Can bring doom and despair
Worse than shell shock in blazing Beirut

The history of TEGS goes back years
when men could drink four or five beers
With the passage of time
Now the beer's become wine
And the poker game no longer appears

Some say that golf makes you think
Though failure can drive one to drink
It's certainly not easy
If the weather is breezy
And a good putt just stops on the brink

The friendship of TEGS has been good
Cemented with good wine and food
The trip has been long
The wit fast and strong
We'd play on for ever if we could

Several of the leading members of TEGS have nicknames which give a flavour of their characters and their role in the group. Phil Webster (ex-chief political correspondent of the Times) is the "Bookie" – we expect honest Phil to set the odds and run the betting each time we meet. (The bets are on who will win the event.) Richard Evans (ex-racing correspondent of the Times) is "The Major" – a man who always dresses in smart county style with polished brown shoes and a charming manner. The Major was often our spokesperson when issues arose requiring diplomacy usually with ex-military club secretaries. "Loopy Roop" is the tag of Rupert Morris (an ex-journalist who runs a successful agency called "Clarity" which teaches bankers how to write good prose). The name conjures up not only Rupert's somewhat excessively wild swing but also his sometimes excitable temperament. Rupert is now firmly committed to working as a humanist celebrant – in which capacity he took a big part in my mother's funeral. This year Rupert is also Chairman of the National Liberal Club in London where he has already made a big impact by abolishing the old-fashioned dress rule that required jackets and ties. "Slo Jo" is Joe Davis – a powerful yet unreliable golfer whose speed around the course is hindered by the large number of shots he has to make and the time he spends looking for lost balls. Jo is a somewhat mysterious figure – often disappearing to remote parts of the world to play bridge or perhaps poker for high stakes. Jo has a sharp and independent mind – providing a personal investment advisory service to various wealthy clients. The "Woodpecker" is Nick Wood who runs a large political lobbying agency – Nick loves his old Jaguar car, his many cigarettes and his large consumption of good red wine – a man who seems totally bullet proof, a keen competitor always using ever bit of the limited golfing skills he possesses. I have always been affectionately known as "The Gorilla" – possibly because of my somewhat agricultural (swashbuckling some call it!) but effective golf swing. In latter years the Gorilla has become "The Time Lord" or the "Cosmic One" because of my sometimes unconventional alternative views and my use of the VW campervan (the Tardis) as a "home from home".

For my 70th birthday celebrations the TEGS group visited the great course at Dornoch in the north east of Scotland. Breezy but sunny, our round was seriously spoiled by the slow play of American groups in front and impatient Scottish golfers behind. This photo shows me driving on the 18th – only to lose a well-hit ball in a deep fairway bunker and, with that, the chance to par the hole and win the event. Such are the vagaries of golf.

At Dornoch, moments before impact!

A “Teenager” at 73!

And so it came to pass that after 45 years looking after (and sometimes worrying about) my 7 kids and 4 years looking after (and worrying about) my elderly Mum, I finally found myself “free like a teenager” with no pressing ties except the Christon Bank garden. This may take a little time to get used to! Ros and I had, 4 years before, decided to live together so it’s wonderful to be able to share our love of the simple life which includes music, golf, camping and gardening in the great outdoors. Ros (after 40 years teaching English in Germany) is the very best of willing editors for my writing. Our wonderful VW campervan gives us the freedom to explore wild places and we are fortunate to be able to rent a comfortable little cottage in the pretty village of Craster. There are, of course, musical commitments with various orchestras/pub folk sessions; Ros and I also play duets regularly at two of the local care homes (Abbeyfield and the Grange). There are also plenty of golfing outings which provide both fun and exercise. The great event of last year was the re-vamping and re-building of my self-sufficiency website. This comes from a new team work which has grown up between myself and two energetic, intelligent and “right thinking” young Bretons (Ariane and Tom). Together with yet another new edition of the “New Complete Book” from Dorling Kindersley, the new website will continue to promote some of my thinking and pondering into the outside world.

MY QUEST 8

As I write this story today (2019), I have been teaching self-sufficiency for more than 25 years. I have had the pleasure of meeting many interesting and well-motivated people. It has been stimulating to share ideas with them. It is 50 years since the publication of “Silent Spring” and “Limits to Growth”. It is 25 years since the Earth Summit at Rio. Many millions of ordinary people have been inspired to think (and worry) about the state of the Earth by TV programmes such as those of David Attenborough. The politicians produced by our populist democracy are increasingly reviled and distrusted. The destructive imperatives created by bank money and corporate profit continue to increase. We have seen the rise and fall of "Occupy". We now have new emerging movements such as the Dark Mountain project, Extinction Rebellion, Post Consumers, Collapsology (inspired by Jared Diamond) and many outspoken critics of "climate change" as well as inspiring activists like Greta Thunberg. Central Banks are desperately trying to keep employment (and economic growth) going by "quantitative easing" (printing more debt). Things don't look good!

What we do not see is any major shift in how humans perceive themselves as part of the natural world rather than being separate manipulators of this world. What we also do not see is any significant understanding of the new, much more magical physical world revealed (over 100 years ago now) by scientists. This is a world where relativity shows time and space can shrink or stretch. It is a world where quantum theory shows that waves can be particles and particles can be everywhere and nowhere all at the same time. It is a world we can never truly manage or control. It is a world (and a cosmos) we can do nothing but wonder at as we do our best to become effective and sympathetic stewards of all life on Earth.

It is complete nonsense, of course, to imagine that humans can destroy life on Earth. Like all previously "successful" life forms, our present extractive civilisation will be replaced one way or another by a no-growth life-enhancing civilisation. Nature has no pity for "out of date" life-forms. There is going to be a challenging and difficult transformation. Many of the present Earth life-forms will be destroyed by this – including our present predatory civilisation. But new life-forms will soon rise from the debris. We still have a chance to make the necessary transition reasonably comfortable both by using our brains but also by learning to listen to deeper feelings within our souls (if you like) about what is life-threatening and what is life-enhancing. Perhaps some new guru will appear to inspire such change – a Karl Marx, Rudolf Steiner, William Blake, Mahatma Ghandi or even Jesus Christ – but time is rapidly running out.

Huge attention is placed on climate change and the limited resource of fossil fuels. This – like so many human pre-occupations – is the fashion of the moment. Certainly if climate change continues (for whatever reason) humans will face discomforts and challenges – as they will if fossil fuels run out (which in fact seems unlikely). But neither of these scenarios really pose any real threat to human survival. Sea levels have changed massively many times and life has adapted. Humans lived quite comfortably for thousands of years without using fossil fuels (dinosaur juice as some call it!). In fact our pre-occupation with climate change and fossil fuels seems to be preventing us realising that what we cannot live without are clean air, drinkable water, healthy soil and fertile oceans. The signals we live by (from our political and economic systems) simply assume there are no costs associated with dumping waste and pollutants into these vital "commons".

Even as early as the 19th century, wise people were pointing out that the results of adopting the flush toilet were likely to be disastrous as vital plant nutrients are continually being transferred from the soil to the sea! Denuding the soil, changing the content of the atmosphere and polluting the sea – it's not a clever idea! In the UK we flush the toilet 90 billion times each year!

So my quest today continues as I do what I can to explain and educate as many ordinary people as possible to the real challenges facing our civilisations. Can we find a way to escape from the dominant cultural institutions which govern what we do. Perhaps we can find some clever (even devious) trick or game which will empower its followers to think and behave differently. Perhaps we can devise forms of cultural engineering which will provide peaceful transition from predation to stewardship. Perhaps we can put together a new "bible" which shows how we could do things differently with our money, land, corporations, democracy, economics and even religion. We certainly cannot expect to solve our problems using the dominant institutions which created them!

More and more I realise that the importance of maintaining the soil through effective composting of what we now call "waste" is the most important challenge for our future.

Compost makes the world go round
In soil that works without a sound
Beasts and bugs grow underground
No better system will be found
Recycling nutrients by the pound

But now we throw our "waste" away
75,000 tons each and every day
Human "waste" flushed out to sea
By the toilets used by you and me
It's cheap and quick for easy money
But our children's children won't think it's funny

We could do better with some wisdom
Managing waste in the United Kingdom
Every house could compost food waste
Learn to live with much less haste
Save the Earth by using less not more
Leave plastic at the super-market door

2018

This year we had a rare gathering of the original family "A Team" – 50 years on as it were! Rupert was over from New Zealand, Gael from Africa/Malta or other exotic places, Sarah from France or New Zealand – the rest of us from the north of England.

WS, Sarah, Gael, Ceri, Dylan and Rupert

In the wider world the UK was battling grimly on with a dysfunctional political system mired in the mess of Brexit. The young teenager (Greta Thunberg from Sweden) was galvanising millions into taking action on climate change and excesses of consumption. Extinction Rebellion (XR) was bringing London to a standstill with multiple peaceful protests. I was getting very frustrated that all the energies released by XR were not being channelled into any constructive actions – like composting, car sharing, use of credit unions not banks, leaving plastic packaging at super-markets, etc, etc. The USA (and UK) continued to provide massive support for the corrosively evil Saudi Arabian regime. China continued to extend its powerful yet stealthy influence throughout the world. Scientists and engineers continued (with miraculously full global support) their work on the greatest machine humans have ever attempted to build – the International Fusion reactor in France (ITER). I continued to be baffled by trying to discover what animals were eating all my peas at Christon Bank.

MY QUEST – FINAL THOUGHTS

As I reach the final phase of my own life here on Earth, I become less and less concerned about the terrible discomforts our present civilisation is bringing upon itself and increasingly confident that nature will, in time, produce something better. Human greed and arrogance will, in the end, bring its own punishment and there will indeed be much weeping and gnashing of teeth. The Earth herself is the only truly living entity in this part of space and she will look after herself as she always has. We are making massive contributions to her future in ways we do not yet understand – computers, the internet, smart phones, genetic engineering, fusion power, crypto-currencies – all these will probably play big roles in the civilisation to come.

I believe that in time the new (more exciting) world revealed by relativity and quantum theory will change the way humans think about themselves and their relationship to the Earth and the natural world. Nation states will ultimately be replaced by much smaller human scale communities, better placed to manage their local and appropriate soil communities. As the comedian Russell Brand has said, the way we think will be changed by adoption of a new spirituality where respect and wonder for the natural world are dominant. With luck we may even realise that as a species we would be wise to learn to share available resources rather than support a "winner takes all" philosophy. None of this is likely to be possible until after the "crash". We don't yet know what form the "crash" will take – war and famine seem very likely. Radical green leaders may well take centre stage. Perhaps some new guru will appear with some tablets of stone and new rules for living! Perhaps the giant corporations, which already rival nation states, will metamorphose into new forms of government – they certainly have an interest in keeping the business of Earth going – how else will they maintain their "top dog" status.

The paradox here is that we already have the means to manage our soil, water and air much better. We can eliminate our dependence on fossil fuel. We can control our population. We can learn to enjoy and treasure the "simple life". We can eliminate most diseases. We could compost or biodigest all our organic waste so nutrients can be returned to the soil. In fact we have all the tools to be able to enjoy a truly fulfilling and sustainable life on a vibrant planet full of the millions of other life forms which are needed for ecological health and stability. What we do not have (yet) are the "tools for living" (institutions) which will enable us to use our knowledge and technology wisely. Exploring and developing such "tools" is the final part of my quest. The quest continues.

2019 – More about Music

In 2019 music continues to play a big part in the here and now of my life in Craster. I play my lovely pink 5-string carbon 'cello in three orchestras as well as enjoying regular folk sessions in the local pubs (Morpeth, Newton, Belford – to name just three). Most evenings Ros and I will play duets together at the piano in our sitting room and we also enjoy taking our music out to two of the local care homes. The old people make a strange and unpredictable audience but they love the excitement of a change of scene and always like to join in the singing of old Scottish songs. It's more than 20 years now since I took up the 'cello again. There have been some mighty sessions of folk music – particularly in Ireland and Brittany.

Skye Fiddle Week

For several years I went along to the energetic fiddle week which takes place on the Isle of Skye each August. The week has become very popular. It is led by Alasdair Fraser (a champion fiddle player) and his beautiful young American playing partner, Natalie Haas, on the 'cello. The week takes place at the Gaelic College and every evening after a day of workshops, the players gather for impromptu concerts, music and dancing in the traditional Scottish way. These ceilidhs are a great opportunity for people to let their hair down and share whatever emotions may be bubbling to get out of them. My own contribution may give you some idea of how things go.

THE HIDDEN FLAME

Both young and old, to Skye we came
*In our search for joy and the hidden **flame***
of insight and music that's far from tame
*They call it "haggis", some strange **name***

To look for a hole in our tantric space
*To escape the tedious fast rat **race***
To play some fiddles, sing some songs
*Forget our worries, rights and **wrongs***

There are some who say it was all John Knox
*That the answer lies outside the **box***
But the Romans too liked nice straight lines
*So we've many to blame for these hard **times***

But fiddles are curvy and models of beauty
*And we all practice hard, it's part of our **duty***
There is dancing and drinking for that's what we do
*in our search for escape to a life which is **true***

There are 'cellos too in our musical zoo
*Their numbers are growing, more than a **few***
Grunty and noisy and not always right
*But a foundation for music late into the **night***

So what does it look like this newfound nirvana
Can it save our souls or enhance our ***karma****?*
Does it come from the dots made of small black notes?
Will it change the world much better than ***votes****?*

So with humour and wit just as sharp as a laser
We're grateful for wisdom from ***Alasdair Fraser***
While sweetness and harmony come from a lass
From the skill and fine 'cello of ***Natalie Haas***

These doggerels usually go down very well because the audience can participate enthusiastically by guessing the rhyming words at the end of the lines (in **bold**).

I do remember one strange and rather wonderful evening where the fates provided a very unexpected and amazing surprise. It had been a tedious day – trying to learn tunes by ear (which I don't find easy) when I knew I could learn them quickly if only I was given the notes. (The leaders normally only gave us the notes after each session had finished because it seems to be a point of honour amongst the "folkies" to learn only by ear.) I had been reading my book in the campervan but eventually decided I had better make the effort to go over to the hall and find out what was going on. As I walked across over the car park I met another latecomer who was also walking (rather purposefully) over to the hall. I asked her where her instrument was – she replied, rather smartly, "my voice is my instrument". We ordered drinks together and fell into what turned out to be a brilliant conversation. Full of sharp repartee and shared opinions, we must have talked intensely for about an hour. It is not often one meets a fellow spirit who shares a lively intellect and a passionate nature. I only found out later that she was one of the most famous Gaelic singers in Scotland – with her own popular radio programme and her own recording studio. I was impressed as you can see from the "poem" I sent her a few days later, together with a copy of the Complete Book (which she was interested in). This is the "poem"…

For Mary Ann

The day was long and my soul was grey
Too many lessons – it was so hard to play
so I slouched in my bunk like a sulking child
deflated and tired, and not feeling wild
'Twas then that it happened, a very strange thing
We met in the car park like birds on the wing
Her smile was sublime, her manner so cheery
I returned her greeting even though I was weary
So we walked to the bar in silent repose
She was pretty down to the end of her nose
I sipped my pint while she tippled on gin
We started to talk for that was no sin
Of gods and religion and Romans and more
as we stood near a table right by the door
Oh what's your name? I heard her say
Still so charming, so clever and always so gay
Then she offered her hand, so firm and so warm
with a smile that struck like a ship in a storm
The night travelled on and the music was roaring
While we talked on and on without ever being boring
Of banking and Cromwell and Napoleon's ships
Such wisdom and insights that came from her lips
Of Patrick O'Brien and dogs with strange names
Perhaps changing the world with internet games
But all things must end or that's what they say
We hugged and we kissed and went on our way

We were never in touch again – so imagine my surprise when, more than 10 years later, I received an email from the very same Mary Ann. She had been reading the Complete Book and wanted to thank me for it by sending me a copy of the book *(fonn)* she had just completed – bringing back memories of those special minutes we spent together on Skye! And a very lovely book it is – with many new Scottish tunes to look at.

There are many other special things to remember about Skye. The scenery is stunning, of course, and often the sea may be alive with whales and dolphins. Then there are the famous midges – which often make life unbearable for those who don't know how to manage them. Fortunately both the campervan and the caravan were pretty resistant – so long as you kept every possible opening closed.

Cobwebs

Soon after arriving back in Northumberland I discovered the strange and rather special music-making group which calls itself "Cobwebs". As the name suggests, Cobwebs brings together a group of musicians many of whom must brush the cobwebs from their instruments before they get back to serious playing. For a small annual subscription, any musician can join Cobwebs. Essentially this is an internet orchestra which has events and members covering the whole area of Northern England, both east and west, from York to the borders. Members receive information about events via the Cobwebs' website and a large email circulation list which contains about 500 names. There are also regional groups who meet regularly each week during school term times.

Cobwebs has sufficient resources to pay professional conductors. Many of the members will be teachers or ex-teachers of music. Many are simply keen amateurs and we all come together, usually just for a day, to play many of the great symphonic works. It is remarkable how effective and capable theses ad hoc orchestras can be – under the helpful guidance of their brilliant chief conductor (Andy Jackson). I quite often find myself sitting in the "hot seat" of the first 'cellist under Andy's watchful eye – perfect concentration is required if I am not to lead the other 'cellists astray! It certainly keeps the brain occupied.

Cobwebs holds two residential weekends each year. Not only do these give us a chance to work more carefully on particular pieces but they also provide opportunities for members to "do a turn" on the Saturday evening. Most of the orchestra are rather shy, worried they may make fools of themselves, but I normally take a chance and play one of the Irish or Northumbrian tunes I like. On one occasion I made this recital – which really sums up the essence of cobwebs.

AN AMAZING CREATION

The Cobwebs's an orchestra that defies time and space
Through email and internet it appears place to place
Its players are varied both in age and in skills
As they tackle great works in search of big thrills
The conductor is Andy who waves a white stick
He helps us much more than a metronome's tick
And there's Lorna who keeps order and sends us the news
When her smile asks for money you just can't refuse
Don't forget dear Anita who planned this weekend
Answering dozens of questions that could drive round the bend
There's a library of music they keep tidy and neat
With all comings and goings now that's quite a feat
And here we have Sheila with fine teas and cake
For the talents of Cobwebs include several who bake
The whole thing is magic, an amazing creation
It's fuelled by your energy with no help from the Nation.

There are two other orchestras which I enjoy playing in. The first is the King Edwards School (KEVI) community orchestra which is run in Morpeth by the head of music at the school. The orchestra gives three concerts each year and it's made up half of pupils from the school and half keen amateurs like myself. This is a great formula which lets the kids play some of the great works and gives players like myself a chance to enjoy playing in formal concerts.

The second is the Northumbrian Symphonietta which is the creation of the irrepressible Bryan Jackson. Bryan is a wonderful enthusiast for music and brings together a scratch group of experienced players to give (usually) two concerts in Alnwick each year where the proceeds go to charity. We only have a couple of rehearsals before each performance so things can be a bit shaky, but we manage and enjoy ourselves while contributing to a good cause.

2019 – More about the Garden

The old walled garden at Christon Bank has now become a magical world – almost another country with its own climate, plants and trees. The trees and hedges we planted in 2013 and 2014 are now beginning to make a real difference – providing shelter and seclusion which was not there before. As I am always telling my self-sufficiency students, trees, when properly looked after, grow much more quickly than most people imagine. Most of our larch trees and birch trees are now nearly 20 feet high – quite an achievement in just 4 years for those one-foot high transplants. The Scotch pines and cedars are not far behind and all provide the "nurse crop" which protects and encourages the oaks, beech and sweet chestnut as well as the giant sequoia and deciduous redwoods which nestle in amongst them. Even the stressed walnuts have managed to grow a good three or four feet in this very wet year of 2019.

The operational part of the garden extends to about 1,200 square yards – with a similar area taken up by soft fruits and orchard trees. This is more than enough to provide temperate vegetables and fruit for several families. In fact, harvesting and preparing food for the deep freeze is the most labour-intensive part of the entire business. We are also able to provide friends and neighbours with plenty of home-grown food!

Cultivation and control of weeds is achieved by rotavating – both at the end of the season (October) and then several times from mid-February until sowing in late April. The health and productivity of the soil is already excellent thanks to the work of many previous gardeners but we keep adding to it by making and applying about 2 tons of compost each year. This is the main task after Christmas and it always brings me great pleasure to see how the magic of a well-managed compost heap turns green vegetation into lovely food for the soil.

Gardening itself is a very pleasant and calming activity – provided, of course, that you have enough experience to know what you are doing. As in so many things in life, there are hard ways and easy ways to get what you want. Pest and weed control are essential. They can be managed easily by good garden design, excellent soil structure (which produces strong, disease-resistant plants), proper protection (netting and greenhouse) and, most important, regular hoeing at the right time. Effective weed control means keeping constant vigilance against establishment of perennial weeds (which cannot be controlled by rotavating) – one digs these out whenever they appear. We do not sow until we are sure our seedbeds are as "clean" as possible (free of weeds) and we sow the same day as we have cultivated – so the weeds have the least possible advantage in terms of time to germinate ahead of our chosen seeds. As soon as we see the tiniest of green shoots (from our chosen seeds) we start to hoe between the rows – but only in the morning of a bright dry day. If we hoe later in the day or there is any rain in prospect then the tiny weeds we have disturbed will simply re-establish themselves before the sun dries and destroys them. It should be obvious that no weeds can grow in soil that is regularly being moved about! We always want to hoe our lovely friable soil so that we never really see any weeds (except within the rows) – and we should hardly ever have to bend down to weed by hand.

Over the 30 or more years I have been growing my own food I have found that managing the garden takes about 10 hours per week during the spring, summer and autumn. There are busy times of sowing and harvesting but also a long period from

November until April when not much needs to be done. Christon Bank is about a 10-minute drive from our home in Craster – so I normally go for a few hours every other day during the growing season. Of course, the garden is something of a tie during the summer – if we go away for a week then the weeds may have a chance to make much more work when we return. And when crops are ready to harvest you have no choice but to act – you can't simply expect the plants to hold back; produce will over-ripen and be ruined. This often means long hours of picking (particularly soft fruits) and late nights processing for the deep freeze.

Every year brings a new pattern of successes and failures – that's just the way gardening is. Usually the weather has a big impact – sometimes it's pests or disease. But it is always magical to see how bare earth is transformed into bountiful production in a matter of a few weeks from the end of April until the middle of June. My self-sufficiency courses now tend to fall into a pattern of having one in late spring (students can help with preparing seedbeds and sowing) and one in July (when students take a big turn in harvesting the blackcurrants and gooseberries). The courses remain popular and we are still amazed to find enthusiastic people arriving at our door from almost any country in the world. Clearly the idea of living more self-sufficiently (what I like to call "right living") has more and more attraction for intelligent people who find themselves trapped in the consumer rat race.

I continue to enjoy a productive working relationship with Ariane and Tom (from Brittany) who share my enthusiasm for wiser ways of living. They discovered my work through the website and we all got together during 2018 to progress the initiative they created to reform and improve the self-sufficiency website. As I write they continue their long exploratory trip visiting alternative lifestyle sites all over the world. From their website at www.alterculteurs.net you can find out more. It is both hopeful and re-assuring to find at least two other active and intelligent people who want to promote the fundamental wisdoms which first found exposure (more than 30 years ago) through the work of people like John Seymour and Bill Mollison. Each month we work together to publish a regular newsletter which appears on the self-sufficiency website and is sent directly to more than 100 people who have subscribed to the website. Not only does the newsletter provide a useful insight into what actually is going on in the garden but we also try to flag up and discuss deeper matters of global political interest.

We have certainly been fortunate to find a mutually beneficial arrangement with Peter Gilbert (who owns the land and farmhouse at Christon Bank). On the frequent occasions when he comes up from London he enjoys the peaceful and ordered environment of the garden which continues a long tradition of growing which his own parents started when they took ownership of the house many years ago. For myself, the garden continues the very long (and important) relationship I have had with the old Christon Bank farmhouse which I first visited in the late 1960s when Sarah was staying there for the summer with her elderly (but quite fierce) grandparents. We spent our wedding night there, which brings back many happy memories.

2019 – More about Golf

Golf serves many functions: a therapy against global madness, a pleasant form of important exercise, a way to interact with the local community, a physical and mental challenge to attain perfection – and it's an interesting game too! Dunstanburgh golf course is sublimely beautiful as it frames Embleton Bay almost under the shadow of the iconic ruins of Dunstanburgh Castle. Our golfing pals are good fun and we all enjoy the friendly (but serious) cut and thrust of regular matchplay golf. Ros and I play perhaps 3 or 4 times each week – it's particularly pleasant to go out late on a long summer evening when we will usually have the place to ourselves. We can smell the sea as we feel the springy seaside turf under our feet and enjoy the occasional good shot or lucky bounce.

I am lucky that all those golfing hours I spent in my youth now bring their reward because my swing remains easy and effective. Many of the golfers much younger than me watch on enviously when, with little fuss or bother, I still hit my drives 250 yards down the middle. Golf, of course, remains a puzzle – how to keep that important concentration and avoid the two or three mistakes which usually spoil each round!

Golf helps to keep the family together too. Dylan and Helen are often staying up at the old family home (The Farmhouse at Low Newton) with their kids – Gustav and Eddie. They have become a very keen golfing family – all playing serious competitive golf to a high standard. We often meet up for a game at Embleton – usually late afternoon before going over for a delicious supper cooked by super-cook Dylan. During summer (the fishing season) Dylan's suppers invariably include fresh caught lobster – much enjoyed by Ros and Gustav! It's great to see the youngsters enjoying the unpredictable challenges of golf without burying themselves in frustration when things go wrong. Playing games has already taught them that life is full of uncertainties – sometimes helpful, sometimes annoying – that's just the way it is. You give it your best shot and either smile or groan at the consequences.

In 2018 I achieved one of golf's more unusual goals – to go round in a score less than your age. It was a tense moment when I holed the final putt on the 18th green. With a bit of luck I may be able to do the same again in 2019 – we shall see. In 2018 we also had an enjoyable re-union of the Oxford and Cambridge teams who played against each other in the great match at Porthcawl in 1968. Once again the Varsity match took place at this great course on the Welsh coast. Once again Cambridge became fairly easy winners. It was a bitter-sweet occasion because rather too many of our number were missing – either from death, from illness or family problems. It seems the ravages of time and life cannot be denied. When I went to watch the University golf match I took a large bag with me; my intention was to collect the masses of plastic waste which wind had blown into grass and bushes around the course. I soon found I had many willing helpers and within a couple of hours we had a full bag which cleared most of the course. It amazed me that nobody else would have lifted a finger if I had not shown a lead. It amazed me too that the young golfers of today can hit the ball probably half as far again as we could in our heydays – clearly modern equipment has really changed the game.

Golf takes us to many interesting and enjoyable places. Over the years golfers have always taken care to provide themselves with comfortable clubhouses and excellent food and drink. We can take our clubs (and our music) off in the camper van – perhaps to Scotland, or Norfolk or, more locally, to neighbouring courses like Goswick, Bamburgh or Eyemouth. One is always sure of a friendly reception. Golf is not quite a religion but it does share some of the same characteristics!

Golf brings us many good friendships as we experience the joys and frustrations of shared exertions on the links. We all know that ultimately it is always "golf" that will win – however hard we try, our human frailties will always stand in the way of perfection.

2019 – More about Politics

It's October 2019 as I attempt to finish this tome! Life, as they say, goes on. I'm still running self-sufficiency course and enjoy the challenge of trying to inspire yet another group of brave people who are trying to change their lives. They bring enthusiasm and energy – many questions – and every course is different. We have a lot of fun but it's "full on" for the whole week from 9.30 am until late each day.

Work in the garden, music and golf take up some time – hopefully keeping me fit as well as playing some part in the local community. I keep writing – often in rather waspish doggerel to the national and local newspapers. I sign myself – AsimpleMan – which, I think, sums up my insights and philosophy. Here's the latest contribution about the mess which is Brexit.

The first Cameron referendum was fatally flawed
They lied and they cheated like a mad mouse that roared
Now Bojo's giant ego sows nought but discord
And poor Corbyn drones on leaving all of us bored

An election won't fix it though Boris may win
And Cummins may laugh as he plots yet more spin
While Boris just plays games to save his own skin
'Cos, in truth, he don't care whether we're out or we're in

The EU's not perfect, as the Greeks know full well
As the power of the Euro sends signals from hell
But to "go it alone" may be the UK's death knell
Can we rely on the "Trump"? It's real hard to tell

So surely the best answer, our "get out of jail"
Is go back to the people, let democracy prevail
and "stick to the facts", this is no car boot sale
Now a new people's vote should end this sad tale

I hear the scientists continually warning our politicians of discomforts ahead. I watch the energetic protests of thousands of climate activists (inspired by young Greta Thunberg). I see the chaos caused by the angry and frustrated demonstrators of Extinction Rebellion. I keep in loose contact with my children and grandchildren as they cut their own swathes through life. I keep my fingers crossed that the ravages of imminent old age do not become too uncomfortable or debilitating. Meanwhile the great wheels of commerce continue to turn faster and faster as the resources available to them become smaller and smaller. Yes – it's an interesting time to be alive.

ANSWERS

Perhaps many readers are wondering just exactly what answers I may have found in my 65 years of "questing"? I will do my best to tell you now.

Answer 1 – We cannot expect our present leaders and policies to solve our problems

Most of our life-threatening behaviours arise because our actions are dominated by cultural institutions which have now become "out of date" and therefore life threatening. Worse still, our so-called leaders are selected by, and must work within, the dictates of these same "out of date" institutions, particularly short-term populist democracy.

The "institutions" I am talking about include fractional reserve banking, fiat money, populist democracy, corporations and "free market" economics (not to mention – religion and consumerism). We cannot expect our leaders to change these systems – this is like asking a man to pull himself up with his own bootlaces. The internal mechanisms of these "systems" were useful when they were invented (that's why they became popular) but now they have become profoundly life threatening. Our banks direct investment into the wrong places. Our money system can only work if there is continued economic growth. Our "populist" democracy gives us the wrong kind of leaders who pursue essentially short-term policies. Corporations can grow indefinitely (they can "live for ever") and their share-holders require them to "mine" the Earth for profit. Economics measures the wrong things and money gives us disastrously wrong signals about what we should do.

I have written extensively about "money" elsewhere but here, at least, is the message I have to give you.

SIGNALS FROM HELL

Those five little letters are all very well
But money is bringing us signals from hell
The fat cats get rich with their banks and their money
But for most life on Earth it's not very funny

We're talking of dustbowls created for cash,
we're screaming with rage at trees burned to ash
We're saddened by seas with no fish to swim
We're maddened by politics, pointless and grim

Quick, dig out the oil, big machines cut out toil
Don't care for tomorrow or the air that we spoil
Devil's dust sours the land, reaping chemical crops
Paying interest to bankers until the fun stops

Why we do it is simple, we've got to pay bills
We do what pays best and enjoy our cheap thrills
Prices and money have tied us up well
Like zombies we're damned by these signals from hell

No doubt it's all fine for the suits guzzling wine
But something is wrong and the Earth's in decline.
We can see it's all mad, a terrible folly
Being trapped and ensnared by the stuff we call lolly

The system is studied by slicks doing tricks
With the sums and equations that's "economics"
And the bankers who smile getting fat on this diet
They're enjoying the fun and ignoring disquiet

While Joe in the street just knows he is beat
In a system all powerful that governs complete
A groan every morning, his routine spells defeat
In a cultural desert with fast food to eat

One man one vote but that's just a joke
A spin doctor's name for an oxen's hard yoke
Egotistical nonsense, hot air like graffiti
But signals from hell, they have no pity

Dress it up smart in fine college courses
Worship its wonder in smart padded bourses
Bow to its power, its sophisticate pleasure
Lavish your soul with greed's transitory treasure

It goes on and on but it won't be forever
This short love affair that's not very clever
This urge to compel with the signals from hell
This romancing with lolly, the ultimate folly

But life's magic rules will not be denied
It won't be long now before our world has died
Then they'll say "when", all those greedy sad men
"Will we re-invent money and start over again?"

So what can be done? First, we would be wise to encourage the expression of new values through "soft cultural engineering" – songs, books, art, music and new positive examples of "right living". Second, we should encourage our scientists to get the message across that the cosmos we live in is a truly magical place (not a simple machine that we can dominate and control) and that we, with our incredible brains, are probably the most magical part of the whole show. Third, our brightest and most independent minds should be working to devise options for new "life-enhancing" cultural institutions to replace money, democracy, corporations, banks and even private ownership. This is what I call the new discipline of "hard cultural engineering".

Answer 2 – Consumerism is addictive and gives power to the "Merchants of Greed"

The economic processes, which now dominate almost everything modern humans do, were initiated by the emerging industrialists of the 17th century through the invention of consumerism. Consumerism is driven by the powerful emotions of human greed. Those who benefit from it (with their helicopters and penthouses) are, in effect, "merchants of greed". Through advertising, education and peer group pressure, they fan the flames of greed in order to keep the wheels of consumerism turning so they can syphon off the profits for their own power and pleasure. In fact, the products they sell are not as significant as the levels of greed they must maintain.

In simple terms, this dynamic makes the "merchants of greed" richer whilst our cultural systems ensure that the majority of the world's population remain as "wage slaves". A large group of associates are well-rewarded for helping the merchants of greed – particularly politicians, bankers, lawyers and accountants. Many young people will face a difficult challenge as they enter adult life as to whether they join the MoGs in well-paid jobs or take less well-paid independent work (as teachers, academics, doctors, for example). The MoGs (in company boardrooms, banks, etc.) do everything they can to attract the brightest brains to join their game.

Answer … what amounts to an "addiction" to consumerism can only be broken by working in self-help groups on the same lines as alcoholics anonymous or weight watchers. But first the "addicts" have to decide they want to escape their dependency.

Answer 3 – The time has come for those seeking change to be positive instead of negative

Day after day it becomes more and more frustrating to see the sadness and anger of right-thinking ordinary people translated into "protest". "Protest" is frequently a negative action when it is always saying we must stop doing this, that or the other. In fact, history shows us that "protest" without vision can be profoundly dangerous – perhaps destroying one hierarchy only to replace it with something worse.

Even when "protest" does succeed in sending a clear message to governments (asking for new laws and regulations) this reflects an old way of thinking because it is essentially a passive way of doing things. We do not need to wait for governments to tell us what to do – the time has surely come when we can see for ourselves how by changing our own lives we can actually make a real difference.

Surely it should be possible to initiate positive social movements which give their followers pride in showing others all the benefits in adopting habits of "right living". It is a hopeless task trying to change the world simply by shouting or lying down in the street. But we can show that the world can be changed by changing our own lives and inspiring others to do the same. And we can do this whilst we make new friends, save money and enjoy a healthier lifestyle!

History also shows us that "protests" (and ultimately revolution) almost invariably lead to violence (with extremely unpredictable results) – sometimes fighting against the system will even make it stronger! The alternative strategy of "withdrawing support for unwanted systems" can bring peaceful and controllable change.

Answer 4 – The mistaken folly of "I"

It is an unfortunate (and potentially life-threatening) fact that the consciousness in our brains produces a dangerously wrong concept of reality. That's a bit of a mouthful! What do I mean?

When we first become aware of our consciousness (as babies) we find we can manipulate the world around us in ways that bring us rewards of all kinds – food, pleasure and excitement. We can rattle our toys, put food into our mouths, build things or smash things, as we choose. This leads our consciousness to have a mental picture of "I" on one side and the external world (which "I" can manipulate) on the other. We take this duality (or separation) with us into adulthood and it prevents us from realising that “I” (we) and the external world around us are all part of the same single complex system of life which comprises the Earth itself. We see the Earth as being “outside of us” when in fact we are “inside of it”. In a true cosmic sense, in the vastness of space it is only the Earth herself that is alive.

Most of the major religions (Buddhism excepted), especially the Romanised version of Christianity, re-inforce this dangerous duality because they teach that the resources of the Earth are simply put there by “God” for humans to use as they please.

So whilst it may be true (and possible) to say that “I” am happy or sad, it is in a real sense misleading and wrong to say that “I” am going out for a walk today. It would be correct to say that the “me part of Earth” is going for a walk. “I” by myself cannot go for a walk unless I have had food to eat and air to breathe – it is Earth that provides these.

And why is our concept of “I” so dangerous? The men and women in suits (mostly) who dominate “management” of the Earth do so in a framework dominated by this false concept of “I”. Their political and economic systems simply assume that:
– they have an infinite pool of Earth’s resources at their disposal
– the Earth’s life support systems will remain unaffected by their actions.

Humans will not have a fruitful and life-enhancing existence unless and until they see themselves not as individuals but simply as parts of the great dynamic web of life which is the Earth. Everything we do which affects our environment may, and often does, have second or third-order consequences which may be uncomfortable or even life threatening. “Climate change” is, of course, an important “wake-up” call but we are still trying to “fix it” using our old mistaken concept of reality! For the most part, we still behave as mindless predators when we would be much wiser to be cautious in our attempts at life-enhancing stewardship.

Answer 5 – We do not live in a deterministic and mechanical world

Not only do we have to suffer the potentially life-threatening consequences of our false concept of "I" but our "managers" are also living in a fictional world where they imagine that all problems can ultimately be solved by science and technology. They still live in what people call a "deterministic" world even though modern science shows us that the cosmos is not a predictable machine. Any experienced gardener can tell you that nature works on the basis of such hugely complex dynamic systems that even the smallest changes can result in runaway unexpected happenings. This is how nature (and life itself) has made itself "anti-fragile" – the challenge of disaster invariably ends up creating new systems of life that are more complex and beautiful than those that may have been destroyed. Nature does this by maintaining massive variety.

Take, for example, the case of the ash tree. Every year each mature ash tree produces (say) 10,000 flying seeds. Each ash tree lives for perhaps 100 years – so that's one million seeds sent off into the environment. But – think about it – only one of those seeds must produce another mature ash tree – if 2 seeds succeed then the planet will very soon be covered in ash trees! Nature finds a way to eliminate 999,999 seeds.

It is true that the amazing insights provided by science (particularly those of Isaac Newton in the 17th century) have empowered great progress in technology and man's control over nature through machines and use of fossil fuels. These insights are the foundation for what remains a dominant world view that the Earth behaves like some gigantic machine which we could, in theory, control with the right levers and buttons. But it is more than 100 years now since the old "machine" version of reality has been de-bunked by the discoveries of relativity and quantum theory. The Universe is much more "magical" than any machine – the way it behaves is, quite literally, fantastic. Space and time can bend and stretch. Particles can be waves and particles at the same time; they can even exist in two places at once! This kind of "magic" is worrying and inconvenient – perhaps that's why it's still not taught in our schools!

So what does this mean? First, it means we must be much more careful and respectful in all our dealings with the natural world. Second, it means we should be wise to retain and encourage a wonderful variety of life forms, including different types of human communities, cultures and religions. Variety brings strength – uniformity brings risk (don't put all your eggs in one basket!). Third, it means that we should be constantly aware of the cosmic magic that is ourselves within the vast unfolding cosmos around us.

Examples of Cosmic Strangeness

Stardust – We are, quite literally, made of stardust. It is a certainly a strange thing that every single atom in our bodies was once created in the centre of a massive event of nuclear fusion which took place in what we call a "star". Somehow (over the 14 billion Earth years we believe our Universe has existed) these atoms came together to form molecules, then the birds and bees – and finally us! Every day when we wake up we should remember this – and the responsibility it now brings with it for us to use our consciousness to promote more "life".

Einstein's Magic – It was really the Scotsman James Clerk Maxwell whose elegant equations showed that light must always move at the same velocity in any frame of reference. Einstein had the genius and independence of mind to work out what the extraordinary consequences of this discovery must mean. Unfortunately we don't really notice these (very) strange consequences in our daily lives – although devices such as GPS must take full account of them to provide accurate positions (the satellites that send signals are moving very fast so time changes for them, and the Earth's strong gravity also "bends" time). Most people (the several billion Earth humans) fail to realise that we live in this magical reality – they simply blunder about trying to earn enough money to pay the rent and hoping governments somewhere will look after the bigger issues of keeping our planet alive! We must hope that somehow scientists can do more to get the true "magical" state of affairs understood! People might behave differently then.

It turns out that the thing we call "space" (the space between stars, planets and galaxies) can stretch and bend – either because of what we call "gravity" or because we accelerate things through it very rapidly. "Space" has to do this to enable the speed of light to remain constant. What we call "time" is also an integral part of "space" – so it too must change if the speed of light is to remain constant. This has some VERY strange consequences – for example, read on…

I have no doubt that in times to come humans will invent nuclear propulsion systems which will allow a spaceship to accelerate constantly for months or even years. Indeed if there are alien advanced life forms out there in space (which does seem almost certain to me – given the billions of other solar systems there must be) then they will almost certainly have already done this. Anyone with this kind of spaceship can actually visit distant stars very easily – yes, even if they are many light years away. As the spaceship continues to accelerate towards its destination Einstein's magic steadily slows time down for those who are travelling faster and faster. The passengers don't notice this – they simply see their destination getting rapidly closer. But a journey which takes our travellers (say) 2 years could see 10,000 years go by both at the destination and the place of departure. This extra-ordinary characteristic of "space/time" has been demonstrated time and time again both in particle accelerators, in GPS devices and even by sending atomic clocks across oceans in jet planes. It may seem stranger than fiction but it really is how our Universe behaves. We can see the phenomenon very clearly in the case of the photons which bring light to us from the sun. In Earth time they take 8 minutes to reach us – but if you were actually sitting on one (going at the speed of light) time would stop and you would reach the Earth instantly.

All this may seem rather fantastic. What you have to come to terms with is that it is not possible to "understand" why the Universe works in this way. This is simply beyond understanding – we just have to accept it and wonder at the strangeness of it all.

One (perhaps peculiar) consequence of Einstein's magic is that IF alien life forms have ever visited Earth (perhaps Earth is simply someone's "garden" experiment) then, whatever they may tell its inhabitants, they cannot revisit (in their fast spaceships) until many thousands of Earth years have passed. They may only have spent a few short spaceship years in fast travel but this will equate to thousands of Earth years – that's just the strange way things are. I do often wonder whether this is the missing logic which has confused rational debate on this question! It does seems odd that so many different civilisations have depended, quite independently, on deeply held myths about Gods arriving in human form!

Answer 6 – How you spend money is more important than how you cast your vote.

Does anyone believe that "voting changes anything"? What we now call democracy began (in 17th century Britain) as government by an exclusive club of rich landowners. As more and more ordinary people were given the vote, the system slowly evolved to become the primary foundation for a "populist" democracy. This is very convenient for the "merchants of greed" because in order to win elections politicians must encourage short-term consumerism and continued economic growth. In effect, our so-called democracy is now the handmaiden of the merchants of greed and, in the process, the "vote" provides them with perfect camouflage for their continued dominance. The one important option which voters are always denied is the chance to vote for "none of the above" – people are simply left with the disempowering prospect of voting for the least worst candidate.

Answer 7 – The forms of human life which matter are not individuals but communities of individuals with shared cultural values (usually religions)

Both history and experience show us that humans can only work effectively if they live in communities which are based on shared beliefs and cultural values. It is clear that the Earth's major religions are no longer "fit for purpose" – indeed they are mostly a cause of conflict rather than a force for good. We humans probably do need "Big Gods" to help us behave well and both Celtic Christianity and Buddhism may indeed provide such "Gods". But the insights and discoveries of modern science show us that "life" itself is something we could worship. In the "religion" of life every follower would carry (on their person, in their house or in their car) a "natural companion" (plant or animal) which they would care for as a constant reminder of their place in the web of Earth's life. As I have already said – we see the Earth as being "outside of us" when in fact we are "inside of it".

Answer 8 – You cannot stamp out an idea by force but only by having a "better" idea

This is a lesson history has demonstrated a thousand times (although the US imperialists and war mongers don't seem to have learned it). The passion, anger and energy of those now seeking change is unlikely to achieve "progress" unless it can be founded on some "better" idea or vision. Michael Davitt with his Land League and Gandhi with his salt protest are the type of examples we should follow. On the one hand you can withdraw support for the existing systems while at the same time putting forward an idealist vision of what might replace them.

Answer 9 – The Earth will look after herself

Like all successful life forms (before and after), our present human civilisation is approaching a critical evolutionary transformation as it reaches the end of the supply of resources it now depends upon for its continued existence. This civilisation's essentially predatory behaviours will soon be replaced by new life-enhancing behaviours and Earth's biome will be re-populated by suitably complementary organisms. Unfortunately the transition will almost certainly be traumatic; millions of humans and other life forms will die.

The Earth, through the humans that live on her, is asking us questions about this now so it's an exciting time to be alive. Will we find new heroes (heroines)? Will we find a new religion? Will we learn the lessons of history? Will we listen to what the Earth is trying to tell us? Somewhere, somehow, the new ideas which will make tomorrow, are stirring. Every single one of us has a role to play in supporting the ideas and the actions which will make a better future.

Answer 10 – We already have all the know-how and technology we need to live in wonderfully productive and life-enhancing ways

Our Earth remains a wonderfully bountiful place despite all our efforts to exploit her. We could control our population, enhance and care for our soil and oceans, limit our use of fossil fuels and give up our mania for "economic growth". Too bad we are trapped in systems of living (cultural institutions) created by, and for the benefit of, the "merchants of greed".

Answer 11 – the big changes which are to come will come from unexpected causes

The plough, gunpowder, the printing press, bank money, the steam engine, railways, radio, the internal combustion engine, computers, the contraceptive pill, the internet, nuclear power, genetic engineering, smart phones – what next? Paganism, Roman Gods, Christianity, Buddhism, Islam. Luther, Marx, Keynes, Thatcher … what next?

A FINAL WORD

I hope, dear reader, that you have enjoyed this "journey" through my life. What great moments of excitement and serendipity there have been! We humans are remarkable creatures – capable both of great creativity and great destruction. The Earth is now poised on a dangerous cusp between well-ordered survival and mindless chaos. Whether I will live long enough to see any resolution of this challenge – that remains to be seen. Certainly the young people of today have a bumpy ride in store. I wish them every success.

The shape of things to come!

Printed in Poland
by Amazon Fulfillment
Poland Sp. z o.o., Wrocław